*Ecofeminism*

In the series Ethics and Action,
edited by Tom Regan

# *Ecofeminism*

## Women, Animals, Nature

EDITED BY

### *Greta Gaard*

Temple University Press

PHILADELPHIA

Temple University Press, Philadelphia 19122
Copyright © 1993 by Temple University
All rights reserved
Published 1993
Printed in the United States of America

Library of Congress Cataloging-in-Publication Data

Ecofeminism: women, animals, nature / edited by
Greta Gaard.
    p.   cm. — (Ethics and action)
    Includes bibliographical references and index.
    ISBN 0-87722-988-0 (cloth). — ISBN
0-87722-989-9 (paperback)
        1. Ecofeminism.   2. Human ecology.
3. Man—Influence on nature.
    I. Gaard, Greta Claire.   II. Series.
    HQ1233.E26   1993
    304.2—dc20
                                        92-6598

Some of the material in Chapter 2 overlaps Janis
Birkeland's essay "Ecofeminism and Ecopolitics," in
*Ecopolitics V Proceedings*, ed. Ronnie Harding (Centre
for Liberal and General Studies: University of New
South Wales, Kensington, NSW, Australia, 1992).

The poem on page 161 is from *Borderlands/La
Frontera*. © 1987 by Gloria Anzaldúa. Reprinted by
permission of Aunt Lute Books (415) 558-8116.

# Contents

# Contents

# *Preface*

The text you hold in your hands represents the culmination of an effort that began in 1989 at the annual convention of the National Women's Studies Association. At that time there was no text that provided a theoretical bridge for women working in the related movements of environmentalism, animal liberation, and feminism. *Ecofeminism: Women, Animals, Nature* is an attempt to build that bridge.

Because a central value of ecofeminism is its plurality of voices, I chose not to write a single-author text, but rather to edit a collection that would present theory as it is lived, in voices both activist and academic. My goal in editing these essays has been to encourage rather than silence the quality of each writer's voice, and to ensure both intellectual rigor and accessibility. Neither the contributors nor I have set as our goal the use of a language available only to a specialized elite; rather, our aim has been to address fairly sophisticated theoretical concepts in plain terms. Addressing both academics and activists requires a delicate balance, but it is imperative, since both types of readers form the movement that is ecofeminism. Ecofeminists strive for inclusivity, in subject matter as well as style of presentation. Because ecofeminism is an interdisciplinary field of inquiry, it needs to use a *lingua franca* if it is to communicate with all those interested in the struggles on behalf of women, animals, and the earth. Ecofeminism requires us to make connections.

I am deeply grateful to both Sandra Eisdorfer and Jane Cullen, editors at the University of North Carolina Press and Temple University Press, respectively, whose continued support has brought this book to completion. For, in the process of editing this book, I have had the good fortune of making connections with the writers and activists whose works are collected here. To them, and to all those working for a healthy planet, this book is dedicated.

*Greta Gaard*

*Ecofeminism*

# CHAPTER I

# Living Interconnections with Animals and Nature

## Greta Gaard

Theory—the seeing of patterns, showing the forest as well as the trees—theory can be a dew that rises from the earth and collects in the rain cloud and returns to earth over and over. But if it doesn't smell of the earth, it isn't good for the earth.

ADRIENNE RICH
"Notes Toward a Politics of Location"

Ecofeminism is a theory that has evolved from various fields of feminist inquiry and activism: peace movements, labor movements, women's health care, and the anti-nuclear, environmental, and animal liberation movements. Drawing on the insights of ecology, feminism, and socialism, ecofeminism's basic premise is that the ideology which authorizes oppressions such as those based on race, class, gender, sexuality, physical abilities, and species is the same ideology which sanctions the oppression of nature. Ecofeminism calls for an end to all oppressions, arguing that no attempt to liberate women (or any other oppressed group) will be successful without an equal attempt to liberate nature. Its theoretical base is a sense of self most commonly expressed by women and various other nondominant groups—a self that is interconnected with all life.[1]

In their analyses of oppression, socialists, animal liberationists, ecologists, and feminists each distinguish between privileged and oppressed groups, where the privileged are upper- or middle-class, human, technologically and industrially "developed," male, and the oppressed are poor or working-class, nonhuman animal, "undeveloped" nature, and female, respectively. Ecofeminism describes the framework that authorizes these forms of oppression as patriarchy, an ideology whose fundamental self/other distinction is based on a sense of self that is separate, atomistic.

As Nancy Chodorow's and Carol Gilligan's studies have repeatedly shown, a sense of self as separate is more common in men, while an interconnected sense of self is more common in women.[2] These conceptions of self are also the foundation for two different ethical systems: the separate self often operates on the basis of an ethic of rights or justice, while the interconnected self makes moral decisions on the basis of an ethic of responsibilities or care. Whether these self-conceptions and affiliated ethical systems are innate or culturally learned is uncertain. Gilligan has noted that while both sexes have the ability to access both types of moral reasoning, the "focus" phenomenon is particularly gender-based: that is, men tend to focus on rights, whereas women tend to focus on responsibilities. What is certain is that a failure to recognize connections can lead to violence, and a disconnected sense of self is most assuredly at the root of the current ecological crisis (not to mention being the root cause of all oppression, which is based on difference).[3]

It is now common knowledge that rights-based ethics (most characteristic of dominant-culture men, although women may share this view as well) evolve from a sense of self as separate, existing within a society of individuals who must be protected from each other in competing for scarce resources. In contrast, Gilligan describes a different approach, more common to women, in which "the moral problem arises from conflicting responsibilities rather than from competing rights and requires for its resolution a mode of thinking that is contextual and narrative rather than formal and abstract. This conception of morality as concerned with the activity of care centers moral development around the understanding of responsibility and relationships, just as the conception of morality as fairness ties moral development to the understanding of rights and rules."[4] Similarly, Karen Warren's "Toward an Ecofeminist Ethic" describes eight boundary conditions of a feminist ethic; that is, conditions within which ethical decision making may be seen as feminist. These conditions include coherence within a given historical and conceptual framework, an understanding of feminism as striving to end all systems of oppression, a pluralistic structure, and an inclusive and contextual framework that values and emphasizes humans in relationships, denies abstract individualism, and provides a guide to action.[5] The analyses of Gilligan and Warren indicate that ecofeminism, which asserts the fundamental interconnectedness of all life, offers an appropriate foundation for an ecological ethical theory for women and men who do not operate on the basis of a self/other disjunction.

In brief, this psychological—and political—construction of the self and the associated ethical system explains why ecofeminists do not find their concerns fully addressed in other branches of the environmental movement. Though some may agree with social ecologists, for example, that the root cause of all oppression is hierarchy, ecofeminists tend to believe hierarchy takes place as a result of the self/other opposition.

Ecofeminists' interconnected sense of self requires us to create a theory that will provide, as fully as possible, an inclusive and global analysis of oppression. To do this, theorists must meet with activists to exchange information and to create political strategy; ideally, theorists must also be activists, thereby enacting the goal of ecofeminist praxis. A meeting of theorists and activists concerned about the fate of women and the earth, the World Women's Congress for a Healthy Planet, took place on November 9–12, 1991. In Miami, Florida, over a thousand women from around the world gathered to create a women's action agenda for presentation at the 1992 United Nations Conference on Environment and Development (UNCED). Throughout the conference, a number of topics reappeared which are of concern within ecofeminism. These included population, global economics, Third World debt, the ideology of development, environmental destruction, world hunger, reproductive choice, homelessness, militarism, and political strategies for creating change globally.

From many respected speakers, the message was the same: the earth is at a turning point, and women's efforts are critical at this time. "Things will not just happen," Wangari Maathai told participants. "Women must make things happen." "It is up to us," said Vandana Shiva, "and not to the heads of state in Rio." One of the participants in Marilyn Waring's workshop on global economics spoke most eloquently. "What you're signing on for here," she said, "if you really care about the issues of this world, is a life sentence. The capacity to weep and then do something is worth everything. We want to remember that emotions are things we value. Creating change globally—this is not something you can do in your spare time. We all have to live it."

In 1983 the first collection of essays on ecofeminism appeared: *Reclaim the Earth: Women Speak Out for Life on Earth*, edited by Leonie Caldecott and Stephanie Leland and published by the Women's Press in London. In this collection, the "Eco-feminist Imperative" was first defined by Ynestra King, and the following chapters described ecofeminism as a theory and practice whose various manifestations included anti-nuclear activism, the international women's health movement, women and land rights, women and world hunger. The collection included the Unity Statement of the Women's Pentagon Action, U.S.A., a document adopted by the original organizers of the largest all-woman protests since 1968.[6] Wangari Maathai described the work of women in Kenya, whose struggle against deforestation is intimately connected to their own survival; Anita Anand described the Chipko movement in India. From the first collection, then, ecofeminism has addressed issues of global concern.

Following Caldecott and Leland, Judith Plant's *Healing the Wounds: The Promise of Ecofeminism* (New Society) appeared in 1989; Irene Diamond and Gloria Orenstein's *Reweaving the World: The Emergence of Ecofeminism* (Sierra Club Books), in 1990. Plant's collection addresses four aspects of ecofeminism: theory, politics, spirituality, and community. Topics in Diamond and Orenstein's collection fall into the categories of history/mystery, politics and ethics, and political activism. Ecofeminist ethics in relation to animals is either marginalized or entirely neglected in both books, but is addressed more fully in Andrée Collard and Joyce Contrucci's *Rape of the Wild: Man's Violence Against Animals and the Earth* (1989), and the relation between the oppression of women and that of animals is developed in Carol Adams' *The Sexual Politics of Meat: A Feminist-Vegetarian Critical Theory* (1990). Finally, the Spring 1991 issue of *Hypatia: A Journal of Feminist Philosophy*, which was devoted to "Ecological Feminism," included essays on ecofeminism's relation to animal liberation, deep ecology, literary practice, environmentalism, and grassroots politics, as well as the relationship between self and nature.

Other texts are devoted exclusively to the relationship of ecofeminism, Third World women, and international "development." Among them are Gita Sen and Caren Grown's *Development, Crises, and Alternative Visions: Third World Women's Perspectives*, published by the Monthly Review Press in 1987, and Vandana Shiva's *Staying Alive: Women, Ecology and Development*, published by Zed Books in 1988. Certain presses, such as Zed Books and Westview, along with ISIS International, have devoted much energy to publishing books on women in development, a topic that is integral to ecofeminism.[7]

Ecofeminists have described a number of connections between the oppressions of women and of nature that are significant to understanding why the environment is a feminist issue, and, conversely, why feminist issues can be addressed in terms of environmental concerns.[8] For example, the way in which women and nature have been conceptualized historically in the Western intellectual tradition has resulted in devaluing whatever is associated with women, emotion, animals, nature, and the body, while simultaneously elevating in value those things associated with men, reason, humans, culture, and the mind. One task of ecofeminists has been to expose these dualisms and the ways in which feminizing nature and naturalizing or animalizing women has served as justification for the domination of women, animals, and the earth.

Another connection between feminism, animal liberation, and environmentalism has been made by documenting the effects of environmental pollution and degradation on the lives of women and animals. Many writers note that toxic pesticides, chemical wastes, acid rain, radiation, and other pollutants take their first toll on women, women's reproductive systems, and children.[9] These hazardous chemicals are often initially tested on laboratory animals to determine levels of toxicity; this practice, together with the enormous environmental costs of factory farming and meat eating, demonstrate the linkages between environmental degradation and the oppression of nonhuman animals (speciesism). The racism and classism inherent in First World development strategies, built on one ethic for economic production at "home" but another ethic for the Third World, have resulted in tremendous hardships for women, who are frequently the major providers of food, fuel, and water in developing countries.[10] By documenting the poor quality of life for women, children, people in the Third World, animals, and the environment, ecofeminists are able to demonstrate that sexism, racism, classism, speciesism, and naturism (the oppression of nature) are mutually reinforcing systems of oppression. Instead of being a "single-issue" movement, ecofeminism rests on the notion that the liberation of all oppressed groups must be addressed simultaneously. It is for this reason that I see coalition-building strategies as critical to our success. For if one thing is certain, it is that women alone cannot "save the earth"—we need the efforts of men as well.

What has kept ecofeminists from joining wholeheartedly with environmentalists thus far is a fear of the ecological "melting pot." Repeatedly, women who join men in progressive movements have been silenced or relegated to traditionally feminine, supportive roles—as noted by the cofounder of Feminists for Animal Rights, Marti Kheel. A movement that sees the concerns of women—or any oppressed group—as something "extra" to be "integrated" cannot hope to enlist our energies or address our needs. Until their analyses take all forms of oppression into account, building coalitions between environmental and social activist groups may be the best way to ensure full representation while maintaining diversity.

Within ecofeminist theory, the place of animals must be addressed. In *Rethinking Ecofeminist Politics*, Janet Biehl charges that while ecofeminists celebrate a plurality of voices and viewpoints in both the formal presentation of the theory (collections rather than single-author texts) and in the voices of the theorists themselves, ecofeminism remains "self-contradictory": "Ecofeminists who even acknowledge the existence of serious contradictions," writes Biehl, "tend to pride themselves on the contradictions in their works as a healthy sign of 'diversity'—presumably in contrast to 'dogmatic,' fairly consistent, and presumably 'male' or 'masculine' theories."[11] Biehl discredits ecofeminism based on what she perceives as its theoretical inconsistencies. And in regard to vegetarianism, she is right: in the three anthologies published at the time of this writing, ecofeminism has failed to locate animals as central to any discussion of ethics involving women and nature.[12] Some theorists, most notably Marti Kheel and Carol Adams, have taken this issue as their special concern, while others dismiss it entirely. Addressing the centrality of all life on earth—which includes all animal species—has been the motivating force for this present collection.

The contributors to this volume reject the nature/culture dualism of patriarchal thought, and locate animals and humans within nature. In essence, this shift involves reconceptualizing the framework of ecofeminism. We are attempting to enter into dialogue with other ecofeminists, building on or challenging this theory as it develops.

The two chapters that follow provide an introduction to ecofeminist theory that places humans and animals within a wider conception of nature. Chapter 2, "Ecofeminism: Linking Theory and Practice," by Janis Birkeland, analyzes the conflict between green politics and ecofeminism. Green philosophy is predicated on the belief that fundamental social transformation is necessary. What appears to be the mainstream in green philosophy holds that anthropocentrism is the root of our social and environmental problems. Ecofeminism, in contrast, views anthropocentrism as a symptom of a much deeper problem: androcentrism. Changing our anthropocentric way of experiencing the world will not exorcise the underlying pathology, our power-based morality or "patriarchy." An ecofeminist paradigm has the potential to help us see and redress the historical split between experiential/individual and critical/institutional approaches in environmental theory.

"Dismantling Oppression: An Analysis of the Connection Between

Women and Animals" by Lori Gruen (Chapter 3) explores the construction of women and animals as dominated, submissive Others in theoretical discourse and everyday practice. In the name of scientific progress, experimenters have (ab)used women's and animals' bodies as the sites of medical research. One of the many implications of this scientific conceptualization of bodies has been an obsession with hygiene and appearance that distances humans from nature. Another implication has been the mechanization of food production and consumption, which negatively affects both women and animals. Gruen places these examples against the background of feminist and animal liberation theories and suggests that these traditional views promote and perpetuate unnecessary and unsustainable dichotomies (between nature and culture, between reason and emotion). Gruen's conclusion illustrates how ecofeminist theory can provide an alternative, inclusive framework for liberation struggles.

The next three chapters discuss various applications of ecofeminist theory, whether in academe or through direct action. Chapter 4, "Roots: Rejoining Natural and Social History," by Stephanie Lahar, offers a foundation for an ecofeminist reading of history. According to Lahar, the human/nature dualism that has been a starting point for ecofeminist theory underlies and undermines our relations to the environment, other people, and that which is embodied and unmediated in ourselves. One effect of this split is that we understand personal and collective histories from a culturally ingrained, dualistic perspective. This perspective perpetuates dynamics that have consistently oppressed women and other nondominant groups, and exploited nonhuman nature. Lahar explores the integration of natural and social history through a primary example of European migrations to lands that were colonized from 1600 to 1900, and uses this example to reframe contemporary questions of historical responsibility, lifestyle choices, and public policy.

"Ecofeminism and the Politics of Reality" by Linda Vance (Chapter 5) connects the theory and practice of ecofeminism. While hiking through the woods, she re-envisions women's history by looking for our place in the natural environment, both past and future. Vance critiques the male environmentalist description of nature as mother, protectress, provider, and nurturer as based primarily in male desire, and argues for a feminist reconceptualization of nature as sister, based on the common oppression shared by women and the nonhuman world. Vance conceptualizes ecofeminism as a sisterly bond, a fundamental rejection of all forms of domination, whose necessary goal is diversity rather than dualism.

7

In Chapter 6, "Questioning Sour Grapes: Ecofeminism and the United Farm Workers Grape Boycott," Ellen O'Loughlin uses the grape boycott as a window for analyzing ecofeminism's potential for being an inclusive, multifaceted philosophy for creating change. O'Loughlin argues that ecofeminist theory must be grounded in material and economic analyses if it is to be a transformative movement to end all oppression, rather than an essentialist equation of women and nature. Her examination of the material realities of women's and men's lives reveals many relations of oppression and exploitation between various groupings of people and the earth. Rather than ignoring the diversity of these oppressions, ecofeminists must actively support movements addressing them. O'Loughlin considers the ways in which the concerns of farm workers in the United States are relevant to ecofeminism. In particular, she explores the UFW-organized grape boycott as an informative example of how ecological and health concerns can link consumers and laborers originally separated by class, color, and culture.

Two chapters give specific focus to animal liberation and its relationship to ecofeminism. "Animal Rights and Feminist Theory" by Josephine Donovan (Chapter 7) provides a feminist framework for interpreting the claims of animal rights theorists. Donovan surveys the theories of traditional male philosophers who have advanced the dialogue surrounding animal rights, and shows how feminist analyses depart from these standard, rights-based ethical systems. Drawing on arguments advanced by Paula Gunn Allen, Marilyn French, Carol Gilligan, Sara Ruddick, and others, Donovan articulates an expanded feminist theory based on human interconnectedness and responsibility to all life.

"The Feminist Traffic in Animals" by Carol Adams (Chapter 8) provides an ecofeminist analysis of the anti–animal rights critique within feminism. Adams speculates about the construction of bodies within ecofeminism, and contrasts this construction with the feminist traffic in animals. As Adams observes, theorizing about difference in terms of species has been positioned as less central to feminism than theorizing about difference in terms of race, class, gender, and heterosexism. But in the self/other dualism of patriarchal thought, "others" are feminized or animalized by the same ideological process in order to make their subordination seem more natural. Adams makes this connection explicitly in terms of the meals served at feminist conferences: arguing against a logic that privatizes food choices by making the political seem personal, or a logic that naturalizes food choices by making the domination and consumption of other species seem inevitable, Adams demonstrates that a feminist meal will be a vegetarian meal.

This collection is also committed to unveiling the harmful implications of the woman-nature association in Western culture. Chapter 9, "For the Love of Nature: Ecology and the Cult of the Romantic" by Chaia Heller, explores the historical relationship between the domination and the romanticization of women, illustrating the functions of the cult of the romantic. Our modern iconography has rendered nature as a victimized woman, an angelic or madonna-like figure to be pitied, romanticized, and "saved." Heller exposes the use of these romantic images to rationalize the domination of women and the devastation of nature. Instead of inciting activism, this portrayal of nature as the modern-day romantic madonna evokes passive, teary sympathy. Heller cites specific examples in which the U.S. government, multinational corporations, liberal environmentalists, and even deep ecologists have used romantic metaphors to obscure the social, patriarchal origins of the ecological crisis. By deromanticizing both women and nature, ecofeminism seeks to build bonds between women cross-culturally in order to end oppression.

"From Heroic to Holistic Ethics: The Ecofeminist Challenge" by Marti Kheel (Chapter 10) describes traditional ethical theories as advocating a type of heroism that needs to be replaced by an ecofeminist ethic of holism. Whereas nature ethicists have tended to concentrate on "saving" the "damsel in distress," ecofeminists have tended to ask how and why the "damsel" arrived at her present plight. This plight, as Kheel describes it, involves a truncated narrative of domination whose missing stories cannot be retrieved using traditional patriarchal ethics. As a holistic ethic, ecofeminism completes the fragmented world view we have inherited by allowing the voices of women and nature to be heard.

Our last two chapters explore the cultural limitations of ecofeminism, for as the philosopher Karen Warren has noted, one of the boundary conditions for a feminist ethic is that it is contextual. In Chapter 11, "A Cross-Cultural Critique of Ecofeminism," Huey-li Li finds that although there are parallels between the oppression of women and the oppression of nature, the woman-nature affinity is not a cross-cultural phenomenon. Moreover, the absence of a transcendent dualism in Chinese society does not preclude women's oppression; in fact, there are no exact parallels between Chinese people's respectful attitude toward nature and the social and political inferiority of women. Li explores the transcendent dualism analyzed by Rosemary Radford Ruether, the mechanism outlined by Carolyn Merchant, and the problem of sexual differentiation described by Elizabeth

Dodson Gray in terms of specific cultural limitations. For non-Western women, the praxis of ecofeminism—which aims to end the interrelated oppressions of racism, sexism, classism, and ecological destruction—is more likely to ensure the solidarity of the global ecofeminist movement than is the culture-specific concept of an affinity between woman and nature.

Finally, my chapter, "Ecofeminism and Native American Cultures: Pushing the Limits of Cultural Imperialism?" (Chapter 12), examines three areas of debate within ecofeminism that have the potential to coopt Native American cultures: the place of animals within ecofeminist theory, the feminization of nature as "Mother Earth," and the movement to reclaim the goddess in an ecofeminist spirituality. Ecofeminists have on occasion resorted to using Native American culture when convenient for building theory. Such use of a marginalized culture by a member of a dominant culture is acontextual and imperialistic. Through a culture-specific discussion of animals, "Mother Earth," and the goddess, I propose that ecofeminism can and must address these topics and others while avoiding cultural imperialism.

As the human species approaches the capacity to annihilate all life on this planet, it becomes imperative that we challenge both the ideological assumptions and the hierarchical structures of power and domination that together serve to hold the majority of earth's inhabitants in thrall to the privileged minority. Ecofeminists seek to articulate this challenge. Our goal in writing this book is to contribute to the evolving dialogue among feminists, ecofeminists, animal liberationists, deep ecologists, social ecologists—in short, all those in the international radical ecology movement who are dedicated to creating a sustainable way of life for all inhabitants on earth.

## NOTES

1. Citing Robert Coles' 1977 study, *Eskimos, Chicanos, Indians*, and John Langston Gwaltney's 1980 text, *Drylongso: A Self-Portrait of Black America*, Joan Tronto suggests that "the moral views of minority group members in the United States are much more likely to be characterized by an ethic of care than by an ethic of justice." See "Beyond Gender Difference to a Theory of Care," *Signs* 12 (1987): 650.

2. See Nancy Chodorow, *The Reproduction of Mothering: Psychoanalysis and the Sociology of Gender* (Berkeley: University of California Press, 1978); Carol Gilligan, *In a Different Voice: Psychological Theory and Women's Development* (Cambridge: Harvard University Press, 1982); Carol Gilligan, Janie Ward, Jill McLean Taylor, and

Betty Bardige, eds., *Mapping the Moral Domain* (Cambridge: Harvard University Press, 1988); and Seyla Benhabib, "The Generalized and the Concrete Other: The Kohlberg-Gilligan Controversy and Feminist Theory," in *Feminism as Critique: On the Politics of Gender*, ed. Seyla Benhabib and Drucilla Cornell (Minneapolis: University of Minnesota Press, 1987), 77–95. Gilligan's theory of moral development has been debated; see "On *In a Different Voice:* An Interdisciplinary Forum," *Signs* 11 (1986): 304–33.

3. "Although detachment connotes the dispassion which signifies fairness in justice reasoning, the ability to stand back from oneself and from others and to weigh conflicting claims even-handedly in the abstract, detachment also connotes the absence of connection and has the potential to create the conditions for carelessness or violation, for violence toward others or toward oneself." See Gilligan et al., *Mapping the Moral Domain*, xxviii.

4. *In a Different Voice*, 19.

5. Karen Warren, "Toward an Ecofeminist Ethic," *Studies in the Humanities* 15 (1988): 140–56.

6. For two days in November of 1980 and 1981, women surrounded the Pentagon to protest the violence of militarism and the sexual and economic violence in the everyday lives of women.

7. Zed Books' impressive list of titles includes Bina Agarwal, ed., *The Structures of Patriarchy: The State, the Community and the Household* (1989); Kumari Jayawardena, *Feminism and Nationalism in the Third World* (1986); Maria Mies, *Patriarchy and Accumulation on a World Scale: Women in the International Division of Labour* (1986); Miranda Davies, ed., *Third World, Second Sex*, 2 vols. (1983); Hikka Pietila and Jeanne Vickers, *Making Women Matter: The Role of the United Nations* (1990). In addition, this press publishes texts on issues involving women, economics, and the land within specific countries. ISIS International is an international nongovernmental women's organization that promotes networking, communication, and cooperation among women and groups working for women's empowerment. They publish *Women in Action*, the *Women's Health Journal*, and other periodicals, and distribute information packets of interest to ecofeminists, such as *Women's Action for the Environment*.

8. See Karen Warren, "Feminism and the Environment: An Overview of the Issues," *APA Newsletter on Feminism and Philosophy* 90 (Fall 1991): 108–16.

9. See Petra Kelly, "Women and Global Green Politics: A Call for the Formation of a New Political Party in the United States," *Woman of Power* 20 (Spring 1991) : 24–25; Lloyd Timberlake and Laura Thomas, *When the Bough Breaks . . . Our Children, Our Environment* (London: Earthscan Publications, 1990).

10. See Bella Abzug, "Women and the Fate of the Earth: The World Women's Congress for a Healthy Planet," *Woman of Power* 20 (Spring 1991): 26–30; Mies, *Patriarchy and Accumulation*; Vandana Shiva, *Staying Alive: Women, Ecology and Development* (London: Zed Books, 1988).

11. See Janet Biehl, *Rethinking Ecofeminist Politics* (Boston: South End Press, 1991), 3.

12. Caldecott and Leland, *Reclaim the Earth* (1983), included one such essay by Norma Benney, "All of One Flesh: The Rights of Animals"; Plant, *Healing the Wounds* (1989), included no essays specifically on animals; and Diamond and Orenstein, *Reweaving the World* (1990), included one, Sally Abbott's "The Origins of God in the Blood of the Lamb." Slightly better presentation of the women-animal connection can be found in *Hypatia*'s special issue on "Ecological Feminism" (vol. 6, Spring 1991), which included two such essays: Deborah Slicer's "Your Daughter or Your Dog?" (108–24), and Carol Adams' "Ecofeminism and the Eating of Animals" (125–45).

# CHAPTER 2

# Ecofeminism:
# Linking Theory and Practice

## Janis Birkeland

> The price of patriarchy is eternal vigilance;
> Ecofeminism is its own reward.

Radical green philosophy is premised on the conviction that the sources of the environmental crisis are deeply rooted in modern culture, and therefore fundamental social transformation is necessary if we are to preserve life on earth in any meaningful sense. This follows from the realization that we cannot rely on patchwork reforms through more appropriate economics, technology, and regulation, or better policies gained through green electoral politics. Our public choice mechanisms and technocratic methods are inherently biased against environmental preservation and conflict prevention.[1] Therefore, the gradual attrition, degradation, and biological impoverishment of the natural environment are inevitable under the existing system. To save a wilderness area is to hold a finger in a bursting dam: it only buys time.

While the recent electoral success of the environmental movement in some parts of the world appears to be grounds for optimism, the system of representational democracy is itself biased toward short-term benefits at long-term cost. Further, better environmental policy means little where powerful resource extraction and development interests are above governments and above the market. Special interests have the ability to create real or apparent threats of resource shortages to disempower the environmental movement, just as they have historically exploited business downturns to weaken the labor movement. But unlike labor, wilderness is not an interest group: it cannot lose political battles and still win the war. Ecosystems cannot be put back.

There is another problem with political "success." Pressure politics is a matter of power, and while power attracts new talent, it also can divide and corrupt. We are beginning to see this in the green movement in Australia. Many "nouveau greens" seeking positions in the public arena lack a deep analysis or an ethical commitment sufficient to prevent the compromise of principles or a latent agenda of personal power. The process of cooptation has begun: a pluralist environmental movement is gradually being transformed into a structure of corporatist representation and mediation.[2] The legitimation of environmental interests by incorporation into existing decision-making structures, as has happened with the labor movement, cannot resolve the underlying psychological and behavioral causes of environmental or social conflict.

The other superficial ground for optimism is the burgeoning number of environmental professionals whose role is to advise government and industry. Environmental specialists are multiplying in all professions, and we now have "environmental" economists, scientists, administrators, lawyers, and planners promoting marginal reforms. The decision-making methodologies these professions use, however, are heavily influenced by concepts derived from the mainstream liberal paradigm and are biased against the preservation of species and ecosystems. For example, because they are geared to analyzing the costs and benefits of development alternatives, they balance off public needs to meet private wants over the long term. Even more fundamentally, an instrumentalist and anthropocentric ethic—whereby human and natural "resources" are construed to have value to the extent that they can be used for human purposes—is endemic to the technocratic methodologies, decision-making processes, and regulatory schemes. This ethic is a natural outgrowth of a "power complex" that is so deeply ingrained in the modern psyche that planners and decision makers who consider themselves environmentally aware continue to make decisions that facilitate the exponential destruction of the nonhuman environment by incremental trade-offs of environmental quality for economic growth.

Thus, while it is important to work for electoral success, environmental consciousness, better policies, and more scientific research, these cannot change the deeply rooted behavior patterns and structural relationships that led to the environmental crisis in the first place. Nor can these change the nature of the decision-making methods and processes that support business as usual. If we value life, then we must transform the cultural and institutional infrastructure[3]—our frameworks of thinking, relating, and acting. The question is, how do we get from here to there? This is where green philosophies divide.

To discuss these differences, we need to establish some terms. For present purposes, there are two basic orientations in the green movement: "masculinist" and "feminist" values, analyses, and strategies. (I use "masculine" and "feminine" as metaphorical icons for systems of value to which people of either sex can subscribe.) Masculinist or "Manstream" theory is that which insists on a gender-blind analysis and disregards the political nature of gender. Because Manstream green thought is gender-blind, it retains some of the basic androcentric or male-centered premises of mainstream theory, which, as we shall see, impedes both green analysis and green strategy.

Two basic orientations within the Manstream itself correspond loosely to left and liberal *strategies* for social change but *not* left and liberal ideology. The "Leftist" approach sees institutional change as preceding personal transformation. Roughly speaking, ecosocialism and social ecology can be placed in this category. I exclude Marxist strategy as it is inconsistent with green principles: an approach that relies on crisis conditions resulting from structural or ecological contradictions is incompatible with environmental protection. The "Liberalist" approach takes the individual as a sovereign actor, and sees changing individual values and perceptions as the primary means toward social transformation. This category includes deep ecologists, New Age, and the majority of those called "greens." (Of course, as Judith Plant reminds us, "we are the social system," (so the split is one of emphasis.)[4] I use the terms "Leftist" and "Liberalist" to convey the notion that green strategies and processes still reflect, in part, the mainstream approach to social change, even though the green movement presents a radical vision for new ecological societies. Both orientations ultimately— though indirectly—rely on persuading enough people to change their beliefs and values and hence public policy.

I will argue that to the extent that environmental academics ignore feminist theory, and activists ignore feminist practice, they are supporting the status quo and impeding social transformation. To this end, I discuss the different schools of green though briefly in terms of their implications for the content and process of social transformation. I will point out some ways in which these biases infect green theory, analysis, and practice. My central concern is to show that green theory in general has not yet come to grips with the deeper impediments to personal and social transformation because it is gender-blind and trapped in an androcentric prism. Because of limited space, however, I will concentrate on the different implications of ecofeminism as compared with the particular Liberalist orientation that centers on human (as opposed to male) chauvinism.[5] As a reference point, I use the literature of deep ecology, which sees anthropocentrism (human-centeredness) as the crucial barrier to social transformation.

The hard distinctions I make between ecofeminist and Manstream radical theory and practice are drawn only for the sake of clarifying concepts. These viewpoints are overlapping and mutually complementary in many ways. However, I will argue that the focus on changing our anthropocentric way of experiencing or perceiving nature is inadequate either as an analysis or a program of action. While human chauvinism must be overcome, it cannot be overcome without addressing male-centeredness and sexism. (I should add that my use of a masculinist style of argumentation is deliberate.)

I will also explain why I believe that, of the many shades of green thought, ecofeminism offers the most comprehensive and incisive sociopolitical analysis to guide both self- and social transformation at this point in history. Just as Leftist green theories do not offer a framework that can adequately theorize the personal dimension of power, the Liberalist green framework cannot adequately theorize the structural dimension. Ecofeminism contributes the necessary insight into the link between the abuse of power on personal and political levels that underlies human oppression and environmental exploitation. On a theoretical level, an ecofeminist paradigm can help us to redress the historical split between experiential/individual (Liberalist) and critical/institutional (Leftist) orientations. On a practical level, it can enable us to link environmental theory and practice, and to develop new strategies for social change.

## An Ecofeminist Paradigm

As I said, there is a prevalent tendency among green theorists to see anthropocentrism as operating behind social and environmental problems, or, at least as providing the legitimation for the exploitation of nature. If this were so, it would follow that the means to create better societies is through changing our perception of our "selves" in relation to nature, or, as deep ecologists would have it, expanding our sense of identification to encompass all life, perhaps even "Gaia" itself. I contend, however, that changing our anthropocentric way of experiencing the world—an objective ecofeminists certainly support—will not exorcise a more crucial pathology of our contemporary culture: our power-based structures and relationships. Nor will it make sufficiently visible the prism that de-forms our attitude toward nonhuman nature. I call this prism the "Power Paradigm," as no existing term encompasses both levels of human relationships: content and process, or ideology and behavior. This concept is not intended to reduce the social/ environmental problem to a culturally encoded power drive, but rather to construct a framework that can unite both power relations (Patriarchy) and personal morality (Power Paradigm)—namely, ecofeminism.

In the vernacular, "Patriarchy" refers to the male-dominated system of social relations and values, and should be distinguished from "hierarchy," which refers to relationships of command and obedience enforced by (Patriarchal) social structures and institutions.[6] In Patriarchy, as we shall see, the systemic devaluation of the "feminine principle" has been a fundamental basis of domination.[7] In Western Patriarchal culture, "masculine" constructs and values have been internalized in our minds, embodied in our institutions, and played out in power-based social relations both in our daily lives and upon the world stage. It is this "masculine" undercurrent, not human-centeredness, which is behind the irrational ideas and behavior displayed on the evening news.

The glorification of what have traditionally been seen as "masculine" values and the drive for power and control are simply maladaptive in an age of toxic waste and nuclear weapons. Healing the powerful psychological undercurrents created by thousands of years of Patriarchy requires rigorous self- and social criticism. We must move beyond limiting conceptions of both masculine and feminine in ourselves and in our societies. This requires not only introspection, but a gender-conscious political analysis, because only through naming the invisible realities can we break "the silent conspiracy that upholds the status quo."[8]

### Ecofeminism Defined

There are many types of "feminisms" (such as liberal, Marxist, separatist, and anarchical feminism), as well as individual interpretations of these positions. Catharine MacKinnon has explained these prefixes by suggesting that "liberal feminism is liberalism applied to women, Marxist feminism is Marxism applied to women, and radical feminism is feminism."[9] Along similar lines, I see ecofeminism as feminism taken to its logical conclusion, because it theorizes the interrelations among self, societies, and nature. Another view, however, is expressed by Anne Cameron:

> The term "ecofeminism" is an insult to the women who put themselves on the line, risked public disapproval, risked even violence and jail. . . . Feminism has always been actively involved in the peace movement, in the antinuclear movement, and in the environmental protection movement. Feminism is what helped teach us all that the link between political and industrial included the military and was a danger to all life on this planet. To separate ecology from feminism is to try to separate the heart from the head.[10]

While I agree with this sentiment, some feminisms are anthropocentric, while ecofeminism is not. In addition, the term "ecofeminism" is more descriptive of a concern with cultivating an ecological ethic that goes beyond concepts of social justice alone. It has also been suggested that the prefix "eco" is a sop to those masculine-identified greens who cannot handle feminism. However, in my experience, such people have a harder time coming to terms with ecofeminism, as it strikes deeper into the core of Patriarchal reason.

We will begin by defining ecofeminism, and then discuss some of the main false stereotypes that are applied to it. Rather than trying to encapsulate the expanding literature on ecofeminism here, I present one perspective. Ecofeminism is a value system, a social movement, and a practice, but it also offers a *political analysis* that explores the links between androcentrism and environmental destruction. It is "an awareness" that begins with the realization that the exploitation of nature is intimately linked to Western Man's attitude toward women and tribal cultures or, in Ariel Salleh's words, that there is a "parallel in men's thinking between their 'right' to exploit nature, on the one hand, and the use they make of women, on the other."[11]

In the dominant Patriarchal cultures, reality is divided according to gender, and a higher value is placed on those attributes associated with masculinity, a construction that is called "hierarchical dualism."[12] In these cultures, women have historically been seen as closer to the earth or nature (perhaps due to childbirth and menstruation). Also, women and nature have been juxtaposed against mind and spirit, which have been associated in Western cosmology with the "masculine" and elevated to a higher plane of being. Although we can only speculate about how Patriarchal consciousness evolved, it is clear that a complex morality based on dominance and exploitation has developed in conjunction with the devaluing of nature and "feminine" values.

This association of women and nature has had tragic consequences for humans and the rest of nature. Some feminists have suggested, however, that this association can be converted into a positive by affirming so-called feminine values, such as caring, openness, and nurturing. This affirmation has been distorted by some who seem to fear that women will somehow take power and do what men have done. However, the very essence of ecofeminism is its challenge to the presumed necessity of power relationships. It is about changing from a morality based on "power over" to one based on reciprocity and responsibility ("power to"). Ecofeminists believe that we cannot end the exploitation of nature without ending human oppression, and vice versa. To do both, they reason, we must expose the assumptions that support Patriarchy and disconnect our concept of masculinity from that of "power over" others and the rejection and denigration of the "feminine."

To this end, as we shall see, feminism challenges the masculine model of Man upon which both mainstream theories and radical critiques depend. Nonfeminist theories generally assume that (male) subjects or decision-makers are unaffected by or (by virtue of their formal positions and responsible perspectives) somehow transcend the personal and nonrational. Psychosexual drives, emotional needs, and personal politics are ignored to the extent that they are incompatible with the archetypal male image. Ecofeminism, in contrast, explains Man's ecocidal behavior in terms of real emotions and life experience, such as sexual identity, the fear of death, the link between personal worth and power, the repressed need to belong, and other expressions of personal insecurity.[13] In Charlene Spretnak's words, "Identifying the dynamics—largely fear and resentment—behind the dominance of male over female is the key to comprehending every expression of patriarchal culture with its hierarchical, militaristic, mechanistic, industrial forms."[14]

While ecofeminism provides a useful framework for political analysis, it is perhaps most fundamentally a process. To ecofeminists, values and action are inseparable: one cannot care without acting. Ecofeminist theory and analysis has only been developing since the 1970s, but the practice has been around for much longer, and has been growing in many parts of the world.[15]

Ecofeminism is also a holistic value system. Some basic precepts to which most ecofeminists would subscribe are set out below.[16] This chapter should clarify their meaning.

1. Fundamental social transformation is necessary. We must reconstruct the underlying values and structural relations of our cultures. The promotion of equality, nonviolence, cultural diversity, and participatory, noncompetitive, and nonhierarchical forms of organization and decision making would be among the criteria for these new social forms.

2. Everything in nature has intrinsic value. A reverence for, and empathy with, nature and all life (or "spirituality") is an essential element of the social transformation required.

3. Our anthropocentric viewpoint, instrumentalist values, and mechanistic models should be rejected for a more biocentric view that can comprehend the interconnectedness of all life processes.

4. Humans should not attempt to "manage" or control nonhuman nature, but should work with the land. The use of agricultural land should be guided by an ethic of reciprocity. Humans should intrude upon the remaining natural ecosystems and processes only where necessary to preserve natural diversity.

5. Merely redistributing power relationships is no answer. We must change the fact of power-based relationships and hierarchy, and move toward an ethic based on mutual respect. We must move beyond power.

6. We must integrate the false dualisms that are based on the male/female polarity (such as thought versus action, the spiritual versus the natural, art versus science, experience versus knowledge) in our perception of reality. The dualistic conceptual framework of Patriarchy supports the ethic of dominance and divides us against each other, our "selves," and nonhuman nature.

7. Process is as important as goals, simply because how we go about things determines where we go. As the power-based relations and processes that permeate our societies are reflected in our personal relationships, we must enact our values.

8. The personal is political. We must change the ideology that says the morality of the (female) private sphere has no application to the (male) public sphere of science, politics, and industry. We must work to rebalance the masculine and feminine in ourselves and society.

9. We cannot change the nature of the system by playing Patriarchal "games." If we do, we are abetting those who are directly involved in human oppression and environmental exploitation. We must therefore withdraw power and energy from the Patriarchy.

## Misconceptions About Ecofeminism

In my experience, ecofeminism is more threatening to masculine-identified men and women than environmentalism because it hits closer to home. Not surprisingly, then, it has been falsely stereotyped to such an extent that most debates about ecofeminism revolve around misconceptions rather than matters of substance.[17] The main misconceptions are that it is dualistic, partial, anti-rational, and "essentialist" (that is, it endorses the idea that women's nature is unchanging and that they are inherently "closer to nature"). However, in each case it is not ecofeminism, but rather Patriarchal theories, to which these adjectives should be applied.

### DUALISM

The misunderstanding that ecofeminism is dualistic probably derives from the ecofeminist suggestion that alternatives to Patriarchy are possible, as evidenced in women's and tribal cultures. That is, some mistakenly construe ecofeminism as conceiving of women as a "homogeneous whole" (in opposition to men) without making adequate distinctions between different races, nationalities, classes, and so on. This, of course, would run counter to the affirmation of cultural diversity by ecofeminists—and by most greens, for that matter. The notion that women could have some similarities in experience and consciousness across national and class boundaries, due to certain shared conditions, is especially troublesome to those who reduce social problems to the existence of classes.[18] This is ironic, as the idea that workers in different industries, cultures, or nations could have a similar consciousness is essential to a class-based analysis.[19] The reality is that men of all classes use and take for granted power over women within their class, workplace, political party, or family structure, even—or especially—when power in the public arena is denied to those men. This is evidenced by the fact that violence toward women is fairly universal in Patriarchal societies and does not differ significantly across class boundaries.[20]

### INCOMPLETENESS

Ecofeminism has also been portrayed as partial or incomplete, as if it were the shadow side of a "real" theory. Similarly, "feminine" cultures or value systems, along with those of tribal peoples, are regarded as childlike, or unworthy of the term "culture." However, in Patriarchal circles, aboriginals and women are credited with a separate experience and value system when this is useful as a basis for asserting control over them, and only denied them in order to delegitimize these groups or their claims. When women begin to evince self-esteem, they are accused of essentialism or reverse sexism. (The arrogance of labeling the idea that women could have thoughts or experience of their own as "sexist"!)

## ESSENTIALISM

The major attack against ecofeminism, however, has been that it allegedly claims that women possess an essential nature—a biological connection or a spiritual affinity with nature that men do not.[21] While perhaps some women believe this, it is not a concept relevant to ecofeminism as such. In the first place, "essentialism" would be inconsistent with the logic of ecofeminism, let alone mainstream ecology. After all, as Ynestra King and others have explained, since all life is interconnected, one group of persons cannot be closer to nature.[22] The assertion of "difference" is based on the historical socialization and oppression of women, not biologism. If gender is shaped by culture, ideology, and history, and how one experiences nature is culturally mediated, then gender conditioning would tend to shape our experience of nature. Of course, the diversity of women and their experience is certainly not denied by ecofeminists. In fact, this diversity is celebrated and seen as a cause for optimism: diversity is vital in the effort to bring about social change.

The accusation that ecofeminism is essentialist, I believe, results from a Patriarchal way of thinking. That is, it presupposes the legitimacy of the Patriarchal construct that sees nature as separate from culture. As Joan Griscom explains, "The question itself is flawed. Only the nature/history split allows us even to formulate the question of whether women are closer to nature than men. The very idea of one group of persons being 'closer to nature' than another is a 'construct of culture.'"[23]

In the second place, whether women are "closer to nature" or generally experience nature differently is a purely academic question. We cannot know if gender differences are due primarily to genes, hormones, an essential nature, culture, or the division of labor.[24] (However, considering that throughout recorded history Mankind has sent forth armies of aggressive males to rape and pillage, it would appear that aggression could not be genetic—or there would be no gentle genes left!) But this is not the issue. What matters is that men and women have shown the capacity consciously to choose other values and behavior patterns. We have seen women adopt "masculine" personal processes to varying extents when they wish to be part of a power structure, and, more optimistically, we have seen some men become caring, gentle, and nondominating. In short, men can subscribe to ecofeminism, and, in fact, their cooperation is necessary if we are to save the planet.

### ANTI-RATIONALISM

Finally, ecofeminism is not anti-rational but rather highlights the patent irrationality of Patriarchy, and the false model of impersonal Man upon which most mainstream theories and radical critiques are based. Despite its political analysis, however, ecofeminism is visionary and shares with deep ecology the advocacy of a "spiritual" identification with nature, by which is meant a reverence for life processes without regard to their usefulness to humans.[25] However, ecofeminism is not a religion, and people of any belief system can take on board the ethical and political insights it offers. As expressed by Starhawk, who is on the spiritual wing of ecofeminism: "Earth-based spirituality influences ecofeminism by informing its values. This does not mean that every ecofeminist must worship the goddess, perform rituals, or adopt any particular belief system."[26]

Those of us who are not religious must recognize that the denial of the apparent spiritual needs of most people is potentially as dangerous as the other extreme—religious dogmatism and/or superstition. Something, it seems, will always fill a spiritual vacuum. A reverence for life processes and a deep sense of interconnectedness with all life forms such as that encouraged by ecofeminism is not soon likely to become a Patriarchal belief system. Even so, the honoring and healing of the earth would come as a welcome relief from bearing witness to the tiresome incantations of economic rationalists on the fantasy of unlimited growth, the atrocious icons of masculinity erected by developers, or the cruel, sacrificial rituals carried out by militarists.

We will now turn to some theoretical problems of Manstream green thought with regard to the environmental problem, and subsequently to problems of Manstream green analysis and practice.

## *Problems of Manstream Theory*

Many have proposed accounts of the historical origins of Patriarchy, but that subject is beyond the scope of this chapter. I will begin with the Enlightenment philosophy of the eighteenth century, in which is embedded the dominant paradigm of modernity, or the growth ethic. The Enlightenment introduced concepts that form the basis of mainstream thought today, elements of which are still found in Manstream green theory. During this Age of Reason, the previous view of history as cyclical was supplanted by a belief in progress: the concept that Society evolves in a forward progression. Progress was thought to be toward individual freedom and self-realization, which meant transcendence from social and natural constraints.

The Enlightenment thinkers held that all "men" possessed the faculty of reason. It was through this "masculinist" notion of reason—removed from emotion and intuition and disciplined by scientific method—that Man could ascertain the knowledge required for human progress. The Enlightenment also celebrated those ideals that were either associated with the masculine self (autonomy, individualism, transcendence) or concepts construed in masculine terms (instrumental rationality, the reductionist scientific method, freedom, and progress). The elevation of these masculine values has been greatly implicated in environmental problems, and it is the resulting imbalance that ecofeminism seeks to redress.

## The Androcentric Premise

The legacy of the history of male dominance, which I call the "androcentric premise," is still evidenced in virtually all modern schools of thought, even "radical" ones, as we shall see. Basically, it is an interpretation of human nature that assumes the universality of a masculine model of Man and its associated values. There are several important aspects to this premise. First is the *polarization* of masculine and feminine archetypes and the elevation of so-called masculine traits and values. Attributes defined as feminine (nurturing, caring, or accommodating) are seen as disadvantages, while those defined as masculine (competitive, dominating, or calculating) are encouraged. To be masculine, after all, is to dissociate oneself from "feminine" attributes.

Second is the historic association of women, nature, and earth. Because it is identified with the "feminine," nature is regarded as existing to serve Man's physical needs (and the reverse). This association of nature and women in Patriarchal societies underwrites *instrumentalism,* whereby things are valued only to the extent that they are useful to Man.

A third element of the androcentric premise is the idea that Man is *autonomous* or independent from both nature and community. This model of Man in Western thought has been described as a "mushroom"; he springs from nowhere as an adult male, with neither mother, nor sister, nor wife.[27] This false sense of masculine autonomy underlies the alienation and anthropocentrism to which many environmentalists trace the modern crisis.

Fourth is the *universalization* of male experience and values. As we will see, the egoistic conception of human nature—the image of Man striving for self-realization through independence from necessity (nature) and freedom from social constraints (community)—becomes the implicit goal of humanity as a whole. Due to this egocentric projection, what men do not experience is regarded as somewhat unimportant, distant, or unreal.

A fifth element is the linkage between masculinity and *power over* others. Masculinity is measured by power as well as distance from the "feminine." And because masculinity is linked with powerfulness and autonomy, dependency and powerlessness are perceived as marks of inferiority and grounds for unequal treatment. In the words of Bertrand de Jouvenel: "A man feels himself more of a man when he is imposing himself and making others the instruments of his will," which gives him "incomparable pleasure."[28]

## Political Implications

What, then, are the implications of the androcentric premise? I have explained elsewhere how this Patriarchal construction of reality is implicated in the behaviors and attitudes that environmentalists cite as underlying causes of the modern crisis: competitive individualism, human chauvinism, instrumentalism, hierarchy, parochialism, and the addiction to power.[29] But perhaps more important is that the androcentric premise prevents our questioning the necessity of power relationships per se.

That is, ostensibly gender-neutral theories protect the power structure by concealing the ideological basis of exploitative relationships. Militarism, colonialism, racism, classism, sexism, capitalism, and other pathological "isms" of modernity obtain legitimacy from the assumption that power relations and hierarchy are inevitably a part of human Society due to Man's "inherent nature." In other words, if Mankind is by nature autonomous, aggressive, and competitive (that is, "masculine"), then psychological and physical coercion or hierarchical structures are necessary to manage conflict and maintain social order. Likewise, cooperative relationships, such as those found among women or tribal cultures, are by definition unrealistic and utopian.

In authoritarian approaches, this essentialist conception of Man has been used to justify hierarchical authority, rules, and the apparatus to enforce them. In more liberal approaches, these same qualities are sometimes revered, even if distrusted. Liberal theory holds that Man's competitive, aggressive instincts should be allowed free rein to pursue His individual interests to the benefit of Society: a social construction of Man that justifies capitalism. In short, the dominant political ideologies, both pluralist and centralist, share the same masculine archetype as representing humanity, although it is used to justify different means of distributing power.

Now, if power relations stem from pre-political or universal truths about human nature, the basis of power relations is removed from the realm of political and social debate. We cannot challenge the legitimating basis of the power structure because we think it cannot be otherwise. Thus, since power relationships are preordained, militarism can be justified as unavoidable or necessary, regardless of its patent irrationality. Likewise, if humans will always compete for a greater share of resources, then the "rational" response to the environmental crisis would seem to be dog-eat-dog survivalism. This creates a self-fulfilling prophecy in which nature and community simply cannot survive.

Ecofeminists have mounted a challenge to this Patriarchal essentialism, or the idea that so-called "masculine" traits are the essence of human nature and that power structures are a necessary concomitant of human Society. First, of course, it would seem from human beings' relative physical weakness that human evolution must have depended on cooperation in its early stages. Second, if women are fully human, then it cannot be argued that humans are innately aggressive, given the Patriarchal conception of women as passive. And even if it is conceded, for argument's sake, that the power drive is intrinsic to all humans, the majority of humans, women, have largely been socialized to suppress it, so men can be too. As Salleh has pointed out, an alternative model to Man exists, but has been backgrounded.[30]

## The Androcentrism of Radical Theories

Because Manstream green theories are gender-blind, they do not adequately challenge the underlying bases of the ethic and ideology that they seek to change. A gender-blind prism hides problems centering on power, dominance, and masculinity, and consequently backgrounds certain realities with an impact upon the environment. Although radical environmental theories contribute important insights into the multifaceted nature of the environmental crisis, their usefulness is therefore limited. To varying extents, as we shall see, they share with mainstream social and political theory the implicit view of humans as masculine, ergo "rational" and/or striving for emancipation from natural and social constraints. I emphasize, of course, that environmentalists, being well-rounded people, do not fit well into square theories: many activists are anti-theory, which means that they are unaware of the extent to which their thinking has been shaped by theory. Finally, this critique applies only to First World environmentalists. We will begin with the least "green."

*Eco-Marxists* are at the fringe of the environmental movement because many have not abandoned their faith in industrial technology and their implicit view of "progress" as emancipation from nature. However, their critique of capitalism is an important component of environmental theory. For Marx, to become free was the ultimate goal of Man's existence, and freedom was to be achieved by mastery of nature through labor. That is, Marx saw human nature in terms of male norms: Man's essence was in "doing" (masculine) rather than in "being" (feminine). This is perhaps why Marx failed to appreciate that Man's freedom through labor and technology are made possible by the expropriation of a surplus from women and nonhuman nature.[31]

Orthodox eco-Marxists have also generally assumed that scientific "laws of nature" and instrumental reason would enable humans to predict and control the consequences of disrupting natural processes. In other words, solutions to environmental problems are dictated by "masculinist" terms (for example, control, choice, and change), rather than the "femininist" concerns of relationship, communication, and caring that are requisite for living in harmony with nature. Thus, eco-Marxists share the approach of mainstream capitalist environmental management, which does not prevent environmental problems but rather predicts, monitors, and mitigates them.

Critical Theorists (such as Jürgen Habermas, Max Horkheimer, and Theodor Adorno) have challenged that desire to control nature and engineer Society which characterizes both capitalism and Marxism. However, they have retained the anthropocentric idea that Man's highest purpose lies in His ability to achieve progress by transforming nature. Generally, the Critical Theorists have failed to appreciate that the reductionist scientific method, instrumental rationality, and bureaucratic institutions that have colonized the human psyche are grounded in, and legitimized by, a Patriarchal construction of reality.

*Ecosocialists* (such as Raymond Williams, Joe Weston, and Martin Ryle) also focus on the effects of capitalist (and state communist) economic and class structures in relation to environmental and social problems. Quite reasonably, they locate the root of social and ecological problems in the control of resources and accumulation of wealth by the few. Their platform is to restructure society and redistribute power to those who will presumably conserve and manage resources in the public interest. Socialists therefore share with liberals the view of social reform as a question of rearranging external social relations. Class relations, however, are better theorized in terms of the underlying logic of oppression—the Power Paradigm.

Socialist critiques do not adequately theorize the personal dimension of power. They fail to link the masculine psyche with the power structures themselves and to recognize that "the personal is political." Ecofeminists, in contrast, argue that if our societies do not move beyond power on *both* political and personal levels, reforms or revolutions will amount to no more than musical chairs over the long term. Whoever is in power will be subject to corruptive influences because of personal insecurity and the need for status and power engendered by a Patriarchal culture.

*Mainstream Greens,* the vast majority of environmental activists, are those who recognize the fundamental interconnections between social justice, peace, democracy, and environmental quality. They have developed policies and programs that would be consistent with an ecologically sustainable society, such as appropriate (small-scale) technologies and recycling, participatory democracy and decentralized communities, redefinitions of work and job sharing. However, the mainstream usually accepts the given political system as adequate, relying on building numbers to bring about better policies. In theorizing the causes of our irrational, lemminglike charge toward biospheric collapse, they, like Leftists, assume that Man is rational. Therefore, they hope to achieve social change by appealing to reason: raising the level of public awareness, lobbying, and promoting an appreciation of the intrinsic value of nature.

This strategy tends to reinforce the credibility of their opponents, who still, by and large, believe in a flat earth. Further, it does not address what really *motivates* people. In other words, the strategy does not look behind "self-interest" to the underlying desire for sex, love, and admiration. For example, Greens implicitly credit parliamentarians with an interest in pushing a particular policy orientation or getting reelected. Thus, they fail to take into account the fact that when parliamentarians "have the courage to make unpopular decisions" as dictated by corporate interests, they can escape via the "revolving door" between business and industry. Acceptance by the big boy's club can be more important than reelection. In short, despite voluminous tomes of mainstream theory to the contrary, Man does not tick by reason alone. But even were it so, numbers games cannot succeed in the long term in a system where the crucial decisions are made outside the political arena.

*Deep ecologists* reason that Man's failure to identify and empathize with the rest of nature results from the way He experiences or visualizes the world (rather than from power relations). They believe it is human chauvinism or anthropocentrism that has led to our separation from nonhuman nature.[32] Hence, personal transformation through the cultivation of a "biocentric" perspective—expanding one's identification to encompass all of nature— would heal Society as a whole. Thus, deep ecologists also rely ultimately on reason to persuade people to take up deep ecology. Once realizing that to harm nature is to harm Himself, Rational Man will then presumably change His ways.

While sharing a biocentric perspective, ecofeminists have criticized deep ecology because of its masculinist bias—because it is abstract, aloof, impersonal, and gender-blind, and it ignores power.[33] Deep ecologists deny the significance of gender and feminist analysis and therefore, in effect, perpetuate the dualistic thinking that they seek to transform. By subsuming women under a gender-neutral model of Man, they paradoxically exclude women and set them apart. A gender-blind analysis that centers on Man's relationship to nature also does little to explain power relations *within* societies. Therefore, deep ecology cannot adequately theorize or remedy the abuse of power. I will discuss at length below this Liberalist approach to social transformation (the strategy that relies on changing individual values).

*Social ecology,* in contrast, does address the issue of dominance relationships. Social ecology is a school of thought that follows the work of Murray Bookchin.[34] It traces the origins of the exploitation of nature to hierarchical social institutions, beginning with gerontocracy and Patriarchy. Social ecologists reason that dominance relationships among humans lead to the objectification, control, and manipulation of others, and hence similar attitudes toward nonhuman nature. As with deep ecologists and ecofeminists, they advocate radical social transformation in the direction of nonhierarchical and more communal, decentralized societies.

Fundamental to Bookchin's theory, however, is a rather masculinist conception of evolution. As humans are integral to nature, their conversion of the nonhuman world is seen as a natural part of an evolutionary progress toward differentiation and complexity to which all life forms subjectively strive. From a scientific standpoint, this view of evolution is rather dated.[35] Also, this masculinist notion of humans as stewards and of an inherent "purpose" in nature does not sit well with deep ecologist and ecofeminist attitudes toward nonhuman nature.[36] But, more importantly, giving pre-eminence and universality to the "masculine" ideals of rationality and freedom reinforces the existing gendered hierarchy of the Power Paradigm, with women fully human only to the extent that they reflect the masculine ideal.

Each of the above "Manstream" environmental theories makes important contributions in analyzing determinants of the environmental crisis. They theorize industrial technology, instrumental rationality, capitalism, anthropocentrism, narrow identification, class, and social hierarchy—which are essential components of any environmental problem analysis. However, these determinants have something in common. They have been embedded and germinated in a Patriarchal construction of reality.[37] Manstream analyses therefore fail to undermine adequately the very pathologies they would exorcise from Society.

To recap, then, some of the shortcomings of Manstream green theory are as follows. First, these radical theories share androcentric assumptions with the dominant paradigm and therefore fail to demystify the ideological props that support the exploitation of nature, such as the idea that humanity is by nature "masculine." This militates against the possibility of an alternative morality based on empathy and cooperation. Second, they fail to explore the implications of the fact that the pathologies identified as "causes" of environmental problems stem from the elevation of values that have been central to "masculine" identity for centuries (in Western culture at least), such as competitive individualism, instrumentalism, and progress as increasing freedom from natural constraints. Third, their problem analyses are one-dimensional in that they reduce social and environmental problems to specific pathologies within Patriarchal Society, while seeing Patriarchy itself as a marginal, coincidental phenomenon. This linearity also leads to a competition among superficially incompatible ideas that can divide the environmental movement. Fourth, because they are gender-blind, they cannot theorize the abuse of power on both personal and political levels. Finally, Manstream theories are partial in that (with the exception of social ecology) they do not really explore or inte-

| | Problem definitions | Dimension of major concern | Instrument of social change | Desired ends |
|---|---|---|---|---|
| Eco-Marxists | Capitalism | Forces of production | Class struggle | Socialism |
| Eco-socialists | Individualism | Economic forces | Political reform | Communi-tarianism |
| "Greens"* | Industrial growth | Government policy | Ecological understanding | Sustainable practices |
| Deep Ecologists | Anthropo-centrism | Perception of world | Expanded identification | Biocentrism |
| Social Ecologists | Hierarchy | Institution forces | Social organization | Anarchism |
| Eco-feminism | "Power paradigm": Androcentrism & hierarchical dualism | Patriarchy: psychosexual motivation and systemic forces | Delinking masculinity as power. Social redesign on feminist principles | Beyond power |

*Note: I distinguish "Green" from the general green movement.

*Figure 1. Radical Environmental Analyses*

grate both individual/perceptual and institutional/structural impediments to social transformation. They offer *either* spiritual strategies (concerned with perception and values) or rationalist strategies (concerned with structure and process). Thus, they fail to satisfy the apparent need for a holistic, integrated approach.

Ecofeminism encompasses both the psychological and systemic manifestations of the androcentric value system and the personal and political expressions of insecurity and dominance. It accommodates both perceptual/spiritual and analytical/rational approaches, and addresses both personal and systemic barriers to social change, as indicated in Figure 1. It therefore provides a holistic framework that can draw upon and integrate the insights developed by Manstream radical critiques. Diversity of theories, views, and approaches is important to preserve, but it is also nice to have a perspective that can weave the threads together. And while internal consistency and comprehensiveness are satisfying, an environmental theory must also provide a framework that can help us to find solutions to specific issues. We now look at the implications of Manstream green thought with regard to the analysis of environmental problems.

## Problems of Manstream Analysis

If we want to get to the bottom of a psychological problem, we must uncover our "blind spot," or what we are denying. The same is true on a social level, and today our crucial blind spot—what we are trained not to see—is the sociopolitical significance of gender. Let us take some examples of how gender blindness limits our understanding of pivotal environmental issues: inappropriate technology, Third World planning and development, population growth, and militarism.

### Technocracy

Gender imbalance and the devaluing of the "feminine" are reflected in all areas of our male-dominant institutions, including those that impact most directly on the environment: science, economics, and planning.[38] For example, these fields elevate abstract, analytical techniques, and focus on objects of study that lend themselves to empiricism and quantification. Intuition, feelings, and empathy, being "feminine," are considered naive or irrelevant. One upshot of this narrow, reductionist method is the all-too-familiar tendency to monitor and record environmental crises, rather than find social solutions. This technocratic approach militates against the holistic understanding of social and ecological interrelations so urgently needed today. Also, technocratic norms and practices create the dangerous illusion of "rationality" and "objectivity." To the extent that scientists and technocrats work in an anti-feminine and anti-natural environment with masculinist concepts and decision rules, they simply cannot be objective.

Moreover, as I have argued elsewhere, these methods are also inherently biased in favor of the existing distribution of power and against the preservation of such meaningful, essential aspects of life as community and nature.[39] In the technocracy, for example, there has been a tendency to define human needs in very limited "masculine" terms that assume individual autonomy. Tangible economic goods and human productivity alleviate physical, impersonal needs and are therefore subjects of public policy. However, when psychological or emotional needs that involve personal relationships—congenial work environments, recognition, and so forth—have been addressed by mainstream theory, it has been basically for manipulative, instrumental purposes, such as increasing worker productivity. This partly explains why, for example, in the name of meeting "human needs," even well-intended development projects have deprived people in the Third World of community, self-reliance, and natural, sustainable lifestyles by displacing them into the consumer economy.

## Third World Development

The interconnection between feminist issues, institutional systems, and environmental desecration is illustrated by the impact of the androcentric international accounting system. The United Nations System of National Accounts selects *which* transactions count as "production" for purposes of calculating Gross Domestic Product (GDP). Feminists have shown how the fact that "women's work" is not counted in international economic balance sheets impacts upon the environment.[40] For example, when women are engaged in argriculture for home consumption, their work is not counted. The accounting system is thus biased in favor of large-scale capital-intensive projects and the replacement of indigenous forests with cash crops, which in turn destroy the local ecology and the self-sufficiency of the population. Marilyn Waring establishes that there is no logical or practical reason for excluding "women's work" from what is measured and therefore counted as contributing to GDP. Only male chauvinism can fully account for it.

Aid and development programs in the Third World have been disastrous for similar reasons, including the failure to consult when planning for development or conservation.[41] The problems created by not looking at the situation of women are exemplified by the failure of a project in Malawi. In brief, agricultural demonstrations were set up to teach men to grow soya beans, while home economics classes were given to teach women to cook them. In the end, the women could not use the recipes because only women did the farming for home consumption and they did not know how to grow soya beans.[42] The men knew how, but they only worked on plantations.

Janis Birkeland

## Population

Because they are gender-blind, nonfeminist environmental theories offer no new insights or answers for the problem of burgeoning human population. They put forth the same answers as the mainstream, like "self-discipline," more economic equality, control of women's reproductive cycle, or naive and paternalistic policy statements like "we must educate women to have fewer children." Some "spokesmen," after much prodding, have begun to acknowledge the need to empower women in the Third World but, in effect, still place the responsibility for the population dilemma upon women. While it will certainly be necessary to redistribute resources and provide for birth prevention, these measures will be insufficient until women have real choices about procreation.

Many leading greens still ignore the crucial fact that in most countries women are treated literally as chattels to be bought and sold. While it is not necessary to recite the atrocities against women in, say, India, Pakistan, Romania, and Iran, it must be recognized that women in most "developed" countries are also regarded as property to varying extents. Even in Australia, for example, one person in four condones violence by husbands against wives, and approximately half the murders of wives occur when they try to leave their "owners."[43] This is not self-determination. It is no coincidence that the Catholic Church, a misogynist edifice, is a proponent of population growth.

If women had physical security (food, shelter, health care) and control over their own bodies, and were not subject to androcentric cultures, then population and child mortality would both decrease. Few would have large families—if only because pregnancy and childcare are simply too much work. Similarly, the liberation of men, an important part of the feminist agenda, would also help to solve the population problem. Patriarchal societies that equate personal worth with success, and success with masculinity, place pressure on men to produce many offspring.[44] Moreover, governments use women to provide children for military strength and markets for growth-based development. Women and colonies are objectified as natural resources. (When in Malaysia in 1985, for example, I heard the prime minister on television urging women to produce more children!) Such culturewide blind spots as the political significance of gender and the invisibility of the values and experience of women exist because they serve the interests of the powerful. And, as we shall see, these blind spots exclude viable common-sense choices from consideration.

## Militarism

Perhaps the most important example of how gender blindness obscures our understanding of environmental problems is militarism. As 90 percent of violent crime is perpetrated by men,[45] and nuclear weapons are a product of the male mind, a gender-blind perspective can only mislead us in our efforts to put an end to militarism. More will be said later about the Manstream analysis of militarism generally. For the moment, it is interesting to note that whereas most discussions of militarism are studiously gender-blind, the military itself understands and manipulates sex roles to benefit the war business, and does so very well indeed. Let us take some examples of how notions of femininity and masculinity are used by militarists to manipulate both soldiers and citizenry.

First, in training, men are taught to despise and distance themselves from their "feminine" side, or their emotions and feelings: "The experience of basic training traditionally implants Patriarchal values by reviling women as a foul and lowly class."[46] In weapons sales, advertising focuses on the sexual association of weaponry and power. As Carol Cohn notes: "Both the military itself and the arms manufacturers are constantly exploiting the phallic imagery and promise of sexual domination that their weapons so conveniently suggest."[47] In recruitment, advertising focuses on "making a man out of you," and the big sexy toys the soldiers will learn to use. In raising armies, citizens are manipulated by conceptions of masculine and feminine stereotypes and sex role expectations. Men should be macho and reckless; they should go to war to prove themselves. Women should be submissive and unquestioning; they should raise sons to be brave soldiers. In quelling dissent, peace activists are characterized in derogatory (read feminine) terms such as "wimps," "sissies," or "poofters." In gaining public support for foreign interventions, the military has found that money, patriotism, and self-interest are not sufficient—but challenging a nation's sense of masculine pride works.[48] Thus many incidents have been engineered to portray the prospective enemy as a bully, such as the alleged encouragement by the United States for Saddam Hussein to invade Kuwait in order to justify a military solution.

Finally, in strategy, masculinity is used to manipulate the enemy. For example, the West insulted Saddam Hussein's masculine pride to induce him to stay in Kuwait so they could attack: it could hardly have been by accident that President Bush told Saddam Hussein publicly that if he did not get out by a certain date, they would "kick his ass." The militarists surely knew that this would make it impossible for Hussein to pull out. His masculinity was at stake, and that is often more important to power-addicted men than life itself—or at least the lives of others. In short, there is little question that the military uses sex and gender, if only for mischievous purposes.

More to the point, the behavior of world leaders, in both personality and strategy, reflects all-too-familiar patterns: building barriers and distancing oneself from the enemy, denying the worth or humanity of the other, attempting to establish dominance and create dependency, and winning at all costs—"sterotypically" masculine forms of conflict resolution. *Preventing* war by promoting world peace, rather than arms sales, subversion, and belligerence, has not really been tried. Perhaps this is partly because the armed forces really exist as an icon: they "represent and defend the masculine ethic," rather than life.[49]

A gender-blind analysis screens out the underlying psychosexual pressures on men. This is one reason that although militarism is probably the biggest threat to the environment—even in peacetime—it seems to be put in the "too hard" basket by most Manstream green theorists, or at least treated as a separate issue. Perhaps it is also because the connections between war and the blueprint for masculinity are too uncomfortable to accept, because it means that the causes of war are "in here" as well as "out there."[50] Attention to androcentrism, on the other hand, contributes to new understanding of militarism. Books such as *Exposing Nuclear Phallacies*, *Missile Envy*, and *Fathering the Unthinkable* make the link between militarism and polarized masculinity clear.[51]

A gender-blind analysis can do more than cloud our understanding of militarism: it also serves to support the status quo. For example, the focus on individual identification and the implicit assumption of rationality dictate the conclusion that the problem underlying world conflict is misplaced self-interest, narrow identification, or nationalism, which in turn leads to distrust or "fear of others."[52] Such an analysis obscures the fact that throughout history, fear and nationalism have been generated by the powerful to control their own populations, and by commercial interests to sell weapons. As (retired) Rear Admiral Gene La Roque says, the Pentagon deliberately "scares the pants off" U.S. politicians each year to encourage more weapons procuring.[53]

Fear, then, should be understood also as a tool and product of manipulation. "Cold war" indoctrination was a deliberate marketing strategy of the corporate/industrial/military/bureaucratic complex.[54] The cold war was a campaign of psychological warfare that instilled the belief that only weapons and strength—that is, threatening and aggressive posturing—could provide national security. In other words, if the Soviet Union had not existed, someone else would have been created to fill that essential role for political and business interests. Here in Australia, for instance, the response to the easing of East-West hostilities was to whip up fear of Indonesians to justify an *increase* in defense spending.

The male-driven militarist complex and weapons trade—the world's largest business—has little to do with narrow identification or anthropocentrism; it is simply organized crime. Even in its public face, it operates outside the public purview. For example, in the 1988/89 fiscal year, 1,500 applications for arms exports were made to the Australian government, and only 5 were rejected.[55] Many of these sales were to regimes that violate human rights: this means that the weapons are used against their own people. There was no public debate on the issue, and public awareness of the potential harm to themselves and the environment was irrelevant to the outcome.

In short, to treat fear of others or individual perception alone is to treat a symptom of psychological warfare. The focus on anthropocentrism, or "them versus us" thinking, conceals the power drive. The arms trade is, for all practical purposes, a global extortion and protection racket. It operates just like that other male enclave, the illegal drug trade, only the damage is far greater, affecting not only immediate lives but the global ecosystem. It is no coincidence, for instance, that drug trafficking was mixed up with arms deals in the U.S. war against Nicaragua: it is known as "vertical integration."

It suits the interests of the powerful if people attribute war to fear of others and nationalism, since they will then believe war is the fault of the voter: that is, a flaw of human nature. Of course, fear and "them versus us" thinking indeed need treating, but treating them as the root problem can be counterproductive. The problem is better understood in terms of the false dualisms that have been used by powerful interests to divide and rule, such as capitalist/communist, male/female, skilled/unskilled, white/black.[56] These divisions are made plausible and encoded by "hierarchical dualism"—the organizing principle of Patriarchal thought. Ideologies that pretend to subsume gender and other differences under a Western model of Man only reinforce the false dichotomy between Man and "Other."

These are just four examples of how gender-blindness is a perceptual barrier to understanding and solving crucial environmental problems. The masculine model of Rational Man is also a barrier to sound strategy. To illustrate this, let us again look at militarism.

## *Problems of Manstream Strategy*

As said above, androcentric green approaches assume, at least implicitly, that Man is rational and will therefore change if He realizes that to harm nature is to harm Himself. While Liberalists focus on the narrow self, many non-Marxist Leftists would maintain that "them versus us" thinking is a result of wealth accumulation induced by life in a capitalist society, and that capitalist imperialism is the major force behind militarism. One cannot argue against the notion that capitalism is integral to military adventurism and the arms race. However, the Leftist green approach, in the West, is to describe the fundamental irrationality of militarism and capitalism and posit a more rational world order. This strategy relies on enlightened self-interest to bring about change, an approach that history has proven futile. It is losing ground everywhere against the more "creative" approach of the capitalist press, the intoxicants of the market bazaar, and the glitz of show biz. Of course, Leftist critiques are certainly useful in describing the "me-chanics" of militarism. Like sports commentators, however, they know the rules of the game and can follow the action, but they cannot determine the outcome.

What I am suggesting is that both Leftist and Liberalist strategies rely upon Rational Man to act differently once He realizes that militarism and its roots (human-centered or capitalist-engendered greed) are not rational. Ironically, then, they ultimately bank upon traditional forms of pluralist political action in the hope that the majority will change the system in the market, the ballot box, or the streets. In short, both rely on reason to persuade Rational Man to act rationally: that is, to think ecologically, end war, and create a just Society.

If the cause of militarism were simply narrow, human-centered but ratio-nal self-interest, then militarism would bear some rational—if misguided—relationship to defense, or some economic or other human benefit. But it does not. Let us first examine the "rationality" of world leaders as reflected in military policy and thus whether rational arguments will persuade them to change. Second, we will look at the green assumption that the populace at large can be persuaded to change their way of thinking and then in turn persuade world leaders to do so, through rational or spiritual means.

## Influencing Leaders

To begin with, militarist policy makes no economic sense. The Worldwatch Institute estimates that 15 percent of the amount spent on weapons in the world could eradicate most of the immediate causes of war and environmental destruction.[57] Further, world leaders know that military spending creates devastating economic problems through the diversion and waste of resources and inflation, and that the spillover costs of domination can never be fully calculated. For example, most global trouble spots today are in areas that were colonized by outside powers. Yet virtually nothing is spent on peace making or eliminating the causes of war. In fact, the United States spends less than one percent of its military budget on either peace making or environmental protection.

Since World War II, many Western governments have become the marketing arm of private arms dealers on alleged economic grounds. Yet this "military Keynesianism" has taken a great toll on the taxpayer as well as the earth. In Iran, for example, billions in U.S. arms passed to the Ayatollah's regime when it took over. When $12 billion worth of weapons were canceled by the Ayatollah, the U.S. taxpayer had to compensate the private arms suppliers to the tune of several hundred million. Yet the United States later sold weapons both to the Afghans, who in turn sold them to Iran,[58] and to the Ayatollah via Israel, while supplying Iraq with weapons to fight Iran!

Thus, apart from a handful of corrupt arms merchants and their puppets, everybody loses financially. Nonetheless, some assume that warfare is rational, in spite of its costs to the taxpayer, because it is supposedly a means to acquire useful resources. However, the recent war with Iraq cost U.S. taxpayers not only countless billions but also an incomprehensible loss of nonrenewable resources. Eight hundred oil wells burned for months in the aftermath of the war. World leaders should know all this, so that the unwillingness of many to negotiate before the war suggests that they do not care about the costs of war or the resources jeopardized in war.

Despite the end of the cold war, militarism and threats of violence are still basic to foreign policy. The alleged defensive reasons for militarism are fallacious. Deterrence and containment, usually of communism, have been the main arguments used to defend the arms race—rather than life. These stated aims, however, are not served by a militarist policy: they are simply rationalizations for dominance. Let us first take nuclear "deterrence." The term is "doublespeak" because it implies self-defense. It is actually a euphemism for a deadly form of aggression—psychological warfare. To most people "deterrence" evokes the idea of (*a*) a retaliatory second strike (*b*) in response to a nuclear attack (*c*) on one's own country. Yet, from the beginning, nuclear deterrence meant threatening a nuclear first strike, not retaliation.[59] Later, in the 1980s, the United States refused to say that it would not strike first, despite the Soviets' promise not to do so: this was not a policy of deterrence. Second, deterrence was never limited to a response to a nuclear attack, but rather was to be used in retaliation for a Soviet encroachment using conventional weapons in Western Europe, or for the prevention of indigenous communist movements elsewhere. Third, it was not, therefore, "self-defense"—a means of defending the territory of the United States. In other words, deterrence was, at best, a tool of foreign policy.

Even if deterrence was a defense strategy, rather than a euphemism for arms sales, psychological warfare, and dominance, deterrence ceased to be U.S. policy in the 1980s. With the new "counterforce" capability came a strategy of "limited nuclear war." The concept of "limited nuclear war" meant striking military targets with tactical (local) nuclear weapons somewhere, while holding in reserve the main strategic force to deter the enemy from responding with a general nuclear attack against the United States. This is apparently what Ronald Reagan had in mind in 1981, when he said that the United States could contain a nuclear war outside its territory. Deterrence, in this context, meant a strategy, not to prevent the other side from using nuclear weapons, but to prevent them from hitting back on U.S. soil.

But even if taken at face value, deterrence theory was also totally irrational: it meant having more weapons than were needed to destroy the planet at least twelve times over, and it meant frightening enemies into building up more arms. Furthermore, deterrence never prevented conventional wars, it increased the risks of nuclear war and terrorism, and it legitimated nuclear proliferation—hardly a human-centered policy.[60] It is, however, very "macho."

"Containment" is the other major defense for militarism. If this excuse were valid, then arms would be used to contain communism, Islam, or whatever. But the West has sold weapons and nuclear technology to Muslim extremists such as the rulers of Iran, to communist countries such as China, and to unstable, unpopular dictatorships that could become communist overnight, such as Marcos' Philippines—with taxpayer subsidies and bailouts. Thus, even if we accept deterrence and containment as substantively rational, these aims have not been furthered by a macho foreign policy.

Finally, the nuclear obscenity bears no resemblance to rationality. Nuclear weapons do not serve the interests of self-defense, deterrence, or containment, and have promoted proliferation, terrorism, global instability, and environmental destruction. Analyses that assume substantive rationality are therefore irrelevant to a useful understanding of Western military strategy—which is based on the notion that the one with the most toys left after much of the world has been destroyed wins. In short, militarism is not a rational means to achieve security (material, ideological, or territorial) because it threatens all life on earth. Alternatively, if military means were indeed "rational," then the *ends* of military action would have to be power for the sake of power, rather than for the sake of resolving the problems cited as reasons for such exploits. The same arguments hold for the rape of the earth.

Yet the Manstream, because of its androcentric model of Man, uses "rational" arguments against the militarist position and for changing the public perception of the "other." Have they not noticed that decades of peace activism, which doggedly pointed out the irrationality of militarism, did little to alter this ecocidal behavior? Arguments that the military causes ozone depletion, fossil fuel consumption, nuclear and toxic pollution, and so forth simply do not impress the male enclave in the corporate / industrial / military / bureaucratic complex. Militarists are not moved by reason: they answer every rational argument with clichés about how Man is essentially aggressive and dominance is natural. Nor are they moved by rarified ideas about expanding our sense of identification to encompass all life forms, which they could see as "effeminate." They are hooked on images of machismo and power.

Even assuming that rational arguments were effective, they would presumably have to be more "rational" and convincing than the militarist's rationale for warfare. The underlying justification for "defense through strength" is that militarism, though itself irrational, is a necessary evil because of Man's "aggressive nature." From this line of reasoning it follows that competition and conquest—winning—is the only means to secure peace. If we accept an androcentric conception of Mankind, it is hard to argue with this logic. However, if instead we recognize the androcentric model to be a social construct, then it becomes clear that masculine identification is alterable. Hence the basic axiom of the militarist's logic is undermined.

In fact, as militarism is inherently irrational, it may be actually counter-productive to defer to de facto proponents of militarism by debating the costs and benefits of war. Such arguments inadvertently give deference and hence credence to militarists and allow them to deny the emotional and irrational in themselves. Militarism cannot be adequately understood outside the psychosexual dimension, and reason alone cannot make militarists act rationally and abandon power-based modes of behavior.

Finally, with regard to the efficacy of reason, it must be remembered that the substance of an argument is often not what is persuasive. It is partly "how" it is said, but mainly "who" says it, that counts. For example, debates about the military are usually couched in technical and strategic terms. People are told that "these issues are very complex" and that they should therefore trust the specialists—the military experts. Moreover, people are conditioned to look down upon or to disregard those outside the power structure. This Patriarchal conditioning must also be addressed directly if activists want people to hear them. It is a value system that builds in and reinforces denial, distancing, fear, greed, and delusion. It must be named if people are to see it. Since reason does not impress those in power, let us turn to strategies for influencing those who empower them.

### Influencing the Populace

Radical environmentalists find much common ground with regard to the sort of societies they would like to live in. However, ecofeminism differs from Manstream theory when it comes to strategy, or how to get there. The Liberalist and Leftist (non-Marxist) approaches in green thought call for changing people's values through reason, education and/or spirituality in order to bring about social change but deny the significance of sex and gender in personal motivation. Put more emphatically by Sharon Doubiago: "Because of sexism, because of the psychotic avoidance of the issue at all costs, ecologists have failed to grasp the fact that at the core of our suicidal mission is the psychological issue of gender, the oldest war, the war of the sexes."[61]

A strategy based on denial is insufficient to achieve social change. Eco-feminist strategy, in contrast, suggests that a deconstructive process is also necessary. Ecofeminists would defuse the ideological and psychological pressures upon the masculine ego that fuel the abuse of power. Manstream green strategy, on the other hand, often fails to deal with problems of politics-as-usual, liberalism, mysticism, identification, power seeking and sexism, and co-optation. In the discussion below, I focus on the Liberalist position, but some points apply to Leftists as well. Again, "Liberalist" refers to *strategies* for social change that begin from the individual—it is not to be confused with liberal ideology.

## POLITICS-AS-USUAL

The Liberalist green orientation stakes its program on the belief that individual change, through a nonanthropocentric perception of reality, can bring about a new political and social order. Seen as a strategy, it is essentially directed at changing people's values or belief systems (rather than at psychological roots), on the assumption that more "aware" individuals will make better decisions or cast better votes. In lieu of challenging the (male-controlled) system directly deep ecologists, for example, advocate developing the capacity to identify and integrate with nonhuman nature, or "Self-realization." It has even been asserted that "ethics follow from how we experience the world," and systemic change will somehow follow from ethical change.[62] However, as I suggest below, our gendered behavioral programing runs far deeper and is much harder to change than are cerebral concepts such as anthropocentrism. Also, people have to *want* to change their beliefs and behavior, and rational arguments and religious exhortations do not carry people over this threshold. People still need to be moved or persuaded to take up deep ecology or different values.

This Liberalist strategy contains vestiges of the dominant liberal political and economic paradigm that, it says, contributes to the environmental problem. Mainstream liberals assume that simply changing people's values will lead to different voting and behavior patterns. Their reasoning is this: values make people prefer certain lifestyle or political alternatives; therefore, political change can be achieved by persuading others to adopt one's own beliefs. This logic is perfectly reasonable—but only in a vacuum unaffected by the media, corporate advertising, a liberal orthodoxy, Patriarchal social conditioning, linguistic patterns, and so on. This is because mainstream liberal philosophy is premised on an image of Man as an autonomous individual, separate from His context. Many Liberalist greens eschew liberalism, yet share its context-free logic, which does not acknowledge the full extent to which our mental processes and values are shaped by the superstructure and infrastructure of our social institutions. Thus, although many Manstream green writers are themselves political activists, the approach is essentially "politics as usual" because it relies ultimately on traditional pressure politics and "numbers" for radical change. They are essentially only advocating public pressure for better goals and policies. However, corporate power is above governments and largely dictates who gets elected and what they do. The Liberalist strategy does not undermine the props or address the emotional "needs" of the powerful.

There is a certain irony in a position that recognizes that the competitive global economic system creates environmental problems but then proposes a solution that is essentially market-based, relying on consumers to change their values and lifestyles. This is analogous to approaching the drug problem by persuading people to "just say no," when we are dealing with something that is profitable precisely because it operates outside the market. The resource extraction and pollution industries do not pay the replacement costs of public resources. Like the illegal drug business, they are lucrative because they do not pay the real costs and they create markets. Likewise, the Green consumer/voter–based strategy encourages us to place a kind of moral responsibility on the victim, distracting attention from the profiteers.[63] Although people demand goods, they do not, for example, demand that these goods be made with new toxic materials and processes that merely replace natural ones. People have not actually been given these kinds of choices.

Recent events illustrate that educating consumers is less urgent than retooling our technocratic, political, and corporate decision-making arenas. Consumers would surely not object, for instance, if their creature comforts were provided via solar energy. In fact, public enthusiasm for recycling centers, environmentally friendly products, and recycled paper has outstripped the supply, yet recycling centers have had to close in Australia. Industry has not been buying the material simply because, in our distorted economy, live trees are cheaper than used ones. This phenomenon is a function of power relations that shape institutions, laws, and economic and planning methods, and only partly a function of chauvinism toward other animals.

Cultivating consumer awareness through grassroots action is no big problem. It has proven relatively easy to legislate to change consumer habits, especially when backed by the ethic-building activities of a diverse environmental peace movement. Car pools, speed limits, tax incentives for energy conservation, water meters, labeling laws, and litter fines are effective interim measures—at least when not blocked by industry lobbies. Unfortunately, the packaging industry in Australia has invested vast sums in campaigns against can and bottle deposit legislation. Thus, power, and not consumerism, is the crucial issue.

## LIBERALISM

Much green strategic thought is still trapped in liberal reformist thought in other ways as well. A liberal paradigm may be adequate for resolving social justice issues, but not preservation ones. This is because it frames all environmental issues in terms of distributional claims among competing interests in resources.[64] That is, reformists tend to equate environmental ethics with "egalitarianism" because it is consistent with the concept of rights, the "social contract," and the "mushroom" model of Man. In this framework, responsibilities are construed as merely mutual rights. If social justice is simply transposed onto animals, however, we would "balance the interests" between humans and animals, or incrementally trade off nature to meet human needs. This limited egalitarian conception of ethics is still commonplace in green thinking.

Similarly, as in liberalism, much green thought has emphasized the self over community. Mainstream liberals devalue the idea of community as being a mere aggregate of individuals, whereas I use "community" to refer to a sense of mutuality and reciprocity (rather than a parochial identification with a particular group). Mainstream liberals hold that Society should not impose a particular conception of the good life or of what constitutes human fulfillment. Though few would quarrel with this proposition, it excludes the idea of community from its conception of what is essential to human well-being. It fails to fully appreciate that we are what we are because of nature, culture, and emotional bonds. Thus, liberalism reflects and reinforces the estrangement of autonomous Man from the feminine, community, and nature. Liberalist green thought does not fully escape this legacy. It is also two-tiered—relating to the self and the biotic community—though it seeks to bridge this Man-made gap. While it attempts to reunite Man with nature, it leaves community and the women's culture in the background.

Furthermore, this Manstream emphasis on the individual "at one with nature" distracts attention from structural and systemic issues. Institutions embody values, so they must be changed as well. Of course, some constructive institutional reforms have been put forth by Manstream theorists, and others: reforms such as bioregionalism, decentralized and direct democracy, and the new economics.[65] These ideas, however, can also be supported by anthropocentric perspectives and in fact draw on the prior work of anthropocentric ecologists, social ecologists, and anarchists.[66] Also, as Judith Plant points out, these new lifestyles and organizational modes require feminism: the revaluing of life-giving values, conflict resolution, physical work, and the reintegration of men into the home:

> One of the key ideas of bioregionalism is the decentralization of power: moving further and further toward self-governing forms of social organization. The further we move in this direction, the closer we get to what has traditionally been thought of as 'woman's sphere'—that is, home and its close surroundings. . . . The catch is that, in practice, home, with all its attendant roles, will not be anything different from what it has been throughout recent history *without* the enlightened perspective offered by feminism. Women's values, centered around life-giving, must be revalued, elevated from their once subordinate role.[67]

Another vestige of liberalism in Manstream thought is the view of political activity as being exclusively a means to an end: a goal-oriented activity. However, grassroots or hands-on community involvement is an important means of self-realization as well. For example, it has often been suggested that people "need to save themselves before they can save the forests." However, in the absence of serious personal problems, it is hard to understand how one can make such a separation: when part of a rainforest dies, part of us dies. Personal development, I believe, requires the sometimes painful process of community participation as well as contemplation. Furthermore, the view of politics as a means to an end is corrosive. When we implicitly suggest "we need power to make change," we have already begun to compromise.

There is certainly nothing wrong with criticizing anthropocentrism in favor of biocentrism per se. The significance of ignoring the very real problems of building community and restructuring institutions, however, is this: an environmental ethic that does not offer a chance of saving the natural environment is not an environmental ethic. The relationship between social change and individual perception or spirituality is, therefore, crucial to the relevance of the Liberalists' program for social transformation. Hence we now embark upon the politics of mysticism and transcendence.

## MYSTICISM

As Helen Forsey notes, "in certain patriarchal philosophies the concept of connectedness, union, nirvana, exists: but it has been narrowly conceived by men in exclusively spiritual terms."[68] Patriarchal spirituality has been transcendent and earth-disdaining rather than earth-honoring. Similarly, mystical transcendent spirituality can be a head trip. In Starhawk's words, "Power-from-within must be grounded, that is, connected to the earth, to the actual material conditions of life."[69] Otherwise it cannot lead to real social change.

First, history does not bear out the presumed causal relationship between "spiritual" change and behavior. Most religions begin as spiritual movements, but they are eventually crystallized and institutionalized to become part of an officially sanctioned power structure (family or state). For instance, Buddhism shares a not too dissimilar spiritual base with much Manstream philosophy, yet does not alter social structures based on dominance relationships. Consider, for example, the position of women and the widespread environmental destruction in Buddhist states and societies.

Second, spirituality, belief systems, or world views do not necessarily improve individual behavior. This is because behavior is not solely a product of either rationality or beliefs. Behavior patterns are so deeply encoded that we often do not perceive them. Ways of acting and relating are ingrained from earliest childhood, a product of habit, role-modeling, social reinforcement, and institutions. This is one reason why there is often a gap between what people believe in and what they will do to get their own way, along the whole spectrum from personal to international relations. I have seen religions reinforce and rationalize prejudice and cruelty, but not cure them.

Third, individual moral behavior is constrained by power relationships and institutional corruption. We observed above that environmental and social problems are underwritten by the profitability of resource exploitation and the arms trade. Even if we had an ecologically sound environmental planning system, the pressures of our militarist economy would nullify any structures, plans, or programs designed to conserve natural resources over the long term.

Fourth, changing people's way of thinking through spiritual or educational persuasion would not reach the prime movers. Even the conversion of five billion people might not reach the top thousand in the transnational resource corporations and the military. There is little point in beseeching the godfathers to adopt a new ethic: in real life, there is always someone to take their place. A case in point is India today. Despite a Gandhi who inspired a mass movement to topple the powerful, one power structure merely replaced another.

Fifth, getting more leaders on one's side would not be enough to change the rules of the game or the umpire's bias. (Even the omnipresent game metaphor itself reflects a "masculine" bias.) More enlightened decision-makers would only slow the rapidly increasing disparity between rich and poor, the plundering of the public estate, and the relentless drive toward market totalitarianism.

Sixth, the insufficiency of spirituality alone to effect social change is obvious when the military industries and arms trade are seen for the international extortion and protection racket that they really are. In this context, spiritual approaches in isolation from gender and institutional factors merely serve the power structure. Can we really expect to prevent institutionalized crime by cultivating inner peace and a mystical appreciation of nature, however important these may be?

Seventh, even if a new perception could change behavior, it is unrealistic to expect people to adopt a new way of "experiencing the world" within the given time frame. Many, for instance, have argued that Christianity, if actually practiced, would prevent the desecration of nature.[70] Perhaps it could, but it took hundreds of years for Christianity to take hold, and it did not work as intended even when whole societies were Christian— and we have only a few years to stop the destruction of the nonhuman environment.

Eighth, many have invested heavily in the hope that the "crisis of life conditions on Earth" could cause Society to choose this new path. But crises cannot be relied upon as a catalyst to positive change, as we saw with the oil crisis of the early 1970s and the U.S.-Iraq crisis of 1991. Crises are, moreover, subject to manipulation, as when the nuclear industry uses its vast resources to promote fear of ozone depletion for the wrong reasons. In addition, as those in the peace movement know all too well, crises create fear and denial, which militate against the cooperation and planning that are necessary to save the planet.

Finally, despite their good intentions, spiritual movements set up a "them versus us" relationship between the believers and the less enlightened, and a conviction that there is one right orientation toward experiencing reality, however personalized it may be. Such movements run the risk of creating a hierarchy of beliefs. For instance, some have implied that it is somehow "deeper" to perceive nature as an extension of the self, rather than, say, as a cathedral or an art gallery. As with some religions, we may begin to judge others by their beliefs, rather than by their deeds. However, we are what we *do* about the desecration of human and nonhuman nature, not what we believe in. In short, personal transformation may be necessary, but it is an insufficient condition for social change.

### IDENTIFICATION

Deep personal and social change require self-criticism. Deep ecologists, however, focus on "identification," reasoning that if people learned to expand their sense of identity to encompass all of nature, they would realize that to harm nature is to harm themselves. Paradoxically, this relies on a person's sense of "self-interest," as opposed to a sense of intrinsic value.

> Altruism implies that ego sacrifices its interests in favor of the other, the alter. . . . The motivation is primarily that of duty. . . . It is unfortunately very limited what people are capable to love from mere duty or more generally from moral exhortation. Unhappily the extensive moralizing from environmentalists has given the public the false impression that we primarily ask them to sacrifice to show more responsibility, more concern, better morals. . . . The requisite care flows naturally if the self is widened and deepened so that protection of nature is felt and perceived as protection of ourselves.[71]

Altruism is a difficult concept for the Manstream to deal with because altruism cannot be squeezed into the "masculine" model of Man. Patriarchal ideology sees altruism in terms of a negation of self-interested Man, just as it defines women's feelings and experience as the absence of real thought and knowledge. "Altruism" is therefore denied or redefined in Manstream theory as self-interest that benefits others, a concept that denies the existence of a "feminine principle." But there is altruism in the work of women (the majority of the human race) who put their own interests behind those of their families, children, and the environment. That energy and good will should be affirmed and nurtured, not exploited and coopted.

Deep ecologists are correct in appreciating that people do not change through reason alone. But would it not be more ethical to develop our faculty of caring for other life forms for their own sake, rather than because we identify with them? Morality and gender are social constructions; if women can be socialized to take pleasure in the happiness of others, men must likewise be capable of these sentiments.

One does not need a new philosophy to realize that self-interest and the well-being of the planet are inseparable. Common sense indicates this, whether one is anthropocentric or not. Some deep ecologists have argued that anthropocentric arguments are self-defeating, since they reinforce human identification and therefore could cause people to eliminate species that are not "useful."[72] This wrongly assumes, however, that some creatures have no survival value to the ecosystems upon which humans depend, a position inconsistent with a biocentric perspective.

In fact, the environmentally concerned are being persuaded that the disruptions to natural systems to date have been so catastrophic that any further tinkering with ecosystems is life-threatening. The problem is that they are *psychologically disempowered,* so that many practice denial. It has become obvious that to fool around with the integrity of the food chain, genetic engineering, and radioactive waste is extremely risky and self-destructive— yet Mankind does it. Self-interest has not prevented Mankind from harming people or nature so far, so it is unlikely that a change in our human identification would lead to a cessation of violence against nature. After all, if "homocentric Man" is bent on homicide (forty thousand children die needlessly each day), then why—in the real world—would the new "biocentric Man" not commit biocide?

Unfortunately, those unsympathetic to a biocentric vision are unlikely to be moved by theories so abstract and detached that they ignore sex and power. Of course, it would be desirable if we all could work toward self-realization through a process of expanding our sense of self, but it is doubtful that real personal change can occur without the conscious and painful process of self-criticism that is required to reject power and ego. In short, gender identification is more central to human behavior than human identification, and the focus on anthropocentrism protects the masculine ego from scrutiny.

There is another issue raised by identification as a means of change. We must ask ourselves if we are really identifying with nature or with an intellectual club. Self-realization or an expanded sense of self may, in real life, be a projecting of the ego rather than a transcending of anthropocentrism. Our tendency to project our egos upon the cosmos is, after all, a time-honored androcentric trait.[73]

Finally, rather than all-encompassing, the vision of deep ecology is a detached world view. To "transcend" is to put oneself above: to separate the self and world problems. There is a tendency to try to transcend our egos, privilege, and dominance relationships by simply "overlooking" them. Anyone who would be reading this (as well as I myself) benefits from and thus perpetuates past exploitative relationships on a personal, class, or national level. So do environmental gurus. One cannot claim to transcend the Power Paradigm while benefiting from Patriarchy. It is not enough to give up materialism: if we do not deal with personal power and dominance relationships, we are part of the problem, regardless of our degree of empathy, political awareness, and transcendental purity.

### POWER SEEKING AND SEXISM

The green movement must be able to set an example if it wishes to claim better societies are possible. A major impediment to social change is an old source of friction found in the green movement itself: Patriarchy within its own ranks. This is revealed in the movement's backgrounding of women, and its distance from the grassroots and people of color.

Some men and masculine-identified women expect to be "spokesmen" and will not lick envelopes, learn from others "beneath" themselves, or share information. Sexism also excludes many selfless volunteers from meaningful participation. A majority of green activists (as opposed to "spokesmen") are women, yet a significant percentage eventually leave the movement because they find that it is a microcosm of Patriarchal Society at large.[74] Very often those women who are "threatening" or who question processes are simply eased out by indirect means. This exclusion is seldom executed in full consciousness, but again, gender blindness is power blindness. If men are sincere about saving the earth, they should be willing to relinquish personal privileges based on sex, and begin listening to women.

There is a related tendency among greens to become estranged from the genuine grassroots and to begin to see themselves as the grassroots instead. Movements that begin through knocking on doors and face-to-face contact with the average citizen can become bureaucratized and hierarchical. Information and assistance tend to flow into environmental organizations, rather than out into the community in ways that can empower people at the periphery. This means losing sight of the essential need for community building. Until the green movement addresses the Patriarchal attitudes in its own backyard, it will not serve as a reliable basis upon which to work for social transformation.

None of these problems of sexism and elitism that are sometimes found in the movement are really corrected by a biocentric vision. Self-realization is no substitute for self-reflexive learning: when we stop asking questions, we become part of the problem. Self-reflexive learning requires immersion in grassroots work as well as contemplation. One learns about oneself by being in the movement—by taking responsibility and working collectively with others—not by contributing as an expert or leader.

## COOPTATION

If people see the environmental movement as a platform for personal and professional advancement, and if they cannot assume leadership roles, they will move on to another forum. Patriarchy thus creates fertile ground for cooptation, which affects both the credibility and the long-term effectiveness of the movement. As long as the green movement remains Patriarchal, government and industry will be able to set the agenda and rules of the game. The unconscious desire to be accepted by the powerful or Society at large means activists can be "bought off" by giving them a stake in the power structure. This is why new forms of "conflict resolution" have been merely means of reducing conflict, rather than means of resolving the problem.

A case in point is the recent trend in Australia toward negotiation and mediation between industry and environmental "spokesmen," which has really been a form of corporatization—that is, a process in which resources are allocated via negotiated arrangements between government and powerful special interest groups. For conservation groups to be included in this process at first blush appears a major victory—the legitimation of environmental concern. And there have been initial positive results, such as access to vital information. However, conflict resolution conducted by power brokers is not a real departure from business as usual. Corporatization is a power-based decision-making mechanism and a means of cooptation: a round table does not change the shape of power relations under the table.

Any power-based decision-making mechanism will be exploited by special interests, as we have seen with the Forest and Forest Industries Strategy in Tasmania. This collaborative effort between Greens and industry served as a smokescreen for the development of draconian "resource security legislation" that has turned 1.7 million hectares of Tasmanian forest *irretrievably* into logging zones. In the long term, the corporatization of the environmental movement is no answer. The process is reminiscent of a board game devised in the United States: "Blacks and Whites" was designed so that the black pieces had all kinds of strategies and maneuvers available to them, but, although the "playing field" looked level, they could never win. Moreover, industry can always counter public demand for wilderness by creating a greater public demand for consumable goods, or as in Tasmania, frightening the country into a depression. Industry knows that the best way to close people's minds is to tighten their belts.

## Conclusion

I have suggested that problems created by power relations cannot be resolved by transcendence, monkey wrenching, or pressure politics alone. Manstream environmentalism is bringing about ecological awareness but not basic social change. To change our way of thinking, relating, and acting requires more than a new self-image, metaphysics, policies, or structures. Because of the realities of power relationships in Patriarchal society, we must recognize that policies will not change until people with power in the military, corporate, and bureaucratic establishments cooperate of their own accord. The trick is how to motivate power-driven men and molls to change their behavior. I have argued that people will not want to abandon personal and political power simply because cooperative, reciprocal relationships are more ecologically sensible or "spiritually sound." Rationalist approaches that appeal to intellect and religious approaches that appeal to spirituality have proven inadequate.

We should look at what *motivates* people in real life. Power has often been called the greatest aphrodisiac, and power is obtained through the control and exploitation of social and natural resources. This suggests that if we are to move beyond power-based relationships, we should work to expose and redress the personal insecurities and unconscious motives underlying the power drive and *demystify the social conception of masculinity as power*. We should work to disassociate masculinity from the images of heroism, conquest, and death defiance so familiar in militaristic fantasies; from the images of competitiveness, individualism, and aggression glorified in sport; from the images of objectivity, linearity, and reductionism exalted by science; and from the images of hierarchy, progress, and control entrenched in the technocracy. If polarized masculinity were revealed in its true form, extreme egocentrism, it might cease to be so "sexy" to both men and women. No heroic social agency is needed to "take power"; we can simply withdraw the power, energy, and deference we unwittingly give to the powerful and the ideology of masculinity that supports them.

With regard to the dominant males, or megalomaniacs, the advice of Barbara Walker is relevant, if excessively colorful:

> Men do not voluntarily relinquish their ego trips, war toys and money games. Like spoiled children, many men push selfish behaviour as far as they can, perhaps secretly trying to reach the point where Mother will clamp down and say "No more," and mean it. . . . When many women together say no and mean it, the whole structure can collapse.[75]

With regard to males who blindly follow, we should appreciate that they see themselves as failures because they do not "measure up" to the masculine stereotype and yet are afraid to deal with their feelings and insecurities for fear of "exposing themselves" as possibly unmasculine.[76] If they were affirmed in terms of a different concept of masculinity or humanity, then they would be more reluctant to blindly follow megalomaniac leaders for reflected glory.

There is hope. Men and women in Western societies are increasingly seeking liberation from their Patriarchal programing. All sexes can work to *affirm* the values of caring, openness, nurturing, and nondefensiveness and the possibility of creating societies in harmony with all living beings. What is needed is more elbow grease. The work, however, is its own reward.

## NOTES

1. See Janis Birkeland, "An Ecofeminist Critique of Manstream Planning," *The Trumpeter* 8 (1991): 72–84; Janis Birkeland, *Planning for a Sustainable Society: An Ecofeminist Map* (Hobart: Department of Geography and Environmental Studies, University of Tasmania, 1991); J. Birkeland-Corro, "Redefining the Environmental Problem," *Environmental and Planning Law Journal* 5 (1988): 109–33.

2. In corporatist decision making, governments negotiate, in a closed process, policies and their implementation with peak organizations that have a monopoly of representation over certain categories of interests. This is discussed toward the end of this chapter, under "Cooptation."

3. By "infrastructure," I mean theories, ideologies, paradigms, organizational culture, methods, techniques, and processes.

4. Judith Plant, "Searching for Common Ground: Ecofeminism and Bioregionalism," in *Reweaving the World: The Emergence of Ecofeminism*, ed. Irene Diamond and Gloria Feman Orenstein (San Francisco: Sierra Club Books, 1990), 155–61, at p. 158.

5. I have critiqued the Leftist approach to social change in *Planning for a Sustainable Society*.

6. "Patriarchy" is capitalized herein to distinguish it from more narrow, anthropological usages. Scholars use "patriarchy" in a variety of senses: for a discussion of these different meanings, see Carol Pateman, "Patriarchal Confusions," *International Journal of Moral and Social Studies* 3 (1988): 127–43. Gerda Lerner defines patriarchy as "the manifestation and institutionalization of male dominance over women and children in the family and the extension of male dominance over women in society in general," in *The Creation of Patriarchy* (Oxford: Oxford University Press, 1986), 239.

The links between hierarchy and Patriarchy are examined in many works, including Dorothy Dinnerstein, *The Mermaid and the Minotaur: Sexual Arrangements and the Human Malaise* (New York: Harper & Row, 1976); Elizabeth Dodson Gray, *Green Paradise Lost* (Wellesley, Mass.: Roundtable Press, 1981).

7. "The feminine principle" refers to that constellation of values associated with the feminine and nature in society. For some feminists this concept has a spiritual dimension: see Vandana Shiva, *Staying Alive: Women, Ecology and Development* (London: Zed Books, 1988), 38–42.

8. Margo Adair and Sharon Howell, "The Subjective Side of Power," in *Healing the Wounds: The Promise of Ecofeminism*, ed. Judith Plant (Philadelphia: New Society Press; Ontario: Between the Lines, 1989), 219–26, at 222.

9. Quoted by Judith Allen in a talk recorded on ABC (Australian public radio), 1990.

10. Anne Cameron, "First Mother and the Rainbow Children," in Plant, *Healing the Wounds*, 64.

11. Ariel Salleh, "Stirrings of a New Renaissance," *Island Magazine* 8 (1989): 26–31.

12. See Karen J. Warren, "Feminism and Ecology: Making Connections," *Environmental Ethics* 9 (1987): 17–18; Karen J. Warren, "The Power and the Promise of Ecological Feminism," *Environmental Ethics* 12 (1990): 121–46. Also Val Plumwood, "Ecofeminism: An Overview and Discussion of Positions and Arguments," *Australasian Journal of Philosophy*, supp. to vol. 64 (1986): 120–38.

13. "Man" is capitalized herein to refer to the dominant culture, rather than the sex of the subject.

14. Charlene Spretnak, "Ecofeminism: Our Roots and Flowering," *Elmwood Newsletter* 4 (1988): 1.

15. See Radha Bhatt, "Lakshmi Ashram: A Gandhian Perspective in the Himalayan Foothills," in Plant, *Healing the Wounds*, 168–73; and Pamela Philipose, "Women Act: Women and Environmental Protection in India," ibid., 67–75.

16. For an exposition of biocentric ethical principles to govern our relations with nature, see Paul W. Taylor, *Respect for Nature: A Theory of Environmental Ethics* (Princeton: Princeton University Press, 1986).

17. See, for example, Janet Biehl, "What Is Social Ecofeminism?" *Green Perspectives* 11 (October 1988); Janet Biehl, *Rethinking Ecofeminist Politics* (Boston: South

End Press, 1991); Dolores LaChapelle, "No, I'm Not an Eco-feminist: A Few Words in Defense of Men," *Earth First!* 9 (March 21, 1989); Susan Prentice, "Taking Sides: What's Wrong with Eco-Feminism?" *Women and Environments* 10 (Spring 1988): 9–10.

18. For example, great discomfort on this point was expressed in numerous workshops at the Socialist Scholars Conference, July 18–21, 1991, University High, Melbourne.

19. Ariel Salleh, "'Essentialism'—and Eco-feminism," *Arena* 94 (1991): 169.

20. Diana E. H. Russell, "Sexism, Violence, and the Nuclear Mentality," in *Exposing Nuclear Phallacies*, ed. Diana Russell (New York: Pergamon Press, 1989), 63–73.

21. For a discussion of women's special relationship to nature, see Susan Griffin, *Woman and Nature: The Roaring Inside Her* (San Francisco: Harper & Row, 1978).

22. Ynestra King, "Feminism and the Revolt of Nature," *Heresies* 13 (1981): 12–16.

23. Joan L. Griscom, "On Healing the Nature/History Split in Feminist Thought," *Heresies* no. 13 (1981): 4–9, at 9, citing Sherry B. Ortner, "Is Female to Male as Nature Is to Culture?" in *Woman, Culture, and Society: A Theoretic Overview* ed. Michelle Z. Rosaldo and Louise Lamphere (Stanford, Calif.: Stanford University Press, 1974), 67–87.

24. See Carol Gilligan, *In a Different Voice: Psychological Theory and Women's Development* (Cambridge: Harvard University Press, 1982).

25. "Spiritual" can mean very different things, from respect for natural life processes to a religious conception. For a discussion of how religion and green thought can come together, see Charlene Spretnak, *The Spiritual Dimension of Green Politics* (Santa Fe, N. Mex.: Bear & Company, 1986).

26. Starhawk, "Feminist, Earth-based Spirituality and Ecofeminism," in Plant, *Healing the Wounds*, 174–85, at 174.

27. Seyla Benhabib, "The Generalized and the Concrete Other: The Kohlberg-Gilligan Controversy and Feminist Theory," in *Feminism as Critique: On the Politics of Gender*, ed. Seyla Benhabib and Drucilla Cornell (Cambridge: Policy Press, 1987; Minneapolis: University of Minnesota Press, 1987), 77–95, at 85.

28. Bertrand de Jouvenel, *Power: The Natural History of Its Growth* (London, 1945), quoted in Hannah Arendt, "On Violence," in *Power*, ed. Stephen Lukes (Oxford: Basil Blackwell, 1986), at 122.

29. *Planning for a Sustainable Society.*

30. Ariel Salleh, "Deeper Than Deep Ecology: The Eco-Feminist Connection," *Environmental Ethics* 6 (1984): 339–45.

31. Maria Mies, *Patriarchy and Accumulation on a World Scale* (London: Zed Books, 1986). See also Maria Mies et al., *Women: The Last Colony* (London: Zed Books, 1988).

32. For an introduction to deep ecology, see Bill Devall, *Simple in Means, Rich in Ends* (Salt Lake City: Gibbs Smith, 1988); Bill Devall and George Sessions,

*Deep Ecology: Living As If Nature Mattered* (Salt Lake City: Peregrine Smith, 1985); Warwick Fox, *Toward a Transpersonal Ecology: Developing New Foundations for Environmentalism* (Boston: Shambhala, 1990); Arne Naess, *Ecology, Community and Lifestyle*, trans. and ed. David Rothenberg (Cambridge: Cambridge University Press, 1989). Reputedly the earliest expression of deep ecology was in 1922: Martin Buber, *I and Thou*, trans. Ronald B. Smith, 2nd ed. (New York: Charles Scribner's Sons, 1958).

33. For example, see Marti Kheel, "Ecofeminism and Deep Ecology: Reflections on Identity and Difference", *The Trumpeter* 8 (1991): 62–72; Val Plumwood, "Nature, Self, and Gender: Feminism, Environmental Philosophy, and the Critique of Rationalism," *Hypatia* 6 (Spring 1991): 3–27; and Ariel Salleh's seminal "Deeper Than Deep Ecology."

34. See Murray Bookchin, *The Ecology of Freedom: The Emergence and Dissolution of Hierarchy* (Palo Alto, Calif.: Cheshire Books, 1982).

35. Stephen J. Gould, *Wonderful Life: The Burgess Shale and the Nature of History* (London: Penguin Books, 1989).

36. See Murray Bookchin's response to such arguments in "Recovering Evolution: A Reply to Eckersley and Fox," *Environmental Ethics* 12 (1990): 253–74.

37. I discuss how these pathologies stem from Patriarchal consciousness in *Planning for a Sustainable Society*.

38. See Judy Wacjman, *Feminism Confronts Technology* (Sydney: Allen & Unwin, 1991).

39. See n. 1.

40. For example, see Susan George, *A Fate Worse Than Debt* (New York: Grove, 1988); Lisa Leghorn and Katherine Parker, *Women's Worth: Sexual Economics and the World of Women* (Boston: Routledge & Kegan Paul, 1981); Marilyn Waring, *Counting for Nothing: What Men Value and What Women Are Worth* (Allen & Unwin, 1988).

41. See George, *A Fate Worse Than Debt*.

42. Waring, *Counting for Nothing*, 190.

43. Federal poll, 1989, reported by ABC television, Australia.

44. Herb Goldberg, *The Inner Male: Overcoming Roadblocks to Intimacy* (Ontario: New American Library, 1987).

45. Australian Institute of Criminology (1992).

46. Charlene Spretnak, "Naming the Cultural Forces That Push Us Toward War," in Russell, *Exposing Nuclear Phallacies*, 53–62, at 57.

47. Carol Cohn, "Sex and Death in the Rational World of Defense Intellectuals," in Russell, *Exposing Nuclear Phallacies*, 127–59, at 134.

48. John Stockwell, speech given at World Affairs Conference, Boulder, Colorado, April 10, 1987. See generally Howard Zinn, *A People's History of the United States* (New York: Harper Collins, 1980).

49. Wajcman, *Feminism Confronts Technology*, 146.

50. Penny Strange, "It'll Make a Man of You: A Feminist View of the Arms Race," in Russell, *Exposing Nuclear Phallacies*.

51. Helen Caldicott, *Missile Envy: The Arms Race and Nuclear War* (New York: Morrow, 1984); Brian Easlea, *Fathering the Unthinkable: Masculinity, Scientists and the Nuclear Arms Race* (London: Pluto Press, 1983); Russell, *Exposing Nuclear Phallacies*.

52. For example, see Fox, *Toward a Transpersonal Ecology*.

53. For example, both the bomber gap of the 1950s and the missile gap of the 1960s, which spurred the arms race and the Cold War, later proved to be hoaxes.

54. Explained in Janis Birkeland, *The Cold War and the Weapons Industry* (Hobart: Department of Environmental Studies, University of Tasmania, 1986).

55. Report on *60 Minutes* television program, February 24, 1991, ABC television, Australia.

56. See Cynthia Enloe, *Bananas, Beaches, and Bases: Making Feminist Sense of International Politics* (Berkeley: University of California Press, 1989).

57. For the costs of war, see Frank Barnaby et al., *The Gaia Peace Atlas* (New York: Doubleday, 1988). Also see Paul Ekins, Mayer Hillman, and Robert Hutchinson, *Wealth Beyond Measure: An Atlas of New Economics* (London: Gaia Books, 1992), 156–59.

58. *The Australian* (newspaper), September 21, 1987.

59. Using the bomb to "deter" potential Soviet aggression was in fact U.S. policy as early as 1945, four years before the Soviets had a bomb, and long before they were expected to have one. See Bernard Brodie, ed., *The Absolute Weapon: Atomic Power and World Order* (New York: Harcourt Brace, 1946).

60. Birkeland, *The Cold War and the Weapons Industry*.

61. Sharon Doubiago, "Mama Coyote Talks to the Boys," in Plant, *Healing the Wounds*, 43.

62. Arne Naess, quoted in Warwick Fox, "Approaching Deep Ecology: A Response to Richard Sylvan's Critique of Deep Ecology," *Occasional Paper* no. 20 (Hobart: Department of Environmental Studies, University of Tasmania, 1986), 46.

63. The adoption of this approach may relate to an implicit assumption among many liberals that institutional change involves either violent revolution or authoritarian repression. An example is William Ophuls, *Ecology and the Politics of Scarcity: Prologue to a Political Theory of the Steady State* (San Francisco: W. H. Freeman, 1977).

64. Birkeland-Corro, "Redefining the Environmental Problem."

65. See Van Andruss et al., *Home! A Bioregional Reader* (Philadelphia and Lillooet, British Columbia: New Society Publishers, 1990); Herman E. Daly and John B. Cobb, Jr., *For the Common Good: Redirecting the Economy Toward Community, the Environment, and a Sustainable Future* (Boston: Beacon Press, 1989); Paul Ekins, ed., *The Living Economy: A New Economics in the Making* (London: Routledge, 1986). Also see Waring, *Counting for Nothing*.

66. For example, see Wendell Berry, *The Unsettling of America: Culture and Agri-*

*culture* (San Francisco: Sierra Club Books, 1977); Murray Bookchin, "Ecology and Revolutionary Thought," 1964 (available from Left Green Network, Burlington, VT 05492); Peter Kropotkin, *Kropotkin's Revolutionary Pamphlets* (New York: Benjamin Blom, 1968); Aldo Leopold, *Sand County Almanac: And Sketches Here and There* (New York and Oxford: Oxford University Press, 1949).

67. Judith Plant, "Searching for Common Ground: Ecofeminism and Bioregionalism," in Andruss et al., *Home! A Bioregional Reader*, 79–85, at 82.

68. Helen Forsey, "Community—Meeting Our Deepest Needs," in Plant, *Healing the Wounds*, 227–34, at 231.

69. Starhawk, "Feminist, Earth-based Spirituality and Ecofeminism," 177.

70. See, for example, Robin Attfield, *The Ethics of Environmental Concern* (New York: Columbia Press, 1983), and H. J. McCloskey, *Ecological Ethics and Politics* (Totowa, N.J.: Rowman and Littlefield, 1983), who argue that traditional ethical precepts, Christian and utilitarian, are sufficient for dealing with environmental problems. For an opposing view, see Henlee Barnette, *The Church and the Ecological Crisis* (Grand Rapids, Minn.: Eerdmans, 1972).

71. Arne Naess, the "father" of deep ecology, quoted in Joanna Macy, "Awakening to the Ecological Self," in Plant, *Healing the Wounds*, 201–11, 209.

72. See, for example, Robyn Eckersley, "The Ecocentric Perspective," in *The Rest of the World Is Watching*, ed. Cassandra Pybus and Richard Flanagan (Sydney: Pan Macmillan, 1990), 68–78.

73. Marilyn French, *Beyond Power: Women, Men, and Morality* (London: Abacus, 1986).

74. See Jane Elix, "Green Girls and Ecological Housewives," *Refractory Girl* 35 (1990): 11–14.

75. Barbara G. Walker, *The Crone: Women of Age, Wisdom, and Power* (San Francisco: Harper & Row, 1985), 175–76.

76. Heather Formaini, *Men: The Darker Continent* (London: Mandarin, 1990), 8.

# CHAPTER 3

# Dismantling Oppression:
# An Analysis of the Connection
# Between Women and Animals

## Lori Gruen

Despite a growing awareness of the destructiveness of the human species and the precarious position in which such destruction puts all inhabitants of the earth, there has been shockingly little discussion of the fundamental forces that have led us to the brink. While multinational corporations and grassroots activists alike have stressed the urgency of a change in behavior, few have stressed the need for a serious change in attitudes and values. Those who do critically examine the underlying motivation for and psychology of destructive action tend to focus their attention on single issues, mimicking, in some ways, the very system at which their critique is aimed. Until recently this has been the trend among those engaged in the struggle for both women's and animal liberation.[1] Feminist theory, in all of its variety, focuses on the primacy of women's oppression, often to the exclusion of parallel concerns. Similarly, animal liberationists, by focusing on the pain and suffering of one group while often ignoring the pain and suffering of others,[2] have situated themselves firmly in the tradition of single-mindedness so common in Western institutions. Such exclusivity not only clouds the expansive nature of oppression, but also hinders the process of undermining such oppression and ultimately liberating all those oppressed.

The emerging discourse of ecofeminism attempts to take up the slack left by those who focus on various symptoms rather than the causes of oppression. In doing this, an often heterogeneous group of theorists have begun analyzing the connections between woman and nature and offering alternative conceptions of how we should live in the world. Whether theoretical, practical, or spiritual, ecofeminists call for a major shift in values. Ecofeminists of whatever variety (and there are many) are united in believing that it is immediately important that we each change our own perspectives and those of society from death-oriented to life-oriented—from a linear, fragmented, and detached mindset to a more direct, holistic appreciation of subjective knowing. How this shift is interpreted, however, varies tremendously within the ecofeminist literature.[3] For present purposes I want to suggest that any interpretation of an ecofeminist vision must include a reexamination of our relationship to nonhuman animals. In fact, I will suggest that an adequate ecofeminist theory must not only analyze the joint oppression of women and nature, but must specifically address the oppression of the nonhuman animals with whom we share the planet. In failing to do so, ecofeminism would run the risk of engaging in the sort of exclusionary theorizing that it ostensibly rejects.

The categories "woman" and "animal"[4] serve the same symbolic function in patriarchal society. Their construction as dominated, submissive "other" in theoretical discourse (whether explicitly so stated or implied) has sustained human male dominance. The role of women and animals in postindustrial society is to serve/be served up; women and animals are the used. Whether created as ideological icons to justify and preserve the superiority of men or captured as servants to provide for and comfort, the connection women and animals share is present in both theory and practice. By examining this connection and the way it sustains the constructed reality of patriarchal society, those struggling for the liberation of women and animals may be better able to reconstruct thought and action in a more balanced, less destructive way.

In this chapter I examine the connection between women and animals by discussing some of the various ways in which it is manifest in contemporary theory and in everyday life. This connection is not to be understood as a "natural" connection—one that suggests that women and animals are essentially similar—but rather a constructed connection that has been created by the patriarchy as a means of oppression. I then analyze the philosophies that serve as foundations for animal liberationist and feminist thought and attempt to show how these theories are inherently exclusionist. I then suggest that ecofeminism can and must remedy the problems with these theories. Finally, I discuss how an appreciation of the connection between women and animals and a renewed understanding of theories that advocate their liberation can enhance strategies of action for change.

Lori Gruen

## *The Connection*

The connection between woman and animal can be located in various strands of an elaborately constructed narrative.[5] In the process of creating what Donna Haraway has referred to as "origin stories,"[6] anthropologists, in this case primarily white, middle-class men, have concocted theories of human cultural development and then attempted to convince themselves and others of the truth or essential nature of one or another of them. In this section, I briefly present four of these theoretical frameworks that serve to justify the oppression of women and animals. While these narratives appear to borrow from and reinforce one another, my presentation is not meant to be a reflection of some true, progressive history.

One of the more popular origin stories suggests that an evolutionary shift occurred as a result of the emergence of hunting behavior in male hominids.[7] According to this theory, the hunter's destructive, competitive, and violent activity directed toward his prey is what originally distinguished man from animal and thus culture from nature. This Myth of Man the Hunter was created by mid-twentieth-century Western minds (influenced by post–World War II political hostilities; the creation, use, and continuing development of nuclear weapons; and increased consumption in "advanced" Western societies); it defined a biologically determined being whose "natural" behavior served as the foundation of culture. It is hardly a coincidence that the act of killing was what established the superiority of man over animal and that the value of such behavior was naturalized and exalted.[8] The myth thus serves not only to posit an essential difference between man and animal but also to elevate man because of his ability to systematically destroy animals.

Theoreticians, by creating a history in which man is separate from and superior to animals, establish a mechanism in which a separation from woman can be grounded. In this account of human social evolution, woman's body (being smaller, weaker, and reproductive) prevents her from participating in the hunt, and thus relegates her to the arena of non-culture. Woman's nonparticipation is conceived as naturally inferior. Her reproductive capacity and life-bearing activities stand in sharp contrast to the death-bringing activities that underlie culture.[9] Constructed in this way, human social evolution establishes the subservient status of woman and animals.

The second framework suggests that as the march of culture continued, nomadic hunting and gathering societies developed into stationary agrarian communities. The advent of agriculture brought with it a decrease in leisure time, the emergence of the process of domestication, and what can be understood as a further distancing of man from woman, animals, and nature. While there is no consensus as to why agriculture replaced foraging, it has been argued that the shift required more, rather than less, labor. As a result of an increased demand for laborers, women came to be thought of as breeders of a workforce. The need for more children to tend the land occurred at roughly the same time as the recognition of the mechanics of reproduction—a recognition that presumably was made possible by the domestication of animals. Once previously nomadic people settled down and began to cultivate the land, the domestication of animals, primarily sheep and goats, soon followed.[10] Before animals were domesticated, it would have been difficult to understand what role the male played in reproduction; observing animal mating may have clarified it. Thus, the domestication of animals, combined with the need for more laborers and the knowledge of how to create them, allowed for the further alienation and oppression of women. As Elizabeth Fisher suggests:

> Now humans violated animals by making them their slaves. In taking them in and feeding them, humans first made friends with animals and then killed them. When they began manipulating the reproduction of animals, they were even more personally involved in practices which led to cruelty, guilt, and subsequent numbness. The keeping of animals would seem to have set a model for the enslavement of humans, in particular the large-scale exploitation of women captives for breeding and labor, which is a salient feature of the developing civilizations.[11]

The shift from nomadic existence to agricultural practices—practices founded on a belief that the natural world could be controlled and manipulated—permitted the conceptualization of animals as sluggish meat-making machines and reluctant laborers, and women as breeders of children.

The third framework, grounded in religious beliefs that developed with the rise of agriculture, also served as a source for separating man from woman and animals. Droughts, storms, and other natural conditions led to the devastation of crops, which in turn caused much suffering. Thus, nature was simultaneously the source of great fear and that which provided the means of survival. Woman, likened to the earth for her ability to bring forth life, was also feared. With the increased risks and uncertainties of the farming life came an intensified desire to dominate. This domination of both

Lori Gruen

natural forces and women was often sought through "divine intervention." In order to enlist the help of the "gods," various rituals were devised. By removing themselves from the natural activities of daily life, men believed they would be in closer touch with the "supernatural" powers that would protect them from nature. In religious mythology, if not in actual practice, women often served as symbols for the uncontrollable and harmful and thus were sacrificed in order to purify the community and appease the gods.[12] Animals too were sacrificed, and it has been suggested that many animals were first domesticated not as food sources but as sacrificial creatures.[13] Religious belief can thus also be seen as a particularly pernicious construction of women and animals as "others" to be used.[14]

During the rise of industrialization, religion based on divine forces was complimented by a fourth framework structured on a belief system that centered on the empirical. The scientific revolution of the sixteenth century established what Carolyn Merchant describes as the "mechanistic world view,"[15] a view that, in combination with the development of the "experimental method," laid yet another conceptual foundation for the manipulation of animals and nature. Domination and the imposition of order were formalized through the scientific objectification of reality. Objective scientists rely on an epistemology that requires detachment and distance. This detachment serves as justification for the division between active pursuer of knowledge and passive object of investigation, and establishes the power of the former over the latter. By devaluing subjective experience, reducing living, spontaneous beings to machines to be studied, and establishing an epistemic privilege based on detached reason, the mechanistic/scientific mindset firmly distinguished man from nature, woman, and animals.[16]

The above-mentioned theoretical frameworks may be seen behind contemporary practices that involve, to varying degrees, the oppression and exploitation of women and animals. While not often explicitly recognized, the theories that separate man from animal and man from woman inform virtually every aspect of daily life. Such ways of constructing reality ground patriarchal conceptions of the world and its inhabitants. Only by critically evaluating the cultural and historical forces that gave rise to current beliefs can we begin to understand the motivations that compel individuals to behave as they do. With this in mind, I will now look at some of the ways in which the oppressive constructions of women and animals affect living beings.

## Exploitation in the Name of Scientific Progress

Between 17 and 70 million animals are killed in U.S. laboratories every year. Under the guise of scientific inquiry, dogs, cats, monkeys, mice, rats, pigs, and other animals are routinely suffocated, starved, shocked, blinded, burned, beaten, frozen, electrocuted, and eventually killed. A majority of the experiments are conducted to satisfy curiosity rather than to improve anyone's health. For example, in a series of experiments conducted at Columbia University's Medical School in New York, experimenters placed pregnant baboons in restraining devices after implanting ten monitoring devices into the bodies of their fetuses. The mothers often gave birth at night, when no one was present, and the infants strangled to death. According to the researchers, "The baboons like to give birth when no one is around. Because of the restraining chair, and the catheters and electrodes, they can't properly tend to the infants . . . and they die."[17] At the University of California at Berkeley, an experimenter genitally masculinized female dogs to test their ability to copulate. The tests were performed before and after the administration of testosterone. The experimenter noted that "animals are unsuccessful in their attempts to copulate with receptive females. They mount and thrust vigorously but do not achieve intromission and establish a copulatory 'lock.'" He "tentatively concluded that the failure . . . of genitally masculinized females to insert and lock when mounting receptive females is due to incomplete penile development."[18] In an experiment conducted at the University of Texas, Dallas, seventy-one kittens aged between 4 and 112 days were given five to eight injections of the hallucinogen LSD. While the experimenters noted that "the behavioral effects of LSD in animals have received monumental attention and literally thousands of studies have dealt with the issue," they decided to go ahead and subject the kittens to the experiments in order to compare the effects on young animals with those on adults. They concluded that the drug "produced a constellation of behaviors [including tremors, vomiting, headshakes, and lack of coordination] that has been previously described in detail for the adult cat."[19]

Literally billions of dollars and countless animal lives have been spent in duplicative, often painful, and generally insignificant animal experiments. While much of the rhetoric employed to justify such experiments is cast in terms of altruistic researchers devoted to the promotion of human health and longevity, the bottom line is often obscured. Animal research in the

United States is big business, and the currency is more than pain and suffering.

Large corporations make enormous profits selling specialized equipment (such as the Columbus Instruments Convulsion Meter), restraining devices, electrically wired cages, surgical implants, and decapitators. Animals themselves, mass produced by corporations such as Charles Rivers, are marketed as commodities that can be modified to consumer specifications. One advertisement likens animals to automobiles: "When it comes to guinea pigs, now you have a choice. You can opt for our standard model that comes complete with hair. Or try our new 1988 stripped down, hairless model for speed and efficiency."[20]

Reducing animals to objects devoid of feelings, desires, and interests is a common consequence of the scientific mindset by which those engaged in experimentation distance themselves from their subjects. Ordered from companies that exist to provide "tools" for the research business, animals' bodies are currently bought and sold in ways that are reminiscent of slave trading in the United States[21] or, more recently, Nazi experiments on women:

> In contemplation of experiments with a new soporific drug, we would appreciate your procuring for us a number of women. . . . We received your answer but consider the price of 200 marks a woman excessive. We propose to pay not more than 170 marks a head. If agreeable, we will take possession of the women. We need approximately 150. . . . Received the order of 150 women. Despite their emaciated condition, they were found satisfactory. . . . The tests were made. All subjects died. We shall contact you shortly on the subject of a new load.[22]

Conceiving of an experimental subject as an inferior, "subhuman" other— as a "specimen" meant to serve—lightens the burden of justifying the infliction of pain and death. Thus, current scientific practices motivate the cultivation of continued detachment.

The detachment is particularly acute in the area of contraceptive research, most of which is done on the female reproductive system. While the risks of childbirth are specific to females, the risks associated with contraception can be borne by either men or women. Yet it is primarily females, both human and nonhuman, who are subjected to risks in contraceptive research, which is controlled by male-dominated pharmaceutical companies. "Third World" women undoubtedly suffer the worst, in terms of both actual experimentation and the subsequent manipulation of reproductive choice.[23] Motivated by the desire for profit and the belief that women's bodies are legitimate sites of experimentation, U.S. contraceptive companies have a history of allowing dangerous drugs to be marketed even after animals have been harmed by them. G. D. Searle, for example, consistently released fraudulent data about the safety of oral contraceptives. In one instance, an FDA investigation revealed that the company secretly removed a tumor from a dog and falsified animal test results. In one of Searles' first human trials for its birth control pill, which took place in Puerto Rico, one woman died of heart failure and another developed tuberculosis, yet such "side-effects" were rarely brought to the users' attention.[24] Upjohn, which manufactures Depo-Provera, found that the drug killed animals in laboratory tests, yet the company continued to market it overseas:

> Animal studies that [showed] Depo caused a significant incidence of breast tumors in beagle dogs and endometrial cancer in rhesus monkeys are downplayed as being irrelevant to humans since the test animals are inappropriate. . . . 'It's no use explaining about beagle dogs,' said one British doctor who had just injected a Bangladeshi immigrant, 'she's an illiterate peasant from the bush.'[25]

Because women and animals are judged unable to comprehend science and are thus relegated to the position of passive object, their suffering and deaths are tolerable in the name of profit and progress.

Often experimenters attempt to justify the use of the bodies of women and animals by touting the benefits that those experimented on receive as a result. This is particularly the case in the area of the new reproductive technologies. Although a few infertile middle-class women have benefited by newly developed procedures such as artificial insemination, embryo transfer, and in vitro fertilization, the overall costs have not been adequately assessed. As we have seen, the suffering of women and animals is devalued from the start. The risks of contraceptives such as DES, the pill, and IUDs, which in many instances have led to the very infertility that the new reproductive technologies are now meant to overcome, were not sufficiently addressed. Further, the success rate of such technologies is often misrepresented, particularly by the media. For every previously infertile woman who is able to reproduce after treatment, there are many others who suffer—both emotionally and physically—in vain. Gena Corea, in *The Mother Machine*, discusses just how women may suffer from reproductive experimentation: hormonal treatment to create superovulation can damage ovaries, with unknown long-term effects; surgical manipulation may damage ovaries and the uterus; and the dangers of anesthetics and the risk of infection are downplayed: "Men are experimenting on women in ways more damaging to women than anyone has publicly acknowledged. It may sound simple to just take a few eggs from a woman's ovary, fertilize them, and return them to her uterus, but in fact the manipulations of the woman's body and spirit involved in this procedure are extreme." [26]

While the risks to women are often overlooked, concern for the fetus is more likely to be the focus of debate. Some researchers suggest that risks to the fetus are minimal, given the results of animal experiments. However, many researchers have questioned the usefulness and applicability of animal studies. [27] As Ruth Hubbard writes, "The guinea pigs for the in vitro procedure are the women who provide the eggs, the women who lend their wombs, and the children who are born." [28]

Often it is not literally women's bodies that are manipulated in laboratories but rather the body of "knowledge" created by Western scientists about women. Many animal experiments are designed to establish essential differences between men and women. Research on intelligence, aggression, competition, dominance, and the effect of various hormones on behavior serves to scientifically establish the lesser status of women. [29] Female animals stand in for human females in a number of experiments that would be too difficult to do with women. [30] One particularly chilling example of such research occurred at the University of Wisconsin Primate Research Center under the direction of Harry Harlow. In over two decades of research ostensibly designed to study affection, Harlow conducted numerous maternal deprivation experiments in which he separated baby monkeys from their mothers and placed the infants with what he called "monster mothers":

> Four surrogate monster mothers were created. One was a shaking mother which rocked so violently that the teeth and bones of the infant chattered in unison. The second was an air-blast mother which blew compressed air against the infant's face and body with such violence that the infant looked as if it would be denuded. The third had an embedded steel frame which, on schedule or demand, would fling forward and knock the infant monkey off the mother's body. The fourth monster mother, on schedule or demand, ejected brass spikes from her ventral surface, an abominable form of maternal tenderness. [31]

Harlow is also known for creating such horrors as the "well of despair," the "tunnel of terror," and living monster mothers who had been brought up in isolation and developed such anti-social behavior that they had to be forcibly tied down in "rape racks" in order to be mated. Harlow's work is objectionable not only because of the extreme cruelty inflicted on animals but also because of its reduction of love, affection, and companionship to manipulatable, reproducible variables that can be tinkered with by scientists. Commenting on Harlow's work, Donna Haraway suggests that "misogyny is deeply implicated in the dream structure of laboratory culture; misogyny is built into the objects of everyday life in laboratory practice, including the bodies of the animals, the jokes in the publications, and the shape of the equipment."[32]

Science, developed and conducted by white, middle-class Western men, has systematically exploited the bodies and minds of women and animals in a variety of ways. These practices, supported in part by a fallacious belief that objective science is value-free, are based on a conception of women and animals as different and lesser beings, beings whose suffering and death are justifiable sacrifices in the name of "progress."

### The Hygiene Fetish and the Great Cover-Up

Most research scientists plead that without animal experiments, human health and life expectancy would not be what they are today. Others argue that progress in these areas is largely the result of improvements in diet and sanitation. It is important to note, however, that advances in hygiene and the resulting decrease in disease have occurred primarily in the more affluent nations. In wealthy countries, billions of dollars are poured into research to find cures for the diseases of affluence, while diseases that we already know how to prevent and cure ravage poor communities, causing the suffering and death of millions. If researchers were really concerned about human health, alleviating the suffering of the poor would surely be one of the top priorities.

Hygiene has unarguably improved the health of those living in industrial societies, yet Western cultures have perverted the need for cleanliness in order to provide manufacturers with profits, subjugate women, and further distance man from nature. The proliferation of cleaning products and their subsequent marketing simultaneously perpetuate the notion that "dirt" and "natural odors" must be controlled and eliminated, and that it is women's job to do this. Thus, women have been placed at the boundary between nature, with its "contaminants," and civilized sterility. In addition to separating man from woman and nature, the production of cleaning products destroys the environment through the creation of toxic chemicals and contributes to the death of millions of animals.

Products ranging from oven cleaner to feminine deodorant spray are placed in every conceivable orifice of animals in order to test their toxicity. Two of the most common toxicity tests are the Draize eye irritancy test and the Acute oral toxicity test. In the former, a rabbit is placed in a restraining device while a substance (bleach, toilet bowl cleaner, air freshener, etc.) is placed in one of her eyes. The animal is then observed for eye swelling, ulceration, infection, and bleeding. The studies can last for as long as three weeks, during which time the eye may lose all distinguishing characteristics. At the end of the study the animals are killed and discarded. In oral toxicity tests, dogs, rats, and monkeys are forced to ingest various products. Often animals will display classic symptoms of poisoning—vomiting, diarrhea, paralysis, convulsions, and internal bleeding—but will be left to die "naturally." Cleaning products must also undergo tests in which the animals are forced to inhale lethal doses of chemicals; tests in which a particular substance is injected under the skin, into the muscle, or into various organs; and tests in which animals are forced to swim in a chemical bath, often drowning before the effect of the chemicals on the animal's system is determined. Ostensibly, these studies are designed to protect the consumer. However, the unreliable nature of such experiments and the difficulties associated with extrapolating data from one species to another make consumer protection doubtful. In addition, as we have seen with contraceptives, companies may determine that a particular product is highly dangerous but nonetheless release it. Animal experiments, regardless of their validity, cannot prevent accidental ingestion or dangerous exposure in humans. No matter how many animals die in attempts to determine the toxicity of furniture polish, for example, the effects on the child who drinks it will be the same.

These methods are also employed to test cosmetics, products primarily designed to mask women's natural appearance. Advertising for lipstick, eyeshadow, mascara, and the like suggests that women must be made up in order to conform to (male) standards of beauty. Contemporary culture constructs men as the lookers and women as the looked at. As John Berger suggests, "Men act and women appear. Men look at women. Women watch themselves being looked at. This determines not only most relations between men and women but also the relation of women to themselves. The surveyor of woman in herself is male: the surveyed is female. Thus she turns herself into an object—and most particularly an object of vision: a sight."[33] By purchasing and using cosmetics, women become complicitous not only in their own reduction to the object of a gaze, but also in the suffering and death of animals.[34]

The same media manipulation of women and physical mutilation of animals are used by the fur industry. This industry, in addition, can also be indicted for playing on class differences for profit. Wearing furs, the industry informs us, not only beautifies and glamorizes women, but also bestows upon them a "high-class status." Wearing the skins of dead animals empowers women, we are told. But, again, all it does is reduce women to objects who inadvertently serve the profit and pleasure interests of men. One fur coat requires the death of 4 to 5 leopards, 3 to 5 tigers, 10 lynx, up to 40 raccoons, or 35 to 65 mink.[35] In order to obtain their skins, animals are either trapped in the wild or raised on "ranches." Trapped animals suffer tremendously when a steel-jaw trap slams tight on one of their limbs. As the animal struggles to break free, she may tear her flesh, break her bones, and severely injure her mouth and teeth. Some may even chew off their limbs in order to escape. Those who do not escape must remain in pain for days—without food or water—until the trapper arrives to kill them. "Ranched" animals are generally confined in small wire cages for their entire lives. When they have grown to full size, they are killed in the least expensive way possible, most commonly by having their necks broken, being gassed or suffocated, or by electrocution.

While women are covering up dirt and odors, masking their natural looks with cosmetic products, and enhancing their status and elegance by draping themselves in furs, animals are living and dying in terrible pain. The real cover-up, however, is the one perpetrated by industries that see both women and animals as manipulatable objects. Women are conditioned to believe that they must alter or disguise what is undesirable—nature—at great physical, psychological, and economic expense to themselves[36] and at immeasurable cost to animals. The end result is an enormous profit by a few individuals and the perpetuation of the notion that the exploitation of women and animals is a legitimate means to such an end.

## Domination in the Kitchen

The traditionally constructed role of woman as cleaner and the sight/site of male pleasure allows for the diminishment of women and the pain of animals. At least since the rise of industrial culture, women have been confined to the domestic sphere, where one of their primary roles is to provide food. Certain animals have been domesticated and forced to provide food in a different sense. Women prepare and cook; animals are prepared and cooked. Both play subservient roles in the male-dominated institution of meat eating.

The practice of meat eating not only relegates women to a particular physical space—the kitchen or its equivalent—but also, as Carol Adams has forcefully argued, places women in a specifically constructed social place:

> People with power have always eaten meat. . . . Dietary habits proclaim class distinctions, but they proclaim patriarchal distinctions as well. Women, second-class citizens, are more likely to eat what are considered to be second-class foods in a patriarchal culture: vegetables and fruits and grains, rather than meat. The sexism in meat eating recapitulates the class distinctions with an added twist: a mythology that meat is a masculine food and meat eating, a male activity.[37]

Men, as those in power, eat meat, and their consumption of flesh in turn perpetuates this power. In the hierarchy of consumption, men are at the top, women are below, and the more than 5 billion animals in the United States that are intensively reared, slaughtered, dismembered, packaged, and sold are lower still.[38]

Of all of the animals that are killed in food production, female animals fare the worst. The egg industry is the most acute example of highly centralized, corporate exploitation of female animals. Over 95 percent of the eggs produced in the United States come from factories that hold captive anywhere from a quarter of a million to five million hens each. These hens live in wire cages, set in rows, stacked five cages or more high. One cage housing four or five hens typically measures 12 by 18 inches, with no room to stretch a wing. In order to produce over 4.2 billion dozen eggs each year, hens are imprisoned in these cages from the time they are ready to start laying until their production rate drops and the factory manager decides it is time to throw them out. This usually occurs after a year, although the confinement may last as long as eighteen months. Since the hens spend virtually all of their lives standing on wire mesh, they often develop painfully malformed feet. Since they are unable to scratch, their claws may grow so long as to curl around the wire, trapping the bird until she dies from starvation or dehydration.

Female pigs, who are considered "hog producing machines," do not rank much higher on the scale of abuse. Any recognition of their high intelligence and intense social desires is absent on sow farms. Sows are kept chained in "iron maidens," 6 by 2 foot metal stalls that are just bigger than the pig herself. Often they are placed in stalls and tethered. One report of what happens when the sows are first placed in confinement suggests how they feel about it:

> The sows threw themselves violently backwards, straining against the tether. Sows thrashed their heads about as they twisted and turned in their struggle to free themselves. Often loud screams were emitted and occasionally individuals crashed bodily against the side boards of the tether stalls. This sometimes resulted in sows collapsing to the floor.[39]

Consider the dairy cow. From conception, the lives of cows are manipulated and controlled. The bucolic picture of the dairy cow playing with her calf in the pasture may be seen only in fairy tales and history books. She is now a living pincushion whose life is painful and poisoned. The industrialization of agriculture has not overlooked the dairy cow. She is put under stresses as severe as any imposed on pigs and poultry in the agribusinessman's quest for ever greater profits.

In order to keep dairy cows in a constant state of lactation, they must be impregnated annually. After her first infant is taken from her at birth, she is milked by machines twice, sometimes three times, a day for ten months. After the third month she will be impregnated again. She will give birth only six to eight weeks after drying out. This intense cycle of pregnancy and hyperlactation can last only about five years,[40] and then the "spent" cow is sent to slaughter. During that five-year period, the overworked cow is likely to be very sick. In order to obtain the highest output, cows are fed high-energy concentrates. But the cow's peculiar digestive system cannot adequately absorb nutrients from such feed. As a result, during peak production the cow often expends more energy than she is able to take in. According to John Webster of the University of Bristol School of Veterinary Science: "To achieve a comparably high work rate, a human would have to jog for about six hours a day, every day."[41] Because her capacity to produce surpasses her ability to metabolize her feed, the cow begins to break down and use her own body tissues; she literally "milks off her own back."

One-third of all dairy cows suffer from mastitis, a disease that infects the udders. The most common mastitis is caused by environmental pathogens that result from squalid housing conditions, particularly from fecal contamination. Treatment includes spraying the teats with disinfectants and injecting antibiotics directly into them. Both treatments are becoming increasingly ineffective as the disease becomes resistant. The result for the cow is bleeding and acute pain, particularly during milking (which is always done by machine). The result for the consumer is contaminated milk.

The assembly-line mentality, which has allowed for herds of more than three thousand animals to be "processed" with minimal human labor, has insinuated itself into the cow's process of reproduction. Dairy cows are always artificially inseminated. According to farmers, this method is faster, more efficient, and cheaper than maintaining bulls. With the use of hormone injections, cows will produce dozens of eggs at one time. After artificial insemination, the embryos will be flushed out of the womb and transplanted into surrogate cows through incisions in their flanks. Since only the best producer's eggs are used, cows can be genetically manipulated to produce more milk. Additional advances may soon force cows to produce even more. The Bovine Growth Hormone (BGH) is being touted as a revolutionary way to increase milk yields without raising feed costs. Cows are already producing more milk than their bodies should and more than the market demands.[42] With the advent of BGH, the already shortened and painful life of the dairy cow may become even shorter and more painful.[43]

Meat eating and the consumption of "feminized protein"[44]—dairy products and eggs—in industrialized countries is perhaps the most prominent manifestation of a belief system in which woman and animals are reduced to objects to be consumed. Animals clearly can be seen as pawns in a power dynamic by which man asserts his superiority. Women too are oppressed by this system, which locates power in the ability to master and consume the flesh of another. In times of shortage, it is men who eat flesh. Indeed, a disproportionate number of women starve or suffer from malnutrition in countries where food is difficult to come by. The number of taboos associated with the foods women are allowed to consume, spanning a variety of cultures, can be seen as yet another way in which consumption—who consumes what—dictates power relations. As we saw with the institutions of science, hygiene, and beauty, it is men who dominate how reality is constructed, and too often it is women and animals who suffer.[45]

## The Philosophy

In the preceding section, I discussed just a few of the countless ways in which women are exploited by men in contemporary Western culture. In response to such oppression, a varied discourse has emerged that attempts to theorize a way of thinking and acting to end the tyranny of patriarchal thought. Similarly, a theory opposed to the vast destruction of animal life has been developed. Both feminist theory and animal liberation theory address ways in which the continuing oppression of women and animals, respectively, can be curtailed and eliminated, yet neither draws on the strengths and insights of the other. By examining the more prominent strains of each of these theories, I hope to establish how each fails to adequately address certain fundamental features of oppression and thereby minimizes the possibility of its successful elimination.[46]

In this section, I examine what I call "anthropocentric feminisms" (liberal feminism, Marxist feminism, and socialist feminism), showing how each elevates humans above animals. I also discuss some of the shortcomings of radical feminism.[47] I then examine two of the most prominent animal liberation theories and trace their failure to provide a sufficient analysis of oppression to the fact that both are firmly situated within what can be considered an oppressive theoretical framework. Finally, I suggest that the shortcomings of the preceding theories can be overcome in the emerging discourse of a truly inclusive ecofeminism.

## Feminist Theory

Liberal feminism locates its critique of patriarchal institutions in their failure to recognize the equal competence and status of women. Following in the tradition of liberal political theory, liberal feminists view the ability to be rational as the basis of moral decision making. Rationality, then, and a respect for autonomy and self-determination are the primary values for liberal feminists. The oppression of women, according to this view, results from depriving women of education and opportunities. Liberal feminists do not provide any deep criticism of particular social institutions, but rather suggest that the problem of women's oppression is one of exclusion. Freedom for the liberals will occur when women are provided with equal access to jobs and positions of power and are protected equally under the law.

The liberal feminist critique is problematic in a number of ways,[48] although for present purposes I want to discuss only one. The liberal feminist vision of liberation does not challenge the underlying structure of patriarchy. Indeed, it operates on the very same Western, rationalist assumptions. This was particularly apparent at a 1991 conference where many African women who espoused a liberal perspective eloquently argued for equal access to resources.[49] They expressed the desire to be able to consume just as much as their Western sisters. Feminists of this sort seek equality in the system as it now exists (or perhaps with minor modification) while failing to consider the way in which consumption patterns, for example, affect the environment. Their position necessarily excludes concern for animals and the planet on which we all live. Criticizing such a view, Dorothy Dinnerstein writes:

> Without hope . . . we are already dead. And an equal-rights-for-women stance that remains oriented to an otherwise unchanged social reality is blind hope: hope resigned, on some silent level of feeling, to the truth of what it denies: the imminence of world-murder. It is a business-as-usual strategy; a self-deceptive device for whiling away time; a blind to-do; a solemn fuss about concerns that make no sense if we have no future.[50]

Regardless of the disagreements that might arise about the underlying principles or assumptions of patriarchy, its implications, at least as they affect animals and many women, are destructive. This system, loosely defined, kills the bodies and minds of millions and threatens to kill the planet as well. Surely an adequate theory of liberation must address this.

Marxist feminists do provide an analysis of the system and suggest that the path to liberation must be cleared of economic inequalities. Following Marx, these feminists maintain that the oppression of women is part of a larger problem—the oppression of the working class by the bourgeoisie. Once private property is abolished and thus the primary mechanism of alienated labor eliminated, once human beings have equal access to the means of production, they will be free. For Marxist feminists, the liberation of women is linked with the process of integrating women into production.[51]

While Marxist feminists begin to address the problem of hierarchies and appreciate the importance of understanding human beings in relation to their particular place in history, they nonetheless elevate human beings over animals and the natural world. In fact, Marx viewed animals and nature as fundamentally distinct from human beings and as "objects" to be used in the service of humanity. In the *Manuscripts of 1844*, Marx distinguishes humans from animals on the grounds that the former not only engage in the activities of life (as do animals) but also can freely and consciously choose that activity: "Conscious life activity distinguishes man from the life activity of animals."[52] Humans are distinct from and superior to animals in that they can transform/exploit the natural world, whereas animals can only fulfill their immediate needs.[53] While quite different in many ways from liberals, the feminists who follow in the Marxist tradition continue to maintain their hierarchical position with regard to animals and the natural world.

Socialist feminists have developed a much more comprehensive theory than the Marxist feminists. While maintaining a strong emphasis on material concerns and historicity, socialist feminists specifically incorporate a gender analysis with a class analysis. They call for a radical transformation of most existing institutions: the family, education, compulsory heterosexuality, government, and industry.[54] For the most part, however, socialist feminists have not yet addressed the institutionalized oppression of animals and its relation to oppression generally. While it need not be exclusionary in this regard, concern for animals and nature is noticeably absent from current socialist feminist discourse.

All of the above-mentioned anthropocentric feminist theories focus on the full integration of women into culture and production, however conceived. A fundamental assumption of each position is that there is a distinction between the cultural and the natural and that women's liberation must occur within the former. Indeed, anthropocentric feminists understand the connection between woman and nature as part of the oppressive system of beliefs that grounds the exploitation of women. Therefore, such a connection must be denied. This view, perhaps unwittingly, reproduces the conception that culture and nature are distinct, a view that grounds much of patriarchal thinking. Failing to challenge this distinction undermines a more complete understanding of the workings of oppression.

Radical feminism, on the other hand, specifically addresses the connection between woman and animals/nature.[55] These feminists embrace the connection and attempt to strengthen it by denying the value of its opposite. In other words, radical feminists see women as closer to nature and men as closer to culture and thereby reject the cultural in favor of the natural. They elevate what they consider to be women's virtues—caring, nurturing, interdependence—and reject the individualist, rationalist, and destructive values typically associated with men. On this view, the widespread slaughter of animals and the degradation of the environment are seen as the responsibility of the patriarchs. Presumably such atrocities would not be committed if women were in control.

The radical feminist position, though at the other extreme from liberal, Marxist, and socialist feminism, also reproduces a particular patriarchal notion: the belief that woman and nature are essentially connected. This

Lori Gruen

view accepts a type of determinism that forever separates woman and man. The difference is that this account turns the hierarchy and power relation on its head. Instead of devaluing women, animals, and nature, radical feminists devalue men. Radical feminism is therefore not a completely liberatory theory, because in its vision of a future the oppressor and the oppressed do not disappear; they simply change their masks.

## Animal Liberation Theory

Two of the most popular theories which call for animal liberation are the rights-based theory of Tom Regan and the utilitarian theory of Peter Singer.[56] Regan's argument, briefly stated, goes as follows. Only beings with inherent value have rights. Inherent value is the value that individuals possess independent of their goodness or usefulness to others, and rights are the things that protect this value. All subjects-of-a-life have such value. Only self-conscious beings, capable of having beliefs and desires, only deliberate actors who have a conception of the future, are subjects-of-a-life. In addition, all beings who have inherent value have it equally. Inherent value cannot be gained by acting virtuously or lost by acting evilly. Inherent value is not something that can grow or diminish according to fads or fashion, popularity or privilege. According to Regan, at the very least all mentally normal mammals of a year or more are subjects-of-a-life and thus have inherent value that grounds their rights.

Singer's view is based not on rights, but rather on the principle of equal consideration. According to Singer, all beings who are capable of feeling pain and pleasure are subjects of moral consideration. In order to determine how to treat others, Singer argues that we must take the like interests of all those affected by an action into account. All like interests are counted, regardless of the skin color, sex, or species of the interest holder. Singer's utilitarian theory maintains that right actions are actions that maximize pleasure and minimize pain. This principle does not apply solely to physical suffering, but also to psychological pain insofar as it can be determined. For Singer, to disregard the pain and suffering of animals when making a decision that will affect them is "speciesist." Speciesism is a bias in favor of one's own species and is considered morally on a par with sexism and racism.

While both of these theories argue for the inclusion of animals in the moral sphere, they rely on reason and abstraction in order to succeed. Regan writes:

We know that many—literally, billions and billions—of these animals are subjects-of-a-life in the sense explained and so have inherent value if we do. And since, in order to arrive at the best theory of our duties to one another, we must recognize our equal inherent value as individuals, reason—not sentiment, not emotion—reason compels us to recognize the equal inherent value of these animals and, with this, their equal right to be treated with respect.[57]

Singer suggests that "an appeal to basic moral principles which we all accept, and the application of these principles to the victims of [Nazi and animal] experiments, is demanded by reason, not emotion."[58] By focusing exclusively on the role of reason in moral deliberations, these philosophers perpetuate an unnecessary dichotomy between reason and emotion. Certainly it is possible that a decision based on emotion alone may be morally indefensible, but it is also possible that a decision based on reason alone may be objectionable. Furthermore, the beings we are considering are not always just animals; they are Lassie the dog and the family's companion cat, bald eagles and bunnies, snakes and skunks. Similarly, humans are not just humans; they are friends and lovers, family and foe. The emotional force of kinship or closeness to another is a crucial element in thinking about moral deliberations. To ignore the reality of this influence in favor of some abstraction such as absolute equality may be not only impossible, but undesirable.

One way to overcome the false dualism between reason and emotion is by moving out of the realm of abstraction and getting closer to the effects of our everyday actions.[59] Much of the problem with the attitudes many people have toward animals stems from our removal from the animals themselves. Our responsibility for our own actions has been mediated. Who are these animals who suffer and die so that I can eat pot roast? I do not deprive them of movement and comfort; I do not take their young from them; I do not have to look into their eyes as I cut their throats. Most people are shielded from the consequences of their actions. As long as the theories that advocate the liberation of animals rely on abstraction, the full force of these consequences will remain too far removed to motivate a change in attitude.

## Ecofeminist Theory

All of the theories just discussed, in one way or another, accept normative dualisms that give rise to a logic of domination.[60] By embracing such a way of thinking, these theories are exclusionist in the sense that each creates or maintains a category of "otherness." In the case of the anthropocentric feminists, "other" is nonhuman animals and nature; for radical feminists, "other" is culture and man; for the animal liberationists, "other" is human emotion and collectivity. The maintenance of such dualisms allows for the continued conceptualization of hierarchies in which a theoretically privileged group or way of thinking is superior. By establishing superiority in theory, the groundwork is laid for oppression of the inferior in practice.

Unlike these theories, ecofeminist theory will recognize sympathy and compassion as a fundamental feature of any inclusive, liberatory theory. An inclusive ecofeminist theory suggests that compassion is crucial to undoing oppression in both theory and practice. "Others" are not only marginalized by contemporary cultural practices, but negated by the process of defining a powerful "self." As Donna Haraway has written, "The construction of the self from the raw materials of the other, the appropriation of nature in the production of culture, the ripening of the human from the soil of the animal, the clarity of the white from the obscurity of color, the issue of man from the body of woman . . . mutually construct each other, but not equally."[61] Ecofeminists must challenge such dualistic constructions and, in so doing, attempt to establish a different system of values in which the normative category of "other" (animals, people of color, "Third World" people, the lower classes, etc.) is reevaluated. By recognizing that the exploitation that occurs as a result of establishing power over one group is unlikely to be confined to that group only, ecofeminists are committed to a reexamination and rejection of all forms of domination.

Revealing and respecting the value of the hitherto inferior "other" is one of the ways in which ecofeminists have attempted to eliminate hierarchies and undo the logic of domination. Constructing, and then naturalizing, hierarchies has been one of the more insidious justifying mechanisms for the oppression of both women and animals. Ecofeminists will thus focus on the elimination of all institutionalized hierarchy as another principle force for ending oppression. As Ynestra King suggests:

Life on earth is an interconnected web, not a hierarchy. There is no natural hierarchy; human hierarchy is projected on to nature and then used to justify social domination. Therefore, ecofeminist theory seeks to show the connections between all forms of domination, including the domination of nonhuman nature, and ecofeminist practice is necessarily anti-hierarchical.[62]

Nonhierarchical analysis, coupled with an expanded conception of moral community, allows ecofeminist theory to overcome the exclusionary pitfalls of both feminist and animal liberation philosophies. By challenging the central assumptions of oppression, an inclusive ecofeminism posits the beginnings of a truly liberatory theory. At the heart of ecofeminist theory and practice lies a vision of a new way of conceptualizing reality, a vision that moves away from rugged individualism and an overemphasis on reason to a more inclusive focus and respectful appreciation of difference.

## Politics and Possibilities

The exclusionary nature of both animal liberation and feminist theory often manifests itself in practice. A number of years ago, I came across a booth of women in Grand Central Station in New York who were collecting signatures for a petition to ban pornographic material. Having just begun to think about the connection between the oppression of women and that of animals, I was quite interested in the cover of a *Hustler* magazine that these women were displaying. The particularly telling image was of a woman being put through a meat-grinder. I approached the women and explained my interest. I was immediately barraged with accusations challenging the sincerity of my feminist sensibilities and was dismissed. I continued to explain my belief that understanding the roots of oppression of all beings was an important way to undermine patriarchal exploitation, but my words fell on deaf ears. Marti Kheel conveyed to me a similarly structured experience, only this time the person who would not listen was an animal liberationist: "A man called me up from a noted animal rights organization requesting items for a garage sale. I was told that magazines such as *Playboy*, *Hustler*, etc. would be welcome. When I reproached him for promoting sexist literature, he accused me of not really caring about animals."[63] Although both of these incidents involved the sensitive topic of pornography, and thus emotions may have been high, feminists working to end the oppression of both women and animals encounter such experiences with remarkable regularity.

Exclusivity and inability to see beyond particular cases of oppression are not limited to personal encounters. Animal rights organizations are, for the most part, run by men, while the bulk of those working for them as employees and volunteers are women. Those organizations that are headed by women continue to adhere to the top-down authoritarianism so common to patriarchal institutions. Decisions are made by a select few, usually without the input of those who will be directly involved in carrying out the decisions. At conferences, demonstrations, and other media events, men are most often represented as the spokespeople and leaders of the movement. At the largest gathering of animal protectionists to that date—the 1990 March for the Animals—the majority of participants were women, but women were vastly underrepresented on the platform of speakers. The *Washington Post* quotes Sukey Leeds, who attended the march, as criticizing march organizers for allowing only three women to speak: "Women have done all the work in the animal rights movement . . . but men really run it and they have for years."[64] While men have made important contributions to exposing the plight of animals, the sentiment that Leeds expresses is common and accurate. Those engaged in work for animal liberation have failed to examine the fundamental roots of oppression and as a result have incorporated oppressive practices into their struggle.[65]

Feminists, too, seldom see the practical connection between the liberation of women and that of animals. Few feminist gatherings are vegetarian, let alone vegan.[66] Often the decision to serve meat and other animal products is based on a reluctance to infringe on women's rights to choose or deference to the cultural traditions of women of color, for example. Such rationalizations ignore the infringement of an animal's "right"[67] to live a pain-free life and fail to recognize that cultural traditions are exactly those institutions at which legitimate feminist critiques are aimed. In an article that grapples with the question of "cultural imperialism" and the accusation that serving vegetarian food at feminist functions is racist, undermining the traditions of women of color, Jane Meyerding writes, "It is a contradiction for feminists to eat animals with whom they have no physical or spiritual relationship except that of exploiter to exploited. . . . I think concern for the lives of all beings is a vital, empowering part of feminist analysis; I don't think we can strengthen our feminist struggle against one aspect of patriarchy by ignoring or accepting other aspects."[68] By failing to take into account the plight of animals, feminists are acting out one of the deepest patriarchal attitudes. Ecofeminists argue that we need not and must not isolate the subjugation of women at the expense of the exploitation of animals. Indeed, the struggle for women's liberation is inextricably linked to abolition of all oppression.

Feminists can complement their work by adopting one of the most striking features of animal liberation practice—the immediate recognition of the consequences of individual action. Animal liberationists are deeply aware of how some of the most basic choices they make—what they eat, what they wear, what they purchase—directly affect the lives of animals. In their everyday practice, vegetarians and vegans live resistance. They simply do not contribute to the suffering of animals and the perpetuation of a system of oppression in this way. This refusal, rather than being antithetical to feminist concerns, in fact promotes them. For some feminists, such as the women at the Bloodroot Collective, taking direct action on behalf of animals was an outgrowth of their feminism:

> Our vegetarianism stems . . . from a foundation of thought based on feminist ethics: a consciousness of our connections with other species and with the survival of the earth. . . . Dependence on a meat and poultry diet is cruel and destructive to creatures more like ourselves than we are willing to admit—whether we mean turkeys and cows or the humans starved by land wasted for animal farming purposes to feed the privileged few.[69]

By refusing to consume the products of pain (not eating animals, not wearing leather, fur, and feathers, not using makeup and household products that have been tested on animals), feminists, like animal liberationists, can directly deny the legitimacy of a patriarchal system that treats sentient individuals as objects to use and profit from.

Similarly, animal liberationists can gain much, both personally and politically, by embracing feminist practices. Ironically, while animal liberation stresses individual responsibility for actions, most people interested in protecting animals abdicate a certain amount of responsibility by sending checks to large, wealthy organizations in the hope that these groups will act on their behalf. While particular issues often require the coordination of many different people and their respective talents (which certainly requires money), much animal abuse can be combatted in the home and local community. The hierarchical structure of animal protection organizations, coupled with often overstated claims of effectiveness, promotes a "follow-the-leader" mentality that devalues individual action. In contrast, feminist practice, which focuses on group decision making and consensus, strengthens the voice of every individual and allows for the often difficult development of cooperative action.

Both feminists and animal liberationists would do well to reflect upon how their inclusion of certain "others" is often accomplished at the expense of other "others." Animal liberation activists strive to set themselves apart from the "lunatic fringe," implicitly declaring that they are just as patriarchal as the next guy. Feminists all too often fail to consider the various ways in which oppression operates, particularly as it affects nonhumans, because, they proclaim, "We are not animals!" While the work of both feminists and animal liberationists has raised awareness of the oppressive conditions under which most women and animals live, and has often led to important reforms to improve these lives, the roots of oppression remain intact.

Ecofeminist practice attempts to dig at these roots. Calling for a fundamental shift in values, ecofeminist practice is a revolt against control, power, production, and competition in all of their manifestations. Such practice embraces a "methodological humility,"[70] a method of deep respect for difference. In action, one must always operate under the assumption that there may be something happening that cannot be immediately understood. This is a particularly useful strategy for developing alliances between animal liberationists and feminists. Methodological humility suggests that there may not be one right answer to the problem of undoing patriarchal oppression. Making connections, between the various ways in which oppression operates and between those individuals who suffer such oppression, will allow all beings to live healthier, more fulfilling, and freer lives.

## NOTES

*Acknowledgments*: I would like to express my gratitude to the following people who provided useful comments on earlier drafts of this work: Ken Knowles, Blueberry and Madeline, Laura Perez, Mary Richards, Ross Swick, Estelle Tarica, and especially Greta Gaard.

1. For the present purposes I will be focusing on the oppression of women and animals, but I believe that the type of analysis I am doing is not exclusive. A similar analysis could be done for oppression of all kinds, but it would be more appropriately accomplished by people of color, the infirm, the colonized, and so on, who are undoubtedly more able than I am to speak of their own oppression.

2. While many animal liberationists deny such a claim in theory, their practice is quite different, as we shall see below, under "Politics and Possibilities."

3. Some of the more recent books on ecofeminism include, Andrée Collard with Joyce Contrucci, *Rape of the Wild: Man's Violence Against Animals and the Earth* (Bloomington: Indiana University Press, 1989); Irene Diamond and Gloria Feman Orenstein, eds., *Reweaving the World: The Emergence of Ecofeminism* (San Francisco: Sierra Club Books, 1990); Judith Plant, ed., *Healing the Wounds: The Promise of Ecofeminism* (Philadelphia: New Society Books, 1989); Vandana Shiva, *Staying Alive: Women, Ecology, and Development* (London: Zed Books, 1988).

4. I would like to differentiate between the constructed category "woman" and

individual "women," who have very different lives and experiences. When I seem to be speaking in more general terms, I do not mean to be overlooking differences between women and thus assuming a universal perspective, but rather am addressing the category. I have not figured out the best way to make this distinction explicit, but will use the term "woman" to indicate the constructed concept, as the text allows.

5. This section is a brief glance at some of the more prevalent theories that have served to establish and/or justify the subjugation of women and animals. For more detailed accounts please see the references.

6. Donna Haraway, *Primate Visions: Gender, Race, and Nature in the World of Modern Science* (New York: Routledge, 1989), 5.

7. For one of the best discussions of the creation of the Myth of Man the Hunter, see Haraway, *Primate Visions*, chap. 6.

8. Marti Kheel's "Ecofeminism and Deep Ecology: Reflections on Identity and Difference," in Diamond and Orenstein, *Reweaving the World*, 128–38, discusses contemporary manifestations of such behavior.

9. Some female anthropologists and other writers have attempted to reconstruct the his-story of early humans by emphasizing the important role women played in the development of culture. See, for example, Adrienne Zihlman, "Women as Shapers of the Human Adaptation," in *Woman the Gatherer*, ed. Frances Dahlberg (New Haven: Yale University Press, 1981). While this is an interesting approach, it ultimately legitimizes the enterprise of constructing essential and deterministic origins.

10. For an examination of some of the theories about how and why animals were domesticated, see Elizabeth Fisher, *Woman's Creation* (New York: McGraw-Hill, 1979), part 4.

11. Fisher, *Woman's Creation*, 197.

12. See, for example, Joan Banberger, "The Myth of Matriarchy: Why Men Rule in Primitive Society," in *Woman, Culture, and Society*, ed. Michelle Z. Rosaldo and Louise Lamphere (Stanford: Stanford University Press, 1974), 263–81.

13. As John Zerzan writes: "Sheep and goats, the first animals to be domesticated, are known to have been widely used in religious ceremonies, and to have been raised in enclosed meadows for sacrificial purposes. Before they were domesticated, moreover, sheep had no wool suitable for textile purposes. The main use of the hen in the earliest centers of civilization 'seems to have been,' according to Darby, 'sacrificial and divinatory rather than alimentary.' Sauer adds that the 'egg laying and meat production qualities' of tamed fowl 'are relatively late consequences of their domestication.'" *Lomakatsi* no. 3, P.O. Box 1920, Boulder, CO 80306.

14. For more on the way in which religion has served as a theoretical framework for oppression, see Mary Daly, *Beyond God the Father* (Boston: Beacon Press, 1973), and *Gyn/Ecology* (Boston: Beacon Press, 1978), and Marilyn French, *Beyond Power* (New York: Ballantine Books, 1985).

15. Carolyn Merchant, *The Death of Nature: Women, Ecology, and the Scientific Revolution* (San Francisco: Harper and Row, 1983).

16. For a more detailed critique of science from feminist perspectives, see my "Gendered Knowledge? Examining Influences on Scientific and Ethological Inquiries," in *Interpretation and Explanation in the Study of Animal Behavior: Comparative Perspectives*, ed. Dale Jamieson and Marc Bekoff (Boulder, Colo.: Westview Press, 1990), 56–73, and the references therein.

17. Quoted in Lori Gruen and Peter Singer, *Animal Liberation: A Graphic Guide* (London: Camden Press, 1987), 65.

18. F. A. Beach, "Hormonal Modulation of Genital Reflexes in Male and Masculinized Female Dogs," *Behavioral Neuroscience* 98 (1984): 325–32.

19. M. E. Trulson and G. A. Howell, "Ontogeny of the Behavioral Effects of Lysergic Acid Diethylamide in Cats," *Developmental Psychobiology* 17 (1984): 329–46.

20. Such advertising copy is the norm in magazines such as *Lab Animal* and others that cater to research laboratories. For a discussion of these sorts of ads, see Peter Singer, *Animal Liberation* (New York: New York Review of Books, 1990), 37–39.

21. Marjorie Spiegel, *The Dreaded Comparison: Human and Animal Slavery* (New York: Mirror Books, 1988).

22. Excerpted from letters from the I. G. Farben chemical trust to Auschwitz, as quoted in Bruno Bettelheim, *The Informed Heart* (New York: Avon, 1971), 243. This example was brought to my attention by Jonathan Glover.

23. Betsy Hartmann, in her carefully researched work *Reproductive Rights and Wrongs: The Global Politics of Population Control and Contraceptive Choice* (New York: Harper & Row, 1987), writes that "in the contraceptive research business, the Third World has long been an important laboratory for human testing." She documents the ways in which many women are exploited and harmed as a result of population control pressures.

24. Ibid., 177.

25. Ibid., 189–91.

26. Gena Corea, *The Mother Machine* (New York: Harper & Row, 1985), 166.

27. For example, Dr. Pierre Soupart has questioned whether the data obtained from lab animals could be extrapolated to human beings, "especially when the extrapolation concerns chromosomes, which are specific for every single mammalian species." As cited in Corea, *Mother Machine*, 151.

28. Ruth Hubbard, *The Politics of Women's Biology* (New Brunswick, N.J.: Rutgers University Press, 1990), 202. Hubbard objects here to the use of women as if they were animals—namely, guinea pigs. This view is anthropocentric, a notion I will discuss below, under "The Philosophy."

29. See for example Hubbard, *Politics of Women's Biology*, and Ruth Bleier, ed., *Feminist Approaches to Science* (New York: Pergamon Press, 1986), chap. 7.

30. One would like to say "too morally objectionable," but given the history of scientific use and abuse of "others," the difficulty undoubtedly lies in negative public opinion and illegality, rather than the experimenter's conscience.

31. Harry Harlow, *Learning to Love* (New York: Aronson, 1974), 38.

32. Haraway, *Primate Visions*, 238. Indeed, the *Laboratory Primate Newsletter* 29, no. 3 (July 1990), ran the following "Research Report":

"Two scientists at the University of Erewhon recently did an interesting study with chimpanzees. The results, published in a report in Reader's Digest point to genetic origins for differences between the sexes.

"Two groups of chimps, one only males, the other only females, were taught to wash dishes after meals. 99% of the females, but only 2% of the males, also washed the stove without being specifically told. In addition, all of the females swept the kitchen floor daily, while none of the males displayed any sweeping behavior at all.

"The experiment might have been more valid if the groups could have been combined. In that way we would have been assured that the males and females were not treated differently by the investigators. Unfortunately, when this was attempted, uncontrollable fighting ensued. The basis for the conflict was never fully determined, but the experimenters noted that it invariably took place near a full bag of garbage.

"Other scientists all over the country are racing to duplicate these results."

33. John Berger, *Ways of Seeing* (New York: Penguin Books, 1972), 47. Many have rightly challenged this way of understanding as overly deterministic. See, for example, the essays in Lorraine Gamman and Margaret Marshment, eds., *The Female Gaze* (Seattle: Real Comet Press, 1989). Nonetheless, it is certainly true that at least some women in the United States and Europe are complicitous in their construction as objects.

34. Many women have suggested that there is an element of self-pleasure in the use of makeup. To examine this perspective here would take us too far afield. However, I would like to suggest that these women consider using cruelty-free cosmetics when they choose to make themselves up. Cruelty-free cosmetics can be purchased from the following distributors, who offer mail order catalogues: Vegan Street, P.O. Box 5525, Rockville, MD, 20855; Earthsafe Products, P.O. Box 81061, Cleveland, Ohio, 44181; A Clear Alternative, 8707 West Lane, Magnolia, TX, 77355; Pamela Marsen, Inc., P.O. Box 119, Teaneck, NJ, 07666; or ask your local grocer to start carrying cruelty-free products.

35. These numbers do not include the "trash" animals that are "accidentally" caught in traps and discarded. For further information about the fur industry, see Greta Nilsson, *Facts About Fur* (Washington, D.C.: Animal Welfare Institute, 1980).

36. Consider the psychological and physical price that is exacted from women who feel compelled to live up to contemporary standards of what is beautiful and in the process starve themselves, subject themselves to such dangerous procedures

as breast augmentation, face lifts, and liposuction. In addition there is the cost of working both inside and outside the home in order to be a "good" woman and afford the products that such a constructed goal requires.

37. Carol Adams, "The Sexual Politics of Meat," *Heresies* 6 (1987): 51–55. See also her book: *The Sexual Politics of Meat: A Feminist-Vegetarian Critical Theory* (New York: Continuum, 1990).

38. For an in-depth look at modern factory farming practices, see Jim Mason and Peter Singer, *Animal Factories* (New York: Crown Publishers, 1990).

39. G. Cronin, "The Development and Significance of Abnormal Stereotyped Behavior in Tethered Sows," Ph.D. thesis, University of Wageningen, Netherlands, p. 25.

40. A cow can, under healthy conditions, live between twenty and twenty-five years.

41. John Webster, "Large Animal Practice: Health and Welfare of Animals in Modern Husbandry Systems—Dairy Cattle," *In Practice*, May 1986, 87.

42. Overproduction in the dairy industry is chronic because of generous federal subsidies. In 1985, approximately 3 billion tax dollars were spent to buy 13 billion pounds of surplus dairy products in the United States.

43. Information reported in this section was discovered while I was doing research for the second edition of Peter Singer's *Animal Liberation*. Much of this and more can be found therein.

44. I first came across this term in Carol Adams' work.

45. Clearly, women too are responsible for the oppression of animals and often are complicitous in their own oppression. My point here, however, is to establish the connection between generic women and animals. In doing this, I do not mean to suggest that women need not think of their responsibilities as consumers, and I address these issues below, under "Politics and Possibilities."

46. My analysis of these feminisms roughly follows Alison Jaggar's characterization of them in *Feminist Politics and Human Nature* (Totowa, N.J.: Rowman and Allanheld, 1983).

47. Karen J. Warren, "Feminism and Ecology: Making Connections," *Environmental Ethics* 9 (1987): 3–21, and Ynestra King, "Feminism and the Revolt of Nature," *Heresies* 13 (1981): 12–16, have both analyzed various feminist frameworks in order to determine how adequately they can accommodate ecological concerns. Building on their discussions I am interested in showing how each feminist framework is inadequate or incomplete not only in addressing the oppression of nature, but specifically in addressing the oppression of nonhuman animals.

48. See Jaggar, *Feminist Politics and Human Nature*, for a discussion of some of them.

49. The World Women's Conference for a Healthy Planet held on November 8–12, 1991, in Miami, Florida.

50. Dorothy Dinnerstein, "Survival on Earth: The Meaning of Feminism," in Plant, *Healing the Wounds*, 193.

51. For a detailed discussion of Marxist feminism and some of the problems associated with it, see Lydia Sargent, *Women and Revolution* (Boston: South End Press, 1981).

52. Karl Marx, First Manuscript, "Alienated Labor," 127.

53. For an interesting critique of Marx's views on nature, see Ward Churchill, *Marxism and Native Americans* (Boston: South End Press, 1982).

54. See, for example, Jaggar, *Feminist Politics and Human Nature*, chaps. 6 and 10.

55. Here I have in mind those feminists whom Ynestra King calls "radical cultural feminists" ("Healing the Wounds: Feminism, Ecology, and the Nature/Culture Dualism," in Diamond and Orenstein, *Reweaving the World*) and Karen Warren calls "nature feminists" ("Feminism and Ecology"). Mary Daly is a leading example of such thinking.

56. See Tom Regan, *The Case for Animal Rights* (Berkeley and Los Angeles: University of California Press, 1983), and Singer, *Animal Liberation*.

57. Tom Regan, "The Case for Animal Rights," in *In Defense of Animals*, ed. Peter Singer (New York: Blackwell, 1985), 23–24.

58. Singer, *Animal Liberation*, iii.

59. Marti Kheel has suggested that even though "in our complex, modern society we may never be able to fully experience the impact of our moral decisions, we can, nonetheless, attempt as far as possible to experience emotionally the knowledge of this fact" ("The Liberation of Nature: A Circular Affair," *Environmental Ethics* 7 [1985]: 148).

60. For a sophisticated discussion of how normative dualisms are related to the logic of domination, see Karen J. Warren, "The Power and the Promise of Ecological Feminism," *Environmental Ethics* 12 (1990): 125–46.

61. Haraway, *Primate Visions*, 11.

62. Ynestra King, "The Ecology of Feminism and the Feminism of Ecology," in Plant, *Healing the Wounds*, 19.

63. Personal correspondence, September 1990. See also Kheel, "Speaking the Unspeakable: Sexism in the Animal Rights Movement," *Feminists for Animal Rights Newsletter*, Summer/Fall 1985.

64. *Washington Post*, June 11, 1990.

65. There are a few exceptions. A number of student organizations and Feminists for Animal Rights have recognized how oppressive theory often translates into oppressive practice and have conscientiously worked to combat both.

66. A "vegan" gathering is one in which no animal products are served. The fact that very few gatherings are vegan may be attributed to oversight or lack of awareness; in some cases, however, proposals to make feminist events cruelty-free have been rejected. For example, at the June 1990 convention of the National Women's

Studies Association, the Coordinating Council rejected the Ecofeminist Task Force recommendation that it "make a strong statement of feminist non-violence, and make NWSA a model of environmental and human behavior by adopting a policy that no animal products—including the flesh of cows, pigs, chickens, and fish, as well as all dairy and eggs—be served at the 1991 conference, or at any future conferences."

67. Rights language is rooted in a predominantly masculinist tradition: see, for example, Josephine Donovan, "Animal Rights and Feminist Theory," Chapter 7 in this volume. In addition, it is a particularly confusing rhetoric that can, in important instances, obfuscate questionable values.

68. Jane Meyerding, "Feminist Criticism and Cultural Imperialism (Where Does One End and the Other Begin)," *Animals' Agenda* 2 (November–December 1982), 22–23.

69. Betsy Beavan, Noel Furie, and Selma Miriam, *The Second Seasonal Political Palate* (Bridgeport, Conn.: Sanguinaria Publishing, 1984), ix–x.

70. Uma Narayan develops this notion in a different context—namely, as a way in which white feminists and others can begin to bridge gaps that divide them from women of color. "Methodological humility," however, seems an appropriate strategy for ecofeminism as well. See "Working Together Across Difference: Some Considerations on Emotions and Political Practice," *Hypatia* 3 (Summer 1988): 31–47.

# CHAPTER 4

# Roots: Rejoining Natural and Social History

## Stephanie Lahar

> Social history, political history, and natural history are the three horses pulling the chariot of the study of human sociology and its relationship with the natural world.
>
> RICHARD WHITE
> *Land Use, Environment, and Social Change*

There is not a place in the world that does not reveal the touch and bear the consequences of human hands and minds—not Antarctica, not the deepest equatorial jungle, and certainly not Tokyo or New York City. At the same time, there are no people who have not been shaped by the effects of landscape and water, the climate and natural features of the area in which they live. These effects are seldom an explicit part of social and political histories, but they are readable by signs. Environments influence survival activities, necessitate closed or open constructions of shelter, which shape social interactions, and prompt understandings of connections with other life forms through predator/prey and interdependent relationships. They contain natural forces, phenomena, and objects that become the basis of religious and cultural symbols, and offer other opportunities for expressions of human creativity through interactions with the nonhuman environment. Nations and cultures have particular characters and cosmologies: compare the intense inward, religious and artistic focus of the people of Bali, living on a small volcanic island for century after century, with individualist and acquisition-oriented white Americans, expanding their frontiers across great tracts of land ranging from coastal flats and mountains to open prairies.

Many Americans of European heritage still believe in "wilderness" and the open spaces that marked their earlier history. Seen from an airplane, however, the United States looks like a crazy quilt, with regular checkerboards of agricultural lands and planned urban areas, irregular polygons marking other urban and suburban areas and ownership boundaries, and spaghettilike swaths trailing down mountains. There are almost no areas empty of transportation corridors and dividing lines laid down by human hands with technological assistance. We do not realize how extensive the effects of our tenure on the land have been.

History has been divided into pieces like the landscape, and it is abstract and apart from us. "Natural history" is a discipline studied by environmental scientists, and "history" is an account of human events both social and political, with notable omissions of women's herstories and the cultural pasts of many other categories of people. Feminists and theorists from the relatively new and interdisciplinary fields of human ecology and environmental history have questioned and criticized from different angles the historical accounts that we have and their underlying value systems, which have written a few people, events, and ecological contexts into historical accounts and written most others out. But will reclaiming what has been left out give us a more meaningful understanding of the past? Can an ecofeminist perspective, which attempts to integrate concepts of ecology with a feminist analysis of interconnected forms of domination, contribute insights that will bring history close enough to our personal and collective experience so that lessons from the past might guide decisions that we have to make now? I believe that an integrated ecological/social context for understanding history can help change the way we think about the past and the present in necessary ways, especially if we include ourselves in the stories—embodied in a time and a place, with the past unfurling behind us and our hands and faces in the future.

## Whose Social History?

If natural and social history have been divided, how has history told the stories of human beings? The major feminist critique that has been offered is that women have been made insignificant if not absent from history. Gerda Lerner explains:

Historical scholarship, up to the most recent past, has seen women as marginal to the making of civilization and as unessential to those pursuits defined as having historical significance. . . . Thus, the recorded and interpreted past of the human race is only a partial record, in that it omits the past of half of humankind, and it is distorted, in that it tells the story from the viewpoint of the male half of humanity only.[1]

Not only have historians been men, but they have been particularly privileged men who have generally recorded events from the point of view of a small elite group. Women are not the only ones who are missing from their accounts. People of color in the West, non-Western peoples, and poor people are also absent as historical subjects. Women's invisibility as a group has, however, been central to modern critiques of history introduced by feminist theory. Many feminists have also extended a critique that starts from the absence of women's herstories to a broader socialist criticism. Adrienne Rich says that "as a woman, as a Jew, as a lesbian, I am pursued by questions of historical process, of historical responsibility, questions of historical consciousness and ignorance and what these have to do with power."[2]

What *do* these questions have to do with power and dominant value systems? Oppression and repression are sustained by individuals and institutions that are also most often sexist and heterosexist, racist and classist, as well as exploitative of the natural world. Radical feminists see the original problem as sexism; the Old and New Left see the problem as economics and government; and other progressive movements and theories point to various "isms" that interconnect, negating and distorting the past—as well as the present—in a way that is damaging to us all.

No matter what the specific focal point of the analysis, most viewpoints critical of mainstream history intersect and are complementary in making one point: history has rendered women and most non-European, non-privileged people invisible or despicable, destroying identities and cultures. Invisibility and violence are strangely and intimately related; refusing to perceive or acknowledge another person is one end of a continuum whose other is murder and genocide. When Europeans began massive migrations in the seventeenth century into North America, Argentina, Australia, and South Africa, they did not regard the aboriginal peoples of those lands as any real obstacle to their settlement of the "New World." The indigenous people, indeed, "disappeared" through death and assimilation in a vast population replacement resulting from a complex web of ecological and social factors in which the cultural narcissism that characterized European consciousness was one part. This narcissism is not so far away as we might think: most of us can remember movie images of cowboys and Indians from our childhoods in America, and most of us cheered for the cowboys. How many socially sensitive political progressives and feminists even now know much about Native American history and culture, save for some appropriated pop ideas about Native American religion and cosmology?

We are *all* impoverished by the loss of cultural histories. When a people's past is lost, everyone's identity is diminished, paths of human possibilities are closed, reservoirs of knowledge vanish. During the Burning Times of the witchhunts in Europe from 1300 to 1700, most of the priceless traditional knowledge about plants, healing, and folk medicine in the West died with thousands of women and men who were murdered precisely because they were the holders of this knowledge.[3]

Alongside human and cultural negations and extinctions runs the parallel of animal and plant extinctions and exploitation. Exploitation is a one-way, nonreciprocal relationship. It is exemplified in "green revolution" intensive agriculture that ruins soils, in the ivory trade's decimation of African elephants for luxury items, and in such subtle everyday practices as discharging sewage into streams and turning scarce wildlife habitat into lawns. Human exploitation of nonhuman communities is not a phenomenon confined to the modern age; the earliest major impacts of humans on the North American continent occurred in prehistoric times. Ian McHarg attributes these effects to "a tool more powerful than required, beyond [human] power to control and of enormous consequence"—huge prairie fires set to drive bison, deer, mammoth, and mastodon into closed valleys or over precipices: "It is thought that it was the combination of human hunters and a hostile climate that resulted in the extinction of this first great human inheritance in North America, the prairie herbivores. Firelike the grasses spread, firelike the herds of grazing animals swept to exploit the prairies—and it was the fire of the aboriginal hunter that hastened or accomplished their extinction."[4]

The original tool that human hunters used to alter an ecosystem is causing global alterations today as millions of acres of tropical rainforest are burned daily. Have we come so far? The quantity, scope, and consequences of contemporary environmental devastation create a situation of global crisis that is radically different from times past. Carolyn Merchant presents the ecological and social history of New England as a microcosm as she examines the compression of natural and social processes in her book *Ecological Revolutions*. What "took place in 2,500 years of European development through social evolution came to New England in a tenth of that time through revolution. . . . Today, capitalist ecological revolutions are occurring in many developing countries in a tenth of New England's transformation time."[5]

Although practices we could define as exploitative were present in very early societies, many if not most of the agricultural, hunting, and other human activities in the aboriginal cultures of North America and elsewhere seem to have been reciprocal in nature.[6] Some of the reciprocity was simply a biological byproduct of small human populations. Richard White notes how human occupation of a site often leads to enrichment of the soil: "The shells and bones, the plant refuse, the ashes from fires, the excrement of humans and animals gradually rotted and provided the surrounding soils with significant amounts of potash, phosphorous, and nitrogen."[7]

Some of the reciprocity, however, was socially structured by cosmologies, religious beliefs, and traditions that limited the taking of plants and animals and promoted practices that sustained ecological communities. For example, in the Salish Indian culture of what is now western Washington, the association of human powers with particular animals blurred the boundaries of human and animal identity, a common phenomenon in pre-modern societies. Hunting rules among the Salish included sanctions against killing young animals, killing more than could be used, and wasting meat. "Fraught not only with economic but also with religious significance, animals were not to be lightly persecuted," White comments. "They were to be treated with respect and were not even to be laughed at, let alone tormented or killed without need."[8]

It is tempting to conclude that aboriginal peoples, exquisitely cognizant of their place in an ecological web, possessed an intersubjective awareness of themselves and of nonhuman life that offers an alternative to the highly self-aware, blind-to-others consciousness that characterizes the most dangerous forms of modern identity. In a way this is true, but there seem to be other differences between pre-modern and modern configurations of consciousness in addition to their different relations to nature, and it would be simply impossible to return atavistically to an earlier mental attitude. There is, for example, evidence that styles and types of consciousness that developed in tribal societies were more focused on collective than individual identities. According to Donald Worster, "most who have studied ecosystem people [tribal societies subsisting on hunting, gathering, and minimal agriculture] believe that the balance between human populations and the resources of their environment is not maintained through conscious decision or overall awareness on the part of individuals."[9] Instead, sustainable relations with the nonhuman environment result from a more collective locus of identity and strong, even rigid, customs and traditions that serve to keep the group in a homeostatic relation to its environment. Sometimes stability and traditions are maintained at the cost of resilience and adaptability. This cost may be one of a complex of biological/social factors that have caused aboriginal peoples to fare so poorly when confronted with "modern" cultures from other lands.

## History's Distortions from an Ecofeminist Perspective

Those who are written out of history are those who suffer at the hands of dominant groups. Invisibility and, ultimately, violence happen most easily within a short-sighted and fragmentary mindset that is isolated from the existence and needs of others, qualities that characterize a modern, reductionist, and patriarchal intellectual and scientific tradition. Modern economic systems, including but not limited to capitalism, feed cycles of alienation and abstraction as living things become commodities, monstrously erasing life and feeling. Within this tradition, pornography and vivisection are products and practices that make up our "entertainment" and routine scientific research.

Ecofeminism sees as destructive not only the perceptual distancing and isolation of different peoples from each other, but also the habits of dualistic thought that separate human society from nature. The human/nature dualism is crucial to address and redress, since it is so fundamental, underlying and undermining our relations to the world around us and to that which is embodied and unmediated within ourselves. When we set ourselves apart from nature, we disembody human experience and sever it from an organic context. This means that we stop being aware of the shapings and natural containments that a particular environment places around human practices and social structures. But of course environmental effects do not cease to exist. Instead, society is shaped by a fractured relation to the ecosystem(s) it inhabits, losing both characteristic bioregional contours and a sensibility for natural limits. Additionally, I suggest that separating ourselves from our natural heritage, which has been a central project of human civilization, also has profound psychological and social implications as it supports our nonperception of others. When we cut off a part of ourselves that we share with all other human beings and, by extension, all of life, it is easier to deny that others, or a particular other, exists.

Is it important to place *when* in the ancient past human beings began to experience personal and collective identities separately from the surrounding environment? We may read clues about the genesis of self-awareness in our cultural myths, which are fraught with ambivalence and religious fear—for example, the "fall" from grace, with its accompanying separation from a divine source of sustenance and from nature. Riane Eisler, in her popular work *The Chalice and the Blade*, suggests that the myth of the garden of Eden indicates an ancient cultural past in which people lived in nondominating partnerships with each other, cutting across gender and other differences, as well as in greater harmony with nature.[10] But perhaps the myth of the fall points to an ancient memory of our phylogeny as a species, emerging out of the oceans and savannahs; or to some primal symbolism we all derive from a sense of separation at birth. Perhaps it is the trace of a decision to take a particular path in the development of human experience made by an archaic and collective subjectivity that is the precursor of what we now recognize as our personalized consciousness.

Is there a way to know whether there were ever times and places when human beings lived in easy cooperation with each other and the nonhuman environment, without the sexist, oppressive, and exploitative complex of power relations we call patriarchy? Is seeking such times and places useful in empowering women today, by portraying model societies in which women either shared or held primary power? There has been a strong initiative in popular feminist thought to do just this, represented most prominently by the writings of Monica Sjöö and Barbara Mor, Riane Eisler and Merlin Stone. In their work a few comparatively recent societies have been presented as models, such as the Native American Iroquois nation, in which women's status in political and tribal life seems to have been near or equal to that of men. But the major focus of this search has been prehistoric human settlements in the Neolithic period.[11]

The Neolithic, or New Stone Age, was marked by the first villages, the development of animal husbandry, and the grinding and polishing of stone weapons. Sjöö and Mor, in *The Great Cosmic Mother*, go so far as to say that the "Neolithic revolution, occurring circa 10,000 B.C., was the creation of women."[12] These authors depend heavily on interpretations of James Mellaart's archeological excavations of the city of Çatal Hüyük (c. 6500–5650 B.C.) in what is now western Turkey, and Marija Gimbutas' excavations of Vinca settlements (c. 5300–4000 B.C.) in what is now Yugoslavia. Their archelogical studies yielded icons, symbols, and statues of female and woman/animal deities, and burials of women in these settlements show evidence of care and ritual treatment. Artifacts or built structures that might indicate war or defense are lacking.[13]

Feminist interpreters of Neolithic history conclude that societies were basically matriarchal (with women having power over men, the reverse of patriarchy) or matricentric (fundamentally egalitarian, but placing great value on women's activities and reproductive functions, with kinship lines traced through women). This line of thinking sees the matricentricity of Neolithic culture as a social arrangement that is not only good for women but also directly related to positive societal characteristics such as peacefulness, cooperation, and benign relations with the natural world.

"Unquestionably," says Janet Biehl, "some Neolithic societies were relatively egalitarian and organic. They may also have been matrilineal, although so far this has been impossible to prove."[14] But shaky conclusions of matriarchy based on the finding of female icons rest on an even shakier assumption: that women's higher status resulted from a belief that women were related in a special and superior way to the earth and to divine power through their childbearing capacity. There are at least two problematic leaps here. First, female religious symbols are not indicative of the status of women in daily life: in Mexico today, for example, extremely sexist social arrangements coexist with local forms of Christianity that center on and revere the Virgin Mary. In fact, the elevation of the Virgin Mary to divine archetype may even help to justify the mistreatment of ordinary, mortal women in such a culture. Gerda Lerner also points to this phenomenon, noting that because of "the coexistence of symbolic idolatry of women and the actual low status of women such as the cult of the Virgin Mary in the Middle Ages [similar to what exists today in Mexico and Central America], the cult of the lady of the plantation in antebellum America, or that of the Hollywood star in contemporary society, one hesitates to elevate such evidence to historical proof."[15]

Second, the beliefs and attitudes of Neolithic peoples toward women's childbearing capacity are unknown to us. Our projections of its enormous importance probably say more about a modern elevation/repression of sexuality and reproduction, in an age when we are alienated from natural functions, than they do about Neolithic sensibilities. Clearly Neolithic peoples celebrated and ritualized birth as well as death and other passages and transitions, as we still do today. Even if many of them did respond to childbearing with mystified awe—and one can imagine that they were very much in tune with a spirit of wonder—speculation that feelings about childbearing and its symbolization were the primary force behind establishing social and political structures is an enormous leap. It supposes that Neolithic peoples simply reversed the biological determinism that is a modern rationale for domination and asserted that "women are better/ stronger" instead of "women are inferior/weaker." To attribute power-over relations to the mystification of childbearing, and men's subsequent jealousies and fears of it, is to reduce problems of domination to sexism. This trivializes other forms of privilege and oppression. New feminist theories, including ecofeminism, must continue to outgrow this categorical exclusivity. Furthermore, by looking only to human subjectivity and symbol systems as explanations for cultural arrangements, we fail to see the full range of natural forces and environmental factors that act through and upon them. By dividing the social and the natural in our understandings of human evolution, we are applying a Cartesian framework, marked by our own modern alienation from nature, to prehistoric peoples.

The human/nature and other dualisms described by Cartesian philosophy are, and were, destructive in their implications. Reinforced by exploitative social and economic systems, the results of such conceptual and cultural splits are human projects that are unsustainable, devoid of reciprocity with the nonhuman environment. Because history has made the nonhuman environment invisible, we do not understand the ecological impact of our social choices, nor how they will come back to haunt us. The invisibility of entire human and animal communities and cultures permits exclusionary and oppressive practices and projects, causing unnecessary and unacceptable suffering. It is, therefore, morally abhorrent. Those on both privileged and undervalued sides of cultural hierarchies are also deprived of models of character, action, and empowerment emerging from lives that have been hidden—darkened, muted, and placed out of our reach. The painstaking work of recovering what has been hidden historically is a critical project, and also one that is particularly susceptible to the biases of privilege. It is not surprising that some of the most powerful work about the recovery of previously invisible lives has been done by African-American women, including Alice Walker and Patricia Hill Collins. In their writing we discover models and inspiration not in an ancient, mythical, and irretrievable past, but in those who have lived just ahead of us and in those who are living now.[16]

How do we, especially those of us who are of European-American descent, escape from our biases in order to understand the past more fully and live better in the present? History is an absolutely subjective human construction or telling. Our purpose cannot be simply to render the accounts "complete" and "objective" by adding on people of non-European descent, women's herstories, and an ecological context. Simply adding on pieces leaves intact the polarized underpinnings of our view and our ways of looking, as well as perpetuating the myth of an "objective" view. In a search for fuller personal, cultural, and natural histories, we must expect and actively seek changes in our own consciousness, as we incorporate our growing understandings of the past and give them expression. To think about the past differently is to burst through the confines of rational analysis; thinking, feeling, and sensing viscerally the presence and movement of molecules, blood, and ideas that physically link us to those of many colors, cultures, and physical forms, even over millennia. This affirms history as an ongoing process. We must take our social analysis down to the nub—beginning with each person's, and humanity's, emergence from and containment within biological existence.

## *An Ecological Context*

The miracle of our origins is enough to create a sense of awe in us today. The earth, in its 4.5 billion year history, has known human-like inhabitants only in the last 2 million years, a period known as the Quaternary.[17] Our evolution and revolutions are far from finished, and the conscious memory we have of our past, relative to the period of evolution, is extremely short. It is hard to imagine the configurations of body, mind, emotion, and spirit our direct ancestors lived in, and even harder to imagine the bodily and subjective experience of their nonhuman ancestors, tracing back through an evolutionary lineage that in its earliest, recognizably animal form begins with an unsegmented worm.[18] We piece together relics and fragments of ancient peoples and the objects they made and lived with, assisting shadows of memories with deductive logic and imaginative speculation—both colored heavily with our current perceptual biases and values. We are now a species with a number of recognizable genetic races, subgroups, and combinations populating every planetary land mass and ecosystem, and traveling across the seas. This is the context that we cannot forget in our telescoped views of human events and historical trends.

One way to approach history is to begin with a particular event or phenomenon and follow its paths backward and forward, exploring nonhuman and human forces that acted upon and resulted from it. These can range from global climatic changes to the intentional act of a single human being.

I would like to follow this approach to examine a historical phenomenon of extraordinary significance to the modern world.

In the years between 1600 and 1900, massive migrations of European Caucasians to temperate regions around the globe changed the patterns by which humans inhabited the earth, and also significantly changed their genetic mix. According to Alfred Crosby, "European whites were all recently (before 1700) concentrated in Europe, but in the last few centuries have burst out . . . and have created vast settlements of their kind in the South Temperate Zone and North Temperate Zone (except Asia, a continent already and irreversibly tenanted)."[19] In a period of about three hundred years—about four human lifetimes, moments in the life of a glacier, an instant in the life of a mountain—Europeans entered North America, sections of South America, Australia, New Zealand, and South Africa, becoming the predominant human inhabitants of most of these areas. Crosby, in *Ecological Imperialism: The Biological Expansion of Europe*, names the totality of these migrations the "Great Demographic Takeover." Crosby's approach is unique because he maintains an ecological frame of reference throughout his exploration of European colonization, providing an excellent counterpoint to social analyses. His work contributes to an integration of biological and social factors that helps us to make sense of the migrations as a whole.

In the centuries before the mass European migrations, social arrangements, patterns of human inhabitation, and human-environmental relations were very different in Europe and in what was to be called the "New World." If we compare, for example, England and New England in the late Middle Ages, we find a system of intensive agriculture versus a combination of hunting and gathering plus light agriculture; settlements clustered around huge estates or manors whose boundaries had changed little for centuries versus tribal communities that often moved seasonally; a feudal system of governance and economics versus communal sharing of resources and political guidance by tribal elders and councils; a population whose numbers dramatically rose and dropped versus a relatively stable population. In England, the primeval forests had long since been pushed back: a good estimate is that at the dawn of the twelfth century, 7 to 8 million acres were in cultivation, equal to the area under the plow early in this century.[20] In New England, 95 percent of the land was covered with forest canopy.[21]

The pressures and impetuses for the modern outflow of European migrants were clearly developing by the late Middle Ages. It is impossible to categorize them as strictly "biological" or "social." Between the Norman invasion and the end of the thirteenth century, England's population tripled to about 6 million inhabitants.[22] Graham Nicholson and Jane Fawcett observe that in a good agricultural year, existing cultivation and fishing practices, along with patterns of land tenure, were probably able to support this larger population, in part because the climate was both drier and warmer than today. But by 1300 the climate became wetter and colder, steadily shortening the growing season. The bioclimatic change in this period is indicated by the rapid decline in English vineyards, the extinction of the Nordic population in Greenland, the cessation of corn growing in Iceland, and documented changes in ice conditions in Scandinavian waters and in rivers on the continent.[23] According to the Swedish oceanographer Otto Pettersson, the climate deteriorated uninterruptedly until the middle of the fifteenth century, perhaps because of the effect on the tides of the positions of the moon and the sun in relation to the earth—a configuration that occurs cyclically about every eighteen hundred years.[24]

The resulting famines weakened the population and intensified class stratifications. Landless peasants were in the worst position, with women being the poorest of the poor, a situation recapitulated in many developing nations today. The following fourteenth-century account vividly describes the misery that many endured:

> The poorest folk are our neighbors . . . in their hovels, overburdened with children, and rack-rented by landlords. For whatever they save by spinning they spend on rent, or on milk and oatmeal to make gruel and to fill the bellies of their children who clamour for food. And they themselves are often famished with hunger, and wretched with the miseries of winter—cold, sleepless nights, when they get up to rock the cradle cramped in a corner, and rise before dawn to card and comb the wool, to wash and scrub and mend, and wind yarn and peel rushes for their rushlights. The miseries of these women who dwell in hovels are too pitiful to read or describe in verse.[25]

In 1349 the Black Death, or bubonic plague, broke out among the weakened populace. By the end of the last outbreak in 1377, 40 to 50 percent of the population in England had been wiped out, and up to a third of the entire population of the continent.[26] There were immediate effects on land tenure and loyalty to the roles and traditions that had supported a manorial economy. People's faith that they would be taken care of by their lord and the land, in exchange for their labor and loyalty, had been shaken to the core. With land available and traditions undermined, there was no basis for obedience to a manorial lord. Many people who had had no land, or little, under feudalism were able to claim enough to grow food for their own comfortable subsistence and have surpluses, to gather materials for housing, and even to experience some leisure. The massive depopulation established a context for the breaking of traditions and alliances in the feudal system and an age of more individual interests and of nuclear families versus manorial families and kingdoms. It also sowed the seeds of a modern European consciousness that spread globally several hundred years later.

It was not until the sixteenth century that the European population had recovered from the losses caused by the Black Death. Population pressures rose again in the context of new patterns of land tenure and the dawn of the industrial and scientific revolutions, with their concurrent changes in knowledge, symbol systems, and awareness of self and others. Between 1500 and 1800 the numbers more than doubled, escalating into rates of population increase that were unparalleled in the world and approached only by China.[27]

Population booms are obvious contributors to social tension and environmental pressures. Historically they are often portrayed as uncontrollable natural phenomena, by-products of unconscious and unintentional sexuality which then prompt a social response. Thus, they sit on the dividing line between the conceptualized worlds of nature and humanity. But there is ample evidence that humans have deliberately shaped their numbers from the most ancient societies to the present, either through social rewards for having many children or through contraception, abortion, infanticide, and other population controls.[28] Although the burgeoning of Europe's population was certainly the result of many interacting forces, values, and institutions, it is of more than passing interest that the period of greatest population increase in Europe coincided with the upsurge of Christianity, which encouraged unlimited reproduction, and the persecution of "witches"—midwives, herbalists, and healers—who knew best how to prevent and abort unwanted pregnancies.

In addition to noting the social forces that are part of population booms, it is important to confront the mistaken assumption that more people equal more pressure on the environment in a simple numerical correlation. Deep ecologists talk about a "carrying capacity" of humans for a region, as if there were a universal increment that could be determined in a value-free and monocultural way. The reality is that pressures on the environment have more to do with human systems of production, reproduction, and consumption than with numbers of people. For example, a tiny proportion of people today consume most of the earth's "resources." The enormous consumption of Americans and other Westerners is the product of knotted practices and institutions: a capitalist economy bent on expansion; a meat-based diet that requires up to twenty times as much land as grain- and vegetable-based diets, and whose supporting industries deplete topsoil and fresh water; and the politics of global imperialism.[29]

The pressures that European peoples faced in past centuries were due not simply to increasing numbers and land scarcity, but to an interaction of particular social values, practices, and institutions with the environment. As a result, European peoples swarmed to other temperate lands along with their domesticated animals, such as horses and cattle, and such "varmints" as European rats. The animals that the immigrants brought with them accomplished their own population replacements. Usually we think of changes in animal habitation during this period as livestock replacing herds of buffalo and bison, but the changes reached into every ecological niche. One of the most successful imports, for example, was the honeybee, a native of the Mediterranean and the Middle East. The first hive in Tasmania swarmed sixteen times in the summer of 1832.[30]

Crosby's thesis is that the European migrations were an ecological phenomenon in which the interaction of humans, animals closely associated with them, weeds, pathogens, and microorganisms brought about a monumental transformation of environments and cultures. He notes that all of these different organisms "accomplished demographic takeovers of their own in the temperate, well-watered regions of North and South America, Australia and New Zealand."[31]

From an ecological standpoint, it is important to note the failures as well as the remarkable successes of the European migrations. The hardiness and adaptability of European people and their entourage of related organisms extended only to temperate regions. In neither Africa nor tropical America did European crops or animals prosper. Crosby writes that "in tropical Africa, until recently, Europeans died in droves of the fevers, in tropical America they died almost as fast of the same diseases, plus a few native American additions."[32]

To the widespread regions in which they were successful, however, Europeans brought intensive forms of agriculture as well as foreign plant and animal species that transformed forests and clearings into networks of fields. This disrupted the subsistence methods of the natives, who then became more receptive to European land-use and social practices. William

Cronon recounts the words of a speech given by the Narragansett sachem Miantonomo in 1642, just a few years after the arrival of English colonists near his people's villages: "Our fathers had plenty of deer and skins, our plains were full of deer, as also our woods, and of turkies, and our coves full of fish and fowl. But these English having gotten our land, they with scythes cut down the grass, and with axes fell the trees; their cows and horses eat the grass, and their hogs spoil our clam banks, and we shall all be starved.[33]

Even more devastating than European land-use patterns to the culture and subsistence of the native peoples were the Old World diseases—smallpox, measles, chicken pox, influenza, plague, and tuberculosis. According to Cronon, mortality rates in the initial onslaughts of these diseases "were seldom less than 80 or 90 percent, and it was not unheard of for an entire village to be wiped out. . . . A long process of depopulation set in, accompanied by massive social and economic disorganization."[34] During the first part of the seventeenth century, certain areas such as Vermont and New Hampshire "were virtually depopulated as the western Abenaki declined from perhaps 10,000 to fewer than 500."[35] These diseases also left their mark on American Indian history and folklore. Crosby writes of a legend from the southern Plains Indians in which a Kiowa meets Smallpox on the plain, riding a horse: The man asks, "Where do you come from and what do you do and why are you here?" Smallpox answers, "I am one with the white men—they are my people as the Kiowas are yours. . . . My breath causes children to wither like young plants in spring snow. The strongest of warriors go down before me. No people who have looked on me will ever be the same."[36]

Cronon's *Changes in the Land: Indians, Colonists, and the Ecology of New England*, like Merchant's *Ecological Revolutions*, examines the mutual transformations of lands and peoples in New England. Merchant's use of the Marxist/socialist categories of production and reproduction as vectors of analysis also helps to amplify gender roles as an explicit factor in, and result of, ecological and social transformations in New England. By primarily viewing history through categories of production and reproduction that are centered in human society and implicitly partake of a nature/culture duality, Merchant's analysis approaches but does not really become an ecofeminist perspective. Her analysis of production and reproduction during the European demographic takeover in New England, and its cultural postscripts, is nevertheless helpful to ecofeminists in sorting out and integrating multiple sites of historical change.

Merchant defines production simply as "the extraction, processing and exchange of natural resources." On the other hand, reproduction is the "biological and social process through which humans are born, nurtured, socialized and governed. Through reproduction sexual relations are legitimated, population sizes and family relationships are maintained, and property and inheritance practices are reinforced."[37]

Merchant traces how biological processes and social traditions of production and reproduction interacted in the colonization of New England, shaping its perpetually expansionist character. For example, European patterns of inheritance and family life meant that each son should, ideally, be given a farmstead large enough to be nearly self-sufficient. As immigration continued, very high birthrates were maintained, and lifespans increased, this became impossible. She explains:

> It was rural New England's failure to reproduce its system of production that initiated the capitalist ecological revolution. Pushed by ecological degradation and stimulated by market opportunities, ordinary farmers took up more quantitative methods of management during the nineteenth century. Urged by elite scientists, improvers, clergy and doctors to abandon their old ways and become entrepreneurs, they were drawn into the mechanistic approach to nature. A participatory consciousness dominated by vision changed to the analytic consciousness required by capitalist agriculture.[38]

Both Merchant and Cronon present the changes that occurred in New England as a gradual but inexorable revolution that permanently altered the landscape and deeply affected both of the human cultures involved, but especially and most obviously the Native Americans. Additionally, Merchant traces how, as colonial subsistence agriculture changed to capitalism, male and female spheres of activity in white society, which had overlapped and intersected, were increasingly pulled apart. As men began to transport their surplus goods to market and work away from their homesteads, women's responsibilities became more and more domestic, contributing to the particular constellation of gender arrangements that has become our modern inheritance.

The case history of New England enables us to see profound changes in a particular place telescoped in time, but changes over larger parts of the globe were just as dramatic and significant in their totality. Only a few centuries after the first Old World arrivals, whites of European heritage amount to nearly 90 percent of the population in Canada and the United

States, 95 percent in Argentina and Uruguay, 98 percent in Australia, and 90 percent in New Zealand.[39] As overwhelming as these statistics are, the transformations that took place between 1600 and 1900 were much more extensive than the human demographics show. In Argentina and Uruguay, for example, only a quarter of the plants growing wild in the pampa (prairie) are native. In an "inundation" of animals from the Old World, "horses, cattle, sheep, goats, and pigs have for hundreds of years been among the most numerous of the quadrupeds"—in lands that before the migrations had never seen such animals.[40] Crosby concludes:

> The demographic triumph of Europeans in the temperate colonies is one part of a biological and ecological takeover which could not have been accomplished by human beings alone, gunpowder notwithstanding. . . . The human invaders have consulted their egos, rather than ecologists, for explanations of their triumphs. But the human victims, the aborigines of the Lands of the Demographic Takeover, knew better, knew they were only one of many species being displaced and replaced; knew they were victims of something more irresistible and awesome than the spread of capitalism or Christianity.[41]

## Revisiting the European Migrations from an Ecofeminist View

Ecofeminism seeks to develop an integrated—but not reductionist—perceptual experience and conceptual view of nature and society. It seeks to move beyond a purely "socialist" analysis (viewing the world primarily as the result of the production and reproduction of human cultures and commodities) or a purely "ecological" analysis (in the sense of a science-based description of organic and inorganic links). It also aims to establish an ethic of responsible action. Part of the way that ecofeminism does this is to emphasize multiple factors in and relations among different phenomena and events. In my definition, ecofeminism does not privilege a single vector of analysis and make other axes of change into secondary effects, as Marxism privileges economic forces of production, for example, and radical feminism privileges gender relations. Thus, an ecofeminist perspective draws from social and ecological contexts in an effort to develop open and evolving, rather than "finished," explanations.

In ecofeminist terms what I have presented as an ecological context for understanding the "great demographic takeover" of white Europeans needs to be further elaborated to adequately confront conceptual dualisms and the effects of power-over relations, but even by itself an ecological framework is expansive and challenges us in several ways. It stretches existing definitions of "social" and "biological" factors and helps us to integrate them. It also makes appallingly clear the simple ecological lessons from the past that have not been incorporated in the meetings of different cultures and ecosystems in the twentieth century—and therefore the degree to which history, unexamined and partial, repeats its failures. We can no longer afford to ignore how fragile, specific, and precious different ecosystems are, including their human inhabitants, and how easily devastated. Diversity in peoples and ecosystems is a natural condition. Temperate regions are not the tropics, Europe is not New England, and the once fertile soils on the banks of the Ganges River in India, ruined by green revolution technology, are not like either of those Western lands. There is no connection between the ability of a particular group of people and/or entourage of organisms to dominate or prevail against others, and the value or sustainability of their culture or tenure upon the land.

An ecological context also brings up difficult questions of historical responsibility that ecofeminism can help us examine more closely. We know that life on the planet comprises phenomena and processes that are perpetually changing, but the influences of human actions on the earth are much greater than those of any other form of life. Does our ability as human beings to wreak radical and irreversible changes in land, sea, and the organic world impart a particularly human responsibility for the earth and its life (including the well-being or suffering of other human beings), or is this capacity a morally neutral by-product of natural and human evolution? Is there a difference between a succession of red cedar and hemlock replacing an old fir forest, a swarm of African bees replacing Mediterranean honeybees, and the European demographic takeover of 1600–1900?

Let us look first at the dualistic way in which we are conditioned to think about these questions. In a world view in which nature and humanity are discontinuous, cedar trees and bees do not partake of any type of subjectivity or consciousness but are driven, without intention or choice, by biological forces. And, of course, since they are both other-than-human and therefore part of a big mossy entity called "nature," there are no significant differences between them. Continuing to think divisively, we would understand human society, in contrast, as independent of nature and its forces, completely intentional and free in its actions. In a historical framework that is *either* natural *or* social, we can choose to collapse the European migrations into the category of a "natural" phenomenon, seeing the trees, bees, and human players as equally unconscious and biologically driven. Or we can choose a social (and by implication anti-natural) perspective, in which the migrations would have to be understood as an intentional choice made by human beings out of at least relative freedom, particularly freedom from biological needs and pressures. "Humanity" also becomes an undifferentiated entity in this case, without distinctions between privileged ruling elite and poor and hungry European peasants, or those who were oppressed on the basis of their ethnicity, religious affiliation, or gender. When humanity is undifferentiated, it is easy to see the European migrants as wholly to blame for decimating peoples and ecosystems in temperate latitudes, and also to see indigenous peoples, animals, and ecosystems wholly as victims. In our historical view this makes some people more powerful than they actually were, some less powerful, and all but a few invisible. Dualistic thinking guides us into polarities in thinking about the European migrations: either the complete absolution of responsibility (in the image of an unconscious swarm) or total blame (the evil empire).

Human beings are not trees or bees, however—whichever species we consider diminished by such analogies. There are meaningful and critical differences in consciousness and intentionality among humans, and among all forms of life.[42] Neither is history, though, the story of a masterminded plan for human civilization independent of the rest of nature. The differences among forest succession, bee swarms, and human migrations can certainly be explored, but not by viewing them through reductionist categories such as nature and culture. Ecofeminism is unique in deconstructing the nature/culture dualism from both sides, unlike such progressive movements as deep ecology and, to a lesser extent, bioregionalism (the latter is less developed as an overall theory). Deep ecology, for example, redefines nature to include humanity and presents environmental degradation as an abhorrent symptom of our alienation from the "wild" parts of ourselves. But in using a universal "we" that is powerful, privileged, and historically alienated from natural processes, it fails to see human diversity (including diversity in human-environmental relations) and abuses of power played out in ethnocentric, classist, and sexist acts and institutions. Therefore, overpopulation and the lack of a proper reverence for nature become the causes of the "environmental crisis" to which social dislocations and human suffering are secondary or incidental.[43] Clearly an ecofeminist examination of history shows that we cannot reduce complex realities in this way.

But let us return to one particular and difficult question. Can and should the European migrants be held morally responsible for the ways in which their mass migrations and individual actions were destructive and caused suffering for others? I would answer this question with an equivocal yes and no—not because I am waffling, but because the question itself is too simple. We must first examine the idea of moral responsibility. It contains two concepts that each have many layers: first, an equation with power, the capacity to effect physical and subjective changes in living and nonliving things and processes; and, second, a relation to a system of ethics that establishes ideals and criteria to distinguish good and evil.

The relative power that different European migrants had to determine their own lives and to affect lives and landscapes around them was extremely varied, as was the power of indigenous peoples and other life forms to shape their surroundings and to resist changes not of their own making. The degree of power that a particular individual could exercise also changed greatly in some cases and very little in others as Europeans traveled to the New World. For example, most women who arrived in North America from Europe found that their surroundings and conditions had changed, but their social position and influence remained much the same, as Old World family cultures were continued and replicated. On the other hand, some minor European lords suddenly controlled huge tracts of land and colonies in the New World, which gave them much greater social status and influence, and convicted criminals imprisoned in European countries became free men in places like Australia.

To consider moral dimensions of responsibility for the flourishing of some people and forms of life and the suffering of others, we must add ethical judgments to an understanding of unequal and changing power relations. But we must also understand the ethical systems that we use as historical in their own right. As Murray Bookchin has observed in his studies in the political history of philosophy, ethics that define individual and collective good usually (if not always) develop partly as a construction of, or as a reaction to, particular political forms and structures. For example, the ethics of Socrates and Aristotle, foundational to Western thought, emerged with and reflect the rise and heyday of the Greek polis, that civic structure which sought to institutionalize a form of democratic governance based on both individual fulfillment and collective well-being *for its elite members*. The polis explicitly excluded women, slaves, non-Greeks, and resident aliens.[44] In the last quarter-century, feminist theorists and activists have accumulated sufficient voice to confront the critical ethical assumption supporting not only the Greek polis but also most Western political, religious, and social institutions in our written history. This assumption is that one group (specifically white male elites) can, through the manipulation of abstract and universal principles such as democracy and justice, provide the greatest good for a society or the world.

Some feminists have sought to define an alternative ethical orientation that is more accountable to women's experience. They have projected an ideal based in a personal sense of relationship and mutual responsibility, a caring for human and nonhuman others described by some as a characteristic of women's personalities.[45] Early descriptions of such an alternative ethic—for example, Carol Gilligan's *In a Different Voice*—emphasize the difference from the traditional ethic that elevates self-fulfillment to the top of a hierarchy of values. Instead, an almost symmetrically opposite ethic of care and relation to others is portrayed as desirable. More recent treatments, especially those with an ecofeminist focus, emphasize a dialectical relationship between individual needs, compassion for others, and collective memberships and realities as a source for ethics.[46]

From ecofeminist guidelines developed by myself, Marti Kheel, and others, I would define an ethical position most simply as this: acting to the best of one's ability from a sensibility that simultaneously knows and values oneself as an individual; is compassionate through identification with human and nonhuman others and caring about others' lives and well-being; and is creative, undergoing self-transformation through cultivating a relation to collectives ranging from human families to the planetary community. I believe that an ethical position becomes a basis for morally responsible action when a person, through the particular form of nature's subjectivity that is human consciousness, fully accepts and exercises her or his personal power to shape lives and events—and also accepts and exercises the *limits* to that power that emerge through mediating one's multiple alliances. The definitions of ethics and moral responsibility I have developed are useful to me in guiding trivial and large decisions, but they would probably not be wholly meaningful to either Native Americans or European migrants several hundred years ago. My definitions, framed in a vernacular that is a product of a specific and contemporary experience, may be a better measure of the quality of the actions I take in my own life than they are of historical events. I would argue that the moral responsibility of individuals and groups in the past depends on their access to power and also on whose ethical standards we use to make such judgments. This means that it is impossible to establish absolute, unmediated accountability, or blame, for historical events. This does not preclude compassion for or identification with people and other living beings in history, and emotional responses to their experience—anger, sadness, joy, hope; nor does it prevent us from passing judgments on historical events and actions. But it does require that we acknowledge that the criteria we are using arise out of our own experience, which both connects with and differs from the experiences of people in other places and times. This is particularly important for white, wealthy, heterosexual, or otherwise privileged ecofeminists, who through refraining from fixing absolute blame may more easily find points of identification with privileged historical groups, as well as those that have been oppressed. This can help us examine more honestly the ways we may be causing suffering through consciously or unconsciously exploiting our own privilege, and explore the combinations and intersections of oppression and privilege that our ethical systems and world views grow from.

## Bringing the Past Into the Present

Issues today present choices that mirror those of times past. These give us the opportunity to notice how we have changed—or stayed the same. In Quebec and New England, for example, a controversy has raged over the last several years about the proposed expansion of an already huge hydroelectric dam project, involving on the one hand descendants of the European colonists in New England and Quebec and, on the other, Native Americans. The backdrop to the economic debate (which has, in keeping with mainstream social values and the concerns of current political systems, emerged as the primary focus of public dialogue and media attention) is the face-off of two different cultural constructs and attendant value systems. Additionally, the future of a large ecosystem in anything like its present form is at stake. If the Canadian provincial utility company, Hydro-Quebec, implements the next proposed phase of its project, it will add thousands of square miles to the 4,600 that have already been flooded in the James Bay region of Quebec, which includes the home territory of the Cree and Inuit people as well as a multitude of plant and animal communities.[47] If the project is not implemented, some consumers of electricity in Quebec, New England, and New York may need either to find alternative supplies of energy, each with their own environmental and social impacts, or to restructure radically their needs for and consumption of electricity.

In New England, recent events have shown that citizens and policymakers have been split in their alliances. Early in 1990 Maine's Public Service Commission rejected the purchase of power from Hydro-Quebec and directed its largest utility to pursue conservation programs instead. Later that year Vermont's Public Service Board approved a contract under which that state's twenty-four electric utilities would buy power from Hydro-Quebec over a period of thirty years. Yet in a special election in October 1991, citizens of Burlington, Vermont's largest city, voted not to authorize its utility's participation in the contract.[48]

What is involved in making choices like the ones that citizens and public officials have faced in this controversy? In the case of Hydro-Quebec, a major (and inconclusive) part of the debate has hinged on economics and whether or not needs for additional power have been accurately assessed. But human rights and environmental impacts have clearly been another key part of the public dialogue and decision-making processes, and these require a different type of consideration. To ignore these latter issues would be to make the Cree and Inuit peoples, the animals, and the environment of the James Bay region invisible, and to cut them off from citizens' and officials' sense of themselves and their communities. This reveals the kind of narrow identifications based on political boundaries and cultural groupings that have enabled the appropriation of "natural resources" throughout history. The choice to perceive and to incorporate indigenous peoples and the nonhuman environment into one's own sense of self and community, as the European colonists of 1600–1900 did not, is a choice to face personal and cultural change oneself. To stand against a project such as Hydro-Quebec's expansion on the basis of its concomitant destruction of human cultures and the environment is an active response to history and the effects of human choices in the past.

To take a morally responsible position means holding a compassionate awareness of others and an understanding of a whole in which one is a part, along with an affirmation of one's own individual integrity. It requires a willingness to undergo self-transformation. Traditionally, in the West, "moral" choices have been regarded as something to be expected only of the most privileged individuals, those educated or gifted in rarefied forms of reason and capable of holding the abstract ideas regarded as necessary to act with more than the most selfish interests in mind. This attitude has both reinforced the classic nature/culture dualism and justified political institutions in which only elites can make large-scale decisions. But in fact the impetus to act in what I have defined as a morally responsible way may be traced to impulses and emotions that are both biological and social by our usual definitions. Emotional experiences similar to what we, in a specific human culture, name compassion, grief, and love are clearly present in some (but not all) animal communities, as well as specifically cultivated in some (but not all) human communities. Abstract reasoning may be one culturally specific path to a sensibility I am portraying as an ecofeminist perspective, and as a morally responsible position. But there are other paths, including some that may be simpler and more direct, to help us live and act in ways that approach a wholly embodied and inspirited state— that of a fully *sensible* human being.

To transform our relationship to the past by learning to understand the interactions and continuity of what has been divided into natural and social history, to establish a personal relation and place in it, is to develop roots—a metaphor that expresses grounding in both the organic world and social communities. This is riskier, more confusing, more exciting, and more transformative than adding on pieces to a purely social construction of history. It involves experiencing viscerally and intuitively, as well as rationally, the genesis of the human body and its organic and subjective evolution out of the oceans and savannahs, as well as through the social milieus of our grandmothers and grandfathers. We simultaneously arrive from the past and depart for the future in each encounter with history and with the decisions that we must make today.

## NOTES

1. Gerda Lerner, *The Creation of Patriarchy* (New York: Oxford University Press, 1986), 4.

2. Adrienne Rich, "Resisting Amnesia," *Woman of Power* 16 (Spring 1990): 15.

3. Herbal healing and the practice of midwifery were clear signs of heresy and witchcraft, according to the *Malleus Maleficarum*, or "Hammer of Witches." I have not been able to find reliable statistics on the number of people burned or hanged as witches. In Rosemary Ellen Guiley, *The Encyclopedia of Witches and Witchcraft* (New York: Facts on File, 1989), estimates range from 30,000 to 100,000 in Germany alone, and I have seen estimates elsewhere of up to 9 million in all of Europe.

4. Ian McHarg, *Design with Nature* (Garden City, N.Y.: Doubleday/Natural History Press, 1969), 67.

5. Carolyn Merchant, *Ecological Revolutions: Nature, Gender, and Science in New England* (Chapel Hill and London: University of North Carolina Press, 1989), 2.

6. Ester Boserup draws on the work of Frank Hole to speculate about evidence of overgrazing and the cultivation of steep hillsides, which resulted in erosion and desertification in southwestern Asia, in periods from 8000 to 4000 B.C.: see "Environment, Population and Technology in Primitive Societies," in *The Ends of*

*the Earth*, ed. Donald Worster (Cambridge: Cambridge University Press, 1988), 28. Evidence has also been found for the extinction of native species through human activities in prehistoric times in New Zealand and Madagascar.

7. Richard White, *Land Use, Environment, and Social Change: The Shaping of Island County, Washington* (Seattle: University of Washington Press, 1980), 20.

8. Ibid., 29.

9. Donald Worster, "Doing Environmental History," in Worster, *The Ends of the Earth*, 279.

10. Riane Eisler, *The Chalice and the Blade* (San Francisco: Harper & Row, 1988).

11. In addition to Eisler, see Monica Sjöö and Barbara Mor, *The Great Cosmic Mother: Rediscovering the Religion of the Earth* (San Francisco: Harper & Row, 1987); and Merlin Stone, *When God Was a Woman* (New York: Dial Press, 1976).

12. Sjöö and Mor, *The Great Cosmic Mother*, 88.

13. Ibid., 88–92.

14. Janet Biehl, "Goddess Mythology in Ecological Politics," *New Politics*, no. 2, (1989): 91. See Biehl's article and her book *Rethinking Ecofeminist Politics* (Boston: South End Press, 1991), for an in-depth critique of the scholarship and popular texts about goddess worship in Neolithic cultures. I disagree with key elements of Biehl's critique from the left, especially her elevation of reason and denigration of feeling, intuition, and other modes of human knowing. I also feel that her polemical attempt to discredit ecofeminism as a whole in *Rethinking Ecofeminist Politics* is misguided; nevertheless, her exposure of logical fallacies in feminist revisionings of the Neolithic period is well formulated and valuable.

15. Lerner, *The Creation of Patriarchy*, 28–29.

16. Patricia Hill Collins collects pieces of a rich intellectual tradition among African-American women in *Black Feminist Thought* (Boston: Unwin Hyman, 1990). Jamaica Kincaid's and Alice Walker's novels, as well as Walker's edited collection of Zora Neale Hurston's work, offer multiple models of powerful women living under oppressive conditions. See Jamaica Kincaid, *Lucy* (New York: Farrar Straus Giroux, 1990), and *Annie John* (New York: Farrar Straus Giroux, 1985); and Alice Walker, *The Color Purple* (New York: Harcourt Brace Jovanovich, 1982).

17. Andrew Goudie, *Environmental Change* (Oxford: Clarendon Press, 1983; New York: Oxford University Press, 1983), 1.

18. See Richard Grossinger, *Embryogenesis: From Cosmos to Creature—The Origins of Human Biology* (San Francisco: North Atlantic Books, 1986).

19. Alfred Crosby, "Ecological Imperialism: The Overseas Migration of Western Europeans as a Biological Phenomenon," in Worster, *The Ends of the Earth*, 104.

20. Graham Nicholson and Jane Fawcett, *The Village in England* (New York: Rizzoli, 1988), 14.

21. Merchant, *Ecological Revolutions*, 31.

22. Nicholson and Fawcett, *The Village in England*, 45.

23. These signs are described in Gustaf Utterstrom, "Climatic Fluctuations and Population Problems in Early Modern History," in Worster, *The Ends of the Earth*, 42, and also in Nicholson and Fawcett, *The Village in England*, 46.

24. Utterstrom, "Climatic Fluctuations," 41.

25. *Piers Plowman*, quoted in Nicholson and Fawcett, *The Village in England*, 11. For additional material on gender and other inequities in the Middle Ages, see Carolyn Merchant, *The Death of Nature: Women, Ecology and the Scientific Revolution* (San Francisco: Harper & Row, 1980). Merchant promotes the view that medieval societies held a more "organismic" view of the world than moderns do, seeing themselves as part of a larger whole. This did not mean, however, that preindustrial society in Europe was egalitarian in either social or human-environmental relations. The feudal system was at least in part justified by the philosophy/cosmology of Aristotle's great chain of being (*scala natura*), in which there was a hierarchy in the heavens and a hierarchy on earth. The pope and then the king were at the top, peasants were at the bottom, and women were below the men of their particular status group.

26. These estimates are from Nicholson and Fawcett, *The Village in England* 46, and Donald Worster, "The Vulnerable Earth: Toward a Planetary History," in Worster, *The Ends of the Earth*, 9.

27. Worster, "The Vulnerable Earth," 9.

28. See Dianne Fenton, "Looking at Issues of Abortion Through an Ecofeminist Perspective," senior thesis, University of Vermont, 1990; Norman Himes, *Medical History of Contraception* (New York: Gamut Press, 1963); Rosalind Petchesky, "Reproductive Choice in the Contemporary United States: A Social Analysis of Female Sterilization," in *And The Poor Get Children: Radical Perspectives on Population Dynamics*, ed. Karen Michaelson (New York and London: Monthly Review Press, 1981). In addition to evidence of early population control in human societies, note that many other animals appear to regulate their population through their behavior (including infanticide) as well as through "unconscious" fluctuations in reproductive capacities.

29. Statistics on resource consumption attributable to a meat-centered diet and its industries are from "Realities 1990: Facts," excerpted from John Robbins, *Diet for a New America* (Walpole, N.H.: Stillpoint, 1987).

30. Crosby, "Ecological Imperialism," 109.

31. Ibid., 116.

32. Ibid., 104–5.

33. William Cronon, *Changes in the Land: Indians, Colonists, and the Ecology of New England* (New York: Hill and Wang, 1983), 162.

34. Ibid., 86.

35. Ibid., 89.

36. Crosby, "Ecological Imperialism," 112. Also see Alfred Crosby, *Ecological Imperialism: The Biological Expansion of Europe 900–1900* (Cambridge: Cambridge Uni-

versity Press, 1986), in which he describes legends about smallpox that arose in other indigenous cultures colonized by Old World societies. For example, "the Yukaghirs, who in the 1630's occupied vast areas of Siberia from the Lena basin east, and of whom there were only 1500 at the end of the nineteenth century, have a legend that the Russians were not able to conquer them until the intruders brought smallpox in a box and opened the box. Then the land was filled with smoke, and the people began to die" (39).

37. Merchant, *Ecological Revolutions*, 11, 14.

38. Ibid., 113.

39. Crosby, "Ecological Imperialism," 114.

40. Ibid., 114.

41. Ibid., 116.

42. Hans Jonas, *The Phenomenon of Life: Toward a Philosophical Biology* (Chicago and London: University of Chicago Press, 1982), provides a fascinating and well-reasoned account of phases in the evolution of plants and animals, and the subjectivity of living organisms.

43. See Bill Devall and George Sessions, *Deep Ecology: Living As If Nature Mattered* (Salt Lake City: Gibbs Smith, 1985), esp. 69–76.

44. Murray Bookchin, *The Rise of Urbanization and the Decline of Citizenship* (San Francisco: Sierra Club Books, 1987), 41.

45. See especially Carol Gilligan, *In a Different Voice: Psychological Theory and Women's Development* (Cambridge: Harvard University Press, 1982); Mary Belenky et al., *Women's Ways of Knowing* (New York: Basic Books, 1986).

46. I have introduced parameters describing and defining ecofeminism, including its moral dimensions, at greater length in Stephanie Lahar, "Ecofeminist Theory and Grassroots Politics," *Hypatia* 6 (Spring 1991): 28–45. Also see Marti Kheel, "Ecofeminism and Deep Ecology: Reflections on Identity and Difference," in *Reweaving The World: The Emergence of Ecofeminism*, ed. Irene Diamond and Gloria Feman Orenstein (San Francisco: Sierra Club Books, 1990), 128–37; Marti Kheel, "The Liberation of Nature: A Circular Affair," *Environmental Ethics* 7 (1985): 135–49.

47. Paul Markowitz, "Energy Efficiency: Vermont's Most Promising Power Source," *Vermont Environmental Report* (Summer 1988): 11.

48. The Burlington special election in October 1991 reversed a March 1990 vote that had been declared invalid because literature supporting Hydro-Quebec had been placed inside voting booths.

# CHAPTER 5

# Ecofeminism and the Politics of Reality

## Linda Vance

### An Ecofeminist at Large

When I leave the road and enter the northern forest, the thick, humid, engulfing northern forest, I always pause, as though at a doorway, as though about to part a curtain, and center myself, and ask permission and safe passage. It is not unlike taking off my shoes when I enter my home, or the homes of my friends; I leave a material world behind to enter into another, more sanctified one.

I live in a town in New England, but the forest is home, in the sense that it provides the continuity in my life, the place I return to, humbly, time and again. But insofar as I view the wild places of my life that way, I am no different from generations of humans, environmental despoilers and conservationists alike, who see the nonhuman world in terms of its value or use for them. I may love it and honor it, but try as I might, I slip continuously into the prevailing Western view of the forest, and nature, as separate, other, a place to go to. I don't plunder its resources, or turn it to the plow, but I inadvertently lapse into metaphors of property and possession.[1] Yet it is hardly surprising that I do so. The forest may be home, but I don't live there, don't exist in a dialectical relationship with it. Instead, my experience of forest is mediated by literature, by religion, by history, by ethnicity, by science, by gender, by class: by all the forces that interact at any given time to form my—or anyone's—conceptual framework. In fact, given the cultural and intellectual baggage I carry into the forest, it's a miracle I can move at all.

I say that facetiously, but it has a hollow and bitter resonance. The bitterness comes because I know, as a feminist, that not only is my immediate experience mediated by excess baggage, but that baggage was largely designed by and for men, to describe and preserve *their* experience, and give it meaning and depth. The literature and the history that purport to record the interactions of human consciousness with the nonhuman world are in fact the records of male consciousness. A man-against-nature theme resonates throughout the dominant white culture of this country, infusing fiction, poetry, art, and popular literature.[2] And even nature writing, a rich literary tradition in the United States, and one often embraced by environmentalists, is hopelessly male-dominated. Thoreau, Emerson, and, to a lesser extent, John Muir shaped the genre, and in the past few decades they have been joined by a profusion of others: scientists like Stephen Jay Gould, Lewis Thomas, and Loren Eisley, who explore "the humanistic dimensions of their disciplines," and humanists like Mark Abley, Edward Abbey, John Burroughs, Robert Finch, Barry Lopez, John McPhee, and David Quaamen, who are "ranging, as impassioned amateurs, through the sciences' disciplines."[3] There are some women, of course: Annie Dillard, Gretel Erlich, and, in a way, Anne LaBastille write in this genre.[4] If I were to expand the field to include writing about adventure, where the focus is purely the individual's challenges and achievements, and spiritual meaning takes a back seat to survival, I could add Judith Niemi and Barbara Weiser's anthology about canoeing, *Rivers Running Free*; Arlene Blum's tales of her mountain climbing exploits in *Annapurna: A Woman's Place*; Cindy Ross's journal of her 2,600-mile hike on the Pacific Crest in *Journey on the Crest*; or Nicolette Walker's account of her solo sail across the Atlantic, *When I Put Out to Sea*. And if I were to expand it in another direction, to include domesticated nature, long the province of women, I could bring Maxine Kumin, Sue Hubbell, or Carol Bly into consideration. But for every woman I can name, there are a dozen or more men.

Moreover, the women rarely write with any degree of gender consciousness, and most, if not all, are white, middle-class, college-educated, physically unchallenged, and heterosexual, hardly a cross-section of America, although it may say something about whose work gets published. And I should note, too, that the reader gains these biographical data from publishers' blurbs and casual remarks in the text; the women, like the men, rarely identify their own history as a context in which vision takes place. Yet it is clear that their lives and choices bias their perspectives. LaBastille contemptuously describes her "slack and unmuscled" city friends,[5] and confides that she would hate herself if she ever "got fat" and that she fears "getting some crippling disease."[6] She unabashedly acknowledges terror at seeing an "enormous black man,"[7] and insists that the majority of wilderness women enjoy heterosexual relationships.[8] Dillard, in *Pilgrim at Tinker*

*Creek*, persistently uses a generic "he" and "man," perhaps forgivable in 1974, but not so in 1982, when she does it again in *Teaching a Stone to Talk*.[9] And Ehrlich, although she claims Indian friends and neighbors, feels compelled to observe in *The Solace of Open Spaces* that "there is nothing in our psyches, styles, or temperaments that is alike," and that although whites may endure the same harsh life as the Native people, they "won't become visionaries, diviners, or healers in the process."[10] Nor, presumably, will they have the "natural horse-handling abilities" with which she claims the Crow Indians were endowed, and which allowed them to become "famous horse thieves."[11]

So what about history? Surely we have a record of the ways in which women of the past interacted with nature; after all, urbanization is a relatively new phenomenon. I took the existence of such a history for granted until an afternoon last winter when I found myself in search of it.

I was clumping through the woods near my house on snowshoes, a gift from a widow whose husband they'd belonged to. "These were Walter's," she told me. "I got no need for them. Maybe you got a boyfriend would like 'em." It was the first time I'd worn them, and I felt clumsy and encumbered. But after an hour or so they began to feel natural, and I bounded along quite freely, pleased by a growing sense of strength and flexibility. I felt the ease that grows with time and distance in the woods, natural in my surroundings, as likely a part of it all as the fox and deer, as though I had been here for years, for generations, as though I had grown up in the north woods, with the smell of balsam and spruce in every breath I took. In fact, I began to feel so comfortable that I started wondering about ancestral memory, some sort of genetic imprinting: who in my family might have traversed the winter woods on snowshoes? My maternal grandfather, no doubt, born in northern British Columbia. My great-uncles from Cape Breton Island, off the coast of Nova Scotia. But who else? Not their parents, Scottish and Irish immigrants whose days were filled with wage labor. Not their children, born and raised in cities. Certainly not my grandmother or great-aunts; all of the stories I remembered from them were set indoors.

I thought about Walter, and the spirit of the snowshoes that bridged the gulf between his life and mine. But I couldn't sustain it. I don't really believe in ancestral memory, or in the memory of snowshoes or footsteps. If I can imagine Walter's experience, or the experience of ancestors I never met or never had, it's not because of mystical connections. It's because I carry around an oral and written and cinematic history of adventure in the woods. In Quebec, I grew up on tales of the Iroquois hunters, the *cour-*

*reurs des bois,* the *trappeurs,* the Jesuit missionaries whose lives were lived out on frozen ground. Blinding, blowing snow exhilarated us as children; we imagined ourselves deep into Hudson's Bay territory, with wolves and wilderness howling all around us. Television, when it came, brought more heroes: the Mounties, Sergeant Preston and his dog King, Davy Crockett. But all these heroes of snow and ice, I realized upon reflection, were male.

As I bounced along, increasingly annoyed by this turn of thought, I came to the edge of a thickly wooded precipice, where my attention returned long enough to keep me from catapulting over. Here, amidst a tangle of downed trees, were the tracks of another set of snowshoes, another solitary walker who had stopped for the view. Which way had he come from, I wondered. *He.* I tried to imagine a woman, and was infuriated when I found it difficult. If I was there, alone in the woods on snowshoes, why couldn't she be?

> After crossing the bleak, snowy plain, we scrambled over another brook and entered the great swamp. . . . It seemed the fitting abode of wolves and bears, and every other unclean beast. . . . Now we stooped, half-doubled, to crawl under fallen branches that hung over our path, then again we had to clamber over prostrate trees of great bulk, descending from which we plumped down into holes in the snow, sinking mid-leg into the rotten trunk of some treacherous, decayed pine-tree.[12]

Thus Susanna Moodie, an Ontario homesteader in the 1830s, described a journey to town in the midst of winter. After coming in from my walk, I spent the afternoon and evening poring over my books, looking for evidence of a long tradition of *women* in the snow and ice. I wanted to find that the tradition was there all along, and that I, a student and teacher of women's history, had simply missed it, as though it were a bird's nest buried deep within a rotting pine, or a larval case indistinguishable from the leafy debris on which it lay.

> It was twilight from the thick snow, and I faced a furious east wind loaded with fine, hard-frozen crystals. . . . [which] beat on my eyes— the only exposed part—bringing tears to them, which froze and closed up my eyelids at once. . . . I had to take off one glove to pick one eye open, for as to the other, the storm beat so savagely against it that I left it frozen.[13]

This was Isabella Bird, an intrepid English traveler who rode alone through the Colorado mountains in 1873. Descending from the rugged cabin where she had spent a month with rough miners and lawless desperadoes, she had been caught in a storm on the plains near Boulder, which she now recounted in a letter to her sister. I found, too, a handful of American westering women whose diaries recorded the hardships of the first winters spent on the prairies and in the mountain towns, in makeshift cabins, boxcars, sod houses. Here and there I encountered references to other exceptional women, like Martha Maxwell, a celebrated taxidermist, hunter, and naturalist of the nineteenth-century Rockies, or Sacajawea, who guided and interpreted for the Lewis and Clark expedition from 1804 to 1806. Beyond that, my books were hollow and dry.

I thought of pursuing it further. A computer search of a women's studies data base might turn up a score of women I'd missed; a hunt through attics and archives might yield a dusty diary or two. But I knew that would miss the point. Tradition is not found in obscure corners. Tradition is the commonplace, the banal, what ordinary people know and recognize, chickadees and robins, black-eyed susans and ragweed, oaks and maples. I have seen Cerulean Warblers, flown off-course in their migration, marveled at mountain laurel and redbud growing in protected pockets of Northern forest, a state-length beyond their range. But these are not the fauna and flora of Vermont, any more than the bold women explorers and adventurers of the nineteenth century are part of a female tradition.

For experience to become tradition, it has to be known, but women's lives have not been seen as important enough to be told. We can search, of course, through the diaries and letters and account books of the past, and try as specialists to reconstruct the details of women's daily lives. Meanwhile, the ordinary stuff of men's lives is passed on to everyone through popular culture. I have never hunted for sustenance or pleasure, yet I know what it is like to kill animals I have never even seen, because men's hunting tales are piled like old magazines in my memory. I have never canoed on anything rougher than a windy lake, yet I can imagine gasping for breath and courage while shooting the wild rapids of an unexplored river, because I have seen the movies and read the books that immortalize those male adventurers, have been taught in school that bravery and adventure is what we mean by history. But I have also never tried to thaw frozen bread or make porridge to feed children screaming of cold and hunger when I had no dry wood for the fire, no water, and no one to help me, and I am not sure I would know where to begin. I could tell you how a man trapped beaver in the mid-nineteenth century, but can do no more than speculate on what his wife, at home, used to catch her menstrual flow.

And what was her experience of the world outside the cabin? Did she put on his extra snowshoes, or her own, when he was gone, and stamp over the drifts to the edge of a frozen lake, where she could see the sky that was denied to her by the sentinel-like firs around their cabin? Did she track deer herself, hoping to find where they had lain the night before, to feel their presence and their wildness? Did she peer into the cavities of fallen trees in the hopes of seeing a sleeping porcupine? Did she part the snow at the base of a trunk, where tiny mouseprints stopped, wondering if there would be a nest? All that evening I sat at my desk, staring through the icy windowpane at distant stars in a deep black winter sky, trying to know a woman's experience through my imagination.

## The Politics of Reality

One of the projects of women's studies since its inception has been to correct the record, to write women back into the history we have been written out of. Feminists both within and outside academia have recognized that purportedly objective knowledge of the world is not objective at all; it is a product with "historically identifiable creators"—that is, privileged white men, those who have had the power both to define a particular conception of reality and to enforce it.[14] Marilyn Frye, in her essay "To See and Be Seen: The Politics of Reality," offered the following semantic reminder:

Reality is that which is.

The English word 'real' stems from a word which meant *regal*, of or pertaining to the king.

'Real' in Spanish means *royal*.

Real property is that which is proper to the king.

Real estate is the estate of the king.

Reality is that which pertains to the one in power, is that over which he has power, is his domain, his estate, is proper to him.

The ideal king reigns over everything as far as the eye can see. His eye. What he cannot see is not royal, not real.

He sees what is proper to him.

To be real is to be visible to the king.

The king is in his counting house.[15]

The lives of women, of working-class people, of people of color, have thus been rendered invisible not by historical accident but by design. We are real only insofar as we are useful objects; our lives are inconsequential, our experiences uninteresting. They do not count. They are unreal. They are untrue. At the same time, the lives and experiences of those who do count are imposed upon the rest of us as "reality." And so in the forest I am doubly burdened: alienated from my own experience, my own reality, and bound to another's.

That is my dilemma in the forest. It is also my dilemma in the classrooms, conference rooms, hearing rooms, and courtrooms where the future of the forest—or the oceans, or animals, or the rivers, or the mountains—gets debated and discussed. Although the actual work of agitating for change is disproportionately done by women,[16] the conceptualization of environmentalism is male-dominated because men are disproportionately valued as spokespersons, theorists, and leaders. As a result, even when environmentalist rhetoric appears feminist-friendly, its underlying assumptions of experience are likely to be male.[17]

Consider, for example, the separation of culture from nature. Radical environmentalists decry the fact that the scientific, intellectual, and industrial revolutions of the past three hundred years have corresponded to a devaluation and objectification of nature, a reduction of nature's role to that of something to be controlled and used by humans. But whose revolutions? For that matter, whose culture, whose nature, whose control and use? Women barely took part in the conceptualization of those revolutions, or, until recently, in the culture that emerged from them. Neither did the poor, or non-Europeans. We have been assigned much of the execution of the culture-building project, but we have had little say in its design. Thus, culture/nature dualism is hardly a shared experience. For privileged white men, the separation of culture and nature means a yearning for that which they have lost. For women and people of color, that same separation means a continual struggle for access to that which defines and controls us. Those men do not realize that a person's perception of culture/nature dualism, and her potential responses to it, are intimately shaped by gender, race, and class. Unfortunately, neither do the rest of us, much of the time. The dominant ideology, the dominant culture shaped by those privileged men, is force-fed to everyone else, and we align ourselves with the "culture" side of the equation even as we urge a greater acceptance of the despised nature with which we are associated. To do otherwise is to accept our role as outsiders.

Many radical, socialist, and cultural feminists have urged women to stop assimilating and to accept the outsider role, identifying that as a necessary standpoint from which to agitate for change. Insofar as we can stand outside dominant ideology, we can see it clearly, and criticize it. We can look at prevailing definitions of reality and ask the essential questions: who benefits from the definition? Who loses? Initially, the definition of nature and culture as separate, and culture as superior, benefited men of privilege because it gave them free rein—indeed, an almost divine mandate—to exploit and subdue the inferior others. Even now, with nature again in vogue, and everyone's voice rising in her defense, the rhetoric seems suspiciously self-interested. Save the rainforest in case valuable medicinal plants lie undiscovered there. Preserve wilderness as part of our "national heritage." Conserve resources for future generations. This is the rhetoric of property and progeny: the two things that matter most to a privileged few.

The application of feminist consciousness to definitions and constructions of nature has led many women to question their own acceptance of prevailing attitudes. Many, if not most, liberal feminists have rejected nature altogether, throwing in their lot with culture; after all, that's where the power is. But some cultural feminists have chosen to reclaim the long association of woman with earth, with nature, with the intuitive and spiritual, and to redefine that association as vital to sanity and survival, celebrating it through ritual and action.[18] Other radical feminists, uneasy about claiming an identity they have been taught to despise,[19] or afraid—justifiably—that such reclamation is often distorted to the advantage of the privileged few, have tried instead to bridge the chasm between culture and nature, working toward a reintegration.[20] But, for the most part, feminists of all persuasions have retained a curious but distant posture around questions of women and nature.

Recently, it seems, curiosity has been on the rise. In 1989 nearly forty women came to the pre-conference meeting of the National Women's Studies Association (NWSA) Ecofeminist Task Force; probably thirty of those said they had come "to find out what ecofeminism is," hoping, I guess, that someone had already decided, and that this would not be yet another tool of understanding that we would have to create from scratch, the way we have had to create feminism. After a while, the deconstruction and reconstruction of reality is tiring work.

Because our experience as women *is* diverse, so too is ecofeminism. Ask a half-dozen self-proclaimed ecofeminists "what ecofeminism is," and you'll get a half-dozen answers, each rooted in a particular intersection of race, class, geography, and conceptual orientation. My answers are particular to my experience as a white academic, as an Anglo, as a lesbian, as an immigrant, as a woman who moved from the working class to the middle class, and from city to country. This particularity doesn't compromise my authority to speak; what it does do, however, is underscore the point that my vision—my reality—is partial and political.

From my vantage point, the project of ecofeminism is understanding, interpreting, describing, and envisioning a past, a present, and a future, all with an intentional consciousness of the ways in which the oppression of women and the exploitation of nature are intertwined. Without an appreciation of the past, we don't know where we've come from. Without knowledge of the present, we can't know where we are. And, most critically, without a vision of the future, we can't move forward.

## *The Ecofeminist Past*

When I teach New England history, I try to convince my students of the importance—and the joy—of reading the past "off the ground," of learning to recognize the stories our physical surroundings tell. It takes a certain amount of booklearning, I assure them, and a lot of patience, but mostly it just means being alert, a skill anyone can learn without benefit of schools. I certainly did.

I grew up in a sooty urban neighborhood where the biggest excitement in the sky came from the sparks the incinerators sent up at night; I couldn't tell one tree from another, didn't know there were any birds other than pigeons and sparrows, and rarely tasted a fresh vegetable. But I did learn to read my own city landscape. I learned that neighborhoods like mine, with their mixes of duplexes and apartment buildings, were wealthier than ones where identical redbrick three-story boxes sprawled over a half-dozen city blocks, and poorer than ones with lawns and trees, and poorer still than neighborhoods that sported single-family homes. With the acute class consciousness of children who want things their families can't afford, my friends and I were experts at decoding architecture. As we grew older, and more sophisticated, we learned to spot ethnicity and religion in the names blazoned across the storefronts in a given neighborhood, in the clothes the old women wore, in the smells that wafted down the streets at dinnertime, in the snatches of mumbled conversation we overheard from the tired adults squatting on stoops. It was a naturalist's education, divorced as it was from nature, because it taught me the habits I would later bring with me to the country: to look for meaning in the everyday as well as the anomalous and, above all, to pay attention.

Over the past twenty years, I have gradually learned the ways the land tells a complex history of natural and social and intellectual change. When I hike through the Green Mountains, I mark changes in elevation by the shift from hardwood to red spruce forests. But I pay attention to more than that. I record the massive hill farm abandonment of the thirties, when rural electrification programs made it possible for lowland farmers to re-frigerate their milk but forced others out of business; their stories are told by the gnarled old apple trees that struggle for light in the midst of second-growth forest. I see the turn-of-the-century craze for "mountain air" among the urban rich in the crumbling foundations of once-grand hotels perched high above the valleys, long since burned to the ground beyond reach of a fire brigade. I remember the first world war in forests where yellow birch and wood sorrel grow alone without their customary associate, hemlock; the hemlock, I know, was logged off to make struts for biplanes. I see other historical patterns in other places: in the high deserts of the Southwest, the deep, winding arroyos remind me of overclearing and overgrazing brought on by greed, indifference, wild promises of irri-gation systems, and the belief that rain would follow the plow.[21] Across this country, or any country for that matter, the land bears the scars of human activity and consciousness.

Traditional histories, with their emphasis on great men and great wars, have tended to ignore the natural environment except as a site where the real drama took place. In the past several years, however, the new field of environmental history has emerged, conceptualizing and analyzing inter-actions between humans and their environment as dialectical and historical, a process of ongoing change. As someone who cares deeply about the land, I am encouraged by this trend toward contextuality; as a feminist, however, I am chagrined to see that even in this new context, "human" all too often means "men," and "human activity" too frequently concentrates solely on modes of production. But at least one historian, Carolyn Merchant, has challenged this approach to ecological understanding, and has tried to for-mulate an ecofeminist framework for understanding how change over time is a function of complex interactions between the ecology of a place, human production and reproduction, and human consciousness.

Merchant proposes a conceptual model of three nesting spheres. In the center lies the ecological core of a particular habitat at a particular time: the relations between humans, animals, plants, and physical objects and forces.

Interacting directly with this core are human production activities such as extraction or processing of "natural resources." Surrounding the perimeter of the core of production and ecology is a sphere of biological and social reproduction. Whether the core will be stable over time depends on this second sphere, since it will be affected by biological reproduction in both humans and nonhumans, and the social reproduction of laws, domestic arrangements, economic structures, and belief systems. The outer sphere represents human consciousness and ideology—the myth, philosophy, science, religion, language, cosmology, and art that shape our perceptions of the environment and dictate our responses to it. Merchant describes the separation between the spheres as a "semipermeable membrane" that allows for interactions between them. Changes in the ecological core, such as desertification, can both be brought about by or contribute to changes in patterns of human and nonhuman reproduction; those changes may have been influenced by, or lead to, changes in consciousness and ideology.

The model works well over a range of applications. Merchant herself uses it to describe ecological change in New England from the pre-colonial period to the industrial/capitalist revolution of the mid-eighteen hundreds. But it could be just as useful for an understanding of Europe in the sixteenth and seventeenth centuries, when, as described by Susan Bordo, a series of plagues, famines, droughts, and floods decimated the population, weakened government and the church, and set the stage for an ideological quest to separate from and dominate the natural world.[22] In the same way, it offers an integrated approach to studying the so-called green revolution of this century, a scheme imposed by Europeans and Euro-Americans on the developing world, which dramatically altered ecological balances, disrupted traditional social patterns, displaced women as primary food producers, and led to sharp ideological conflicts.[23] Over and over, an ecological/environmental approach to history illustrates the major "laws" of ecology that Barry Commoner described over twenty years ago: everything is connected, everything goes somewhere, nature knows best, and there is no such thing as a free lunch.[24]

Nonetheless, even Merchant's approach to history has limitations for ecofeminists. Like traditional history, environmental history focuses more on change within a system than on stability, emphasizing shifts in consciousness, or in modes of production, or in the ecology of a region. More importantly, it centers primarily on human actions and their impact. Nonhuman initiation of ecological change is relatively rare. Certainly the environment, left undisturbed, undergoes change over time: for instance, ponds fill in, grow to fields, then forests. But these are gradual changes, and are more likely to be the result of shifting patterns of human activity, such as urbanization, than to be catalysts for change in other spheres. The only "natural" change that truly alters production, reproduction, and consciousness is catastrophic: earthquakes, volcanic eruptions, and, to a lesser extent (because their impact is often increased by earlier short-sighted human acts), floods, drought, and disease. Thus, like traditional history, ecological history is often a history of events and drama.

An even more important limitation of ecological history, however, is that it is by and large an academic field, and therefore is loyal to certain norms of "evidence." Its practitioners are creative and conscientious in exploring a range of sources to determine what a given people believed at a given time—religious tracts, farmers' almanacs, diaries and letters, popular literature, land records, and so on—but the less literate a culture, the less "complete" a picture one can draw of it. Consequently, ecological history, in its endeavors to "prove" what was, tends to be confined to explorations of European and Euro-American consciousness and, even within that realm, to the consciousness of those people whose position in the culture allowed them to leave records of their thought—once again, privileged white men.

And, finally, ecological history, despite its insistence on considering how the land and human consciousness interact, is still reductionist, still leaves no room for magic. The boyfriend of one of my students, a forester, upon hearing that I planned to hike a section of trail through southern Vermont, mentioned that he would be interested in hearing my impressions of Glastonbury Forest when I returned. He didn't offer more in the way of information, and I forgot about it until I found myself in a deep emerald world of maple and beech trees towering over a tumble of mossy boulders and a carpet of arching ferns. I was stunned, overwhelmed, infused with a sense of awe and reverence I could not explain. It was not only the size of the trees, but their sheer majesty, and the quality of the light, and a silence that seemed to stretch for a thousand years. "That forest," I told Sharon when I got back, "it felt enchanted." She laughed. "When Kevin was managing it," she said, "he couldn't get guys to cut in there. They thought it felt haunted." I could, I suppose, reduce that experience to issues of gender, history, cosmology, class, and so on, could explain why *my* response was to feel blessed by the presence in that forest, and the woodcutters' response was to feel intimidated. But the fact remains: there *was* a presence.

Many ecofeminists therefore find greater satisfaction in stories of the past that acknowledge the intangible, the magical. And many of us want more from history than a cautionary reminder of what we already know. We want inspiration and alternative ways of knowing. For that reason we sometimes turn to more admittedly conjectural histories than those which purport to portray the past "objectively", gleaning knowledge from reports of archeological findings, oral traditions, remnants of earlier cultures, intuitive readings of myth and ritual, and sheer speculation. Particularly popular in this respect are histories of matriarchal or matrifocal cultures in which women enjoyed positions of equality or superiority vis-à-vis men, and nature was seen as a collaborator or benefactor, not as a foe to conquer.[25] In the past ten years, there has been an abundance of work in this area, both scholarly and popular, and it seems to have attracted a wide following. Within the academy, such histories are of course suspect, since they rest heavily on icons portraying women and animals as deities or symbols of fertility and abundance, and tend to ignore the fact that female idolization/idealization seems quite able to coexist with actual low status (see the chapter by Stephanie Lahar in this volume). But this is no reason to dismiss them. All history is conjectural and subjective; complete pictures are virtually impossible. The value of speculative histories is that they offer a sense of possibility, a sense that what might have been might also yet be. And because they draw on myth and ritual, they offer models of consciousness that help us to create cosmologies and rituals for our own time.

## The Ecofeminist Present

The ecofeminist present, for me, is a recent arrival. My nonfeminist friends started talking about environmental problems in the mid-seventies. I was unmoved. Even though I spent all my free time in the forest and dreamed of the day when I could at last move to the country and live in harmony with the land, I thought that environmentalism, as a political focus, was utterly and unredeemably out of touch with the real world, a bourgeois, materialist, self-indulgent pastime for people who didn't have to work for a living and didn't know a thing about life. I was a recent lesbian, still identified as working-class, was going to law school while working as an organizer in an inner-city neighborhood, and was heavily involved in the women's movement, which made me especially contemptuous of women who were working on environmental issues: didn't they recognize their own oppression?

Perhaps because I jumped class, perhaps because I *did* move to the country, perhaps simply because I realized, as millions of other people have, that environmental degradation has proceeded to a point where everyone is threatened regardless of race, class, or gender, I became involved with environmental struggles. And almost immediately my feminst ideology crashed headlong into a wall of middle-class, masculinist behavior, thinking, and politics. Environmental philosophy and action, I discovered, are hopelessly male-oriented, with heavy emphasis on concepts of rights and obligations, and what often appears to be excessive loyalty to both patriarchy and capitalism.[26] Even the governing metaphors of environmentalism bespeak the lack of shared experience between men and women. I have heard altogether too many men speak of "the rape of the wilderness." When a man says that the land or the forest or the mountain has been raped, he is speaking of despoliation. He may deplore it; he may mourn the loss of what was; he may rage and rail in helpless fury at the despoiler; but no matter how great his sense of loss may sound, he is still speaking from a man's cultural experience of rape: namely, having something he considers separate from but proper to him—his reality—taken away. He feels the violation of *that which is his,* its loss to him. And women? For us, rape is a different metaphor entirely. We feel the violation, not of that which is proper to us, but of our very selves. When *we* refer to the rape of nature, it is, I believe, with the same sort of empathy for *nature* as we feel for our sisters who are victimized by male violence—that is, a pain in our own bodies, a sense that nothing can be kept sacred, a despair and a loss of self.[27] This is quite different from the masculinist lament about a rape, the sense that something— someone—is now less than she was, meaning, of course, less useful, less valuable as property.

I have also heard too many so-called radical white male environmentalists speak of Mother Nature: the protectress, the provider, the nurturer. They invoke that sacred image freely, usually against other men who are bent, speaking still in their metaphorical terms, on rape. No one has much sympathy for virgins these days, but everyone knows you shouldn't rape your mother. Perhaps this image works on men, as clumsy crosses are thought to work against the undead. I don't know; but I do know what this white man's image of nature-as-mother says to women. On a general, cultural level, it is a reminder that our primary role is as caretakers and providers, and that our only source of power is to threaten to become angry and withhold our bounty. But on a more immediate and practical level, it sounds like a not very subtle warning to us that only mothers, only women who nurture and provide, deserve to be safe from rape.

After all, anyone who spends much time in the natural world knows full well that nature is no June Cleaver. I wrote the first version of this chapter while hiking in the forests and mountains of Vermont, where—in June—hail, thunder, rain, and lightning assailed me; where I slipped and slid over moss-covered boulders and slime-covered roots; where I toppled into a crevasse on a mountainside when loose gravel gave way under my boot; and where, at last, I was driven from a rocky summit by seventy-miles-per-hour winds, sleet and snow, and cloud cover too thick to see through. This nature—my nature—was a wild and rowdy woman, a bad and unruly broad with no concern for her children, and of no use to anyone but herself. This is the nature you will rarely hear men celebrate as female: it represents, after all, an unsuitable role for a woman.

I think about all this as I hike through the woods: no man's mother, or wife, or virgin, but merely a bad and unruly broad, am I safe? The answer, of course, is no. I am not safe in the woods, and I am not safe in the contemporary environmental movement, where men continue to dominate, and to use metaphors that are at once sexualized and sexist as a reminder to women of our place. I make this statement about the entire movement, even about self-styled radicals like the men of Earth First!, those macho-outlaw bad boys of environmentalism, so glibly eloquent about imperialism and racism, with such a tenacious grip on three or four key elements of quantum physics, Native American teachings, and Buddhism. In a pinch, they will admit to a passing similarity between the subjugation of women and the subjugation of nature, but they don't take the former seriously enough to fight it, either in their lives or as part of an integrated political struggle. In theory, these men have the power to dominate nature; by renouncing that theoretical power, they derive another sort of power, moral superiority over their fellows. In both theory and practice, however, they have the power to dominate women; that very real privilege is something they don't want to give up.

So men in the environmental movement would prefer that women take their issues elsewhere, for example, to the feminist movement, except that we should call ourselves "ecofeminists" so that everyone knows that we aren't only for ourselves, we're for nature too. How do women in the feminist movement feel about all this? Some women oppose the term "ecofeminist," insisting that because feminism is already against oppression, against domination, against violence, we don't need a special word to describe our politics.[28] Some, I think, are suspicious of any word that seems to modify an unqualified commitment to feminism alone: when the chips are down, they wonder, will we be "eco" or "feminist"? After all, political resources are scarce in the waning years of the twentieth century (Kaye/Kantrowitz).[29] And some just don't want to hear any suggestion that women are angry about issues other than our own. After a century of being angry on be-half of other downtrodden beings, women have finally become righteously angry on our own behalf; the term "ecofeminism," with its implied con-cern for the nonhuman environment, can easily be construed as signaling a backsliding, a lapse, once again, into concern for others.

On a bad day, then, say when she's hiking through a spruce bog trying to convince herself that being a food source for mosquitos and black flies is an ecologically sound role, an ecofeminist can despair, and start to feel like she is the least loved cousin of just about everyone, and sister to no one. Except, of course—and here she pauses, a boot heavy with black muck ar-rested in mid-step, and she looks around—except, of course, nature. Sister. Sister Nature. Separate from me, and part of me at the same time. Utterly loyal and totally unreliable. Fully known, and always a mystery. Ready to die for me and kill me. Needing me desperately and completely self-reliant. Accomplice and traitor. Harmony and struggle. Sisterhood: this was the ideal we brought with us to feminism, that women were sisters to each other. We believed that women, however diverse, shared a common op-pression—namely, that we were perceived as the known and shaped objects in a world where the knowers and shapers are men. This is precisely the oppression we share with the nonhuman world, and why, as ecofeminists, we assert that the domination of women and the domination of nature go hand in hand.

I do not mean to suggest that a simple metaphorical shift can usher in sweeping change, nor am I entirely oblivious to the dangers of seeing nature as a "sister." After all, white women in the feminist movement have often been all too ready to assume that "sisterhood" means we know and can speak for the experience of women of color, of native women, of rural women. But at its best, sisterhood has been an ideal, a way to describe and nourish the bond and the dynamic tension between women. In the same way, I think, it can now describe and nourish our bond with the natural world, and the dynamic tension between human and nonhuman nature.

Seen in this light, ecofeminism, rather than being a poor relation of the feminist and ecology movements, is a synthesis, the sibling connection between that which is fundamental to both movements. The ideology of ecofeminism demands opposition to domination in all its forms,[30] and a rejection of the notion that any part of the world, human or nonhuman, exists solely for the use and pleasure of any other part. This is a deceptively simple-sounding assertion; but if you contemplate it for a moment, you will realize that it has the entire weight of the Western cultural tradition against it. Until the last two decades, even the most radical environmentalists accepted the idea of human superiority over nature; they urged only that we be responsible, that we not abuse our rights to shape nature to human ends.[31] Ecofeminism goes further, and relinquishes all claims to inherent human power-over.[32]

Rejection of power-over is the starting point; the second aspect of ecofeminism is a replacement paradigm, an alternative world view. Here, ecofeminists draw on the better aspects of ecological science[33] to emphasize the value of diversity, interdependence, sustainability, cooperation, and renewal. At the same time, we are nourished by the hard-learned lessons of the better part of feminism,[34] particularly the lesson that all oppressions intersect, and that no one—human or animal—can be free unless we all are. Recognizing that, and rejecting simple-minded masculinist dualisms like the nature/culture split, we understand that virtually any topic is suitable for ecofeminist discussion. Ecofeminism is not "only" about nature, then, but rather about contextuality, about understanding our lives and our struggles in their broadest form. It is about reclaiming and reconstructing reality—including but not limited to the "reality" men have imposed on nature—through women's experience and women's perceptions.

So how does one "do" ecofeminism? Does it mean we all hang out in the wilderness? No: ecofeminism is essentially a conceptual framework that can suggest a number of courses of action. Its third aspect, then, is an analytic methodology. To be an ecofeminist means to be constantly aware of relationships—between humans, between humans and nonhumans—and to be keenly attuned to the patterns of domination that may be at play. In any instance of domination, it means asking: Is some party to this relationship disadvantaged vis-à-vis the other(s)? If so, can that disadvantage be embraced within a larger vision of nonviolence, diversity, cooperation, and sustainability? If not, how can the relationship be changed? And, finally, what is the relationship between this and other forms of dominance?

These are hard questions. When we ask if a relationship of dominance can be embraced—not merely accepted, but embraced, as critical to a yet-unrealized future goal—we don't always get yes and no answers, and everyone doesn't necessarily agree. There is a continuum of certainty about what is acceptable and what is not. For instance, on one end, I think—I hope—we find everyone in agreement that certain practices are wrong:

things like vivisection, oppression on the basis of skin color, strip mining. On the other end, I think we find most people agreeing that even some destructive acts are acceptable in the broader context: the eradication of some life forms, like harmful viruses or bacteria, or the harvesting of plants for food. But in the middle, on issues like rodent and insect control, or the clearing of new farmland in response to human population growth, we get disagreement. Women do not agree on the middle, and the middle continues to shift. A commitment to ecofeminism means we have to accept a degree of uncertainty and disagreement.[35] In particular, I think it means we have to trust women who say they are dedicated to social justice and equality, and not administer a political litmus test.

This suggests, for me, a fourth element of ecofeminism: a process that respects difference and encourages discussion, and that embraces a range of praxis. Diversity of experience and expression, like diversity of life forms, is a necessary goal of ecofeminism. There can be no single set of answers, no one portal through which to enter. To insist on a single ideology, or a single praxis, is to deny the tremendous complexity of the problems that centuries of patriarchy have created. And it denies the dialectic realities of the complicated, interconnected life on this planet. Consequently, in some ways it doesn't matter where one's ecofeminist praxis begins. Some of us may be closer to mainstream environmentalism, working to save open spaces or wildlife habitat. Some of us may be integrating feminist and animal liberation goals in our opposition to genetic engineering and biotechnology. Others may be creating new forms of spirituality that celebrate and foster woman's connection with natural processes. Yet others may be struggling against the vicious anti-woman, anti-nature maldevelopment schemes proliferating in the First World. The point is that we don't have to be in the same place; we simply have to be doing something, and seeing the connectedness of it all, and not undoing or denying each other's work. Even though I sometimes despair at what I think are trivial efforts—including my own—and wish we could agree to work first on the threats to global survival, I know that we can only come to consciousness through the things we feel in our gut.

And so for me the fifth element of ecofeminism is empathy. When I presented a first draft of this chapter at a panel on ecofeminism at the NWSA 1990 meeting, Donna Hughes observed that I was following in the Western cultural tradition by continuing to personify nature as female, and asked if, given the negative associations at play there, I could not consider some other characterization. Somewhat flippantly, I answered that if I didn't think of nature as female, I wouldn't be able to feel such enormous pleasure in her presence. A wisecrack, but with a lot of truth to it. Giving nature a female identity reinforces my sense of solidarity with the nonhuman world. Indeed, as Marti Kheel pointed out during that same exchange, more genderization, not less, might be a good thing: meat-eaters might be less sanguine about consuming parts of dead animals if they had to ask someone to "pass me one of her ribs, please," or "slice off one of her wings for me, would you?" For many of us, empathy toward the nonhuman world is the heart of our political stance. We are not persuaded to be vegetarians only because someone argues that animals have inherent rights too, but also by feeling an intuitive kinship with them, or with the land that has been so cruelly ravaged by grazing, or by recognizing that the degree of disassociation and objectification necessary to eat meat is both symptomatic and productive of deep alienation from others.[36] Similarly, we do not fight for the preservation and protection of wild rivers just so that present and future generations of affluent tourists can raft them, but also because their wildness resonates so deeply with our own, because we know ourselves what a joy it is to follow one's own course. Identification and empathy may be dismissed by rationalists as sentimental—as feminine—but passionate convictions, beliefs from the heart, can always get us through the hard times when reason and argument fail.

## The Ecofeminist Future

With a sense of where we've come from, and a feeling for where we are, we can begin to ask where we're going and how to get there. This work is both personal and collective.

On both levels, action requires a set of goals or objectives, or, in short, a vision of the future, a plan for how we want the world to be. One vision often appearing in ecofeminist thought and writing is bioregionalism, a commitment to living harmoniously with the ecology of a given area.[37] As I finish the revision of this chapter, another winter is beginning to grip New England. Although an enormously brutal and costly war has stabilized oil prices for the moment, the relentless recession, brought on, in part, by fears of spiraling prices and fuel shortages eighteen months ago, continues. Many of my neighbors, my friends, my students—even my university colleagues—are fearful about losing their homes and livelihoods. Only some make the connection between the recession/war and the lack of a sound energy policy, one that would have encouraged us to live cooperatively within the limits set by the land. On a smaller scale, a friend has just called me from New Mexico to report that days of rain and flooding have destroyed houses, bridges, roads, the gardens that she and her friends rely on for sustenance. The problem, of course, is not the rain itself, but the severe depletion of western land by years of overgrazing, to the point where in many areas nothing remains to absorb the rainfall, or to stop the raging runoff.

Despite a heightened environmental consciousness at the grassroots level, responses to global environmental crisis have been mostly bandaid solutions designed to maintain, with only minor modifications, the wasteful lifestyles and preposterous consumption habits of the affluent Western world. Americans still act as though we were only renting the planet and could move if things get bad, or get the landlord to fix it. New England imports food from California and Arizona, which import water from Colorado and Utah, which import clothing from southern and foreign textile mills, and so on. We are out of balance with our environment, have contorted the land to make it fit human desires, instead of the reverse.

The lessons of ecological history teach us that such practices are doomed to failure. Past human generations, having destroyed or exceeded the capacities of the land to support us, have moved on, or have tried exporting environmental problems while importing solutions, but because everything *is* connected, such solutions are short-lived, and the consequences ultimately return, boomeranglike, to us. What a commitment to bioregionalism requires, then, is an acceptance of limits. In the United States, the desert will not support agriculture without massively destructive irrigation projects. The Northeast cannot sustain its present population concentrations without imperialistic energy ventures in foreign countries. The Midwest cannot manage to produce enough grain and legumes to feed meat animals without heavy infusions of petrochemical fertilizers and insecticides, and a resultant loss of topsoil and fertility. The Northwest cannot maintain an economy based on wood products without losing biotic diversity and sustainability.

Clearly ecofeminists cannot expect to initiate huge demographic transitions within our lifetimes, or, most likely, within the imaginable future. What we can do, however, is make the need for responsible cooperation with the land known, and use our own lives to model the possibilities.

We have to begin, I firmly believe, with a commitment to knowing the ecology of our immediate environment, and to understanding the impact of our present lifestyles both on that environment and on other regions and peoples. As ecofeminists, we can and should be organizing study groups so that we can educate ourselves about the soil, water, plant and animal life, and climatic patterns within our region, asking not only what the land can provide for us in terms of sustenance, but what the land itself requires to maintain its sustainability, diversity, and beauty. At the same time, we need to be investigating where our food, clothing, energy, communications, and health care systems come from, where our waste goes to, and at what environmental, nonhuman, and human cost.[38] Once we begin to acquire that awareness, we can implement change in our own lives, and suggest alternatives that others can also pursue.

Even at the simplest level, we can adapt our diets to local, seasonal fruits, vegetables, seeds, and grains, and give up meat, both because of its demands on space, water, and vegetation and because killing animals for food is disconsonant with principles of empathy. We can change our patterns of fuel consumption, explore domestic architecture and living/working arrangements that make more efficient use of space, energy, and water, stop buying things we don't need, stop discarding things we can reuse. These are simple solutions, a variation on the ones found in the proliferation of books and pamphlets advising us on "X ways you can save the earth." But simple solutions are nothing to shun; they are immediate and manageable, give a sense of accomplishment, and encourage personal responsibility as the core of political action.

At the same time, acting locally cannot mean becoming indifferent to the ecological crises of other areas, whether or not those crises have extraterritorial consequences. All too frequently, environmental activists want only to get a given threat—a waste dump, a mine, a dam, a power plant— to disappear from their own town, county, state, or nation. If we believe what we say, that everything is connected, that everything comes around, we cannot dismiss danger simply because it becomes invisible. We are obliged to extend our attention to acting collectively across borders and geographic regions, sharing expertise, resources, ideas, appropriate technology, and time.

On a more abstract level, ecofeminists need to begin imagining more large-scale and long-range solutions. On the bioregional level, how could a community, a region, be organized to bring it into harmony with its ecology? What would its borders be? What would it produce to meet the needs of its inhabitants? What sort of relationships of production and reproduction would exist in it? What kind of human, animal, plant associations could it sustain? How would inhabitants of one region communicate and interact with inhabitants of another? What kind of social and political organization would be necessary to make it work? What historical injustices need to be corrected to build cooperation and respect, both within a given region and in the broader world? On a global level, how can patterns of exploitation and domination by Europeans and Euro-Americans be reversed? How can indigenous populations be empowered—not just psychologically, but politically and economically—to balance ecological and economic development needs?

Many of the questions I raise here, and the approaches I suggest, are no different from those proposed by progressive elements of the environmental movement.[39] What sets ecofeminists apart? The answer lies in both our experience and our perspective. We know, because we have lived it, that men and women have been disparately treated within patriarchy and capitalism, with women receiving the worst treatment. We know what it means to be exploited, to be forced to yield and produce against our will. We know what it means to be made invisible, to have our reality denied. Because we know all this from our experience, and know from a study of history that the domination of women and the domination of nature have long been politically, philosophically, and economically linked, our perspective differs from that of the men. In the first place, our experience with oppression allows us to speak forcefully and empathically about injustice, to know from the heart what disregard for the integrity of land and nonhuman life means; our experience gives our ethics and philosophy a critical grounding. It also shapes our perspective. Women in Western culture have been caretakers, and like others who have been forced into roles of subservience and nurturing, we have learned sensitivity to values of preservation, protection, dependence, connection. We have learned a type of attentiveness that allows us to move back and forth between seeing the needs of an individual and seeing the needs of a larger community.[40] These are ideas that privileged white men are just beginning to learn, and anyone who has tried to work with those men knows that they don't quite have it down yet. That leaves us a choice: to work within the progressive environmental movement, acting as a conscience and a scout for signs of meaningful change, or to work outside it, as women, putting our experience and perspective to work without interference.

This is not the sort of choice that can be legislated by any one woman for all women, nor is it a choice to be made for all time. Some may choose never to work with men, or to form loose coalitions, or to decide on an issue-by-issue basis. Nevertheless, it is critical for ecofeminists to work together as women at least some of the time. Global ecological salvation will require a transformation of masculinist consciousness, a rejection of ideologies of mechanism, reductionism, and human superiority over nature. The progressive environmental movement recognizes that, but I am not as convinced that the men in it recognize that they will also have to reject the practice of male superiority. But even more important for women is our need to know our own experience with nature more fully. Many of us are separated from everything that is natural—including our own bodies—by centuries of patriarchal domination. Even those of us who wander or work in the nonhuman environment do so in the context of recreation, production, and knowledge-gathering patterns that have been established by men. As women, we lack the body of literature, history, ritual, myth, song, healing practices, games, art, and spirituality that could give the kinds of depth and meaning to *our* lives that men take for granted. We need to explore women's ways of knowing and interacting with the land. To speak of a transformation of consciousness when we have barely explored a consciousness of our own is to become trapped once again in a male-conceived and male-executed reality. And so I would like to see us take on the challenge of exploring our own reality as free as possible from the constraints of masculinist ideology, whether that means something as simple as creating rituals to honor transitions in our lives, or as demanding as establishing intentional communities built on ecofeminist principles.

An ecofeminist future, then, requires us to be visionary and patient at the same time. We need to imagine far-reaching change, and to move slowly, step by step. We need to demand perseverance and dedicated effort from ourselves, and we need to understand that women are already wearied from struggle. We need patience. We cannot build a movement or a future by denouncing other women's efforts, or dismissing them as trivial. Wherever we begin, what unifies us as ecofeminists—as feminists—is a commitment to bringing together all group oppressions to fight domination collectively, because as diverse as our struggles are, the source of our oppression is patriarchal and capitalist privilege. Our goal is not to seize a piece of it for ourselves, but rather to rid ourselves of its scourge before it is too late.

\*      \*      \*

I began writing this essay while hiking in the northern forest, the engulfing northern forest, my home, but my heart was somewhere else, as it almost always is. As much as I love the forest, I am less drawn to its embrace than I am to other, more inhospitable environments: the rocky shores of the

North Atlantic, the arid deserts of the Southwest, the rugged summits of the Appalachians and the Rockies. I used to think it was about the sky, the vast and yawning sky, the sky that puts to shame the English language, with its altogether too few ways to say "blue." But lately I have come to recognize that what compels me to this wilder nature, this inaccessible or dangerous or remote nature, is indeed its wildness, its disobedience, its rowdiness, its resistance to the domination of men. This nature, this sister nature, is where I gain my courage and patience. It is the model for what I want all my sisters to be able to choose to be, without fear or retaliation: useless, unyielding, and free.

## NOTES

1. One can also not ignore the fact that the metaphor of parting a curtain to approach or enter nature is both gendered and sexualized, reflecting a particularly heterosexual male viewpoint in which he, the active knowing subject, stands in front of her, the passive soon-to-be-known object. I recognized this after writing it; since my spontaneous use of such a metaphor is a testament to the power of a nonconscious ideology, I have chosen to leave it in place.

2. A number of studies deal with the man-against-nature theme. Among them, I have found several to be especially useful: Wilson O. Clough, *The Necessary Earth: Nature and Solitude in American Literature* (Austin: University of Texas Press, 1964); Annette Kolodny, *The Lay of the Land: Metaphor as Experience and History in American Life and Letters* (Chapel Hill: University of North Carolina Press, 1975); Roderick Nash, *Wilderness and the American Mind* (New Haven: Yale University Press, 1967).

3. Judy Anhorn, "From Natural Fact to Spiritual Fact in the Writings of Annie Dillard," *Letterature d'America: Revista Trimestrale* 9 (1990): 37–56.

4. Ann LaBastille, *Woodswoman* (New York: Dutton, 1978); and Ann LaBastille, *Beyond Black Bear Lake* (New York: W. W. Norton, 1987). LaBastille is not a great literary talent, nor do I consider her to be, strictly speaking, a nature writer, but whenever I speak on the theme of women and nature in the Northeast, someone is bound to bring up her name; her work enjoys a wide and faithful audience, and so I include her here. I am defining the genre of nature writing, or, as it is more frequently called now, "the literature of natural fact," as that tradition of writing in which the author uses nature as a pathway to spiritual/political meaning or insight. For this reason I would exclude from it the authors, both men and women, who write more as observers of nature than interpreters. An earlier practitioner of the genre whose work is coming back into print, and who displayed wonderful feminist consciousness, is Mary Austin; in particular I would recommend her books *The Land of Little Rain* (Albuquerque: University of New Mexico Press, 1974) and *The Land of Journey's Ending* (Tucson: University of Arizona Press, 1983). See also Judith

Niemi and Barbara Weiser, eds., *Rivers Running Free: Stories of Adventurous Women* (Minneapolis: Bergamot Books, 1987); Arlene Blum, *Annapurna: A Woman's Place* (San Francisco: Sierra Book Club, 1980); and Nicolette Walker, *When I Put Out to Sea* (Chelsea, MI: Scarborough House, 1975).

5. LaBastille, *Woodswoman*, 34.

6. LaBastille, *Beyond Black Bear Lake*, 239.

7. Ibid., 132.

8. Anne LaBastille, *Women and Wilderness: Women in Wilderness Professions and Lifestyles* (San Francisco: Sierra Club Books, 1984), 290.

9. Annie Dillard, *Pilgrim at Tinker Creek* (New York: Bantam, 1975); and Annie Dillard, *Teaching a Stone to Talk* (New York: Harper & Row, 1982).

10. Gretel Ehrlich, *The Solace of Open Spaces* (New York: Penguin, 1986), 105.

11. Ibid., 119.

12. Susanna Moodie, *Roughing It in the Bush* (Boston: Beacon/Virago Press, 1987), 468.

13. Isabella Bird, *A Lady's Life in the Rocky Mountains* (Norman: University of Oklahoma Press, 1986), 16.

14. Sandra Harding, *The Science Question in Feminism* (Ithaca: Cornell University Press, 1986), 16.

15. Marilyn Frye, *The Politics of Reality: Essays in Feminist Theory* (Freedom, Calif.: Crossing Press, 1983), 155.

16. By "actual work," I mean the letter-writing, postering, demonstrating, picketing, public education, conferencing, reading, pamphleting, and so on that are so critical to political activism. I am grateful to Helen Caudill for pointing this out to me in relation to the animal rights movement; she further observed that at the June 10, 1990, March for Animals in Washington, at least 75 percent of the marchers were women, while most of the speakers were male. Peg Millett, recently convicted in Arizona on a trumped-up charge of conspiracy, made a similar claim about Earth First! "Earth First! is held together and run by women. The power of the movement comes from women. You don't see that in the media. All you see are a bunch of redneck men and their girlfriends running around and beating their chests." Quoted by David Quaamen, "Reckoning," *Outside*, November 1990, 51–54, 134–39, at 54.

17. By this point it is probably an axiom of feminism and women's studies that there is no such thing as an "objective" viewpoint, but that every position will be shaped by the experience, desires and perspective of the group or class of persons espousing it. For fuller discussion of this point, see, for example, the various contributions to *Feminism and Methodology*, ed. Sandra Harding (Bloomington: Indiana University Press, 1987).

18. See generally the essays collected in Charlene Spretnak, ed., *The Politics of Women's Spirituality* (Garden City, N.Y.: Anchor/Doubleday, 1982).

19. This is a paraphrase of Michelle Cliff's *Claiming an Identity They Taught Me to Despise* (Watertown, Mass.: Persephone Press, 1980).

20. Ynestra King is the one who pointed out these three options for feminists: sever the woman-nature connection and align with culture; reinforce the spiritual/intuitive aspects of the woman-nature connection; or use the woman-nature connection as a starting point for the creation of a new politics and culture that integrate science and magic, intuition and reason. See Ynestra King, "The Ecology of Feminism and the Feminism of Ecology," in *Healing the Wounds: The Promise of Ecofeminism*, ed. Judith Plant (Philadelphia: New Society Press, 1989), 22–23.

21. The ecological history of New England is described at length in Carolyn Merchant, *Ecological Revolutions: Nature, Gender and Science in New England* (Chapel Hill and London: University of North Carolina Press, 1990), and in William Cronon, *Changes in the Land: Indians, Colonists, and the Ecology of New England* (New York: Hill and Wang, 1983). For a popular account of the ecological history of the Southwest, and particularly its water projects, see Marc Reisner, *Cadillac Desert* (New York: Penguin, 1986).

22. Susan Bordo, "The Cartesian Masculinization of Thought," in *Sex and Scientific Inquiry*, ed. Sandra Harding and Jean F. O'Barr (Chicago: University of Chicago Press, 1987), 247–64.

23. One excellent account of the impact of the green revolution on women can be found in Vandana Shiva's *Staying Alive: Women, Ecology, and Development* (London: Zed Books, 1988).

24. See generally Barry Commoner, *The Closing Circle: Nature, Man and Technology* (New York: Knopf, 1971).

25. Among these histories are Riane Eisler, *The Chalice and the Blade* (New York: Harper and Row, 1988); Monica Sjöö and Barbara Mor, *The Great Cosmic Mother: Rediscovering the Religion of the Earth* (New York: Harper & Row, 1987); and Merlin Stone, *When God Was a Woman* (New York: Harcourt, Brace, Jovanovich, 1978).

26. The masculinist orientation is clear in such works as Tom Regan, *The Case for Animal Rights* (Berkeley: University of California Press, 1984); Christopher O. Stone, *Earth and Other Ethics: The Case for Moral Pluralism* (New York: Harper and Row, 1987); Paul W. Taylor, *Respect for Nature: A Theory of Environmental Ethics* (Princeton: Princeton University Press, 1986). The philosophy of deep ecology is a little more refreshing, although the personal behavior of men who profess it is often stale. For the philosophical position, see Bill Devall and George Sessions, *Deep Ecology: Living As If Nature Mattered* (Salt Lake City: Peregrine Smith Books, 1985).

27. I recognize that men are sometimes the victims of rape, and I imagine that such an experience may bring an individual man closer to the position I herein ascribe to women. Nonetheless, I believe that virtually all women, whether they have been raped or not, identify with the victim, because we live our entire lives conscious, in a way that men are not, of the possibility of rape. See, for example,

Andrée Collard with Joyce Contrucci, *Rape of the Wild: Man's Violence Against Animals and the Earth* (Bloomington: Indiana University Press, 1989).

28. Anne Cameron, "First Mother and the Rainbow Children," in Plant, *Healing the Wounds*, 63–64.

29. This is Melanie Kaye/Kantrowitz's somewhat sardonic observation about "the scarcity assumption" in her essay "To Be a Radical Jew in the Late Twentieth Century," in *The Tribe of Dina: A Jewish Women's Anthology*, ed., Melanie Kaye/Kantrowitz and Irene Klepfisz (Montpelier, Vt.: Sinister Wisdom Books, 1986), 264–87, esp. 273–74.

30. I am attempting here to define what Karen Warren has called the "boundary conditions" of a feminist ecological ethic. Although I believe our positions are substantially similar, we express them in different ways, and so I refer the reader to Warren's excellent article, "The Power and the Promise of Ecological Feminism," *Environmental Ethics* 12 (1990): 125–46.

31. For a history of environmental ethics, see, for example, Roderick Nash, *The Rights of Nature* (Madison: University of Wisconsin Press, 1989). This work emphasizes intellectual history over political history, leaving a naive reader with the impression that the evolution of environmental consciousness has been nothing more than a bunch of educated white men writing philosophy that gets read by a bunch of other educated white men, and so on, but it is a useful summary of the chronology of ideas.

32. The discussion of power-over versus power-from-within can be found in Starhawk, *Dreaming the Dark: Magic, Sex and Politics* (Boston: Beacon Press, 1982).

33. By "better aspects" I mean the holistic vision of the interconnectedness of natural processes, rather than those elements of ecological science that stress "producer" and "consumer" relations, and speak of ecosystems in terms of their "net primary productivity" as measured by "biomass." The growth of ecology as a science paralleled the growth of capitalism at the turn of the century, and adopted much of its language. For a history of ecology, see Donald Worster, *Nature's Economy: A History of Ecological Ideas* (Cambridge: Cambridge University Press, 1985).

34. Implied here is the existence of certain "worse" parts of feminism; I leave the reader to her own assessments of where those lie.

35. The commitment to disagreement, which is another way of saying "pluralism," has its drawbacks: Janet Biehl, in *Rethinking Ecofeminist Politics* (Boston: South End Press, 1991), repeatedly cites instances of disagreement in an effort to sustain her snide dismissal of ecofeminism as incoherent.

36. The feminist argument for vegetarianism is made persuasively by Carol J. Adams in *The Sexual Politics of Meat: A Feminist-Vegetarian Critical Theory* (New York: Continuum, 1990).

37. The most comprehensive discussion of bioregionalism as a principle can be found in Kirkpatrick Sale, *Dwellers in the Land: The Bioregional Vision* (San Francisco: Sierra Club Books, 1985). Unfortunately, Sale does not take into account the

spiritual aspects of place, nor could his discussion of bioregionalism be seen as particularly feminist.

38. It is incredibly difficult to begin to unravel the ecological ramifications of even the most seemingly innocuous acts. When I asked a group of students, half of whom were wearing stone-washed jeans, whether they had ever wondered where the stone came from, they looked at me as though I were crazy. "Isn't it just stone?" one asked. Yes; but the stone is pumice stone, obtained by strip-mining techniques.

39. See particularly Devall and Sessions, *Deep Ecology*, and Brian Tokar, *The Green Alternative: Creating an Ecological Future* (San Pedro, Calif.: R & E Miles, 1987).

40. For a fuller development of this theme, see Sara Ruddick, "Preservative Love and Military Destruction: Some Reflections on Mothering and Peace," in *Mothering: Essays in Feminist Theory*, ed. Joyce Trebilcot (Totowa, N.J.: Rowman and Allenheld, 1983).

# CHAPTER 6

# Questioning Sour Grapes: Ecofeminism and the United Farm Workers Grape Boycott

## Ellen O'Loughlin

Sour grapes. What an expression (on your face). Sour grapes are unexpected and unwanted. You pick a grape, bite through the skin to the fleshy fruit expecting sweetness. Perhaps you anticipate seeds, but more likely not (seedless reigns). Expecting sweetness, you are disappointed by the sour grape. Say "yuck" and spit it out if you can; if not, grimace and swallow. The grape is rejected. Is it bad? Or just not what you wanted? Not what you paid for? Were you deceived by the unblemished appearance of the fruit? Can you trust the next one?

Sour grapes: the expression refers to someone who is dissatisfied, holds a grudge, doesn't have a sense of humor, won't go along with the crowd, a sore loser. Sour is crabby, sullen, surly, as well as acerbic. Adjectives to put down, as well as to describe. Adjectives used to describe feminists, troublemakers. Sour grapes is an expression to describe something that leaves a bad taste in your mouth (another expression), in someone's mouth. The question that no one asks is, how does the grape feel? How does being sour feel? How does being spat out feel? How does being rapidly gulped feel? Does the grape feel rejected or glad to get away? Really now, does the grape feel at all? Hey, are any grapes reading this chapter? Grapes, get together.

This chapter is about grapes. It's about attitudes, about people, about oppression, about resistance. About sour grapes in various forms. In this essay I plan to begin to explore the United Farm Workers' grape boycott from an ecofeminist perspective. Ecofeminism is a philosophy that, through analysis of the connectedness of the oppressions of women and nature, demonstrates the necessity of a connected liberation from domination. The UFW grape boycott is part of an activist-labor struggle in which women and environmental concerns are central. The boycott is an effort to connect the oppression of farm workers to health concerns of grape consumers and to free both from danger. This boycott against California table grapes demands from growers "the elimination of dangerous pesticides from all grape fields . . . [a] joint testing program for poisonous substances in grapes sold in stores . . . free and fair elections for farm workers, and good faith collective bargaining in the grape industry."[1] These issues, and others addressed by the UFW, such as clean air and water, sexual harassment, poverty, nondomination, and self-determination, are also ecofeminist topics. I am not saying that the UFW is ecofeminist; I wish, rather, to show that the movements share common concerns and can learn from each other. Through my interest in ecofeminism, I have been motivated to learn more about the UFW; in learning about the UFW, I am encouraged to think critically about ecofeminism.

My particular focus here is on what ecofeminism can learn from the UFW grape boycott. I have chosen this angle partially because of my own positionality. I am white, lacking money but well-educated and so endowed for success, and ecofeminist. In other words, I am relatively privileged. I am particularly interested in agricultural issues, but at this point have more book learning than practical experience. So while I am in the land of books and papers, I want especially to learn from those who have more hands-on, feet-in experience. I am not writing from an expert position; rather, I am writing as a student, as a seeker of additional understanding, a student who wishes to share as she learns.

Additionally, I am concerned about ecofeminism's potential to be essentialist and racist. I do not think ecofeminism is essentialist or racist, but overemphasis on women's biological connectedness to nature and woman/female as a singular symbolic category can leave out the many important differences among women and the many ways women's various oppressions are related to the domination of nature.

Increasingly, however, I see ecofeminism fulfilling its potential to be a transformative feminism.[2] Karen Warren in "Feminism and Ecology: Making Connections" states that

a transformative feminism would expand upon the traditional conception of feminism . . . by recognizing and making explicit the interconnections between all systems of oppression. In this regard, a transformative feminism would be informed by the conception of feminism which has been advanced by many black feminists and Third World feminists articulating the needs and concerns of black women and women in development. These feminists have argued that because of the basic connections between sexist oppression and other forms of systemized oppression, feminism, properly understood, is a movement to end *all* forms of oppression.[3]

I think ecofeminism, to be truly transformative, must also listen to Zuleyma Tang Halpin, who argues in "Scientific Objectivity and the Concept of 'the Other'" that

> women have been oppressed, not so much because they have been equated to nature, but rather because *both* women and nature have been equated to "the Other" [and also that] . . . the same dynamic that has resulted in labeling women as inferior and justified society's domination of women and nature, has done the same during most of our history, to Blacks and other people of color, Jews, the poor, and gay or lesbian persons.[4]

Since the dynamic of oppression is similar (though not identical or interchangeable) among oppressed peoples, and since most women experience this dynamic in more than one way (that is, through the dynamics of racism, classism, heterosexism, and ageism, as well as sexism), ecofeminism, in order to fight the oppression of women and nature, must look at more than just the ways in which sexism is related to naturism. Rather, we have to examine how racism, heterosexism, classism, ageism, and sexism are *all* related to naturism. Then we have to see how compound, multiple oppressions relate to naturism and actually affect women's lives.[5]

In a related vein, Warren's second criterion for a transformative feminism is that it "must provide a central theoretical place for the diversity of women's experience."[6] It must "be a call to oppressed groups to collectively assert *for themselves* their felt experiences, needs, and distinctiveness."[7] I agree that diversity must be central to ecofeminism, but rather than calling to oppressed groups, ecofeminism should be, as Lee Quinby writes, "listening to all voices of subjugation and hearing their insurrectionary truths [in order to] make us better able to question our own political and personal practices."[8] And question we must, especially when our privileges (for example, whiteness of skin, educational achievements) suggest that we know more, and when our differences (that is, female biology) suggest that we know better. Gloria Anzaldúa writes in *Borderlands/La Frontera: The*

*New Mestiza* that in a New Consciousness (I'd say inclusive of and analogous to a transformative feminism), whites "come to see that they are not helping us but following our lead."[9] This she writes in the context of alliance, the context of whites setting up committees "to help Big Mountain Navajos or the Chicano farm workers or *los Nicaraguenses*."[10] Alliance will not work, coalition will not work, if seen as charity, if not undertaken in the spirit of learning and gaining from the experience. What I can learn, am learning, and what ecofeminism can learn, from studying the actions and strategies of the UFW is the subject of this chapter.

The present UFW boycott, begun in 1984, continues the UFW's tradition of innovative organizing techniques. Originally a part of the wide demands for social justice that characterized much of the 1960s, the union has continued to forge a progressive path. Throughout its history the UFW has combined conventional labor demands for unionization with, for example, campaigns to get DDT and other dangerous pesticides out of the fields. In the 1970s the union was successful in organizing labor on farms and in vineyards. The conservative 1980s saw both the creation of a pro-management Agricultural Labor Relations Board in California and renewed political activity on the part of the UFW. Soliciting support from outside the fields, the UFW works with other labor organizations, with community and religious organizations, with school boards and city councils, and focuses on consumer health as well as labor conditions. Health, in the face of pesticide use, is an issue that transcends social boundaries and provides a unique space for communication and coalition.

Lin Nelson's "The Place of Women in Polluted Places" explains that "health as an ecological process is the visceral daily reality that forces us to face the crossroads at the end of the twentieth century."[11] The article looks at various ways in which women, ecology, and health are related. Some of the angles she looks at include environmental illness, reproductive hazards and fetal protection policies, mothers of children exposed to toxics, women as test objects, women polluters and women in complicity with polluters, activists and kitchen-table researchers. Nelson suggests that women have many places in our social ecology, places that we must explore.

If we recognize that women are in many places, we have little need for monolithic categories such as "woman." The concept of ecology can guide us in our attempts to see how our different places are connected. Ecology helps explain the various oppressions women face as a network, as a web, without ranking and without additive approaches.[12] An ecologist cannot just add up the parts of a pond and think she is coming close to describing that ecosystem and how it functions. A fish in a pond and a fish in an ocean, looked at ecologically, must be understood as inhabiting different, maybe similar but not the same, places. Likewise, women are in different places: in pesticide-sprayed fields, in supermarkets, in agribusiness management. Women are also in different places in terms of class, race, sexuality, culture, and age. Whether I am in a field or an office, what I do there, my niche, is at least partially determined by the interconnection of societal environmental factors. My position when choosing whether or not to eat a grape at a friend's house is not the same as that of the worker who picked and packed that grape. But our positions are connected, and in more than one way. Furthermore, our respective positions are not determined simply by sex or sexism or women's relation to nature. If so, we'd be in the same place. Or that farm worker would have to be male (but then why do I seem to be in the better position?). Obviously there are many factors at work, intersecting in many ways. By using ecology as a model for understanding connections and diversity, ecofeminism can be transformative. Thinking ecologically thus helps me to include supporting the UFW grape boycott as a part of my understanding of ecofeminism and makes an examination of the boycott a critical educational opportunity for ecofeminism.

In her examination of women's many places, Nelson is particularly concerned with women who would not label themselves "ecofeminist" (probably never heard the term), "feminist," or "ecologist"—yet "without these women we would have no resistance and little knowledge about what ails us."[13] Many farm worker women are these women; many UFW women are these women. The fact that they fight in association with men, are concerned about men's health too, certainly should not make their experiences, their knowledge, their leadership, less important to ecofeminism.

Nelson concludes that "we must not, and we must not let others, ghettoize environmental health as a 'women's problem'" and that "our sense of ecology must include where people spend most of their waking hours—the workplace."[14] Certainly the UFW has been a leader in both of these areas. The UFW's focus on environmental health as a concern to both consumers and laborers, as well as their concern for men, women, and children in the fields and living near farms, is a strategy to counter ghettoization—whether by sex, ethnicity, or occupation. The focus of the grape boycott can be summarized as "Our concerns are yours too." The problem of pesticides does not stop at the harvest, does not affect only fieldhands. And, even more clearly, the UFW has been a leader in making the workplace part of ecology. From the earliest bans on DDT, Dieldren, and Aldrin (in 1970, years before the federal government acted), to the present campaign to ban Captan, Parathion, Phosdrin, Dinoseb, and methyl bromide,[15] the UFW has been a leader in fighting for an ecologically safer and healthier workplace. Thus, ecofeminism can certainly learn from the UFW, as our literature says now what the union has demonstrated for years.

The UFW has a strong history of fighting, one ecofeminist women and men can learn from. Its grape boycott is a movement that not only addresses the various exploitations involved in farm labor but also has an expanded vision that confronts the many ways the capitalist agribusiness structure oppresses people throughout the system. The connection of exploitations is the baseline of the grape boycott. From studying this movement and participating in it, ecofeminists learn more about how oppressions are related and how to fight domination.

The UFW grape boycott asks consumers not to buy California table grapes until the growers agree to the elimination of dangerous pesticides from all grape fields, a joint testing program for poisonous substances in grapes sold in stores, free and fair elections for farm workers, and good-faith collective bargaining in the grape industry. The UFW brings together consumers and laborers, consumer and labor issues, with these three demands. A UFW brochure asks consumers, "What Do You and a Farm Worker Have in Common?" and then answers, "Exposure to Poisonous Chemicals!"[16] Health concerns about pesticide oppression are the explicit connection that the UFW focuses upon to unify consumer and laborer.

The UFW film *The Wrath of Grapes* (1986) points out that the farm workers are the canaries for all of us. Just as canaries in cages were lowered into the ground so that their death from bad gases would warn miners that the mine was unsafe, so farm workers are indicators of the toxicity of pesticides. According to the UFW,

> 78% of Texas farm workers surveyed had chronic skin rashes; 56% had kidney and liver abnormalities; and 54% suffered from chest cavity problems. . . . The miscarriage rate for female farm workers is 7 times the national average. . . . More than 300,000 farm workers are made ill every year through pesticide exposure.[17]

The UFW alerts consumers that a great deal of this poison cannot be washed off, thus suggesting that consumers should pay close attention to farm workers' concerns. Throughout their literature, the UFW links the worker in the field and the consumer in the grocery store through the common threat of pesticides, and educates consumers about pesticides and the toxic dangers workers and consumers face. For instance:

> 344,000 pounds [of Captan] are used annually on table grapes, and residue of this compound is the most frequently discovered material on grapes in stores. Not only can Captan cause cancer, it also causes birth defects and changes in body cells. It is structurally similar to Thalidomide, which caused thousands of babies in Europe to be born without arms and legs.[18]

This theme, found throughout UFW literature, is an attempt to break down the barriers of capitalist-industrial society, to reveal a hidden social ecology, and to forge opposition to the current oppressive system of agriculture.

Besides connecting consumer and labor interests, the UFW also makes connections with larger environmental issues and community-organized environmental movements:

> Parathion and Phosdrin . . . can be rapidly fatal, producing illnesses in workers in as little as 20 minutes. Usually sprayed aerially, these poisons cause populations surrounding agricultural areas the same problems as they cause farm workers, since as much as 90% of aerially sprayed pesticides miss their target area. . . . Pesticides are now thought responsible for groundwater contamination in 23 states . . . and groundwater provides 50% of our country's drinking water supply.[19]

By incorporating information about resource and environmental pollution into the arguments about worker health, the UFW specifically allies itself with more conventional environmental and conservation causes. Again, this type of argument is meant to break down walls of classism and racism and evoke a true sympathy between farm workers and the rest of us.

*The Wrath of Grapes* and UFW newsletters publicize those central California valley towns where children, in the 1980s became the flags of cancer clusters. In McFarland, eleven children living within six blocks of each other were found to have cancer. In Fowler, a town of 3,000, there were seven children with cancer. More recently, a third community, Earlimart, was identified as yet another cluster site. Here the UFW believes the incidence of cancer is 1,200 times the "normal" rate.[20] With these stories of poisoned children, the UFW incorporates maternalism, and parentalism, into its multifaceted environmental politics, but as a partial strategy that does not exclude women, and men, in their other roles. As ecofeminists struggle with interpretations of the meanings of nurturance, the significance of reproduction, and the usefulness of metaphors such as "Mother Earth," we need to look around us for examples of how other groups have used maternalism and parentalism. In particular, we need to be able to fully integrate maternalism into our theories without making it the core of ecofeminism. Relating workers in the fields, consumers in the stores, and children in the neighborhoods, the UFW's educational and fundraising material points to many connections between various environmental and health crises by illustrating several ways and places in which pesticides affect our lives.

The UFW's experience in dealing with California agribusiness has potential repercussions and affinities worldwide. Vandana Shiva's study of women and development in India, *Staying Alive: Women, Ecology and Development*, shows the full scope of agribusiness. She explains how "twenty years ago, forty centuries of knowledge of agriculture began to be eroded and erased as the green revolution, designed by multinational corporations and western male experts, homogenised nature's diversity and the diversity of human knowledge on a reductionist pattern of agriculture."[21]

Agriculture is a primary category of internationalized capitalism, along with electronics, the sex trade, and handicrafts production.[22] Much U.S. food comes from exploitation of Third World people and land. Many of us became aware of where beef came from through concern over the tropical rainforests. Other luxury foods, many of them fruits, are grown in huge plantations, from the Caribbean (continuing from the days of the African slave trade) to the Philippines. In the 1960s a lot of U.S. fruit companies moved south of the border, trying for a longer growing (and selling) season so Americans could eat (and buy) fresh strawberries in the winter. They were additionally motivated by the fact that "irrigation water, land, and labor were much cheaper in Mexico than in the United States. There were also fewer restrictions concerning the use of pesticides and fertilizers than in the United States. Even though most of the mechanical equipment had to be imported from the United States, it was the Mexican farm owner or manager who paid for this, not the fruit company."[23] The UFW negotiates a difficult path through this web of internationalized agriculture.

One of the United States' most important agricultural producing areas is California, also the home of the UFW. Mainly fruit and vegetable crops are grown there, and many farm workers are needed during the critical seasons. California has bright sun and flat and fertile land, but instead of coming in the growing season, California rain falls in the winter.[24] The answer to this dilemma was and is irrigation. In 1987 the national census of agriculture counted over 17 million acres of irrigated farmland in California.[25] What does irrigation mean to this land and the people working it?

Donald Worster, author of *Rivers of Empire: Water, Aridity, and the Growth of the American West*, argues that the West is "a culture and society built on, and absolutely dependent on, a sharply alienating, intensely managerial relationship with nature."[26] Throughout the book he traces the promises of irrigation as democratizer of resources into the realities of empire wherein the power elite of the capitalist state apparatus "go on appropriating every available drop of water for its canals and pipelines, while providing the masses with a few dribbles to support them in their managed oasis life,"[27] and wherein the water is poisoned with pesticides, salinized, and simply disappearing. In the San Joaquin Valley of California, 1981 saw 400,000 acres of brackish water tables heralding the threat of desertification of a million acres within a hundred years. The danger salinization poses to life was also illustrated by the discovery, in 1983, of fledgling coots, stilts, grebes, and ducks with stumps for feet and missing eyes and beaks, dying soon after birth in the Kesterson National Wildlife Refuge. It was revealed that the "birds were the victims of selenium compounds and other salts leaching from nearby irrigated fields."[28]

After organizing irrigation, farmers established cooperative marketing and then coordinated "labor recruitment and control."[29] Once expensively constructed water systems mandated cash-cropping, California began to specialize in high-profit crops that created the need "for harvest hands who would come running, get the crop in efficiently, and then leave before they became a useless burden on a grower's income."[30]

In "The Ecology of Feminism and the Feminism of Ecology," Ynestra King speaks of an ecofeminist belief in a "healthy, balanced ecosystem, including human and nonhuman inhabitants, [which] must maintain diversity."[31] She explains further:

Ecologically, environmental simplification is as significant a problem as environmental pollution. Biological simplification, i.e., the wiping out of whole species, corresponds to reducing human diversity into faceless workers, or to the homogenization of taste [e.g., no sour grapes] and culture through mass consumer markets. Social life and natural life are literally simplified to the inorganic for the convenience of market society.[32]

The connection between the monocultures in the fields and the mono-cultures in the stores is forged through the capitalist creation of faceless workers. In industrial capitalist agriculture this is especially clear in the case of seasonal farm workers. Not only are workers disempowered and faceless, but, if the system could have its way, workers would be bodyless during off-peak seasons. And so we must all listen to the farm workers who have been putting together the interests of the worker, the consumer, and the environment, symbolized and actualized most potently by pesticides. Pesticides and farm workers are presently used as controllable and manu-factured inputs designed to produce standardized and profitable goods. The land and the people working the land are used, but not replenished or nurtured. Compost for soil and prenatal care for workers and their children are not considered worthwhile in the prevailing narrow economic view of agriculture. The exploitation of farm workers is clearly related to patterns of natural resource abuse. Farm workers' lives and bodies demonstrate the interconnections of ecology and social justice that ecofeminism seeks to understand.

In California (at least), the history of farm labor can be examined in terms of changing tides of exploitable immigrant labor that have been played against each other, sometimes to the benefit of one ethnic group over another, always to the benefit of the capitalist agricultural state system.[33] Today in California most farm workers are Chicano, as yesterday they were Chinese, Japanese, Mexican, Filipino, or white Dust Bowl refugees. The main concern of agriculturalists was always to have a large supply of cheap and amenable labor. If labor seemed to be gaining strength through labor movements or ethnic solidarity, business interests were threatened. The UFW came into being toward the end of the Bracero era (1942–1964), a period of government and agribusiness importation of Mexican labor to bring down and keep down farm workers' wages and ensure control. Just as big business plays American workers against their Third World counter-parts by moving operations to cheap-labor free-trade zones, so agribusi-ness brought in floods of poor potential laborers to keep all farm labor cheap and under control. In fact, the *maquiladora* system of twin factories (officially known as the Border Industrialization Program) that now lines the Mexican–U.S. border began in 1965 as an incentive to the Mexican government to agree to the ending of the Bracero program.[34]

The dangers to which farm workers are subjected, and which the UFW addresses, obviously include more than pesticide issues. The UFW is a labor organization confronting the fact that "farm workers are the poorest workers in America. Our members not only do the most dangerous work in the country . . . they also receive the lowest wages."[35] The UFW seems to downplay economic issues when going after public support, yet acknowledges them as baseline when, for instance, Cesar Chavez, organizer and leader of the UFW, says in the literature, "I'm sure I don't have to tell you that farm workers are the poorest workers in America."[36] The farm worker force is poor, primarily people of color; the owners are increasingly wealthy, increasingly absentee.[37]

Mechanization also threatens farm workers. Worster notes that the successes of the UFW[38] through the seventies created a backlash of mechanization.[39] " 'The machine won't strike,' noted the chairman of an engineering department at the University of California at Davis . . . , 'it will work when [the growers] want it to work.' "[40] Worster connects increasing mechanization to the totalization of the process of dominating the earth. "If one could make water run uphill for hundreds of miles, one could do more, much more. One could turn over the whole job of irrigated cropping to genetics, to electronics, to robotics, doing away with the need for almost all field labor, completing man's triumph over the desert."[41] The UFW's fight to hold on to jobs, and to make the jobs better, is connected through such American icons as the rubber tomato, designed for mechanized picking rather than good eating, to ecological justice. The expensive machines of mechanized picking are available only to the biggest and wealthiest growers, so smaller farmers are forced out, monoculture increases, and genetic diversity shrinks.

The history of capitalism has been one of shifting control over knowledge and skills from workers to capitalists. The removal of skills from work leads to lower wages and decreased security for workers and increasingly centralized power for capitalists/growers. Working people become "factors of production and instruments of capital."[42] Growers have been willing to increase wages occasionally, but have fought much harder on issues like pesticide use that directly impinge on the right of management to control. Linda and Theo Majka, farm labor historians, conclude that pursuit of

control issues . . . has placed farm workers in an offensive rather than defensive position; it raised consciousness and increased workers' competence and knowledge of the agribusiness system. . . . The struggle for pesticide restrictions, the hiring hall, and the elimination of the labor contractor have not aimed to abolish profits or give political control to the working class. Where successfully implemented, however, they have provided a meaningful link between the union's daily actions and the goals of reducing exploitation, guaranteeing stable employment, elevating the standard of living, and eroding the domination of grower profit over the human needs of workers.[43]

Thus the Majka analysis, without being ecologically motivated or concerned with the connections the boycott attempts to build around pesticide issues, nonetheless reveals the deep threat that even a small fight for control poses to the domination complex of capitalist agribusiness. Despite the fact that they are "low-skilled workers" and supposed to be almost "exclusively concerned with wage issues," the UFW has elaborated control issues to "an unprecedented extent," consistently fighting on such issues as job safety, work timing and production levels, tools and equipment, hiring and seniority, labor camp conditions, pesticide bans.[44] If domination is about control—control of nature, of women, of poor people—then the fight to end domination must confront issues of control, must try to regain autonomy, self-control.

The UFW, with the leadership of Cesar Chavez and Dolores Huerta (the union's first vice president and chief contract negotiator),[45] has always used nontraditional labor tactics to improve the lot of farm workers. Chavez, Huerta, and Gilbert Padilla (a later vice president) had worked as community organizers for the Community Service Organization before turning to farm worker issues. In 1962 Chavez began organizing the National Farm Workers Association (NFWA), forerunner of the UFW. Three years later, the union faced its first big test: a strike in the Delano area, center of table grape operations and a region with many resident farm workers.[46] Even in this first effort, Chavez and the NFWA actively sought outside support from students and the media. To back up the strike, the union called for a boycott, concentrating its attention on Schenley Liquor and later DiGiorgio (with its subsidiaries S & W Fine Foods and TreeSweet Products). After Schenley gave in, DiGiorgio tried to bring in Teamster unionization to crush the NFWA. The NFWA then merged with the Filipino group AWOC (Agricultural Workers Organizing Committee) and affiliated with the AFL-CIO under the name NFWA-UFWOC; in 1972 they officially became the United Farm Workers of America.[47] NFWA-UFWOC won the elections over the corporate-sponsored Teamsters.

Through the late 1960s and 1970, UFWOC concentrated on organizing the table grape segment of California agribusiness. The boycott of table grapes was built with boycott organizations and committees across the country. Help came from other unions, religious and civic organizations, and individuals. New York grape sales dropped 90 percent in the summer of 1968.[48] Chavez fasted, committing himself further to a "Gandhian nonviolent militance."[49] Anti-boycott activities included a sudden increase (from 555,000 to 2,167,000 pounds in a single year) in Defense Department purchases of grapes to ship to Vietnam.[50] In 1969 the union began to make the pesticide connection, getting increasing reports of worker illness from contamination and connecting this information to tests on grapes in stores that showed residues of Aldrin (later banned by the Food and Drug Administration as a carcinogen).[51]

The boycott is one of the alternative strategies used successfully by the UFW. The boycott, like the march, like the fast, has been used successfully many times in this century in struggles for social change. Gandhi led India to independence with boycotts and marches. The Indian salt march, for instance, protested against British attempts to monopolize the production of salt for their profit, a part of the British exploitation and domination of India and Indian people. Martin Luther King and the American civil rights movement used marches and boycotts to fight segregation of schools, restaurants, and buses. Gandhi, Andrei Sakharov, members of the Irish Republican Army, and woman suffragists have gone on hunger strikes or fasts, often when imprisoned, to raise public consciousness and to force the government to respond. Cesar Chavez and the UFW have successfully converted these methods to the farm labor movement. The use of these tactics illustrates the broader political nature of the UFW.

In 1966 Chavez led the UFW version of the Freedom March and the Indian salt march. The farm workers' march was called a *peregrinación* and was wrapped up in religious and cultural connotations. Led by la Virgen de Guadalupe, patron saint of the *campesinos,* the march was penitential and set to arrive in Sacramento on Easter Sunday. Besides being a labor action, the march was an affirmation of the cultural values of Chicanos, a statement of resistance to racism as well as economic oppression. As Gloria Anzaldúa writes, "Chicanos did not know we were a people until 1965 when Cesar Chavez and the farm workers united and *I Am Joaquin* was published and *la Raza Unida* party was formed in Texas." "Chicano," she observes, specifically refers "to a politically aware people."[52]

The boycott is a more practical labor tool for the farm workers than the strike alone. The effectiveness of the strike tool for farm workers has often been undermined by the readily available pool of replacement workers and strikebreakers that agribusiness has used to undercut potential reforms.

The boycott, as used by the UFW over the last twenty-five years, is also necessary and sometimes successful because of the corporate, diversified, and fragmentary nature of modern agribusiness. In the mid-1960s the UFW won some relatively quick victories because it was able to latch on to the Schenley Industries Scotch and Bourbon Corporation, which as a corporate giant stood to lose more in bad grape publicity than it would gain in worker exploitation. Other battles, too, the UFW won and lost as a result of the mobile nature of capital interests. During the 1979 lettuce strikes, a threat to boycott Chiquita Bananas in order to increase pressure on Sun Harvest, the United Brands subsidiary that grew lettuce, helped get a good union contract settlement quickly. But within a few years Sun Harvest went out of business, and the contract died with it.

The boycott is also a more effective tool than the strike for the UFW because many farm workers cannot afford, financially or legally, to become involved in strikes. Because much of the work is seasonal, farm workers are under pressure to make as much money as they can when work is available. Additionally, since many farm-working families include members who are not in the United States legally, there is extra pressure to keep quiet and play by the growers' rules. When people risk being stopped and checked in the supermarket or on the highway just because of how they look or speak, they often cannot afford to call attention to themselves by protesting against conditions. The UFW's use of boycotts puts pressure on the growers and the industry while protecting the farm workers from some direct attacks. For organizing farm workers or voting for the UFW can be dangerous. When Chavez received the Gandhi Peace Award in May 1989, he accepted it on behalf of five UFW martyrs killed in the last twenty years: Nan Freeman, Nagi Daifallah, Juan de la Cruz, Rufino Contreras, and, most recently, Rene Lopez.[53]

Boycotts are feminist tools also. At the end of *Patriarchy and Accumulation on a World Scale*, a book that pulls together ecofeminist analyses of the destruction of European witches, the creation of modern Western science and capitalism, and the colonialist conquest of most of the non-European world, Maria Mies includes a chapter entitled "Towards a Feminist Perspective of a New Society." This chapter deals with the question of activism, of feminist practice. In a discussion of intermediate steps, steps in which we begin to refuse our allegiance to and complicity with the existing destructive order, steps that begin to get us from here to there, Mies advocates boycotts as a path of conscientization that can "revive awareness of all exploitative relations in the commodities."[54] In so doing, boycotts can link the self-interest of the consumer to the exploitation of others and allow consumers to address their own role in exploitative systems. The generic "consumer" is a feminized position, a category still populated largely by women. As an example, Mies mentions boycotting Unilever cosmetics as a statement about sexist images of women, exploitation of tribal women in India, and the torture of lab animals. Mies sees the boycott path as "a de-mystification of the commodities, a re-discovery of the exploitation of women, nature, colonies, inherent in these commodities, and an effort to transform the market relations which link us de facto to women, men, animals, plants, the earth, etc., into true human relations."[55] Eventually boycotts should lead to increasing worker and consumer control over production decisions.

A weakness in Mies's discussion is that, because she is consciously speaking to Western feminists about what they can do, the consumer seems to be the more active party.[56] But, generally speaking, boycotts are going to affect the people involved in production much more than the consumers. Therefore, boycott decision making and leadership must come from within the most exploited group, the group with more to lose and more to gain. The grape boycott is farm worker–led and organized. Farm workers are pointing out to the rest of us the exploitative relations inherent in the production of California table grapes, pointing out the true sourness in the grapes, and working to transform the oppressive market relations into better human and ecological ones.

The more I listen to the UFW, the more I can taste the sour grapes, the more I become sour myself. The UFW exposes the *carrilla,* the pressure, growers use to force workers to meet unreasonable quotas by starting early and quitting late, by working through lunch and rest breaks, and by not going to the bathroom. Portable toilets often are not accessible, clean, or provided with toilet paper. The inconvenience is particularly problematic for women, but there is more than inconvenience involved. At least one farm worker was forced to abort her pregnancy because she had used some grape-packing paper that turned out to be treated with "medicine"—that is, pesticide—when there was no toilet paper available.[57] Many women are sexually harassed by foremen and can lose their jobs for resisting the boss's advances. Often workers have to give bribes to supervisors. In August 1989 the UFW sponsored a conference and speak-out about conditions. Five hundred came to share stories about *carrilla,* sexual harassment, poor sanitary conditions, and pesticides.[58] The Farm Worker Education and Legal

Defense Fund and the UFW filed lawsuits in October 1989 on behalf of workers at several vineyards.[59]

These varied forms of systemic violence and exploitation on an everyday basis are symptomatic of a racist, classist, sexist society. As Dolores Huerta explains in the film *Troubled Harvest* (1990),[60] people of color in the United States suffer from racial discrimination as well as economic discrimination and develop psychological scars from racism, but working with/in the UFW helps Chicano people realize that there is nothing wrong with them. Anzaldúa's poem *"sus plumas el viento"* tells of a farm worker and her lack of access to real choices; one section describes her situation:

> Burlap sack wet around her waist,
> stained green from leaves and the smears of worms.
> White heat no water no place to pee
> the men staring at her ass.
>
> *Como una mula,*
> she shifts 150 pounds of cotton onto her back.
> It's either *las labores*
> or feet soaking in cold puddles *en bodegas*
> cutting          washing          weighing          packaging
> broccoli spears carrots cabbages in 12 hours          15
> double shift the roar of machines inside her head.
> She can always clean shit
> out of white folks' toilets—the Mexican maid.
> You're respected if you can use your head
> instead of your back, the women said.
> *Ay m'ijos, ojala que hallen trabajo*
> in air-conditioned offices.[61]

This poem, with its objective and not-pretty picture of a female farm laborer's day, bluntly illustrates many reasons for women farm workers' involvement in the UFW. From this vantage, ecology is not a concern for romanticized nature; it is about transforming drudgery into respected and healthful occupations.

Many farm worker families live in migrant camps or, increasingly, in their cars or fields.[62] Camp conditions often leave a great deal to be desired. Workers may have running water, but they do not know if it is free of pesticide contamination. Keeping field clothes away from dishes and other clothes is often difficult, and of course means extra work for women. For those without camps:

> This is the life of the working homeless: laboring nine or ten hours in the hot sun for about $15; washing in a drainage ditch or, if they are lucky, in a public restroom; eating out of cans in makeshift kitchens; sleeping in cars, under vines, anywhere they can; worrying about food and shelter, about their health and pesticides, about the future.[63]

The issues farm workers are concerned about are ones we should all be concerned about: health, poverty, racism, working conditions, and pollution, as well as sexism. The UFW's grape boycott is not the solution to all these problems. But it is a good intermediate step worth the investment of ecofeminist time, energy, and interest. Because so many issues intersect within the oppressions faced by farm workers, we can begin to confront the many systems of domination that structure society through participating in the grape boycott and through studying acknowledged leaders like the UFW.

Many of Anzaldúa's poems in *Borderlands* illustrate the terror of racism and sexism, as well their connections to imperialism, capital accumulation, and attitudes about the land. For instance, "We Call Them Greasers"[64] devastatingly relates the oppressor's view of rape, lynching, and murder as justified by the worthlessness of people who "weren't interested in bettering themselves, why they didn't even own the land but shared it." Her poems illustrate just a little of the complexity of relationships between women and nature: a complexity influenced by history, by cultural values, by racism, by sexism, by capitalism, by innumerable factors. Indeed, women are in many polluted places, facing many pollutions. Ecofeminism must listen to all these voices and hear their truths in order to be truly transformative.

As an ecofeminist I need to know not only Rachel Carson's contributions to publicizing the dangers of DDT, but also that the United Farm Workers got the first bans on DDT, DDE, and Dieldren instituted in UFW-contracted fields. With guides to socially responsible investment and green consumption increasing in popularity, all people must acknowledge the UFW's leadership in developing these strategies for creating a better world. When I consider the variety of sponsors and supporters of the grape boycott—people of many races, religions, and organizations—I see further evidence that the UFW has a lot to teach about successful coalition politics. Today I need to know that the UFW is continuing to develop as a leader in the area of social ecology and green expertise. For instance, the UFW

> has a seven-acre demonstration farm on which farmworker families learn how to make the small plots surrounding their homes more productive. Rebecca Flores-Harrington, a UFW organizer, stresses that the key to success for their experiment lies in being able to make money for poor people to live on. "When people see that you can do that, they will get serious about this organic farming."[65]

In addition, the UFW has helped Los Angeles and Orange County citizens protesting against malathion spraying.[66] The UFW's commitment to uncovering and fighting oppression as a system of exploitative relationships has put it at the forefront of ecological politics. The grape boycott is an action we can all support and learn from as our struggle(s) to end oppression continue along many paths, through many fields. *Viva la Causa!*

\*   \*   \*

A sour grape is a prism. The UFW boycott holds the grape up high so the sun can stream through it and reveal the cross-currents of our society flavoring the fruit. See the glitter of industrial capitalism, the dust of degraded soils, the poverty of hard-working people, the shrinking spectrum of life. See the poisons flowing into the water, into the animals, and into our mouths.

Now put the grape to your eye and take a look at ecofeminism. What do you see? Is it easy to focus? Do you get only one picture? Hold the grape there for a minute and think about what you can see. Sure, everything looks different. Maybe you are getting multiple images when you try to focus on the woman/nature connection. Maybe the ecology you are seeing does not quite fit your old definition. Maybe you can see a little bit more.

### NOTES

1. United Farm Workers, Summer 1989 fundraising letter, p. 2.

2. Karen Warren, "Feminism and Ecology: Making Connections," *Environmental Ethics* 9 (1987) : 17–20.

3. Ibid., 18. Warren cites bell hooks, *Feminist Theory: From Margin to Center* (Boston: South End Press, 1984), 17–31; "The Combahee River Collective Statement," in *Home Girls: A Black Feminist Anthology*, Barbara Smith, ed. (New York:

Kitchen Table Women of Color Press, 1983), 272; Gita Sen and Caren Grown, *Development, Crises and Alternative Visions: Third World Women's Perspectives* (New Delhi: DAWN, 1985; New York: Monthly Review Press, 1987), 13.

4. Zuleyma Tang Halpin, "Scientific Objectivity and the Concept of 'The Other,'" *Women's Studies International Forum* 12 (1989) : 286.

5. On the concept of multiplicity, see, for instance, Deborah K. King, "Multiple Jeopardy, Multiple Consciousness: The Context of a Black Feminist Ideology," in *Feminist Theory in Practice and Process*, ed. Micheline R. Malson, Jean F. O'Barr, Sarah Westphal-Wihl, and Mary Wyer *Feminist Theory in Practice and Process* (Chicago: University of Chicago Press, 1989), 75–105.

6. Warren, "Feminism and Ecology," 18.

7. Ibid., 19.

8. Lee Quinby, "Ecofeminism and the Politics of Resistance," in *Reweaving the World: The Emergence of Ecofeminism*, ed. Irene Diamond and Gloria Feman Orenstein (San Francisco: Sierra Club Books, 1990), 127.

9. Gloria Anzaldúa, *Borderlands/La Frontera: The New Mestiza* (San Francisco: Spinsters/Aunt Lute, 1987), 85.

10. Ibid.

11. Lin Nelson, "The Place of Women in Polluted Places," in Diamond and Orenstein, *Reweaving the World*, 175.

12. King, "Multiple Jeopardy," 80.

13. Nelson, "The Place of Women," 175.

14. Ibid., 185.

15. United Farm Workers of America, AFL-CIO, "Straight Talk on the Fresh Grape Boycott" (New York: UFW, AFL-CIO, n.d.).

16. UFW, "What Do You and a Farm Worker Have in Common?" brochure (New York: UFW, n.d.).

17. UFW, Summer 1989 fundraising letter, 3.

18. Ibid., 2.

19. Ibid., 2–3.

20. UFW, "UFW Finds Cancer in Earlimart," *Food and Justice* 6 (November 1989): 3.

21. Vandana Shiva, *Staying Alive: Women, Ecology and Development* (Atlantic Highlands, N.J., and London: Zed Books, 1989), 98–99.

22. Maria Mies, *Patriarchy and Accumulation on a World Scale* (Atlantic Highlands, N.J., and London: Zed Books, 1986), 127.

23. Sonja Williams, *Exploding the Hunger Myths: A High School Curriculum* (San Francisco: Institute for Food and Development Policy, 1987), 106.

24. Donald Worster, *Rivers of Empire: Water, Aridity, and the Growth of the American West* (New York: Pantheon Books, 1985), 98.

25. *Statistical Abstract of the United States 1990* (Washington, D.C.: U.S. Government, Department of Commerce, 1990), 643, chart 1112.

26. Worster, *Rivers of Empire*, 5.

27. Ibid., 330.

28. Ibid., 323.

29. Ibid., 215.

30. Ibid., 218–19.

31. Ynestra King, "The Ecology of Feminism and the Feminism of Ecology," in *Healing the Wounds: The Promise of Ecofeminism*, ed. Judith Plant (Philadelphia: New Society, 1989), 20.

32. Ibid.

33. See, for example, Linda C. Majka and Theo J. Majka, *Farm Workers, Agribusiness, and the State* (Philadelphia: Temple University Press, 1982).

34. Fuentes, 27–28.

35. UFW, Summer 1989 fundraising letter, 4.

36. Ibid.

37. See, for example, Bruce W. Marion, *The Organization and Performance of the U.S. Food System* (Lexington, Mass.: D. C. Heath, 1986), 22–23, for statistics showing that 49 percent of U.S. farm production as of 1982 occurred on "larger than single family farms, with sales of at least $200,000," and that as of 1978 only one-third of U.S. farms were operated by their owners.

38. And its earlier constitution, the National Farm Workers Association.

39. Worster, *Rivers of Empire*, 296.

40. Ibid., 297. Worster cites Bernard Taper, "The Bittersweet Harvest," *Science 80* (November 1980): 82.

41. Worster, *Rivers of Empire*, 297.

42. Theo Majka and Linda Majka, "Power, Insurgency," 9, analysis cited there as drawing from Harry Braverman, *Labor and Monopoly Capital: The Degradation of Work in the Twentieth Century* (New York: Monthly Review, 1974), 113–19; David Brody, *Workers in Industrial America* (New York: Oxford, 1980), 9–14; David Montgomery, *Workers' Control in America* (New York: Cambridge University Press, 1979), 101–3.

43. Majka and Majka, *Farm Workers, Agribusiness, and the State*, 282–83.

44. Ibid., 7.

45. Ibid., 170.

46. Ibid.

47. Ibid., 182–83.

48. Ibid., 188.

49. Ibid., 189.

50. Ibid., 193.

51. Ibid., 194.

52. Anzaldúa, *Borderlands/La Frontera*, 63.

53. Cesar Chavez, "The Core of Nonviolence," speech excerpt printed in the *Catholic Worker* 57 (June–July 1990).

54. Mies, *Patriarchy and Accumulation*, 224, 227. "Conscientization" is the English version of Paulo Freire's word *conscientizacão,* meaning "learning to perceive social, political and economic contradictions and to take action against the oppressive elements of reality," according to an editor's note in Maria Mies, "Towards a Methodology for Feminist Research," in *Theories of Women's Studies*, ed. Gloria Bowles and Renate Duelli Klein (Boston: Routledge & Kegan Paul, 1983), 126.

55. Mies, *Patriarchy and Accumulation*, 227.

56. This is not a weakness found in her other work, such as "Towards a Methodology for Feminist Research."

57. "Victims of Carrilla," *Food and Justice* (magazine of the United Farm Workers of America, AFL-CIO) 7 (January 1990): 5.

58. "Law Suits Expose Unsanitary, Slave-like Conditions in California Grape Fields," *Food and Justice* 7 (January 1990): 8.

59. "News from UFW," press release, October 25, 1989.

60. *Troubled Harvest* (film), Rainbow Film and Video Production, 1990.

61. Anzaldúa, *Borderlands/La Frontera*, 117–18.

62. "While the Rich Get Richer," *Food and Justice* 6 (September 1989): 8–9.

63. Ibid., 9.

64. Anzaldúa, *Borderlands/La Frontera*, 134–35.

65. Emma Torres, "Traditional Culture, New Agriculture," *Green Letter in Search of Greener Times* 6 (Winter 1990): 19.

66. Ibid.

# CHAPTER 7

# Animal Rights
# and Feminist Theory

## Josephine Donovan

Peter Singer prefaces his groundbreaking treatise *Animal Liberation* (1975) with an anecdote about a visit he and his wife made to the home of a woman who claimed to love animals, had heard he was writing a book on the subject, and so invited him to tea. Singer's attitude toward the woman is contemptuous: she had invited a friend who also loved animals and was "keen to meet us. When we arrived our hostess's friend was already there, and . . . certainly was keen to talk about animals. 'I do love animals,' she began . . . and she was off. She paused while refreshments were served, took a ham sandwich, and then asked us what pets we had."[1] Singer's point is not only to condemn the woman's hypocrisy in claiming to love animals while she was eating meat but also to dissociate himself from a sentimentalist approach to animal welfare. Speaking for his wife as well, he explains: "We were not especially 'interested in' animals. Neither of us had ever been inordinately fond of dogs, cats, or horses. . . . We didn't 'love' animals. . . . The portrayal of those who protest against cruelty to animals as sentimental, emotional 'animal lovers' [has meant] excluding the entire issue . . . from serious political and moral discussion." In other words, he fears that to associate the animal rights cause with "womanish" sentiment is to trivialize it.[2]

Singer's concerns about the image and strategies of animal rights activists are shared by another major contemporary theorist of animal rights, Tom Regan. In his preface to *The Case for Animal Rights* (1983), Regan stresses that "since all who work on behalf of the interests of animals are . . . familiar with the tired charge of being 'irrational,' 'sentimental,' 'emo-

*Source:* Reprinted from *Signs: Journal of Women in Culture and Society* 1990, vol. 15, no. 2. Published by and © 1990 by The University of Chicago. All rights reserved.

tional,' or worse, we can give the lie to these accusations only by making a concerted effort not to indulge our emotions or parade our sentiments. And that requires making a sustained commitment to rational inquiry."[3] In a later article Regan defends himself against charges of being hyperrational by maintaining that "reason—not sentiment, not emotion—reason compels us to recognize the equal inherent value of . . . animals and . . . their equal right to be treated with respect."[4] Regan's and Singer's rejection of emotion and their concern about being branded sentimentalist are not accidental; rather, they expose the inherent bias in contemporary animal rights theory toward rationalism, which, paradoxically, in the form of Cartesian objectivism, established a major theoretical justification for animal abuse.

Women animal rights theorists seem, indeed, to have developed more of a sense of emotional bonding with animals as the basis for their theory than is evident in the male literature. Mary Midgley, for example, another contemporary animal rights theorist, urges, "What makes our fellow beings entitled to basic consideration is surely not intellectual capacity but emotional fellowship." Animals, she notes, exhibit "social and emotional complexity of the kind which is expressed by the formation of deep, subtle and lasting relationships."[5] Constantia Salamone, a leading feminist animal rights activist, roundly condemns the rationalist, masculinist bias of current animal rights theory.[6] In the nineteenth century, women activists in the anti-vivisection movement, such as Frances Power Cobbe, viewed as their enemy the " 'coldly rational materialism' " of science, which they saw as threatening " 'to freeze human emotion and sensibility. . . . Antivivisection . . . shielded the heart, the human spirit, from degradation at the hands of heartless science.' "[7]

Yet Singer's anecdote points up that one cannot simply turn uncritically to women as a group or to a female value system as a source for a humane relationship ethic with animals. While women have undoubtedly been less guilty of active abuse and destruction of animals than men (Virginia Woolf observes in *Three Guineas*: "The vast majority of birds and beasts have been killed by you; not by us"),[8] they nevertheless have been complicit in that abuse, largely in their use of luxury items that entail animal pain and destruction (such as furs) and in their consumption of meat. Charlotte Perkins Gilman, an animal welfare crusader as well as a feminist, criticized such hypocrisy decades before Singer in "A Study in Ethics" (1933). Condemning women's habit of wearing "as decoration the carcass of the animal," Gilman remarks the shocking inconsistency that "civilized Christian women, sensitive to cruelty, fond of pets, should willingly maintain the greatest possible cruelty to millions of harmless little animals. . . . Furs are obtained by trapping. Trapping means every agony known to an animal, imprisonment, starvation, freezing, frantic fear and pain. If one woman hung up or fastened down hundreds of kittens each by one paw in her backyard in winter weather, to struggle and dangle and freeze, to cry in anguish and terror that she might 'trim' something with their collected skins . . . she would be considered a monster."[9] Recognizing that such problems are involved in women's historical relationship with animals, I believe that cultural feminism, informed by an awareness of animal rights theory, can provide a more viable theoretical basis for an ethic of animal treatment than is currently available.

Contemporary animal rights theory includes two major theoretical approaches, one based on natural rights theory and the other on utilitarianism. The major theoretician for the natural rights position is Tom Regan, whose primary statement appears in *The Case for Animal Rights*. In this lengthy, impressive, but sometimes casuistical document, Regan argues that animals—in particular, adult mammals—are moral entities who have certain inalienable rights, just as humans do, according to the natural rights doctrine enunciated in the eighteenth century (particularly by Locke).[10]

Regan builds his case primarily by refuting Kant, who had stipulated in his second formulation of the Categorical Imperative that "man and generally any rational being *exists* as an end in himself, *not merely as a means*," that rational beings possess "*absolute worth*," and that therefore they are entitled to treatment as ends.[11] It is on the basis of their rationality that humans are identified by Kant and other Enlightenment thinkers as moral agents who are therefore entitled to such natural rights as to be treated as ends.

In the articulation of Locke and the framers of the U.S. Declaration of Independence and Constitution, not all humans were in fact considered sufficiently rational as to be held "persons" entitled to rights: only white, male property-holders were deemed adequately endowed to be included in the category of personhood. Indeed, much of the nineteenth-century women's rights movement was devoted to urging that women be considered persons under the Constitution.[12] Here as elsewhere in Western political theory, women and animals are cast together. Aristotle, for example, linked women and animals in the *Nicomachean Ethics* by excluding them from participation in the moral life. As Keith Thomas points out, the centuries-long debate over whether women have souls paralleled similar discussions about the moral status of animals.[13]

In building his case for animal rights, Regan extends the category of those having absolute worth or inherent value to include nonrational but still intelligent nonhuman creatures. He does this by elaborating the distinction between moral agents (those who are capable of making rational, moral judgments) and moral patients (those who cannot make such formulations but who are nevertheless entitled to be treated as ends). This is contrary to Kant, who maintains that "animals . . . are there merely as a means to an end. That end is man."[14]

Regan makes his case by countering Kant's theory that human moral patients (i.e., those who are severely retarded, infants, or others unable to reason) need not be treated as ends. This to Regan is unacceptable. Therefore, if one accepts both moral agents and moral patients as entitled to the basic respect implied in the notion of rights, Regan argues, it follows that nonhuman moral patients (animals) must be included in the category of those entitled to be treated as ends. To argue otherwise is speciesist; that is, it arbitrarily assumes that humans are worth more than other life forms. Speciesism is a concept borrowed from feminist and minority group theory. It is analogous to sexism and racism in that it privileges one group (humans, males, whites, or Aryans) over another.[15] Regan, therefore, maintains an absolutist deontological nonconsequentialist position; treating animals as ends is, he insists, a moral duty. It is a matter of justice, not kindness.[16]

Although Regan rejects Kant's determination of rationality as the basis for entry into the "kingdom of ends," he specifies that those who have "inherent value" must have a subjective consciousness (be "subject of a life") and/or have the kind of complex awareness found in adult mammals.[17] This criterion leaves open the question of severely retarded humans, humans in irreversible comas, fetuses, even human infants. Regan's criterion in fact privileges those with complex awareness over those without.[18] Therefore, though it rejects Kantian rationalism, Regan's theory depends on a notion of complex consciousness that is not far removed from rational thought, thus, in effect, reinvoking the rationality criterion. I do not quarrel with the idea that adult mammals have a highly developed intelligence that may be appropriated to human reason; rather, I question the validity of the rationality criterion. Regan's difficulty here stems in part, it seems, from natural rights theory, which privileges rationalism and individualism, but it may also reflect his own determined exclusion of sentiment from "serious" intellectual inquiry.

From a cultural feminist point of view, the position developed by utilitarian animal rights theorists is more tenable in this regard because it dispenses with the higher-intelligence criterion, insisting instead on the capacity to feel—or the capacity to suffer—as the criterion by which to determine those who are entitled to be treated as ends.

The utilitarian position in animal rights theory has been developed principally by Peter Singer. Indeed, it is his admirable and courageous book *Animal Liberation* that largely galvanized the current animal rights movement. Singer's central premise derives from a key passage in Jeremy Bentham's *Introduction to the Principles of Morals and Legislation* (1789). During a high tide of the natural rights doctrine, the French Revolution, Bentham wrote:

> The day *may* come when the rest of the animal creation may acquire those rights which never could have been withholden from them but by the hand of tyranny. . . . It may one day come to be recognized that the number of the legs, the villosity of the skin, or the termination of the *os sacrum,* are reasons . . . insufficient for abandoning a sensitive being to the same fate. What else is it that should trace the insuperable line? Is it the faculty of reason, or perhaps the faculty of discourse? But a full-grown horse or dog is beyond comparison a more rational, as well as a more conversable animal than an infant of a day, or a week, or even a month, old. But suppose the case were otherwise, what would it avail? The question is not, Can they *reason?* nor, Can they *talk?* but, *Can they suffer?*[19]

A similar passage occurs in Rousseau's *Discourse on the Origin of Inequality* (1755). It seems in part to be a rejoinder to the Cartesian view of animals as machines, discussed below.

> We may put an end to the ancient disputes concerning the participation of other animals in the law of nature; for it is plain that, as they want both reason and free will, they cannot be acquainted with that law; however, as they partake in some measure of our nature in virtue of that sensibility with which they are endowed, we may well imagine they ought likewise to partake of the benefit of natural law, and that man owes them a certain kind of duty. In fact, it seems that, if I am obliged not to injure any being like myself, it is not so much because he is a reasonable being, as because he is a sensible being.[20]

Thus, both Bentham and Rousseau advocate that natural rights, or entrance into Kant's kingdom of ends, be accorded to creatures who can feel.

Their assumption is that the common condition that unites humans with animals is sensibility, the capacity to feel pain and experience pleasure.

The utilitarian position proceeds from this premise to establish that if a creature is sentient, it has interests that are as equally worthy of consideration as any other sentient creature's interests when humans make decisions about their well-being. In Singer's words, "The capacity for suffering and enjoyment is *a prerequisite for having interests*.[21] A stone, for example, does not have interests in the question of being kicked because it cannot suffer, whereas a mouse does have such interests because it can experience pain as a result. "If a being suffers," Singer maintains, "there can be no moral justification for refusing to take that suffering into consideration. . . . The principle of equality requires that its suffering be counted equally with the like suffering . . . of any other being." In short, "pain and suffering are bad and should be prevented or minimized, irrespective of the race, sex, or species of the being that suffers."[22] This is the essence of the utilitarian animal rights position.

Utilitarian animal rights theory has the virtue of allowing some flexibility in decision making, as opposed to Regan's absolutist stance that no animal's suffering is justifiable under any circumstances. As a utilitarian, Singer insists, for example, that an awareness of consequences can and should influence the evaluation of an individual's fate in any given situation. This leads him to admit that "there could conceivably be circumstances in which an experiment on an animal stands to reduce suffering so much that it would be permissible to carry it out even if it involved harm to the animal . . . [even if] the animal were a human being."[23] Elsewhere he says that if the suffering of one animal would have the result of curing all forms of cancer, that suffering would be justifiable.[24] Singer's basic position is that "similar interests must count equally, regardless of the species of the being involved. Thus, if some experimental procedure would hurt a human being and a pig to the same extent, and there were no other relevant consequences . . . it would be wrong to say that we should use the pig because the suffering of the pig counts less than the suffering of a human being."[25]

Therefore, although Singer also uses the term "animal rights," his modifications take it even farther from traditional natural rights doctrine than do Regan's reconceptions. It is not a matter of political rights of a rational citizen, such as the right to free speech or to vote, nor is it the right of an intelligent creature to be treated as an end (in Kantian terms). Rather it is the right of a sentient creature to have its interests in remaining unharmed considered equally when weighed against the interests of another sentient creature.[26]

Singer's insistence that animals have interests equal to humans makes his argument as morally compelling as Regan's contention that animals have rights. Nevertheless, there are some weaknesses in the utilitarian position. One is that a precise value standard for decision making or weighing of interests is not provided, which allows unacknowledged prejudices to intrude. Second, it requires a quantification of suffering, a "mathematization" of moral beings, that falls back into the scientific modality that legitimates animal sacrifice. Thus, while it recognizes sensibility or feeling as the basis for treatment as a moral entity, the utilitarian position remains locked in a rationalist, calculative mode of moral reasoning that distances the moral entities from the decision-making subject, reifying them in terms of quantified suffering. Just as the natural rights theory proposed by Regan inherently privileges rationality, Singer's utilitarianism relapses into a mode of manipulative mastery that is not unlike that used by scientific and medical experimenters to legitimate such animal abuses as vivisection. It is for this reason that we must turn to cultural feminism for alternative theory.

Cultural feminism has a long history. Even during feminism's "first wave," thinkers otherwise as diverse as Margaret Fuller, Emma Goldman, and Charlotte Perkins Gilman articulated a critique of the atomistic individualism and rationalism of the liberal tradition.[27] They did so by proposing a vision that emphasized collectivity, emotional bonding, and an organic (or holistic) concept of life. In *Woman in the Nineteenth Century* (1845), for example, Fuller argued that the "liberation" of women and their integration into public life would effect a feminization of culture, which would mean a reign of "plantlike gentleness," a harmonic, peaceful rule, an end to violence of all kinds (including, she specifies, the slaughter of animals for food), and the institution of vegetarianism (substituting, she urges, "pulse [beans] for animal food").[28] Gilman put forth a similar vision in her utopian novel *Herland* (1915). Indeed, in addition to Fuller and Gilman there is a long list of first-wave feminists who advocated either vegetarianism or animal welfare reform, including Mary Wollstonecraft, Harriet Beecher Stowe, Lydia Maria Child, Elizabeth Blackwell, Elizabeth Stuart Phelps Ward, Susan B. Anthony, Victoria Woodhull, Elizabeth Cady Stanton, the Grimké sisters, Lucy Stone, Frances Willard, Frances Power Cobbe, Anna Kingford, Caroline Earle White, and Agnes Ryan.[29]

In the second wave of feminist theory, the main work to date linking feminism with animal rights has been done by Carol Adams.[30] There have been a number of other works that link feminism more generally with ecology, such as those by Susan Griffin, Carolyn Merchant, Rosemary Radford Ruether, Marilyn French, Paula Gunn Allen, Chrystos, and Ynestra King.[31]

From the cultural feminist viewpoint, the domination of nature, rooted in postmedieval, Western, male psychology, is the underlying cause of the mistreatment of animals as well as of the exploitation of women and the environment. In her pathbreaking study, *The Death of Nature: Women, Ecology, and the Scientific Revolution* (1980), Carolyn Merchant recognizes that "we must reexamine the formation of a world view and a science that, by reconceptualizing reality as a machine rather than a living organism, sanctioned the domination of both nature and women."[32]

Critiques of the logical fallacies inherent in the scientific epistemology are not new. Ludwig Wittgenstein demonstrated the tautological nature of the analytic judgment in his *Tractatus* in 1911, indeed, a point Hume made in the *Enquiry Concerning Human Understanding* in 1748; but it was the critique offered by Max Horkheimer and Theodor Adorno in their *Dialectic of Enlightenment* (1944) that first made the connection between what Husserl called the "mathematisation of the world"[33] and the derogation of women and animals.[34]

The scientific or experimental method converts reality into mathematical entities modeled on the physical universe, which, as seen in Newton's laws, is cast in the image of a mechanism that operates according to fixed repetitions. No distinction is made between life forms such as human and animal bodies, which are seen as machines in the Cartesian view, and nonlife forms such as rocks.

Horkheimer and Adorno argue that the imposition of the mathematical model upon reality reflects a psychology of domination. "In [scientific] thought, men distance themselves from nature in order thus imaginatively to present it to themselves—but only in order to determine how it is to be dominated." Using the term "enlightenment" to refer to the scientific viewpoint, they note that "enlightenment is as totalitarian as any system"; it operates "as a dictator toward men. He knows them in so far as he can manipulate them."[35]

The pretensions of universality of scientific knowledge and the generalizing character of the machine metaphor mean that differences and particularities are erased, subdued, dominated. "In the impartiality of scientific language, that which is powerless has wholly lost any means of expression."[36] As Max Scheler noted, "Those aspects which cannot be represented in the chosen symbolic language of mathematics . . . are assigned a fundamentally different status: they belong to the realm of the 'subjective' and 'unscientific.'"[37] Thus, all that is anomalous—that is, alive and nonpredictable—is erased or subdued in the Newtonian/Cartesian epistemological paradigm. The anomalous and the powerless include women and animals, both of whose subjectivities and realities are erased or converted into manipulable objects—"the material of subjugation"[38]—at the mercy of the rationalist manipulator, whose self-worth is established by the fact that he thus subdues his environment. "Everything—even the human individual, not to speak of the animal—is converted into the repeatable, replaceable process, into a mere example for the conceptual models of the system."[39]

Horkheimer and Adorno conclude that this scientific epistemology is an ideological form that is rooted in the material conditions of social domination—particularly that of men over women. In "their nauseating physiological laboratories," scientists "force [information] from defenseless [animals]. . . . The conclusion they draw from mutilated bodies [is that] . . . because he does injury to animals, he and he alone in all creation voluntarily functions. . . . Reason . . . belongs to man. The animal . . . knows only irrational terror."[40] But the scientist feels no compassion for or empathy with his victims because "for rational beings . . . to feel concern about an irrational creature is a futile occupation. Western civilization has left this to women . . . [through] the division of labor imposed on her by man."[41]

The association of the postmedieval split between reason and the emotions with the division of labor and in particular with the rise of industrial capitalism is a well-developed thesis, particularly among Marxist theorists. Eli Zaretsky, in *Capitalism, the Family and Personal Life* (1976), suggests that the reification of public life occasioned by alienated industrial labor meant personal relationships were relegated to the private sphere: "The split in society between 'personal feelings' and 'economic production' was integrated with the sexual division of labour. Women were identified with emotional life, men with the struggle for existence."[42]

Women's connection with economic life has been nearly universally "production for use" rather than "production for exchange"—that is, their labor has prepared material for immediate use by the household rather than for use as a commodity for exchange or for monetary payment. Such a practice, theorists have argued, tends to create a psychology that values the objects of production emotionally in a way that alienated production for exchange cannot. Since in the capitalist era it is largely women who engage in use-value production, it may be a basis for the relational, contextually oriented epistemology that contemporary theorists ascribe to Western women.[43] The relegation of women, emotions, and values to the private sphere, to the margins, allowed, as Horkheimer, Adorno, and others have noted, masculine practices in the public political and scientific sphere to proceed amorally, "objectively," without the restraint of "subjective" relational considerations, which are in any event elided or repressed by the dominant disciplines.

Like Carolyn Merchant, Horkheimer and Adorno recognize that the witchhunts of the early modern period were symptomatic of the new need to erase and subdue anomalous, disorderly (and thus feminine) nature. Horkheimer and Adorno consider that the eradication of witches registered "the triumph of male society over prehistoric matriarchal and mimetic stages of development" and "of self-preserving reason . . . [in] the mastery of nature."[44] Merchant suggests witches represent that aspect of nature that did not fit into the orderly pattern of the mathematical paradigm; they therefore were seen as dangerously rebellious: "Disorderly woman, like chaotic nature, needed to be controlled."[45]

Merchant notes that Bacon, one of the formulators of the experimental method, used the analogy of a witch inquisition to explain how the scientist manipulates nature in order to extract information from it. He wrote: "For you have but to follow it and as it were hound nature in her wanderings, and you will be able when you like to lead and drive her afterward to the same place again."[46] The image of nature as a female to be dominated could not be more explicit.

The mathematical paradigm imposed the image of the machine on all reality. It was Descartes who most fully developed the idea that nonmental life forms function as machines, which some of his followers (La Mettrie, e.g., in *L'homme machine*) carried to its extreme. Tom Regan critiques the Cartesian view at length in *The Case for Animal Rights*;[47] it is clear that the notion of animals as feelingless, unconscious robots (which Rousseau, among others—see above—rejected) legitimated (and continues to legitimate) atrocious scientific experimentation. One early anonymous critic of Descartes noted: "The [Cartesian] scientists administered beatings to dogs with perfect indifference and made fun of those who pitied the creatures as if they felt pain. They said the animals were clocks; that the cries they emitted when struck were only the sound of a little spring that had been touched, but that the whole body was without feeling. They nailed the poor animals up on boards by their four paws to vivisect them to see the circulation of the blood which was a great subject of controversy."[48]

In "The Cartesian Masculinization of Thought," Susan Bordo describes Cartesian objectivism as an "aggressive intellectual 'flight from the feminine.'"[49] "The 'great Cartesian anxiety' [seen especially in the *Meditations* is] over separation from the organic female universe of the Middle Ages and the Renaissance. Cartesian objectivism [is] a defensive response to that separation anxiety."[50] In the process "the formerly female earth becomes inert *res extensa:* dead, mechanically interacting nature. . . . 'She' becomes 'it'—and 'it' can be understood. Not through sympathy, of course, but by virtue of the very *object*-ivity of 'it.'"[51]

Natural rights theory, likewise an expression of Enlightenment rationalism, similarly imposes a machine grid upon political and moral reality. Recent feminist theorists have criticized the neutral and objective pretenses of the liberal theoretical tradition for leaving out the anomalous context in which events occur, inscribing them instead in an abstract grid that distorts or ignores the historical environment. For example, Catharine A. MacKinnon has criticized the traditional liberal interpretation of U.S. constitutional law for its neutral approach to justice. She urges that we "change one dimension of liberalism as it is embodied in law: the definition of justice as neutrality between abstract categories," for this approach ignores the "substantive systems"—that is, the real conditions in which the abstractions operate. MacKinnon therefore rejects, to use her example, the idea that "strengthening the free speech of the Klan strengthens the free speech of Blacks."[52] This thesis is invalid, she maintains, because it equates "substantive powerlessness with substantive power"[53] through the use of a mechanistic conceptual model. Thus, MacKinnon, like the cultural feminists discussed below, rejects the "mathematizing" elisions of Enlightenment rationalism in favor of a view that "sees" the environmental context. Had the vivisectionists described above allowed this epistemological shift, they presumably would have "seen" the pain—the suffering and emotions—of the animals, which the machine abstraction through which they were viewing them ignored.

Unfortunately, contemporary animal rights theorists, in their reliance on theory that derives from the mechanistic premises of Enlightenment epistemology (natural rights in the case of Regan and utilitarian calculation

in the case of Singer) and in their suppression/denial of emotional knowledge, continue to employ Cartesian, or objectivist, modes even while they
condemn the scientific practices enabled by them.

Two of the earliest critics of Cartesian mechanism were women: Margaret Cavendish, the Duchess of Newcastle (1623–73), and Anne Finch,
Lady Conway (1631–79). Finch emphatically rejected the Cartesian view;
she felt that animals were not "composed of 'mere fabric' or 'dead matter,' but had spirits within them 'having knowledge, sense, and love, and
divers other faculties and properties of a spirit.'"[54] Cavendish, an un-
tutored genius, challenged Descartes directly. She met him while she and
her husband were in exile in France in the 1640s, and she later exchanged
letters with him about his *Treatise on Animals*. In one of his letters, dated
November 23, 1646, he is prompted by her to defend his notion of animals
as machines: "I cannot share the opinion of Montaigne and others who
attribute understanding or thought to animals."[55]

As Keith Thomas (in *Man and the Natural World*) recognizes, Cavendish
was one of the first to articulate the idea of animal rights.[56] Her biographer,
Douglas Grant, notes: "Her writings . . . constantly illustrate her sensibility to nature [and] its creatures: how she felt for 'poor Wat,' the hunted
hare . . . the stag; her pity for their unnecessary sufferings making her
speak out in a century when cruelty to animals was all too common."[57] "As
for man, who hunts all animals to death on the plea of sport, exercise and
health," she asked, "is he not more cruel and wild than any bird of prey?"[58]

The resistance of Finch and Cavendish to the impositions of early modern science were not isolated accidents, I propose. Indeed, if we accept
Michel Foucault's contention that the ascendancy of the scientific disciplines and their attendant institutions was a historical process of colonization that intensified through the postmedieval period, reaching a height
in the late nineteenth century, we must read Finch and Cavendish's critiques as an early feminist resistance to a process that inevitably meant the
destruction of women's anomalous worlds. The suppression of women's
social realities effected by the pseudo-scientific medical theories (especially
those of the sexologists) of the late nineteenth century was the final stage
in what Foucault has labeled the "medicalisation de l'insolite"—the medi-
calization of the anomalous.[59] This process itself involved the social imposition of sexologist paradigms analogous to the scientific imposition of the
mathematical machine paradigm on all living forms.

Perhaps this is why many women of the period seem to have felt a kinship to animals. Both were erased (at best) or manipulated (at worst) to

behave in accordance with paradigms imposed by the rationalist lords—whether vivisectors or sexologists. Women in fact became the primary activists and energizers of the nineteenth-century anti-vivisection movement, which should be seen, I propose, as one manifestation of a counter-hegemonic resistance undertaken by women against the encroachments of the new disciplines. Just as sexologists anatomized women's world "of love and ritual," "entomologizing" it (to use Foucault's term) into various species and subspecies of deviance, so vivisectors turned animal bodies into machines for dissection.

In her study of the nineteenth-century English anti-vivisection movement, *The Old Brown Dog*, Coral Lansbury argues that women activists thus identified with the vivisected dog: "Every dog or cat strapped down for the vivisector's knife reminded them of their own condition." It was an image of dominance. Indeed, pioneer woman doctor Elizabeth Blackwell saw ovariectomies and other gynecological surgery as an "extension of vivisection." For the suffragists, "the image of the vivisected dog blurred and became one with the militant suffragette being force fed in Brixton Prison."[60]

The dominance over nature, women, and animals inherent in this scientific epistemology, which requires that the anomalous other be forced into ordered forms, may be rooted in the Western male maturation process that requires men to establish their autonomous identity against the maternal/feminine. Hanna Fenichel Pitkin's recent analysis of the psychological development of Machiavelli, a prototypical formulator of postmedieval secularism, is most instructive in this regard. She reveals that "Machiavelli's writings show a persistent preoccupation with manhood."[61] "If *virtù* [manliness] is Machiavelli's favorite quality, *effeminato* . . . is one of his most frequent and scathing epithets."[62] In *The Prince* Machiavelli asserts that a leader rules "either by fortune or by ability (*virtù*)."[63] *Virtù* implies manipulative rationality and a certain macho willingness to exert military control. *Fortuna,* on the other hand, represents the nonrational, that which is unpredictable, all that is other to the exertion of rational control and masculine domination. In another celebrated passage in *The Prince*, Machiavelli asserts: "Fortune is a woman and in order to be mastered she must be jogged and beaten."[64]

In an unfinished poem that treats the Circe legend, Machiavelli opposes the world of women, nature, and animals to the civilized world of public order, the world of men. Pitkin notes that Circe is seen as a witch who has the power to turn men into beasts; much is made by Machiavelli of the "contrast between her feminine, natural world, and the world of men which is political and the product of human artifice. . . . Juxtaposed to the masculine world of law and liberty [is] the forest world where men are turned into animals and held captive in permanent dependence."[65] "Male culture," therefore, "symbolizes control over nature."[66]

Pitkin concludes, "Civilization . . . history, culture, the whole *vivere civile* that constitute the world of adult human autonomy are . . . male enterprises won from and sustained against female power—the engulfing mother . . . women as the 'other'. . . . The struggle to sustain civilization . . . thus reflects the struggle of boys to become men."[67] In "Gender and Science," Evelyn Fox Keller similarly argues that the autonomy and objectivity of the male scientist reflect the basic dissociation from the feminine affective world required in the male maturation process.[68]

Beyond this ontogenetic theory is the phylogenetic thesis developed by Rosemary Radford Ruether that patriarchal civilization is built upon the historical emergence of a masculine ego consciousness that arose in opposition to nature, which was seen as feminine. Sexism, she notes, is rooted in this "'war against the mother,' the struggle of the transcendent ego to free itself from bondage to nature."[69] Developing the existentialist notion of the transcendent masculine *pour soi,* and the immanent feminine *en soi,* Ruether urges (thereby rejecting Simone de Beauvoir's thesis in *The Second Sex*) that the continual cultural attempt to transcend the feminine is what has led to our present ecological and moral crisis.

The fundamental defect in the "male ideology of transcendent dualism" is that its only mode is conquest. "Its view of what is over against itself is not that of the conversation of two subjects, but the conquest of an alien object. The intractability of the other side of the dualism to its demands does not suggest that the 'other' has a 'nature' of her own that needs to be respected and with which one must enter into conversation. Rather, this intractability is seen as that of disobedient rebellion." Thus, "patriarchal religion ends . . . with a perception of the finite cosmos itself as evil in its intractability" to technological, scientific progress.[70]

In *Beyond Power* (1985) Marilyn French argues that "patriarchy is an ideology founded on the assumption that man is distinct from the animal and superior to it. The basis for this superiority is man's contact with a higher power/knowledge called god, reason, or control. The reason for man's existence is to shed all animal residue and realize fully his 'divine' nature, the part that *seems* unlike any part owned by animals—mind, spirit, or control."[71] French sees a sadomasochism inherent in this cultural impulse to mutilate or kill off the animal/feminine in the self. According to French, patriarchal society has reached a frightening impasse: "Our culture, which worships above all else the power to kill, has reached the point of wishing to annihilate all that is 'feminine' in our world."[72]

Recent cultural feminist theorists have identified alternative epistemological and ontological modes that must, I believe, replace the mode of sadomasochistic control/dominance characteristic of patriarchal scientific epistemology. Ruether, for example, urges the development of new ways of relating to nature and to nonhuman life forms. "The project of human life," she says, "must cease to be seen as one of 'domination of nature.'. . . Rather, we have to find a new language of ecological responsiveness, a reciprocity between consciousness and the world systems in which we live and move and have our being."[73] In *Sexism and God-Talk* (1983), Ruether suggests that human consciousness be seen not as different from other life forms but as continuous with the "bimorphic" spirit inherent in other living beings:

> Our intelligence is a special, intense form of . . . radical energy, but it is not without continuity with other forms; it is the self-conscious or "thinking dimension" of the radial energy of matter. We must respond to a "thou-ness" in all beings. This is not romanticism or an anthropomorphic animism that sees "dryads in trees," although there is truth in the animist view. . . . We respond not just as "I to it," but as "I to thou," to the spirit, the life energy that lies in every being in its own form of existence. The "brotherhood of man" needs to be widened to embrace not only women but also the whole community of life.[74]

Ruether calls for "a new form of human intelligence," one based on a relational, affective mode popularly called "right-brain thinking," which moves beyond the linear, dichotomized, alienated consciousness characteristic of the "left-brain" mode seen in masculinist scientific epistemology. Linear, rationalist modes are, Ruether enjoins, "ecologically dysfunctional."[75] What is needed is a more "disordered" (my term—if order means hierarchical dominance) relational mode that does not rearrange the context to fit a master paradigm but sees, accepts, and respects the environment.

In *The Sacred Hoop: Recovering the Feminine in American Indian Traditions* (1986), Paula Gunn Allen finds in those traditions attitudes toward nature that are quite different from the alienation and dominance that characterize Western epistemology and theology. God and the spiritual dimension do not transcend life but rather are immanent in all life forms. All creatures are seen as sacred and entitled to fundamental respect. Allen, herself a Laguna Pueblo-Sioux, recalls that "when I was small, my mother often told me that animals, insects, and plants are to be treated with the kind of respect one customarily accords to high-status adults." Nature, in her culture, is seen "not as blind and mechanical, but as aware and organic." There is "a seamless web" between "human and nonhuman life."[76]

Rather than linear, hierarchical, mechanistic modes, Allen proposes a return to the achronological relational sensibility characteristic of her people. Recognizing that "there is some sort of connection between colonization and chronological time," Allen observes that "Indian time rests on a perception of individuals as part of an entire gestalt in which fittingness is not a matter of how gear teeth mesh with each other but rather how the person meshes with the revolving of the seasons, the land, and the mythic reality that shapes all life into significance. . . . Women's traditional occupations, their arts and crafts, and their literatures and philosophies are more often accretive than linear, more achronological than chronological, and more dependent on harmonious relationships of all elements within a field of perception than western culture in general. . . . Traditional peoples perceive their world in a unified-field fashion."[77]

In her study of contemporary women's art, *Women as Mythmakers* (1984), Estella Lauter has identified the contours of a new myth that involves women and nature. "Many of these artists accept the affinity between woman and nature as a starting point—in fact, creating hybrid images of woman/animal/earth until the old distinctions among the levels in the Great Chain of Being seem unimportant."[78] Recognizing Susan Griffin's *Woman and Nature* (1978) as prototypical, Lauter detects in contemporary women's literature and art "an image of relationships among orders of being that is extremely fluid without being disintegrative."[79]

In these works, boundaries between the human world and the vegetable and animal realm are blurred. Hybrid forms appear: women transform into natural entities, such as plants, or merge with animal life. Lauter finds "surprising numbers of women" poets have a "high degree of identification with nature, without fear and without loss of consciousness." Many of these artists have revalidated ancient mythic figures that emblematize aspects of women's relationship with nature: Demeter/Kore, Artemis/Diana, Daphne, Circe. The earth is seen not as "dead matter to be plundered, but wounded matter from which renewal flows. The two bodies, women's and earth's, are sympathetic."[80]

The women artists and the feminist theorists cited here point to a new mode of relationship; unlike the subject-object mode inherent in the scientific epistemology and the rationalist distancing practiced by the male animal rights theorists, it recognizes the varieties and differences among the species but does not quantify or rank them hierarchically in a Great Chain of Being. It respects the aliveness and spirit (the "thou") of other creatures and understands that they and we exist in the same unified field continuum. It appreciates that what we share—life—is more important than our differences. Such a relationship sometimes involves affection, sometimes awe, but always respect.

In "Maternal Thinking" Sara Ruddick urges that a maternal epistemology, derived from the historical practice of mothering—that is, caring for an other who demands preservation and growth—can be identified. She calls it a "holding" attitude, one that "is governed by the priority of keeping over acquiring, of conserving the fragile, of maintaining whatever is at hand and necessary to the child's life." Ruddick contrasts the "holding" attitude to "scientific thought, as well as . . . to the instrumentalism of technocratic capitalism." Maternal practice recognizes "excessive control as a liability," in sharp distinction to scientific modes of manipulation.[81]

The maternal ethic involves a kind of reverential respect for the process of life and a realization that much is beyond one's control. Citing Iris Murdoch and Simone Weil as her philosophical predecessors, Ruddick calls this an ethic of humility. It is an attitude that "accepts not only the facts of damage and death, but also the facts of the independent and uncontrollable, developing and increasingly separate existences of the lives it seeks to preserve." Ruddick calls such an attitude "attentive love," the training to ask, "What are you going through?"[82] Were vivisectionists to ask such a question, we would not have vivisection.

Evelyn Keller draws similar distinctions to Ruddick's in her observations of Nobel prize winner Barbara McClintock's "feminine" scientific practice (which contrasts so markedly to the aggressive manipulation of nature proposed by Bacon, seen at its worst in lab animal experimentation). McClintock believes in "letting the material speak to you," allowing it to "tell you what to do next." She does not believe that scientists should "impose an answer" upon their material, as required in the mathematical paradigm of traditional scientific epistemology; rather, they should respond to it and retain an empathetic respect for it.[83] It is interesting that numerous women scientists and naturalists who have worked with and observed animal life for years—such as Jane Goodall, Dian Fossey, Sally Carrighar, Francine Patterson, Janis Carter—exhibit this ethic implicitly: a caring, respecting attitude toward their "subjects."[84]

Finally, Carol Gilligan's *In a Different Voice* (1982) suggests that a feminine ethic is one rooted in a "mode of thinking that is contextual and narrative rather than formal and abstract."[85] What she names a "morality of responsibility" is in direct contrast to the "morality of rights" seen in Regan's animal rights theory. In the former, a feminine mode, "morality and the preservation of life are contingent upon sustaining connection . . . [and] keeping the web of relationships intact." She contrasts this with the "rights" approach (which is seen in her study as more characteristically masculine) that relies upon "separation rather than connection," and on a "formal logic" of hierarchically ranged quantitative evaluations.[86]

Gilligan, Ruddick, Lauter, Allen, Ruether, and French all propose an ethic that requires a fundamental respect for nonhuman life forms, an ethic that listens to and accepts the diversity of environmental voices and the validity of their realities. It is an ethic that resists wrenching and manipulating the context so as to subdue it to one's categories; it is nonimperialistic and life-affirming.

It may be objected that this ethic is too vague to be practicable in decisions concerning animals. My purpose here, however, is not to lay out a specific practical ethic but, rather, to indicate ways in which our thinking about animal-human relationships may be reoriented. Some may persist: suppose one had to choose between a gnat and a human being. It is, in fact, precisely this kind of either/or thinking that is rejected in the epistemology identified by cultural feminism. In most cases, either/or dilemmas in real life can be turned into both/ands. In most cases, dead-end situations such as those posed in lifeboat hypotheticals can be prevented. More specifically, however, it is clear that the ethic sketched here would mean feminists must reject carnivorism; the killing of live animals for clothing; hunting; the trapping of wildlife for fur (largely for women's luxury consumption); rodeos; circuses; and factory farming; and that they must support the drastic redesigning of zoos (if zoos are to exist at all) to allow animals full exercise space in natural habitats; that they should reject the use of lab animals for testing of beauty and cleaning products (such as the infamous "LD-50" and Draize tests) and military equipment, as well as psychological experimentation such as that carried out in the Harlow primate lab at the University of Wisconsin; that they should support efforts to replace medical experiments by computer models and tissue culture; that they should condemn and work to prevent further destruction of wetlands, forests, and other natural habitats. All of these changes must be part of a feminist reconstruction of the world.

Natural rights and utilitarianism present impressive and useful philosophical arguments for the ethical treatment of animals. Yet it is also possible—indeed, necessary—to ground that ethic in an emotional and spiritual conversation with nonhuman life forms. Out of a women's relational culture of caring and attentive love, therefore, emerges the basis for a feminist ethic for the treatment of animals. We should not kill, eat, torture, and exploit animals because they do not want to be so treated, and we know that. If we listen, we can hear them.

## NOTES

*Acknowledgment:* This essay is dedicated to my great dog Rooney (1974–87), who died as it was being completed but whose life led me to appreciate the nobility and dignity of animals. I would also like to acknowledge the contributions of Gloria Stevenson, who introduced me to the concept of animal rights years ago, and my dog Jessie.

1. Peter Singer, *Animal Liberation* (New York: Avon, 1975), ix–x. Throughout I use the shorthand term "animal rights theory" to refer to any theorizing about humane treatment of animals, regardless of its philosophical roots.

2. In the *Ethics* Spinoza remarked that opposition to animal slaughter was based on "superstition and womanish pity" rather than on reason (as cited in Mary Midgley, *Animals and Why They Matter* [Athens: University of Georgia Press, 1983], 10). This is the kind of charge that disconcerts Singer.

3. Tom Regan, *The Case for Animal Rights* (Berkeley and Los Angeles: University of California Press, 1983), xii.

4. Tom Regan, "The Case for Animal Rights," in *In Defense of Animals*, ed. Peter Singer (New York: Blackwell, 1985), 24.

5. Mary Midgley, "Persons and Non-Persons," in Singer, *In Defense of Animals*, 60.

6. Constantia Salamone, xeroxed form letter, July 1986.

7. Quoted in James Turner, *Reckoning with the Beast: Animals, Pain and Humanity in the Victorian Mind* (Baltimore: Johns Hopkins University Press, 1980), 101, 103. Roswell C. McCrea, *The Humane Movement: A Descriptive Survey* (1910; reprint, College Park, Md.: McGrath, 1969), 117, notes that sentimentalism versus rationalism as a basis for animal rights theory was an issue in the nineteenth-century animal rights campaign: "As a rule humane writings [and] work, are based on a 'faith' rather than any rationalistic scheme of fundamentals. The emotional basis is a

common one, and the kind treatment of animals is assumed to be a thing desirable in itself." The exception was the Humanitarian League under Henry Salt, which tried to place "humane principles on a consistent and rational basis." It was based "not merely on a kindly sentiment, a product of the heart rather than of the head." However, Frances Power Cobbe and other women theorists of the time were not afraid to privilege the heart. For an introduction to their ideas see Coral Lansbury, *The Old Brown Dog: Women, Workers, and Vivisection in Edwardian England* (Madison: University of Wisconsin Press, 1985).

8. Virginia Woolf, *Three Guineas* (1938; reprint, New York: Harcourt, Brace, 1963), 6. Woolf's note to this passage indicates she had done some research on the issue.

9. Charlotte Perkins Gilman, "A Study in Ethics" (typescript, Schlesinger Library, Radcliffe College, Cambridge, Mass., 1933); published by permission of the Schlesinger Library. It must be noted that the women criticized by Singer and Gilman are guilty of sins of omission rather than commission; they are not actively conducting atrocities against animals. Their failure is due to ignorance and habit, traits that are presumably correctable through moral education. In this article I focus mainly on the rationalist ideology of modern science because it is the principal contemporary legitimization of animal sacrifice and because its objectifying epistemology, which turns animals into "its," has become the pervasive popular view of animals, thus legitimizing other forms of animal abuse such as factory farming.

10. Despite his accent on rigorously rational inquiry, Regan throughout uses the term "counterintuitive" as a kind of escape clause whenever deductive reason per se proves inadequate. An example of where Regan's argument becomes (to me at least) illogical is his lifeboat hypothetical, where he maintains that with four normal adult humans and one dog, it is the dog who must be sacrificed. His reasoning here suggests an unacknowledged hierarchy with humans still at the top. See Regan, *The Case for Animal Rights*, 324–25. See also Peter Singer's critique in "Ten Years of Animal Rights Liberation," *New York Review of Books*, January 17, 1985, 46–52, esp. 49–50, and Peter Singer and Tom Regan, "The Dog in the Lifeboat: An Exchange," *New York Review of Books*, April 25, 1985, 57.

11. Immanuel Kant, "Theory of Ethics," in *Kant Selections*, ed. Theodore M. Greene (New York: Scribner's, 1927), 308–9.

12. See further discussion in Josephine Donovan, *Feminist Theory: The Intellectual Traditions of American Feminism* (New York: Ungar, 1985), 4–5.

13. Keith Thomas, *Man and the Natural World: A History of the Modern Sensibility* (New York: Pantheon, 1983), 43. For further thoughts on the "cultural symbolism" that links women and animals, see Midgley, *Animals and Why They Matter*, 78–79.

14. Immanuel Kant, "Duties to Animals and Spirits," as cited in Regan, *The Case for Animal Rights*, 177.

15. Ibid., 155; the term "speciesist" was coined, according to Regan, by Richard D.

Ryder in *Victims of Science* (London: Davis-Poynter, 1975). See also Singer, *Animal Liberation*, 7, 9.

16. Regan, *The Case for Animal Rights*, 280.

17. Ibid., 243.

18. Ibid., 77, 247, 319.

19. Jeremy Bentham, *Introduction to the Principles of Morals and Legislation* (1789), in *The English Philosophers from Bacon to Mill*, ed. Edwin A. Burtt (New York: Modern Library, 1939), 847, n. 21.

20. Jean-Jacques Rousseau, *The Social Contract and Discourse on the Origin and Foundation of Inequality Among Mankind*, ed. Lester G. Crocker (New York: Washington Square, 1967), 172. See also Midgley, *Animals and Why They Matter*, 62.

21. Singer, *Animal Liberation*, 8.

22. Ibid., 8, 18.

23. Singer and Regan, "The Dog in the Lifeboat," 57. It should be noted that however much Regan and Singer disagree in theory, in practice their positions are similar: each opposes animal experimentation, exploitation of animals for food and clothing, factory farming, trapping, hunting, rodeos, and circuses.

24. Singer, "Ten Years of Animal Rights Liberation," 48.

25. Ibid.

26. Peter Singer, "Ethics and Animal Liberation," in Singer, *In Defense of Animals*, 1–10. Historically, utilitarianism developed as part of the wave of sentimentalism that emerged in late eighteenth-century Europe, which paved the way intellectually for the animal protection movement of the nineteenth century. See Turner, *Reckoning with the Beast*, 31–33; and Thomas, *Man and the Natural World*, 173–80. Of course, women's increasing participation in cultural life in the eighteenth century undoubtedly contributed to the emergence of sentimentalism and to the growing empathy for animals seen in Bentham's and Rousseau's statements.

27. For a full discussion, see Donovan, *Feminist Theory*, 31–63. The other major theoretical tradition that one might wish to turn to for alternative ideas about human relationship with the natural world is Marxism; however, as Isaac D. Balbus perceptively points out in *Marxism and Domination: A Neo-Hegelian, Feminist, Psychoanalytic Theory of Sexual, Political and Technological Liberation* (Princeton, N.J.: Princeton University Press, 1982), Marxism is rooted in a philosophy of domination. Marx indeed saw human identity as formed through labor that manipulates an objectified physical world. Balbus turns instead to Hegel, who urged that "all substance is subject," that is, motivated by a specific teleology, but all subjects are not identical (285). "Neither instrumental reason nor mere intuition or feeling but rather a new form of instrumental, empathic reason will guide the interactions between humans and the world on which they depend" (286). Such a "postobjectifying consciousness" (285) will emerge, Balbus believes, when new child-rearing practices are developed that intervene in the present male maturation process, which requires the development of enmity for the mother. Thus, Balbus turns in

the latter part of his book to neo-Freudian cultural feminist theory—specifically that developed by Dorothy Dinnerstein—to substantiate his position.

28. Margaret Fuller, *Woman in the Nineteenth Century* (1845; reprint, New York: Norton, 1971), 113.

29. Charlotte Perkins Gilman, *Herland* (1915; reprint, New York: Pantheon, 1979); Mary Wollstonecraft, *A Vindication of the Rights of Woman* (1792; reprint, Baltimore: Penguin, 1975), 291–92, and *Original Stories from Real Life* (London: J. Johnson, 1788); Harriet Beecher Stowe, "Rights of Dumb Animals," *Hearth and Home* 1 (January 2, 1869): 24; Elizabeth Blackwell, *Essays in Medical Sociology* (London: Longmans Green, 1909); Elizabeth Stuart Phelps Ward, "Loveliness: A Story," *Atlantic Monthly* 84 (August 1899): 216–29, " 'Tammyshanty,' " *Woman's Home Companion* 35 (October 1908): 7–9, *Trixy* (Boston: Houghton Mifflin, 1904), *Though Life Do Us Part* (Boston: Houghton Mifflin, 1908), and various articles on vivisection; Frances Power Cobbe, *The Modern Rack* (London: Swann, Sonnenshein, 1899), and *The Moral Aspects of Vivisection* (London: Williams & Margater, 1875); Anna Bonus Kingford, *The Perfect Way in Diet*, 2d ed. (London: Kegan, Paul, Trench, 1885), and *Addresses and Essays on Vegetarianism* (London: Watkins, 1912). Anthony, Woodhull, the Grinké sisters, Stone, and Willard are mentioned by various sources as being vegetarian, and Child as being concerned with animal protectionism. See Singer, *Animal Liberation*, 234. Elizabeth Griffith, in her biography *In Her Own Right* (New York: Oxford, 1984), notes that Elizabeth Cady Stanton followed the Grahamite (largely vegetarian) regime in her youth, following the practices of the Grimkés (34–35). Ruth Bordin, in *Frances Willard: A Biography* (Chapel Hill: University of North Carolina Press, 1986), 122, says Frances Willard believed flesh eating was "savagery" and that the "enlightened mortals of the twentieth century [would] surely be vegetarians." Indeed, there is an interesting connection between the nineteenth-century temperance and humane movements. In 1891 the WCTU in Philadelphia (probably under the aegis of Mary F. Lovell) developed a Department of Mercy dedicated to anti-vivisectionism. According to Turner, *Reckoning with the Beast*, 94, it was virulently anti-science. In *Letters of Lydia Maria Child* (1883; reprint, New York: Negro Universities Press, 1969), Child says she is a member of the SPCA and supports the humane movement. She stresses the close kinship between animals and humans as her rationale (letter of 1872, 213–14). Caroline Earle White was a leading animal protectionist in nineteenth-century Philadelphia; she wrote numerous articles on the subject. Much of Agnes Ryan's material is unpublished; the Schlesinger Library in Cambridge includes the typescript of an "animal rights" novel, "Who Can Fear Too Many Stars?" Charlotte Perkins Gilman wrote numerous articles on animal issues, including "The Beast Prison," *Forerunner* 3 (November 1912): 128–30, and "Birds, Bugs and Women," *Forerunner* 4 (May 1913): 131–32. A further useful reference on women in the U.S. nineteenth-century animal welfare movement is Sydney H. Coleman, *Humane Society Leaders in America* (Albany, N.Y.: Humane Association, 1924).

30. Carol Adams, "The Oedible Complex: Feminism and Vegetarianism," in *The Lesbian Reader*, ed. Gina Covina and Laurel Galana (Oakland, Calif.: Amazon, 1975), 145–52, "Vegetarianism: The Inedible Complex," *Second Wave* 4, no. 4 (1976): 36–42, and *The Sexual Politics of Meat: A Feminist-Vegetarian Critical Theory* (New York: Continuum, 1990). See also Constantia Salamone, "The Prevalence of the Natural Law: Women and Animal Rights," in *Reweaving the Web of Life: Feminism and Nonviolence*, ed. Pam McAllister (Philadelphia: New Society, 1982), 364–75; the articles by Janet Culbertson, Cynthia Branigan, and Shirley Fuerst in "Special Issue: Feminism and Ecology," *Heresies* 13 (1981); Joan Beth Clair (Newman), "Interview with Connie Salamone," *Woman of Power* 3 (Winter–Spring 1986): 18–21; Andrée Collard, "Freeing the Animals," *Trivia* 10 (Spring 1987), 6–23; Karen Davis, "Farm Animals and the Feminine Connection," *Animals' Agenda* 8 (January–February 1988): 38–39, which provides an important feminist critique of the macho vein in the ecology movement; and Andrée Collard with Joyce Contrucci, *Rape of the Wild: Man's Violence Against Animals and the Earth* (Bloomington: Indiana University Press, 1989). Alice Walker has also embraced the animal rights cause. See her "Am I Blue?" *Ms.* (July 1986), reprinted in *Through Other Eyes: Animal Stories by Women*, ed. Irene Zahava (Freedom, Calif.: Crossing, 1988), 1–6; and Ellen Bring, "Moving Toward Coexistence: An Interview with Alice Walker," *Animals' Agenda* 8 (April 1988): 6–9.

31. Susan Griffin, *Woman and Nature: The Roaring Inside Her* (New York: Harper & Row, 1978); Carolyn Merchant, *The Death of Nature: Women, Ecology, and the Scientific Revolution* (New York: Harper & Row, 1980); Rosemary Radford Ruether, *New Woman/New Earth: Sexist Ideologies and Human Liberation* (New York: Seabury, 1975), and *Sexism and God-Talk: Toward a Feminist Theology* (Boston: Beacon, 1983); Marilyn French, *Beyond Power: On Women, Men and Morals* (New York: Summit, 1985); Paula Gunn Allen, *The Sacred Hoop: Recovering the Feminine in American Indian Traditions* (Boston: Beacon, 1986); Chrystos, "No Rock Scorns Me as Whore," in *This Bridge Called My Back: Writings by Radical Women of Color*, ed. Cherríe Moraga and Gloria Anzaldúa (Watertown, Mass.: Persephone, 1981); Ynestra King, "Feminism and the Revolt of Nature," *Heresies* 13 (1981): 12–16. The most recent works include Irene Diamond and Gloria Feman Orenstein, eds., *Reweaving the World: The Emergence of Ecofeminism* (San Francisco: Sierra Club, 1990); and Judith Plant, ed., *Healing the Wounds: The Promise of Ecofeminism* (Philadelphia: New Society, 1989).

32. Merchant, *The Death of Nature*, xviii.

33. As cited in Colin Gordon's afterword to *Power/Knowledge: Selected Interviews and Other Writings, 1972–1977*, by Michel Foucault (New York: Pantheon, 1980), 238.

34. Max Horkheimer and Theodor F. Adorno, *Dialectic of Enlightenment* (1944; reprint, New York: Herder & Herder, 1972).

35. Ibid., 39, 24, 9.

36. Ibid., 23.

37. As cited in William Leiss, *The Domination of Nature* (New York: Braziller, 1972), 111. Sandra Harding similarly observes that "it is the scientific subject's voice that speaks with general and abstract authority; the objects of inquiry 'speak' only in response to what scientists ask them, and they speak in the particular voice of their historically specific conditions and locations": *The Science Question in Feminism* (Ithaca, N.Y.: Cornell University Press, 1986), 124.

38. Horkheimer and Adorno, *Dialectic of Enlightenment*, 84.

39. Ibid.

40. Ibid., 245.

41. Ibid., 248; see also 14, 21.

42. Eli Zaretsky, *Capitalism, the Family and Personal Life* (New York: Harper & Row, 1976), 64.

43. Nancy C. M. Hartsock, *Money, Sex and Power: Toward A Feminist Historical Materialism* (New York: Longman, 1983), 152, 246. On use-value production, see Karl Marx, *Capital*, in *Karl Marx: Selected Writings*, ed. David McLellan (Oxford: Oxford University Press, 1977), 422–23. See Harding, *The Science Question*, 142–61, for a useful summary of what she calls "feminist standpoint epistemologies." They are rooted, she notes, in the assumption derived from Hegel's notion of the master/slave consciousness that "women's subjugated position provides the possibility of a more complete and less perverse understanding" (26). Women's historical experience of silence, of being in the "slave" position vis-à-vis the "master," may provide a basis for empathy with other silenced voices, such as those of animals.

44. Horkheimer and Adorno, *Dialectic of Enlightenment*, 249.

45. Merchant, *The Death of Nature*, 127.

46. Ibid., 168.

47. Regan, *The Case for Animal Rights*, 3–33.

48. Ibid., 5.

49. Susan Bordo, "The Cartesian Masculinization of Thought," *Signs* 11 (1986): 439–56, esp. 441.

50. Ibid., 441.

51. Ibid., 451.

52. Catharine A. MacKinnon, "Pornography, Civil Rights, and Speech," *Harvard Civil Rights/Civil Liberties Law Review* 20, no. 1 (Winter 1985): 4.

53. Ibid., 15. See also Donovan, *Feminist Theory*, 2–3, 28–30.

54. [Anne Finch], *The Principles of the Most Ancient and Modern Philosophy* (1690), as cited in Merchant, *The Death of Nature*, 260.

55. Descartes, *Philosophical Letters*, trans. and ed. Anthony Kenny (Oxford: Oxford University Press, 1957), 44.

56. Thomas, *Man and the Natural World*, 128, 170, 173–74, 280, 293–94.

57. Douglas Grant, *Margaret the First* (Toronto: Toronto University Press, 1957), 44.

58. Ibid., 124. The principal sources of Margaret Cavendish's writings on animal

rights are her *Poems and Fancies* (1653; 2d ed., 1664), *Philosophical Letters* (1664), and *The World's Olio* (1655). Her empathetic imagination extends to plant life, to which she also imputes a form of consciousness (see esp. "Dialogue *between* an Oake, *and a* Man *cutting him downe*," in *Poems and Fancies*).

59. Michel Foucault, *La Volonté de savoir*, vol. 1 of *Histoire de la sexualité* (Paris: Gallimard, 1976), 61 (my translation). For studies of female sexual deviance as defined by nineteenth-century sexologists, see George Chauncey, Jr., "From Sexual Inversion to Homosexuality: Medicine and the Changing Conceptualization of Female Deviance," *Salmagundi* 58/59 (Fall 1982–Winter 1983): 114–45; and Lillian Faderman, "The Morbidification of Love Between Women by Nineteenth-Century Sexologists," *Journal of Homosexuality* 4, no. 1 (Fall 1978): 73–90.

60. Lansbury *The Old Brown Dog*, 82, 89, 24.

61. Hanna Fenichel Pitkin, *Fortune Is a Woman: Gender and Politics in the Thought of Niccolò Machiavelli* (Berkeley and Los Angeles: University of California Press, 1984), 125. Pitkin's analysis relies on the work of "object-relations" neo-Freudian feminists such as Nancy Chodorow, Dorothy Dinnerstein, and Jane Flax.

62. Ibid., 25.

63. Machiavelli, *The Prince and Selected Discourses*, ed. Daniel Donno (New York: Bantam, 1966), 13.

64. Ibid., 86–87.

65. Pitkin, *Fortune Is a Woman*, 124, 128.

66. Ruether, *Sexism and God-Talk*, 76.

67. Pitkin, *Fortune Is a Woman*, 230.

68. Evelyn Fox Keller, "Gender and Science" (1978), in *Discovering Reality: Feminist Perspectives on Epistemology, Metaphysics, Methodology, and the Philosophy of Science*, ed. Sandra Harding and Merrill B. Hintikka (Dordrecht: Reidel, 1983), 187–205, esp. 197. Hunting is, of course, the quintessential rite of passage in the male maturation process. As Barbara A. White notes in *The Female Novel of Adolescence* (Westport, Conn.: Greenwood, 1985), 126–27, "many initiation stories [involve] a hunt [where] the protagonist destroys a 'feminine principle.'" Numerous feminist theorists have connected hunting with male dominance. See Charlotte Perkins Gilman, *His Religion and Hers* (1923; reprint, Westport, Conn.: Hyperion, 1976), 37–38. A more recent scholarly study is Peggy Reeves Sanday, *Female Power and Male Dominance: On the Origins of Sexual Inequality* (Cambridge: Cambridge University Press, 1981), 66–69, 128–30.

69. Ruether, *New Woman/New Earth*, 25.

70. Ibid., 195–96.

71. French, *Beyond Power*, 341. Coral Lansbury recognizes the inherent connection between vivisection and sadomasochistic pornography and, indeed, analyzes a number of late nineteenth-century works of pornography that include scenes of vivisection: *The Old Brown Dog*, chap. 7.

72. French, *Beyond Power*, 523.

73. Ruether, *New Woman/New Earth*, 83.

74. Ruether, *Sexism and God-Talk*, 87.

75. Ibid., 89–90. See also Gina Covina, "Rosy Rightbrain's Exorcism/Invocation," in Covina and Galana, *The Lesbian Reader*, 90–102.

76. Allen, *The Sacred Hoop*, 1, 80, 100; see also 224.

77. Ibid., 154, 243, 244.

78. Estella Lauter, *Women as Mythmakers: Poetry and Visual Art by Twentieth-Century Women* (Bloomington: Indiana University Press, 1984), 18. A separate study could be written on animals in women's fiction. In a number of works animals are used to avenge injuries done to women; e.g., Edith Wharton's "Kerfol" (1916), in *The Collected Short Stories of Edith Wharton*, ed. R. W. B. Lewis (New York: Scribner's, 1968), 282–300; or Sylvia Plath's "The Fifty-ninth Bear" (1959), in *Johnny Panic and the Bible of Dreams* (New York: Harper & Row, 1979), 105–14. In others the woman/animal identification is explicit. See Mary Webb, *Gone to Earth* (fox) (1917; reprint, New York: Dalton, 1974); Radclyffe Hall, *The Well of Loneliness* (fox) (New York: Covice, Freed, 1929); Ellen Glasgow, *The Sheltered Life* (ducks) (Garden City, N.Y.: Doubleday Doran, 1932); Zora Neale Hurston, *Their Eyes Were Watching God* (mule) (1937; reprint, Urbana: University of Illinois Press, 1978); Willa Cather, *A Lost Lady* (woodpecker) (New York: Knopf, 1923); Harriette Arnow, *Hunter's Horn* (fox) (New York: Macmillan, 1949). In many of Glasgow's novels the animal-woman connection is a central issue. See Josephine Donovan, *The Demeter-Persephone Myth in Wharton, Cather, and Glasgow* (University Park: Pennsylvania State University Press, 1989), esp. chap. 5. In many works by women, animals are women's closest companions and often there is a kind of psychic communication between them (especially when the women are witches). See Annie Trumbull Slosson, "Anna Malann," in *Dumb Foxglove and Other Stories* (New York: Harper, 1898), 85–117; Mary E. Wilkins (Freeman), "Christmas Jenny," in *A New England Nun and Other Stories* (New York: Harper, 1891), 160–77; Sarah Orne Jewett, "A White Heron," in *The Country of the Pointed Firs*, ed. Willa Cather (1925; reprint, Garden City, N.Y.: Doubleday Anchor, 1956), 161–71; Virginia Woolf, "The Widow and the Parrot: A True Story," in *The Complete Shorter Fiction of Virginia Woolf*, ed. Susan Dick (San Diego: Harcourt Brace Jovanovich, 1985), 156–63; Rose Terry (Cooke), "Dely's Cow," in *"How Celia Changed Her Mind" and Selected Stories*, ed. Elizabeth Ammons (New Brunswick, N.J.: Rutgers University Press, 1986), 182–95; Susan Glaspell, "A Jury of Her Peers," in *American Voices: American Women*, ed. Lee R. Edwards and Arlyn Diamond (New York: Avon, 1973), 359–81. Sarah Grand's *The Beth Book* (1897; reprint, New York: Dial, 1980) and various works by Elizabeth Stuart Phelps Ward (see n. 29 above) are explicitly anti-vivisectionist. See Lansbury for further works in this area. Flannery O'Connor exposed the male hubris involved in hunting; see "The Turkeys," in *Complete Stories* (New York: Farrar Straus & Giroux, 1971), 42–53. Other significant works include Colette's *Creatures Great and Small*, trans. Enid McLeod (London: Secker & Warburg, 1951); Virginia

Woolf's *Flush: A Biography* (London: Hogarth, 1923); and May Sarton's *The Fur Person* (1957; reprint, New York: New American Library, 1970). See also Zahava, *Through Other Eyes*. Ellen Moers in *Literary Women* (Garden City, N.Y.: Doubleday, 1977) notes "a rich untapped field remains to yield a fortune in scholarly dissertations, and that is the animals in the lives of literary women. George Sand had a horse . . . named Colette; Christina Rossetti had the wombat; Colette had all those cats; Virginia Woolf was positively dotty about all sorts of animals. But it is their dogs who will serve the purpose best—Elizabeth Barrett's spaniel named Flush; Emily Dickinson's 'dog as large as myself'" (260). The most promising recent theoretical approach to the issue of women's connection with animals is that proposed by Margaret Homans in *Bearing the Word: Language and Female Experience in Nineteenth-Century Women's Writing* (Chicago: University of Chicago Press, 1986). Using Lacanian theory, Homans urges that women and nature are linked as "the absent referent" in patriarchal discourse. Her discussion of Heathcliff's sadistic treatment of birds in *Wuthering Heights* is especially suggestive. She observes that Cathy's aim is "to protect nature from figurative and literal killing at the hand of androcentric law" (78).

79. Lauter, *Women as Mythmakers*, 19.

80. Ibid., 177, 174.

81. Sara Ruddick, "Maternal Thinking," *Feminist Studies* 6 (1980): 350–51. See also her *Maternal Thinking: Toward a Politics of Peace* (Boston: Beacon, 1989).

82. Ruddick, "Maternal Thinking," 351, 359.

83. Evelyn Fox Keller, "Feminism and Science," *Signs* 7, no. 3 (1982): 599.

84. See Jane Goodall, *In the Shadow of Man* (Boston: Houghton Mifflin, 1971), *The Chimpanzees of Gombe: Patterns of Behavior* (Cambridge: Harvard University Press, 1986); Dian Fossey, *Gorillas in the Mist* (Boston: Houghton Mifflin, 1983); and Sally Carrighar, *Home to the Wilderness* (Boston: Houghton Mifflin, 1973). See Eugene Linden, *Silent Partners* (New York: Times Books, 1986), on Patterson and Carter. Janis Carter spent eight years trying to reintroduce Lucy, a chimpanzee who had learned sign language, to the wild in West Africa. She tells her moving story in "Survival Training for Chimps," *Smithsonian* 19 (June 1988): 36–49. Goodall has issued a sharp condemnation of the treatment of chimpanzees in American laboratories. See her "A Plea for the Chimps," *New York Times Magazine*, May 17, 1987. Also of interest is Cynthia Moss, *Elephant Memories: Thirteen Years in the Life of an Elephant Family* (New York: Morrow, 1988); and Sue Hubbell's relationship with her bees, seen in *A Country Year: Living the Questions* (New York: Random House, 1986).

85. Carol Gilligan, *In a Different Voice: Psychological Theory and Women's Development* (Cambridge: Harvard University Press, 1982), 19. For a further discussion of the ethic proposed in cultural feminist theory, see Donovan, "The New Feminist Moral Vision," in Donovan, *Feminist Theory*, 171–86.

86. Gilligan, *In a Different Voice*, 59, 19, 73. Another important work that de-

velops a cultural feminist ethic is Nel Noddings, *Caring: A Feminine Approach to Ethics and Moral Education* (Berkeley and Los Angeles: University of California Press, 1984). Unfortunately, however, while Noddings believes the caring ethic she endorses is enhanced by a celebratory attitude toward the female domestic world, which includes, she notes, "feeding the cat," she nevertheless specifically rejects the main tenets of animal rights theory, including not eating meat. It is clear that her "caring" ethic extends only to humans; the arbitrariness of her position can only be attributed to an unexamined speciesism. Nodding's book, while admirable in other ways, is weakened by this bias, thereby illustrating how feminist theory must be informed by animal rights theory if we are to avoid the hypocrisies and inconsistencies of the tea ladies condemned by Singer (for Noddings evinces affection for her pets even while endorsing carnivorism [154]).

For further discussion of this issue, see Nel Noddings, "Comment on Donovan's 'Animal Rights and Feminist Theory,'" and Josephine Donovan, "Reply to Noddings," in *Signs* 16, no. 2 (1991): 418–25.

# CHAPTER 8

# The Feminist Traffic
# in Animals

## Carol J. Adams

> [The question is] how to effect a political transformation when the
> terms of the transformation are given by the very order which a
> revolutionary practive seeks to change.
>
> JACQUELINE ROSE
> *Sexuality in the Field of Vision*

Should feminists be vegetarians? This question has appeared more and
more frequently in recent years. Claudia Card offers one opinion: "Must we
all, then, be vegetarians, pacifist, drug-free, opposed to competition, anti-
hierarchical, in favor of circles, committed to promiscuity with women,
and free of the parochialism of erotic arousal? Is this too specific? These
values are not peripheral to analyses of women's oppressions."[1]

Another feminist, Joan Cocks, critically refers to the ideas that she sees
informing feminist cultural practice: "The political strategies generally are
non-violent, the appropriate cuisine, vegetarian."[2] Whether or not all ecofeminists should be vegans is in fact one of the current controversies within
ecofeminism.[3] The answer implied by one group of ecofeminists is yes;
they proposed to the 1990 National Women's Studies Association meeting
that its conferences be vegan.[4]

Many believe that feminism's commitment to pluralism should prevail
over arguments for vegetarianism. This position sees pluralism as applying
only to an intra-species women's community. It defends personal choice
as an arbiter of ethical decisions and limits pluralistic concerns to those of
oppressed human beings. Pluralism is used to de-politicize the claims of
feminist vegetarianism.

This chapter offers an interpretative background against which the de-politicizing of feminist moral claims on behalf of the other animals can be perceived. Since feminists believe that the personal is political, it appears that many do not think their personal choice of animal foods reflects a feminist politics. But what if the values and beliefs imbedded in the choice to eat animals are antithetical to feminism, so, that, in the case of meat eating, the personal *is* political? Feminist theory offers a way to examine and interpret the practice of eating animals that removes vegetarianism from the category of "lifestyle" choice. In this chapter I provide a feminist philosophical exploration of the claim that animal rights should be practically enacted through all-vegetarian conferences by examining the dialectic between "the political" and "the natural."

In focusing on the need for feminist conferences to be vegetarian, I am not required to address at this time the necessary material conditions for an entire culture to become vegetarian and whether all members of our society have the economic option to be vegetarian. Indeed, while tax subsidies, free natural resources, and our government's financial support of the animal-industrial complex keep the cost of animal flesh artificially low,[5] vegetarianism has often been the only food option of poor people. Were government support to producers not available, animal flesh would be even more costly than vegetarian food. In the absence of neutrality on the part of the government, a grassroots resistance is demonstrating that, as more and more people adopt vegetarianism and de facto boycott the "meat" industry, vegetable proteins are becoming more prevalent and less costly. In addition, as the existence of a coercive government policy on "meat" eating is recognized, alternative political arrangements may become more feasible.[6]

Another reason for my focus on making feminist events completely vegetarian is the fact that most ecofeminists who include animals within their understanding of dominated nature have made this their position— as in the 1990 proposal. Furthermore, the conference proposal removes the vegetarian debate from the realm of personal decisions and relieves it of some of the emotional defensiveness that accompanies close examination of cherished personal practices. Moreover, the eating of animals is the most pervasive form of animal oppression in the Western world, representing as well the most frequent way in which most Westerners interact with animals. It carries immense environmental consequences in addition to the destruction of six billion animals yearly in the United States alone. Yet those living in the United States do not require animal flesh to ensure adequate nutrition; indeed, evidence continues to accumulate that "meat" eating is actually injurious to human health. Lastly, this topic provides an opportunity to respond to anti–animal rights statements by feminists.

## *Defining the Traffic in Animals*

Through the use of the phrase "feminist traffic in animals," I wish to politicize the use of animals' bodies as commodities. The serving of animal flesh at feminist conferences requires that feminists traffic in animals—that is, buy and consume animal parts—and announces that we endorse the literal traffic in animals: the production, transportation, slaughter, and packaging of animals' bodies.

Trafficking in animals represents a dominant material relationship in our culture. The animal-industrial complex is the second-largest industry, and the largest food industry, in the United States. Currently 60 percent of American foods come from animals, including eggs and dairy products (or "feminized protein") and animal corpses (or "animalized protein").[7] These terms disclose that the protein pre-exists its state of being processed through or as an animal; in other words, vegetable protein is the original protein. Trafficking in animals relies on this vegetable protein as well, but requires that it be the raw material, along with animals, for its product. Feminized protein and animalized protein come from terminal animals.

For feminists to traffic in animals, we must accept the trafficking in ideas, or the ideology, about terminal animals. These ideas form the superstructure of our daily lives, a part of which involves the presumed acceptability of this traffic. The difficulty is that the coercive nature of the ideological superstructure is invisible and, for trafficking to continue, must remain invisible.

When I use the phrase "traffic in animals," I deliberately invoke a classic feminist phrase, appearing in works such as Emma Goldman's "The Traffic in Women," and Gayle Rubin's "The Traffic in Women: Notes on the 'Political Economy' of Sex."[8] By choosing the word "traffic," I imply that similarities in the treatment of "disposable" or "usable" bodies exist.

To "traffic in animals" involves producers *and* consumers. Whatever "objects" we determine to be worth purchasing become included within our moral framework, and the production of these objects, too, becomes a part of such a framework, even if this aspect remains invisible. While numerous books on the animal-industrial complex are available,[9] they rarely are cited in feminist writings other than those by vegetarians, thus ensuring the invisibility of trafficking in animals for those who do so. The phrase "traffic in animals" is an attempt to wrest discursive control from those who wish to evade knowledge about what trafficking entails.

## Discursive Control and Ignorance

No objective stance exists from which to survey the traffic in animals. Either we eat them or we do not. Not only is there no disinterested observer, but there is no impartial semantic or cultural space in which to hold a discussion. We live in a "meat"-advocating culture. Conflicts in meaning are resolved in favor of the dominant culture. Whatever our individual actions, the place from which we stand to survey the eating of animals is overwhelmed by the normativeness of "meat" and the (supposed) neutrality of the term "meat."

The contamination of the discursive space in which we might discuss the matter of cross-species consumption is further complicated by ignorance. Vegetarians know a great deal more about the material conditions that enable "meat" eating than "meat"-eaters do. But discursive power resides in those with the least knowledge. Lacking specific information regarding the topic, the people with the most ignorance set the limits of the discussion.[10] Thus, when Ellen Goodman argues that "people make choices in these matters [animal rights] from the first time they knowingly eat a hamburger or catch a fish," she is making an epistemological claim without defining it.[11] She also assumes that this claim dispenses with the challenges of animal rights. What exactly do "meat"-eaters know? That a hamburger is from a dead animal? The details of the literal traffic in animals that has brought the dead animal into the consumer's hands? Goodman implies that people have specific knowledge about "meat" production that in reality they do not have and usually do not want.

## Discursive Privacy

It is necessary to politicize the process of obtaining animal bodies for food by using terms like "trafficking" because of the prevailing conceptual divisions of our culture. The context for talking about our use of animalized and feminized protein is one of rigid separation between "political," "economic," "domestic," and "personal." As Nancy Fraser explains in *Unruly Practices*: "Domestic institutions depoliticize certain matters by personalizing and/or familiarizing them; they cast these as private-domestic or personal-familial matters in contradistinction to public, political matters."[12]

The result of this social division is that certain issues are banished to zones of discursive privacy rather than seen as foci of generalized contestation. For instance, purchasing, preparing, and eating food is cast as a private-domestic matter. A similar separation exists between "economic" and "political":

> Official economic capitalist system institutions, on the other hand, depoliticize certain matters by economizing them; the issues in question here are cast as impersonal market imperatives, or as "private" ownership prerogatives, or as technical problems for managers and planners, all in contradistinction to political matters.[13]

Thus, while issues associated with *marketing* and *purchasing* dead animals become privatized to the domestic sphere of individual choice, issues involving the *production* of animals are *economized*, such as when the rise of "factory farms" is attributed solely to the demands of the market, or it is argued that we cannot interfere with the prerogatives of the animals' "owner."

When issues are labeled "domestic" or "economic," they become enclaved, shielded from generalized contestation, thus entrenching as *authoritative* what are actually only *interpretations* of issues. Furthermore, "since both domestic and official economic institutions support relations of dominance and subordination, the specific interpretations they naturalize tend, on the whole, to advantage dominant groups and individuals and to disadvantage their subordinates."[14] This is precisely what happens with the consumption of animals' bodies: it has been naturalized to favor the dominant group—people—to the disadvantage of the other animals.

As feminism demonstrates, the divisions between politics, economics, and domestic issues are false. The problem that an analysis such as mine faces is that these divisions continue to be accepted even by many feminists when the issue is animals; and the response by dominant groups is to banish the issue back to a zone of discursive privacy. When the issue is people's oppression of the other animals, this tendency to enforce discursive privacy when issues are being politicized is further complicated. Another social division exists—that between nature and culture.

We do not think of the other animals as having social needs. Since animals are ideologically confined to the realm of nature, making any sort of social claim on their behalf already introduces dissonance into established discourses. It appears that we are confusing the categories of nature and culture. But this in itself is a cultural classification enabled by predetermined ideologies that maintain a narrow, uncontextualized focus. Thus, any feminist animal rights position—by which I mean any argument for the freedom of the other animals from use by human beings—must challenge what has been labeled "natural" by the dominant culture.

## Ideology: Hiding the Social Construction of the Natural

Any debate about the place of animals in human communities occurs within a cultural context and a cultural practice. Here ideology pre-exists and imposes itself on individual perceptions, so that what is actually a problem of consciousness—how we look at animals—is seen as an aspect of personal choice and is presented as a "natural" aspect of our lives as human beings. Claiming human beings to be predators like (some of) the other animals (fewer than 20 percent of animals are actually predators) is an example of naturalizing the political. Distinctions between people's carnivorism and carnivorous animals' predation are ignored in such a claim: human beings do not need to be predators, and there is no animal counterpart to human perpetuation of the grossly inhumane institutions of the animal-industrial complex. Nel Noddings summons natural processes when she states that "it is the fate of every living thing to be eaten,"[15] implying a similarity between the "natural" process of decay and the activity of slaughterhouses (which remain unnamed). Eating animals is also naturalized by the glamorization of hunting as an essential aspect of human evolution or as representing the true tribal relationship between indigenous people and animals, even though gathering cultures could be hearkened to as well. The result is that exploitation of animals is naturalized as intrinsic to people's relationships with the other animals. The "naturalization" of the ways in which we are socialized to look at animals affects how we act toward animals—that is, if we see animals as "meat," we eat them. Thus we can read in a letter responding to an article on "political correctness": "None of us has the whole picture. For one woman, vegetarianism is an ethical imperative; for another, eating meat is part of the natural world's give and take."[16]

Attempts to make the ideology and the material reality of "meat" production visible, to denaturalize it, result in responses by feminists who through further promulgation of the superstructure and its importance for individual, or certain groups of, feminists, uphold the trafficking in (traditional) ideas about animals and actual trafficking in animal flesh. "Meat" is thus an *idea* that is experienced as an *object,* a *relationship* between humans and the other animals that is rendered instead as a *material reality* involving "food choices," a social construction that is seen as natural and normative. When we see the concept of species as a social construction, we are enabled to offer an alternative social construction that is morally preferable, one that recognizes animals as a subordinated social group, rather than naturally usable.

To understand why feminists defend their trafficking in animals, we must perceive the dialectic that is at work between the "political" and the "natural."

## Naturalizing the Political: I

In a "meat"-advocating culture, decisions that are actually political are presented as "natural" and "inevitable." When Ellen Goodman argues that "we acknowledge ourselves as creatures of nature" in "knowingly" eating a hamburger or catching a fish, she presumes that her readers share with her an understanding that "creatures of nature" eat dead bodies. She also assumes that we will find it acceptable to be likened to the other animals when the issue is the consumption of animal flesh, even though so much of human nature (and justification for such consumption) is precisely defined by establishing strict notions of differentiation between humans and the other animals. Two prevalent conceptualizations assist in the naturalizing of the political choice to use animals as food and explain Goodman's confidence in her defense of such actions.

### The Case of the False Mass Term

The existence of "meat" as a mass term contributes to the naturalizing of the phenomenon of eating animals' bodies.[17] Mass terms refer to things like water or colors; no matter how much you have of it, or what type of container it is in, water is still water. You can add a bucket of water to a pool of water without changing it at all. Objects referred to by mass terms have no individuality, no uniqueness, no specificity, no particularity.

When we turn an animal into "meat," someone who has a very particular, situated life, a unique being, is converted into something that has no distinctiveness, no uniqueness, no individuality. When you add five pounds of hamburger to a plate of hamburger, you have more of the same thing; nothing is changed. But if you have a living cow in front of you, and you kill that cow, and butcher that cow, and grind up her flesh, you have not added a mass term to a mass term and ended up with more of the same.[18] Because of the reign of "meat" as a mass term, it is not often while eating "meat" that one thinks: "I am now interacting with an animal." We do not see our own personal "meat"-eating as contact with animals because it has been renamed as contact with food. But what is on the plate in front of us is *not* devoid of specificity. It is the dead flesh of what was once a living, feeling being. The crucial point here is that we make some*one* who is a unique being and therefore not the appropriate referent of a mass term into some*thing* that is the appropriate referent of a mass term. We do so by removing any associations that might make it difficult to accept the activity of rendering a unique individual into a consumable thing. Not wanting to be aware of this activity, we accept this disassociation, this distancing device of the mass term "meat."

## Ontologizing Animals as "Naturally" Consumable

The prevailing ideology ontologizes animals as consumable, as mass terms.[19] This ontology is socially constructed: there is nothing inherent in a cow's existence that necessitates her future fate as hamburger or her current fate as milk machine. However, a major way in which we circumvent responsibility for terminal animals' fate at the hands of humans is to believe that they have no other fate than to be food, that this is their "natural" existence. As a result, certain positions regarding animals' ontology—that is, the normativeness of "meat" eating—are embraced by people across the divisions of race, class, and sex. Unless some factor dislodges these positions and brings about consciousness, these positions will continue to be held and, when under attack, fiercely defended as natural, inevitable, and/ or beneficial.

The existence of "meat" as a mass term contributes to the ontologizing and thus "naturalizing" of animals as intrinsically consumable. The ideology becomes sanctioned as eternal or unalterable, rather than suspect and changeable. To be a pig is to be pork. To be a chicken is to be poultry. When Nel Noddings raises the issue of the possible mass extinction of certain domesticated animals if humans were to stop eating them, she is reproducing this ontology. She continues to see the animals as being dependent on their relationship to us, as literally existing (only) for us. To be concerned about whether animals can live without us needing (eating) them continues their ontologized status as exploitable. Indeed, it clearly evokes this ontology: without our needing them, and implicitly, using them as food, they would not exist.

Warehousing animals (the term I prefer to "factory farming") is inevitable in a "meat"-advocating, capitalist culture such as ours. It has become the only way to maintain and meet the demand for flesh products that currently exists and must be seen as the *logical outcome* of this ontology. Warehoused animals account for 90 to 97 percent of the animal flesh consumed in the United States. Thus, those who argue that warehousing is immoral but alternatives to obtaining animal flesh are acceptable deny the historical reality that has brought us to this time and place. They conceive of some "natural" practice of flesh consumption that is free from historical influence, that is essentially atemporal and thus apolitical. Thus they naturalize the political decision to eat other animals.

## *Politicizing the Natural: I*

Animal rights discourse refuses to see the consumption of dead animals as a natural act and actively asserts it to be a political one. It does so by refusing to accept the discursive boundaries that bury the issue as "natural" or "personal." In doing this, animal rights discourse exposes a matrix of relations that are usually ignored or accepted as implicit, the matrix that I call trafficking in animals, by proposing three interrelated arguments: other species matter, our current ontology of animals is unacceptable, and our current practices are oppressive.

### Other Species Matter

Central to the process of "naturalizing" the political is the human/other dialectic in which "human" de facto represents white (human) maleness and "other" represents that which white human maleness negates: other races, sexes, or species. The process that Zuleyma Tang Halpin observes in scientific objectivity is generalizable to the view of anyone in a dominant position in a class-, race-, sex-, and species-stratified culture: "The 'other,' by definition, is the opposite of the 'self,' and therefore comes to be regarded as intrinsically of lesser value."[20] Caroline Whitbeck identifies this as a "self-other *opposition* that underlines much of so-called 'western thought.'"[21] This opposition has been identified in ecofeminist discourse as a set of dualisms: culture or nature, male or female, mind or body, and, importantly, human or animal. In the prevailing dualistic ontology, equation of any human group with the other animals serves to facilitate the humans' exploitation. As Halpin points out, "Even when groups labeled 'inferior' are not explicitly equated with women, they are often compared to animals, usually in ways designed to make them appear more animal than human (using white males as the prototype of humanity)."[22]

In her discussion of the representation of African-American women in pornography and its enabling of the pornographic treatment of white women, Patricia Hill Collins identifies the sexual and racial dimensions of being treated like an animal: "The treatment of all women in contemporary pornography has strong ties to the portrayal of Black women as animals. . . . [Cites an example.] This linking of animals and white women within pornography becomes feasible when grounded in the earlier denigration of Black women as animals."[23] The traditional feminist response to the equation of femaleness with animalness has been to break that association, to argue in a variety of ways for women's work and lives as representatives of culture rather than nature. It has most often left undisturbed the notion that animals represent the natural. In other words, while feminism has liberated white women and people of color from the onerous equation with animals and otherness, it has not disturbed the equation of animals with otherness.

What we have for the most part in feminism is a species-specific philosophical system, in which (an expanded) humanity continues to negate the other animals precisely because their otherness is located in the natural sphere. This species-specific tendency in feminist philosophy is evident, for instance, in Elizabeth Spelman's important article "Woman as Body." After discussing the equation of women, slaves, laborers, children, and animals with the body and how this equation facilitates their oppression, she goes on to offer theoretical redress only for the human animals so oppressed.[24] Barbara Noske points out that "as yet there exists in our thinking little room for the notion of a non-human Subject and what this would imply."[25] Nancy Hartsock wonders "why there must be a sharp discontinuity between humans and [the other] animals. Is this too an outgrowth of the masculinist project?"[26] As if in reply, Noske suggests that "even if there is such a thing as a species boundary between ourselves and *all* animals, might this discontinuity not exist on a horizontal level rather than on a vertical and hierarchical level?"[27] A species-neutral system would recognize each animal as a person, "and to some extent as an Alien person."[28]

## Our Current Ontology of Animals Is Unacceptable

Resisting the current ontology of animals as consumable is central to animal rights. Once the human-animal division is perceived to be as corrupt and as inaccurate as the other dualisms closely examined by ecofeminism, the re-Subjectification and denaturalization of animals can occur. This involves accepting them ontologically on their own terms and not on the basis of our interests. The current ontology requires that we acquiesce to the hierarchical structure that places humans above animals and defines "human" and "animal" antithetically. The current ontology continues to subordinate nonhuman nature—in this case the other animals—to people's whims.

The ontology of animals that accompanies animal rights theory involves distinguishing between reforms of certain practices that accept animals as usable and abolition of these practices. The goal is not bigger cages, but *no* cages; not bigger stalls, but *no* veal calves; not mandated rest stops, but *no* transporting; not careful placement of downed animals into frontloader buckets, but *no* system that creates downed animals; not "humane" slaughter, but *no* slaughter. Reform of the current system still subordinates animals to humans. Reform situates itself within the issue of animal *welfare* rather than animal rights, and the concern becomes the *appropriate* use of animals rather than the elimination of humans' use of animals. Often when feminists respond to animal rights, they attempt to dislodge the ontological claims of animal rights and argue for the reformist acceptance of animals' exploitation. Ellen Goodman argues for the "intelligent, responsible use of animals." Mary Zeiss Stange wants hunters to "promote positive public images of animal use and welfare, as opposed to animal protectionism."[29] In upholding the dominant ontology, the promotion of responsible use of animals grants charity where liberty is needed. Or, as Paulo Freire puts it, such paternalism—taking better care of terminal animals—enacts the "egoistic interests of the oppressors":[30]

> Any attempt to "soften" the power of the oppressor in deference to the weakness of the oppressed almost always manifests itself in the form of false generosity; indeed, the attempt never goes beyond this. In order to have the continued opportunity to express their "generosity", the oppressors must perpetuate injustice as well. An unjust social order is the permanent fount of this "generosity", which is nourished by death, despair, and poverty. That is why its dispensers become desperate at the slightest threat to the source of this false generosity.[31]

What is required is both an acceptance of the ontological integrity of those who are different from the "normative" human and a recognition of animals' consciousness and cultures. As much as men's accounts of women's lives have been partial, false, or malicious lies, so too have humans' accounts of the other animals' lives. In resisting the "naturalization" of animals, we need, as Noske argues, to develop an anthropology of the other animals that encounters them on their terms. A false generosity only serves to restrict animals to the natural realm that enables their ontologizing as usable.

## "Predation" Is Oppressive

Claiming that human consumption of the other animals is predation like that of carnivorous animals naturalizes this act. But if this predation is socially constructed, then it is not a necessary aspect of human-animal relations. Instead it is an ongoing oppression enacted through the animal-industrial complex.

Using the three-part definition of oppression proposed by Alison Jaggar,[32] we can see its applicability to the experience of the victims of the traffic in animals.

First, the "oppressed suffer some kind of restriction on their freedom."[33] Terminal animals suffer literal constraints upon their freedom: most are unable to walk, to breathe clean air, to stretch their wings, to root in the dirt, to peck for food, to suckle their young, to avoid having their sexuality abused. Whether warehoused or not, all are killed. They are not able to do something which is important for them to do, and they lack the ability to determine for themselves their own actions.

Second, "oppression is the result of human agency, humanly imposed restrictions."[34] Humans have a choice whether to eat animals or not. Choosing to purchase flesh at a supermarket or have it served at a conference represents human agency; such human agency requires that the other animals lose their freedom to exist independently of us.

Third, "oppression must be unjust."[35] Injustice includes the thwarting of an individual's liberty because of her or his membership in a group that has been targeted for exploitation. From the perspective of human-skin privilege, the oppression of other animals is seen as just, even though it arises from targeting for exploitation specific groups—in this case, the other animals. In a species-neutral philosophical system, such as the one that I believe is integral to ecofeminism, human skin should not be the sole determinant of what is moral. Viewed from a philosophical system that rejects the intertwined human/animal and subject/object dualisms, humans' treatment of terminal animals is unjust. Beverly Harrison proposes that "no one has a moral right to override basic conditions for others' well-being in order to have 'liberty' inconsistent with others' basic welfare."[36] This is what people are doing when they traffic in animals. As Alice Walker observes, "The oppression that black people suffer in South Africa—and people of color, and children face all over the world—is the same oppression that animals endure every day to a greater degree."[37]

## *Naturalizing the Political: II*

In response to efforts to re-Subjectify the other animals and label our treatment of them as oppression, people who do not wish to give up human-skin privilege seek ways to banish animal rights discourse from the political realm, to reprivatize and re-"naturalize" it. Reprivatization defends the established social division of discourses—that is, the personal is not the political, the natural is not the social, the domestic is not the political—thus denying political status for animal rights. For instance, when Ellen Goodman contends that animal rights are "unnatural," she implicitly accepts discursive boundaries she otherwise finds disturbing. If animal rights are unnatural, then animal oppression is natural; if it is natural, it is not political. She is attempting to encase the debate once again in discursive privacy. Or, when a feminist refers to the "so-called animal liberation movement,"[38] she implicitly denies political content to this movement. When Nel Noddings claims that domestic animals do not have meaningful relationships with other adult animals nor do they "anticipate their deaths,"[39] she delimits their lives within the sanctity of the "natural," which it is presumed we can identify (and control), rather than the social. It may be reassuring to believe that animals have no social network and do not object to their deaths; however, these beliefs are possible only as long as we do not inquire closely into the lives of animals as subjects. Then we see that certain cultural structures facilitate these efforts at depoliticizing and renaturalizing animals' oppression.

Feminist theorist Nancy Hartsock observes that ruling-class ideas "give an incorrect account of reality, an account only of appearances."[40] Our discourse about animals has been determined largely by the appearance of "meat" in animals' marketable form—T-bone, lamb chops, hamburger, "fresh" chickens—an appearance positing that "meat," like George Eliot's happy women, has no history. As long as "meat" has no past, its identity will come only from the constructed context of appetites and appearances. This permits what I call the flight from specificity.

The flight from specificity favors generalities instead of engaged knowledge, mass terms over individual entities. To be specific would require confronting the actual practice and the meaning of what is done to animals. Generalities safely insulate one from this knowledge, keeping debates at a predetermined, unbloodied level. Most frequently they do not pinpoint the victim, the perpetrator, or the method. Just as most feminists would recognize that the statement "Some people batter other people" is imprecise—who and how left undefined—so is the statement "We eat 'meat.'"

When, for instance, in her defense of eating animals, Nel Noddings refers to ensuring that domestic animals' "deaths are physically and psychically painless,"[41] she presumes that such a practice exists and that we all sufficiently understand what she means so that we can *agree* that such a practice either exists or is attainable for terminal animals. In this view, ignorance about the act of slaughtering prevails, though it remains unexposed.[42] In fact, such a practice neither exists nor is attainable.[43]

Another example of the flight from specificity occurs when the term "meat eating" is applied transhistorically, transculturally, implying that the means by which "meat" is obtained have not changed so much that different terms are needed, or else that the changes in the means of production are immaterial to a discussion. Consider Luisah Teish's encouragement to feed the ancestors "meat" if this is what they want:

> I have said that cooking for your ancestors is simple. It is, with one exception. Do not think that you can *impose* your diet on them. It won't work for long.
>
> I knew a woman who tried to force her ancestors to keep a vegetarian diet. The oracle kept saying that they were not satisfied. I suggested she make some meatballs for them. She did and got "great good fortune" from the oracle. I could advise her this way because I'd tried to impose a pork-free diet on my ancestors, but much to my disgust they insisted on pork chops to accompany their greens, yams, and cornbread.[44]

How can the flesh obtained from mass-produced, warehoused, terminal animals in any way duplicate the flesh eaten by the ancestors when they were alive, when a different material reality constructed the meaning of "meatballs"? "Meat" is not an ahistorical term, though it functions here as though it were, as representation. Surely the ancestors know that "pork" obtained from a twentieth-century warehoused animal—who was pumped full of chemicals, who never saw the light of day until transported to be butchered, whose relationship with other animals, including mother and/ or children was curtailed, and who never rooted in the earth—is not at all the "pork" they ate.

In each of these cases, terms such as "painless" or "meatballs" or "pork" convey little specific knowledge about the production of "meat." Those aspects unidentified or misidentified are then presumed to be unproblematic or inconsequential. The result of this discursive control is that "meat"-eaters can set the limits on what sort of information about "meat" eating is allowed into a discussion.[45] What Sally McConnell-Ginet observes about the sexual politics of discourse holds true, too, for the debate over animal rights: "The sexual politics of discourse affects WHO can mean WHAT, and WHOSE meanings get established as community currency."[46]

The meanings that are established regarding "meat" are almost always general, rarely specific. They recognize neither the specific animal killed to be food, nor the specific means for raising, transporting, and killing this animal. This flight from specificity regarding "meat" production bars from the discourse matters that in other areas of feminist theory are considered the basis for making ethical decisions: material reality and material relationships.

## Feminist Defenses of Trafficking in Animals

Before examining specific feminist defenses of trafficking in animals, some general problems of discursive control must be identified. Feminists, like nonfeminists, generally seek to banish animal rights by reprivatizing decisions about animals and renaturalizing animals' lives as subordinate to humans'. In this, several factors function in their favor. They assume that their predefined understanding of the issue is adequate: for example, that it is correct to label animal rights as being in opposition to pluralism because their definition of pluralism excludes animal rights. Any predefined feminist principle that is established as in opposition to animal rights requires closer examination: does it presume that the socially authorized forms of feminist debate available for discussing this issue are adequate and fair? To paraphrase Fraser, does it fail to question whether these forms of public discourse are skewed in favor of the self-interpretations and interests of dominant groups (including human females)—occluding, in other words, the fact that the means of public discourse themselves may be at issue?[47]

Hidden ethical stances prevail even in pluralistic feminisms. In an evolving community of individuals who share ideas and goals for changing patriarchal society, some values are so given, so taken for granted, that we never examine them. For instance, we agree that cannibalism is not a legitimate way to obtain nutrition, even though human flesh can be very tasty. Cannibalism is not a question of individual tastes, appetites, autonomy, or ritual; it is a forbidden activity whose forbiddenness appears obvious to almost everyone, and therefore this forbiddenness disturbs very few. Clearly this is not so when it comes to eating nonhuman animal flesh. In this case the flesh is considered both tasty and acceptable, based on a decision individuals and cultural traditions have made about nutrition and ethics. To suggest that nonhuman animal flesh be forbidden disturbs many.

The differing ethical stances regarding the flesh of human animals versus the flesh of nonhuman animals illustrates that the issue is not whether a community can forbid an action but who is to be protected from being consumed. Since a communitywide vegetarianism is seen as problematic but a community ban on cannibalism is a given, it is obvious that theorizing about species is at this point in time receiving different discursive space from theorizing about race, class, gender, and heterosexism.

## Autonomy

The invocation of autonomy—the insistence that enforcing vegetarianism at a conference restricts an individual's autonomy—presumes that no one else's liberty is at issue in food choices. This is simply not so. The invisibility of animals' oppression permits the debate to be about individual human's liberties, rather than making animals' oppression visible. Staking a preeminent claim for autonomy is an attempt at reprivatization. As Ruby Sales remarked during the 1990 NWSA conference: "Privilege is not a condition. . . . It is a consequence of the condition of oppression."[48] From this politicized perspective, eating animals is a privilege humans have granted themselves, and this privilege is called "autonomy." The ideology that ontologizes animals as consumable pre-exists and provides the foundation for the easy confusion of privilege with autonomy.

## Pluralism

The position that feminist conferences (and theory) should be pluralistic also is seen to be at odds with any universal claim for vegetarianism. Imposing one's dietary decision on all races or ethnic groups is viewed as racist, because the inability to exercise personal food choices severs an individual from her racial/ethnic tradition. I deeply respect the need to preserve nondominant cultures. However, I do not believe that pluralism requires siding with human-skin privilege in order to avoid white-skin privilege. We do not embrace nondominant cultural traditions that, for instance, oppress women. An unspoken "in-order-to" is buried in this assumption: We want feminism to be pluralistic; in order for this to be, we must be species-exclusive in our theory. From this context, we can see that a politicized issue, pluralism, is made to contest with a yet-unpoliticized issue, the traffic in animals. Moreover, we see that pluralism is defined in such a way that it applies only to other human beings. Conventional wisdom implies that for the one issue to prevail, the other must be kept in the realm of discursive privacy. In other words, pluralism becomes a boundary enforcer rather than a boundary destabilizer. Pluralism in food choices, including eating dead animals, can be argued in this way as long as the dominant culture's current ontology of animals remains unchallenged.

Through reprivatization, a universal vegetarianism is seen as a white woman's imposing her "dietary" concerns on women of color. However, since I am arguing on behalf of vegetarian feminist conferences, let us agree that at present the foods offered at most conferences represent the dominant culture. They already ignore ethnic and racial traditions around food.

In addressing the right of racial and ethnic groups to eat animals, we are not talking about food as nutrition but food as ritual. The poet Pat Parker argues that her "meat" eating is literally soul food.[49] But the ritual meaning of a meal may serve to reprivatize something that has broken away from discursive privacy. Alice Walker can see barbarity in her childhood diet in which "meat was a mainstay"[50] and yet still respect rituals that were not barbarous—her mother's gardening, for instance.

The "naturalizing" of the other animals as consumable is inimicable to feminist pluralism—a true pluralism that seeks to recognize the other as a subject rather than an object. This pluralism would acknowledge that the social constructions of race, class, and sex are related to the social construction of species and must be confronted as such.

## Politicizing the Natural: II

A species-exclusive philosophy establishes human and animal as antithetical categories, and naturalizes human beings' use of the other animals. In contrast, a species-neutral philosophy would not exaggerate differences between humans and the other animals, or imply that singular human evils such as warehousing animals or rape represent some residual "natural" or "animal-like" tendency. As the "natural" is politicized and labeled "oppression," "meat" will no longer be an idea that is experienced as an object. Trafficking will be destabilized by consciousness and solidarity.

### The Politics of Consciousness

Consciousness of oppression requires responses. Alison Jaggar observes that to "talk of oppression seems to commit feminists to a world view that includes at least two groups with conflicting interests: the oppressors and the oppressed"[51]—or, to put it more bluntly in the terms of this chapter, "meat"-eaters and their "meat." Paulo Freire suggests that we can respond to these conflicting interests either as critics/radicals, for whom "the importance is the continuing transformation of reality," or as naive thinkers/sectarians, who accommodate "to this normalized 'today.'" Naive thinkers/sectarians accept prevailing ideological barriers and discursive boundaries; critical consciousness can find no hold here: "sectarianism, because it is myth-making and irrational, turns reality into a false (and therefore unchangeable) 'reality.'"[52] Ellen Goodman accepts an unchangeable "reality" when she argues that

> environmental purity, the ability to live a life without a single cruel act against nature, is impossible. . . . The only answer is to avoid the use—or exploitation—of any other species. . . . We acknowledge ourselves as creatures of nature. . . . The anti-fur extremists prefer to win by intimidation. They have staked out a moral position that leaves no room for the way we live. It is, in its own peculiar way, unnatural.[53]

Goodman both reprivatizes and renaturalizes the normalized "today." The alternative to this accommodation of and mythicizing of reality is to accept the process of radicalization, an actual engagement in the efforts to transform concrete reality. This transformation aligns one with the oppressed rather than the oppressor, the "meat" rather than the "meat"-eater.

Breaking down ideological boundaries requires that those who are the oppressors must stop "regarding the oppressed as an abstract category,"[54] must stop seeing "meat" as a mass term.

### The Politics of Solidarity

Critical consciousness makes us aware of ourselves as oppressors. It transforms our understanding of a reality in which the political has been naturalized. But then what? Freire observes:

> Discovering her or himself to be an oppressor may cause considerable anguish, but it does not necessarily lead to solidarity with the oppressed. Rationalizing one's guilt through paternalistic treatment of the oppressed, all the while holding them fast in a position of dependence, will not do. Solidarity requires that one enter into the situation of those with whom one is identifying; it is a radical posture. . . . True solidarity with the oppressed means fighting at their side to transform the objective reality which has made them these "beings for another."[55]

Trafficking in animals oppresses them, ontologizing them as "beings for another." In other words, trafficking in animals makes us oppressors.

The necessary precondition for animals to be free is that there be no trafficking in animals' bodies. The ontology will not collapse upon itself until the actions that the ontology upholds—for example, "meat" eating—are stopped, and until we stop being animals' oppressors.

## Consciousness, Solidarity, and Feminist-Vegetarian Conferences

A feminist conference is an action—an action made up of people gathering to plan, educate, and network around issues of justice for women. Alice Walker, reporting on her evolving feminist consciousness, comments: "I think about how hard it would be for me to engage in any kind of action now for justice and peace with the remains of murdered flesh in my body."[56] Walker's thoughts pose a question: Should the remains of murdered flesh be available for consumption during feminist conferences? We live in a "meat"-advocating culture. But should feminist conferences be "meat"-advocating? If I recall correctly, a letter to a feminist publication a few years back queried: "Why are we going home for the holidays to watch our families eat dead animals?" No one has to go home for the holidays to see the traffic in dead animals—they can come to feminist conferences.

The assumption that feminist conferences should have an all-inclusive menu has been tacit, a given, and thus untheorized. Feminist conference organizers think they are assuming a neutral role in the debate about the consumption of animals by offering a vegetarian option that can be adopted personally if desired. In Freire's terms, they are naive thinkers. They wrongly conclude that there is such a thing as neutrality, that they are not de facto taking an ontological stance that aligns them with the dominant culture. A feminist conference that includes the vegetarian option presumes "meat" eating as normative. As Nancy Fraser argues, "Authoritative views purporting to be neutral and disinterested actually express the partial and interested perspectives of dominant social groups."[57] An all-vegetarian conference thus destabilizes what is claimed to be neutral and comprehensive, demonstrating instead its partiality. It says that if feminists want to traffic in animal bodies, they must be deliberate and not passive about it. It resists the naturalizing of the political.

The individual vegetarian option at a conference is inadequate because it perpetuates the idea that what we eat and what we do to animals (a simultaneous act if we traffic in dead animals) are solely personal concerns. It reprivatizes a political issue, making "meat" the default diet. It removes the actions of a community from the consciousness of that community. Issues such as the environment, women's health, and the politics and ethics of conflicting ontologies are rendered invisible. As the Ecofeminist Task Force Recommendation to the 1990 NWSA conference argues,[58] "meat" eating has dire environmental consequences such as deforestation, soil erosion, heavy water consumption, unrecyclable animal excrement, and immense demands on energy and raw materials.[59] Trafficking in animals also has consequences for our health. The recommendation identified the correlation between flesh consumption and heart attacks, breast cancer, colon cancer, ovarian cancer, and osteoporosis.[60]

Trying vegetarianism at a feminist conference could be a catalyst for a changed consciousness about animals. The only way to experience vegetarian nourishment is by eating vegetarian food. The feminist-vegetarian conference proposal recognizes the practical hurdles to moving away from a flesh diet: many worry that they will not feel full after a vegetarian meal; that the dishes are unappetizing; or that insufficient protein will be ingested. Vegetarian meals therefore speak to practical fears: one *can* feel full; food *can* be tasty; vegetarians *do* get the same amount of protein each day that "meat"-eaters do—twice as much as our bodies require. As the Ecofeminist Task Force urged, conference organizers should "make every effort to provide meals that satisfy the health, conscience, and palate"[61] of feminist conference participants.

Reprivatizers insist that the eating of animals is not a legitimate subject of feminist discourse, but a personal decision. Whether we eat blood and muscle or not is seen solely as an individual act, rather than a corporate one. This attitude toward flesh eating as solely personal is then enacted as individuals are given the choice between competing meal options. Reprivatizers, keeping the debate at the personal level, also keep the debate about the issue of *food*. Animal rights discourse argues that the debate is a political one and the issue is *ontology*. "Meat" at a meal automatically undermines a discussion of vegetarianism because the prevailing consciousness about animals—ontologizing them as consumable—is literally present.

The inappropriateness of this ontology, the naturalizing of it by humans' self-interest, the consequences of it for our health and the environment— the entire oppositional discourse that vegetarianism represents—can only become apparent in an atmosphere that respects animals. The current ontology will never offer this. It is an ontology at odds with feminist ethics.

## NOTES

*Acknowledgments:* Josephine Donovan, Greta Gaard, Mary Hunt, Melinda Vadas, and especially Nancy Tuana have been supportive critics as I developed the ideas in this essay. My thanks to them.

1. Claudia Card, "Pluralist Lesbian Separatism," in *Lesbian Philosophies and Cultures*, ed. Jeffner Allen (Albany: State University of New York Press, 1990), 139.

2. Joan Cocks, *The Oppositional Imagination* (London: Routledge, 1989), 223, n. 3.

3. Noel Sturgeon, "Editorial Statement," *Ecofeminist Newsletter* 2 (Spring 1991): 1.

4. See excerpts from the 1990 NWSA Ecofeminist Task Force Resolution, *Ecofeminist Newsletter* 2 (Spring 1991): 3.

5. Barbara Noske uses the term "animal-industrial complex" in *Humans and Other Animals* (London: Pluto Press, 1989), 24.

6. On government coercion through "meat"-advocacy in the four basic food groups, see my forthcoming "Eating Animals," in *Eating Cultures*, ed. Brian Seitz and Ron Scapp.

7. See Carol J. Adams, *The Sexual Politics of Meat: A Feminist Vegetarian Critical Theory* (New York: Continuum, 1990), 80–81.

8. Emma Goldman, "The Traffic in Women," in *The Traffic in Women and Other Essays on Feminism* (New York: Times Change Press, 1970); Gayle Rubin, "The Traffic in Women: Notes on the 'Political Economy' of Sex," in *Toward an Anthropology of Women*, ed. Rayna R. Reiter (New York and London: Monthly Review Press, 1975), 157–210. See also Janice Raymond, "The International Traffic in Women," *Reproductive and Genetic Engineering* 2, no. 1 (1989): 51–70.

9. See C. David Coats, *Old MacDonald's Factory Farm: The Myth of the Traditional Farm and the Shocking Truth About Animal Suffering in Today's Agribusiness* (New York: Continuum, 1989); Jim Mason and Peter Singer, *Animal Factories* (New York: Crown Publishers, 1980); John Robbins, *Diet for a New America* (Walpole, N.H.: Stillpoint, 1987).

10. As Eve Kosofsky Sedgwick observes in *Epistemology of the Closet* (Berkeley and Los Angeles: University of California Press, 1990): "The simple, stubborn fact or pretense of ignorance . . . can sometimes be enough to enforce discursive power" (6).

11. Ellen Goodman, "Debate Rages Over Animals: Where Do Ethics End and Human Needs Begin?" *Buffalo News*, December 20, 1989.

12. Nancy Fraser, *Unruly Practices: Power, Discourse, and Gender in Contemporary Social Theory* (Minneapolis: University of Minnesota Press, 1989), 168.

13. Ibid., 168. While a case could be made that animal rights discourse represents a runaway need in accordance with Fraser's analysis of needs, to establish the way in which animal rights follows Fraser's analysis is beyond the scope of this paper. The following argument uses Fraser's analysis of the way that issues become politicized and then reprivatized, but it will not establish a direct match between her categories and animal rights discourse. I wish to thank Nancy Tuana for calling my attention to Fraser's work.

14. Fraser, *Unruly Practices*, p. 168.

15. Nel Noddings, "Comment on Donovan's 'Animal Rights and Feminist Theory,'" *Signs* 16 (1991): 420.

16. Susanna J. Sturgis, "Arsenal of Silencers," *Sojourner: The Women's Forum*, December 1991, 5.

17. On "mass terms," see Willard Van Orman Quine, *Word and Object* (Cambridge: MIT Press, 1960), 99ff. Nancy Tuana pointed out that Quine's explanation of "mass term" was applicable to the cultural construction of animals as edible, and her interpretation of his work has greatly influenced my description in this article.

18. This example is based on an explanation offered by Nancy Tuana.

19. On the way that ontology recapitulates ideology, see Carol J. Adams, "Ecofeminism and the Eating of Animals," *Hypatia* 6 (1991): 125–45.

20. Zuleyma Tang Halpin, "Scientific Objectivity and the Concept of the 'Other,'" *Women's Studies International Forum* 12 (1989): 286.

21. Caroline Whitbeck, "A Different Reality: Feminist Ontology," in *Women, Knowledge, and Reality: Explorations in Feminist Philosophy*, ed. Ann Garry and Marilyn Pearsall (Boston: Unwin Hyman, 1989), 51.

22. Halpin, "Scientific Objectivity," 287–88.

23. Patricia Hill Collins, *Black Feminist Thought: Knowledge, Consciousness, and the Politics of Empowerment* (Boston: Unwin Hyman, 1990), 172.

24. Elizabeth V. Spelman, "Woman as Body: Ancient and Contemporary Views," *Feminist Studies* 8 (1982): 109–31.

25. Noske, *Humans and Other Animals*, 157.

26. Nancy C. M. Hartsock, *Money, Sex, and Power: Toward a Feminist Historical Materialism* (Boston: Northeastern University Press, 1983, 1985), 302, n. 9.

27. Noske, *Humans and Other Animals*, 125.

28. Ibid., 138.

29. Mary Zeiss Stange, "Hunting—An American Tradition," *American Hunter*, January 1991, 27.

30. Paolo Freire, *Pedagogy of the Oppressed* (New York: Penguin, 1972, 1978), 30.

31. Ibid., 21.

32. See Alison M. Jaggar, *Feminist Politics and Human Nature* (Totowa, N.J.: Rowman & Littlefield, 1988), 6–7. Thanks to Nancy Tuana for her suggestion of Jaggar's text.

33. Ibid., 6–7.

34. Ibid.

35. Ibid.

36. Beverly Harrison, *Making the Connections: Essays in Feminist Social Ethics*, ed. Carol S. Robb (Boston: Beacon, 1985), 255.

37. Ellen Bring, "Moving Towards Coexistence: An Interview with Alice Walker," *Animals' Agenda* 8 (April 1988): 6–9.

38. Stange, "Hunting," 26.

39. Noddings, "Comment," 421.

40. Hartsock, *Money, Sex, and Power*, 9.

41. Noddings, "Comment," 421.

42. Indeed, Nodding's entire response to Donovan on animal rights is contaminated by this refusal to engage the actual issues. While admitting that the greatest difference between herself and Donovan is their position on the eating of animals, she continually strays from that issue. Diversionary issues such as a discussion of whales and dolphins (who are rarely eaten by Americans), and her cats' predatory nature (which has no resemblance to the human traffic in animals), have little to do with the social construction of flesh consumption.

43. See Carol J. Adams, work in progress, "'Physically and Psychically Painless Animal Deaths': A Tolerable Standard for Feminist Ethics?"

44. Luisah Teish, *Jambalaya: The Natural Woman's Book of Personal Charms and Practical Rituals* (San Francisco: Harper & Row, 1985), 92–93.

45. This problem is discussed at length in Adams, *Sexual Politics of Meat*, 63–82.

46. Sally McConnell-Ginet, "Review Article on Language and Sex," *Language* 59 (1983): 387–88, quoted in *A Feminist Dictionary*, ed. Cheris Kramarae and Paula A. Treichler (Boston: Pandora, 1985), 264.

47. Fraser, *Unruly Practices*, 164.

48. Jennie Ruby, Farar Elliot, and Carol Anne Douglas, "NWSA: Troubles Surface at Conference," *off our backs*, August–September 1990, 11.

49. Pat Parker, "To a Vegetarian Friend," in *Womanslaughter* (Oakland, Calif.: Diana Press, 1978), 14.

50. Alice Walker, *Living by the Word: Selected Writings, 1973–1987* (San Diego: Harcourt Brace Jovanovich, 1987), 172.

51. Jaggar, *Feminist Politics and Human Nature*, p. 7.

52. Freire, *Pedagogy of the Oppressed*, 65.

53. Goodman, "Debate Rages Over Animals."

54. Freire, *Pedagogy of the Oppressed*, 29.

55. Ibid., 26.

56. Walker, *Living by the Word*, 182–83.

57. Fraser, *Unruly Practices*, 181.

58. Summarized in the *Ecofeminist Newsletter* 2 (Spring 1991): 3.

59. The recommendation contained twenty-two *whereas*es; eleven of them concerned environmental consequences, based on material derived from John Robbin's *Diet for a New America*. For a discussion of the environmental consequences of eating animals, see Adams, "Ecofeminism and the Eating of Animals," and Robbins' book.

60. The health consequences of flesh consumption are reviewed in Robbins, *Diet for a New America*, part 2.

61. See *Ecofeminist Newsletter* 2 (Spring 1991): 3.

# CHAPTER 9

# For the Love of Nature: Ecology and the Cult of the Romantic

## Chaia Heller

Awareness of the ecological crisis peaked in 1972 when the astronauts first photographed the planet, showing thick furrows of smog scattered over the beautiful blue and green ball. "The planet is dying" became the common cry. Suddenly the planet, personified as "Mother Earth," captured national, sentimental attention. In our modern iconography, nature became rendered as a victimized woman, a madonna-like angel to be idealized, protected, and saved from society's inability to constrain itself. Some twenty years later we witness a resurgence of environmental concern. As we observed on Earth Day 1992, politicians, corporate ringleaders, and deep ecologists are leaping into the romantic, ecological drama, becoming "eco-knights" ready to protect and save helpless "Lady Nature" from the big, bad dragon of human irresponsibility.

The cult of romantic love, which emerged first in the twelfth-century poetry of the French troubadours of Languedoc, still serves as a steamy cauldron of image and metaphor for today's depictions of woman and nature.[1] Our current representations of "Mother Nature" emerge out of a romantic tradition based on a male, disembodied fantasy of the ideal woman. This "cult of the romantic" has also been extended to nature. The metaphors and myths of this eco-drama are plagiarized from volumes of romantic literature written about women, now recycled into metaphors used to idealize nature. Recently, the environmental and ecology movements have been expanding and updating their library of romantic images and metaphors. Everywhere, the cult of the romantic is elbowing "humanity" to take pity on poor, ideal "Mother Nature."

But romantic ecology has a sinister side. While emphasizing nature as worthy of love and admiration, it ignores the parallel devaluation of women. Romantic ecology fails to challenge the patriarchal, state, and capitalistic ideologies and institutions of domination that legitimize the denigration of women. Ironically, romantic ecologists also fail to recognize that the same ideologies that "justify" the domination of women are used to legitimize the denigration of nature. Instead of challenging these institutions and ideologies of domination within society in general, romantic ecology points its sword toward a mythical dragon called "human nature," "technology," or "Western civilization," all of which are allegedly responsible for slaying "Lady Nature."

Perhaps most lethal, however, romantic ecology often veils a theme of animosity toward woman under a silk cloak of idealism, protection, and a promise of self-constraint. It not only refuses to make the liberation of women a priority, but in some cases actually holds women responsible for the destruction of nature.

This chapter is an exploration of the cult of the romantic. First I examine the romantic posture of idealization, protection, and constraint toward women as depicted in medieval romantic poetry; then I illustrate how environmentalists and ecologists today unknowingly extend this romantic posture to nature. I explore how the cult of the romantic perpetuates the exploitation of both woman and nature, while also impeding an authentic love for and knowledge of women and the natural world. Finally, this chapter proposes a postromantic, authentic way of knowing and caring for nature that requires a radical reconstruction of our idea of love.

Before exploring the romanticization of nature, it is essential first to look briefly at the romanticization of women in the Middle Ages as depicted in romantic love poetry. Unlike "modern romance," which consists of moon-lit dinners, crimson sunsets, and sexual contact, medieval romanticism represents an unconsummated love. As in the story of Tristan and Iseult, lovers rarely if ever express their love for each other physically. Instead, knightly and courtly romance is a love of the mind, expressing its desire in the form of passionate love poetry.

Many historians situate the origin of romantic love within Plato's concept of love.[2] Platonic love emerges out of Platonic dualism, which divides the world into two discrete spheres, material and spiritual. The realm of spirit, or "idea," is regarded as superior to the transient and perishable realm of the body, or matter. Therefore, intellectual and sexual "knowledge" is most valuable when it is gleaned in a way that is independent of physical experience. Ideal love is "unpolluted" by physical contact. For Plato, the highest form of love was intellectual fondling of the eternal, rational ideas found in geometry, philosophy, and logic. For the romantic, however, ideal love is the exercise of sexual restraint and an intellectual expression of passion through love poetry.

## *Medieval Romanticism*

### Idealization, Protection, and Constraint

Romantic poetry often conveys the wistful longing of a man for an idealized woman to whom he rarely, if ever, gains sexual access. This "noblest love" thrives in a realm of purity, in contrast to marriage, which is seen as base, lowly, and merely reproductive. Courtly romance consists of elaborate rituals of devotion in which the lover promises to protect the beloved lady from human and mythical villains while also promising to restrain his sexual desire for her.

The idealization of the beloved by the lover is reflected in the incongruity between the content of the poetry and the actual social context in which it is written. Certainly the idealized, "pedestaled" position of the women in the poetry does not reflect the actual status of the majority of women in feudal society, where most held a lowly position, bound as always to the compulsory patriarchal institutions of reproduction and productive labor.

The theme of romantic protection serves as another projected fantasy of the male romantic. Even when the lady's actual lack of social power leaks through into the poetry, her powerlessness is framed as a need for "protection" by a man. The romantic fantasizes that the woman needs knightly protection from predators instead of recognizing her desire for social potency. The combined elevation and protection of the woman in romanticism allow the male to sustain his fantasy of the woman-on-a-pedestal while indirectly acknowledging her low social status. In this way, the romantic becomes the "protector of the pedestaled woman," creating a subtle amalgamation of male fantasy and social reality.

This fantasy of romantic protection is predicated on the lover's promise of sexual self-constraint. However, romanticism never questions the social conditions that make such constraint necessary. A romantic story would lose its charm if the knight were to challenge the society that renders the lady powerless in the first place. Romanticism patently accepts that men inherently desire to plunder women while regarding male promises of self-control as heroic acts of self-mastery.

Why does romanticism fail to critique the social conditions that regard idealization, protection, and male constraint as good and necessary? Surely the lover wishes his beloved to be truly free! Perhaps it is because the function of romanticism is to camouflage the lover's complicity in perpetuating the domination of his beloved. Perhaps idealizing, protecting, and promising to constrain the desire to denigrate the beloved emerge out of a power structure the lover wishes to maintain.

In the name of protecting the beloved from the dragon that threatens to slay her, the knight actually slays his beloved himself. He slays "his lady's" self-determination and agency in the world. In this way, the knight is really the dragon in drag.

### Love, Knowledge, and Romance

In addition to prescribing idealization, protection, and self-constraint, romanticism also prescribes a particular form of love and knowledge. First, romantic love is a love based on the lover's desires, rather than on the identity and desires of the beloved. The romantic's love depends on his fantasy of his beloved as inherently powerless and good as he defines good. He views his beloved through a funnel, focusing only on a minute, vulnerable section of her full identity. He uses the rest of her body as a screen for the projection of his fantasy of the ideal woman. In this way, the romantic glosses over information about his beloved that contradicts his personal desires. Romantic love is a form of reductionism, reducing woman from her full range of human potential to a tiny list of male desires.

Romanticism is also a way of knowing that is wedded to ignorance. Certainly the romantic does not know his lady to be a woman capable of self-determination and resistance. Clearly he does not recognize her ability to express what is most human, including her capacity for culture-creating, rationality, self-consciousness, and compassion. Most significantly, the romantic is unaware of woman's capacity for self-assertion through sabotage and resistance. The subject of romantic poetry rarely includes stories of "good" women poisoning their romantic lover's food, or stories of admirable women being emotionally unavailable to their lover. Few are the poems or stories that tell of strong, lovable women resisting compulsory motherhood, marriage, and yes, even heterosexual romance. The cult of the romantic erases woman's identity as a wrench in the machine of male domination.

Romantic love is a pitiful attempt to love and know another from behind the wall of domination. True love and understanding can only occur when both subjects are free to express and explore their own desires. The knight can only love the lady if he is willing to completely relinquish his power over her, and commit his life to supporting her struggle if and when she requests it. Once she is free to pursue her struggle for liberation, then and only then, can they begin to talk about love.

## Contemporary Ecology and the Cult of the Romantic

Many ecology and environmental movements unknowingly carry on the romantic tradition, obstructing the possibility for an authentic love and knowledge of nature. Once again, the romantic themes of love through idealization, protection, and constraint pervade—this time in the form of ecological "love poetry."

Even environmental New Age-ism has gotten into the romantic play. I recently saw a slick, high-design button put out by "Affirm It" from Manchester, Massachusetts, with a picture of the earth floating in space. Under the picture was the caption "Love Our Mother," with the following quotation beneath the button on the cardboard backing:

I hold in my mind a picture of perfection for Mother Earth.
I know this perfect picture creates positive energy from
my thought, which allows my vision to be manifested in the
world.

—WILLIE C. HOOKS
Messages from Mother Earth
Daily Affirmations

I choose this as but one example of the kind of romantic New Age "nature idealism" that is steadily creeping into the ecology movement. The quotation vividly demonstrates the romantic idealization of nature. Once again, the romantic expresses his love through "perfect thoughts" rather than through authentic knowledge or action. Hooks' idea, or "perfect picture," becomes a sufficient expression of his knowledge of or love for nature. Mentioning the social context of his beloved nature, or the necessity of social action, would not be nearly as romantic.

Nature is also idealized in the metaphors of deep ecology. "Mother Earth" and "Mother Gaia" reflect an idea of nature as the pure, ideal, all-giving woman for whom every ecologically minded knight should willingly risk his life. The opening paragraph of Kirkpatrick Sale's *Dwellers in the Land* refers to nature in an almost sexual tone as "a vibrant globe of green and blue and grey binding together in a holy, deep-breasted synchrony . . . a pulsing body . . . Gaia, the earth mother."[3] Sale's second chapter, entitled "Gaia Abandoned," further demonstrates this sentimental, idealized posture: the very title personifies nature as an abandoned, helpless woman. In the chapter, Sale expresses concern that "the ways of Gaia have been forgotten" and tells of the decimation of forests and groves over the centuries. But like a true romantic, he focuses his funnel only on a small part of the picture. Rarely if at all does he mention the social conditions that surround his beloved Gaia. Sale fails to mention the declining social position of women within the emerging patricentric societies that plundered natural ecosystems: he focuses only on the degradation of his beloved "woman/nature," named "Gaia."

If ideal love is a longing for a "pure" woman, then surely "Mother Nature" is the woman that *nobody* can screw! Through the lens of romanticism, nature becomes the ultimate "Platonic woman," a distilled idea who has no physical dimensions. She is pure symbol. Therefore, when a bumper sticker commands you to "Love Your Mother," how can you resist? It is far easier to love an abstract idea of an earth mother than it is to love your own mother, who struggles perhaps unflatteringly in a web of patriarchal oppression.

### Ecology and the Cult of Romantic Protection of Nature

The tendency to idealize nature is coupled with the fantasy of protecting an image of nature that is portrayed as weak and vulnerable. During Earth Week 1990, an epidemic of tee-shirts hit the stores depicting sentimal images of a soft blue and green ball of earth being held and protected by two white man's hands. Huddled around the protective hands was a lovable crowd of characteristically wide-eyed, long-lashed, feminine-looking deer, seals, and birds. Underneath the picture was the caption "Love Your Mother." The message was clear: nature is ideal, chaste, and helpless as a baby girl. We must save "her" from the dragon of "Everyman."

However, this romantic posture toward nature has an even nastier side. Romantic protection of nature often hides men's underlying desire to control and denigrate women and people of color. For example, members of Earth First! and others in the deep ecology movement have been quoted as blaming nature's woes largely on "population." The Earth First! journal regularly advertises a sticker that says, "Love Your Mother, Don't Become One." Paradoxically, the same men who romantically express love for "Mother Earth" suggest that mothers are to blame for the denigration of nature. In the name of "protecting Mother Earth," women are reduced to masses of brainless, brown women breeding uncontrollably in the Third World. Meanwhile "Gaia," the idealized mother herself, sits elevated on her galactic pedestal awaiting knightly protection from women's insatiable wombs.

The fantasy of romantic protection blends male perceptions of social reality with male fantasy. The romantic can remain disdainful and ignorant of women's oppression within society while maintaining his fantasy of protecting "woman-nature": in this way, the romantic can love his cake and hate her too. However, removing the veil of romantic protection from the population discussion reveals population imbalances to be the result of patriarchy, colonialism, and capitalism. These institutions disenfranchise women from their own indigenous cultures and their traditional techniques of reproductive control. Throughout history, women have ingeniously managed to control population. However, once women are robbed of cultural knowledge and self-determination, they lose the cultural practices vital to population control. Additional factors, including high infant mortality and the family's need for child labor for survival, contribute to women's having more children than they would ordinarily desire.

Population fetishists rarely point out that "overpopulation" in the Third World contributes little to the overall depletion of the earth's resources. It is rarely considered that one white middle-class person in the United States consumes three hundred times the food and energy mass of one Third World person.[4] In addition, it is widely known that First World corporations are the biggest resource-consumers while also being the biggest polluters. However, those who consume the least are blamed the most, leaving the perpetrators of ecocide sitting under an invisible shroud of feigned innocence.

Deep ecologists, such as Bill Devall and George Sessions, have also been guilty of ignoring the social conditions of women. In many of their writings, they express a particular concern for protecting nature. Often, however, the sweet perfume of romantic ecology disguises a particularly foul-smelling, woman-hating analysis of the origins of and solutions to the denigration of nature, as illustrated in this passage from Devall and Session's *Deep Ecology*:

> Humans are valued more highly individually and collectively than is the endangered species. Excessive human intervention in natural processes

has led other species to near-extinction. For deep ecologists the balance has long been tipped in favor of humans. Now we must shift the balance back to protect the habitat of other species. . . . Protection of wilderness is imperative.[5]

A careful analysis of this passage reveals the sexism and racism that often underlie a sentimental desire to "protect" nature. The romantic ecologist constructs a big, flat category called "human" and holds this abstract human responsible for the destruction of nature. However, it is unclear just who is subsumed under this category of human. Are the authors referring to women, who, rather than participating intentionally and profitably in "human intervention" in nature, are reduced to "bodies of natural labor" and plundered along with nature? Women do 80 percent of the world's labor while owning and controlling less than 1 percent of the world's "resources" and capital. Who indeed is profiting?

Blaming "humanity" for nature's woes blames the human victims as well as the perpetrators of the ecological crisis. Certainly the human victims of capitalism are not to blame for ecological destruction. For example, laborers in Third World countries are reduced by multinational conglomerates to instruments of ecocidal destruction. Like laborers in Auschwitz, they labor to bury a culture and history they love. These laborers fight daily to survive the low-pay slavery that subjects them to deadly working conditions, yet they too are subsumed under the sloppy category of "the accountable human." Failing to expose the social hierarchies within the category of "human" erases the dignity and struggle of those who are reduced to and degraded along with nature. But, again, the struggles of "ladies," women, or people of color are never quite so romantic as those of the knight who protects his beloved nature. And clearly, in the romantic drama of deep ecology, it is the beloved "Lady Gaia" the eco-knight wishes to save, not people.

### Environmentalism as Romantic Constraint

It is commonly held that an environmentally moral society would restrain its capacity to degrade nature. Just as the courtly troubadour demonstrates love for his lady by promising sexual constraint, individuals in society should show their love for nature by promising to constrain their inclination to spoil and deplete the environment. The U.S. media try to promote popular constraint toward nature in a variety of contexts. Advertisers use emotionally laden images of nature in their attempt to evoke in individual Americans a sense of shame and accountability for the destruction of the natural world. For example, a recent television campaign by Pepsi depicts a sentimental image of baby ducks swimming in a reedy pond with small children playing in the sand nearby. The caption urges in pink script, "Preserve It: They Deserve It." Through the use of soft lenses and white children, Pepsi effectively associates the idea of "nature preservation" with an underlying injunction against defiling children.

The Environmental Defense Fund had a recent television campaign showing the "whole earth" photograph suddenly and audibly crumpled by two white man's hands. A stern voice stated dryly, "If you don't recycle, you're throwing it all away." In both instances, the message is clear: If individuals do not constrain their desire to "trash" nature, the natural world is done for.

The theme of romantic constraint is problematic in two ways. First, it actually increases alienation within society and between society and nature. Second, it camouflages the true enemies of both nature and social justice. Western, industrial capitalist society is alienated from nature. To heal this alienation, ecological theory must invite people to come to terms with their distinctive place and role in natural evolution. To accomplish this, ecological theories must help people to recognize and express the human potential for sociability and cooperation both within society and with nature. We need to uncover our ability to be humans-in-nature and humans-as-nature in a new, creative, and liberatory way.

However, the environmental call for individual constraint implies a pessimistic view of society's potential relationship with nature. It suggests that our relationship with the natural world is inherently predicated on a repression of a desire to destroy nature rather than on a desire to enhance nature. "Love as constraint" portrays love only as a holding back, a repression of a destructive desire, rather than as a release of human desire to participate creatively in the natural world. Loving nature through constraint keeps us from identifying and demanding our distinctively human potential to love nature through creativity and cooperation within society. Thus, we fail to see that we can actually release our desire to create a just society where there would be neither "helpless ladies" nor a "helpless Mother Nature" to protect. Focusing on self-restraint obscures the potential for self-expression that we need to create a society free of all social and ecological degradation.

"Love-as-constraint" suggests that we are inherently destructive to each other within society and toward nature. "Love as an enhancement of free-dom" means we can actually enrich the development of other humans as well as nature. This leads to the second point. "Romantic constraint" masks the face of the true destroyer of nature and social justice. Its warped logic runs in this way: If true love is demonstrated through constraint of the desire to defile, then a defiled nature results from the refusal of the lover to constrain her/himself. Thus, in the case of environmental degradation, nature's destruction results from the refusal of individuals to restrain them-selves. In this way, each individual is chastised and shamed for betraying nature.

But is the cause of environmental degradation the failure of individual constraint, and the betrayal of nature? Or is it a few elite men's betrayal of the world? It is essential to distinguish between desire and greed. Desire does not inevitably ravage the earth or its peoples. Desire has the poten-tial to be expressed in liberatory ways that can actually enhance social and ecological relationships. It is the greed for power over others that reduces women, the poor, and all of nature to booty to be bought, sold, and dumped in a landfill.

However, greed is a far less romantic cause for ecocide than is unre-strained "desire." It is much more seductive to wear a button that says, "Love Your Mother" than it is to carry a banner saying, "End Domina-tion and Greed Within Society!" We must uncover the perpetrators of this greedy war against oppressed humanity and nature. We must renounce our vows of "constraint" toward nature while releasing our desire for both a free nature and a free society.

It is time for a radical concept of the love of nature that goes beyond cur-rent romantic notions of idealization, protection, and self-constraint. First, we must explore a "postromantic" concept of "authentic love," grounded in true knowledge of nature. Second, we must explore the idea of "allied resis-tance," a radical alternative to the romantic protection of nature. Third, it is necessary to examine an alternative to "conservationist constraint," draw-ing from the anarchist imperative for the release of creative and cooperative potential within society.

We have already explored the limits of romantic love of nature, show-ing how it often sweetens and camouflages the oppression of women and other oppressed peoples. It is now vital to look more closely at the idea of romantic love within society to clarify and reconstruct a new idea of authentic love of nature within society.

## Romance, Hierarchy, and Alienated Love

Romantic love is predicated on a hierarchical separation between the lover and the beloved. In society, there are a myriad of such hierarchies, based on divisions such as sex, age, and class. Traditionally, men romanticize women, adults romanticize children, and the rich romanticize the poor, just as the master romanticizes the slave. These separations are reinforced by institutions and ideologies that exaggerate differences between groups within the hierarchy. Gender is polarized and exaggerated by rigid gender roles, children are segregated in school ghettos, while their parents are ghettoized in workplaces often segregated by race, class, and sex. These structural and ideological barriers facilitate the condition of social alienation. Within this context, oppressors know very little about the history and lives of the oppressed. Romantic love flourishes between the walls of hierarchy, allowing the oppressor class free reign to paint its own romantic image of the lives and condition of the oppressed.

Romantic love naturalizes and glorifies social domination, making the relationships between oppressor and oppressed appear inevitable, desirable, and even "complementary." It assigns romantic images of both the oppressor and the oppressed that obscure the mutual identification, compassion, and rage that might bring individuals to challenge the social order. Romanticism allows the oppressor to dominate without guilt, and attempts to seduce the oppressed into accepting and even rejoicing in their lot.

Society's increasing alienation from nature has left the idea of nature as fair game for romantic love. Increasing urbanization, suburbanization, and the demise of the family farm leave many of us with little direct participation in the organic cycles of planting and harvesting. Our relationship with the natural world is largely mediated by industries of production and consumption that shape our appetites, tastes, and desires. More and more, the nature we know is some market researcher's romantic idea of a "nature" he thinks we would be likely to buy. The less we know about "the rural life," the more we desire it. So many of us long wistfully for a life we have never lived, but hope to find someday on vacation in Vermont, or rumbling sweetly in a box of wholesome, grainy cereal.

Murray Bookchin, creator of the theory of social ecology, said to me years ago that the more the rural disappears into poverty and agribusiness, the more we would see romantic images of the rural in the media.[6] Sure enough, just as the family-farm crisis peaked, commercials and magazine ads were suddenly riddled with rural images. Grandfathers were every-where, rocking on ruddy porches saying something wise about the good-ness of oat bran, or microwave instant apple pie. Red-cheeked kids began running down dirt roads after a day of hard, wholesome play, ready for Stove-Top Stuffing. Just as the Vermont family dairy farm dissolves, Ben and Jerry's buys the rights to the Woody Jackson cow graphic, transform-ing the Holstein cow image into the "sacred calf" of Vermont.

We are a society of individuals alienated from each other and from nature. If we are not careful, romantic love will continue to rush in, drown-ing out the motivation and analysis necessary for radical social and ecologi-cal change. Authentic love must dissolve hierarchical separations within society and between society and nature. It must undermine social divi-sions—including sex, age, and race—to establish the possibility for mutual understanding, active compassion, and cooperation.

## Knowing Self, Knowing Other

In love, there is a paradox. In order to know and understand that which we love, we must first know ourselves. We must engage in a continual process of becoming conscious of our own beliefs, prejudices, and desires if we are to truly see that which we love. When we fail to know ourselves in this way, the beloved can be nothing more than a mirage of our own desires, a mirage that obstructs our vision of the desires, history, and distinctiveness of our loved one.

For example, the romantic plantation owner in the South certainly never really loved or knew "his" slaves, although many men wrote sentimen-tally of their plantation memories. Romantic love conveniently blots out a recognition of the rage and resistance of oppressed peoples. When the southern master looked out over "his" plantation and romantically ob-served the "innocence" and "loyalty" of the "happy slave singing in the fields," he did not hear the messages of rage and resistance in the slave spirituals, nor did he taste the slave's spit in his soup. Instead, he knew his own desire for the slave to be docile and expedient.

Similarly, when some deep ecologists attempt to understand nature and the causes of ecocide, they project their beliefs about women and oppressed peoples into their understanding of the issues. Many deep ecologists are ignorant of their own sexism and racism. Unknowingly, this sexism and racism surface in their blaming women for depleting the earth by "over-populating." As discussed earlier, the myth that "overpopulation" is the primary cause of ecocide reflects neither knowledge nor love of nature. Instead, such myths reflect the ruling class's desire to blame vulnerable social groups for nature's destruction.

In order to truly love nature, society must know itself. Our idea of nature has become the small, blue pool into which Narcissus gazed, enamored of his own reflection. Narcissus neither saw the color of the water nor felt its coolness on his fingers. When we look into the "pool of nature," we too, cannot see what grows there. We cannot see the creatures, the layers of diversity, or the possibilities of what could emerge. Instead, we see only the romantic reflection of ruling men's desires to preserve the institutions and ideologies that uphold their social power. We see only their desire for women and "Mother Earth" to be nurturing, helpless, and in need of their "protective" control.

The ability to really know nature requires a continual process of critical self-consciousness. We are social creatures looking at the world through social eyes. In order to see nature, we must be increasingly conscious of our social desires and anxieties, our reluctance to relinquish power within society. If we are not conscious of our own greed, then we will see nature as a greedy force from which we must continually steal in order to survive. Similarly, if we are not conscious of the social-religious causes of our own guilt and self-hatred, we will romanticize nature as a "superior" being before which we feel tiny and wretched. Love of nature is a process of becoming aware of and unlearning ideologies of racism, sexism, heterosexism, and able-ism so that we may cease to reduce our idea of nature to a dark, heterosexual, "beautiful" mother. If we do not expel what I call "internalized capitalism," we will continue to see nature as a Darwinian nightmare, a romantic drama in which only the strongest or those best able to make a buck can survive.

In particular, we must extend this critical self-consciousness to our poetic and visual expressions of our love of nature. We must be critical in our use of metaphors and nature images, making sure that they do not reflect racist, sexist, or able-ist beliefs about society. Certainly there are nonpatriarchal, indigenous cultures, such as many Native American cultures, which use female images of nature in a nonsexist way. However, when those who are not from these indigenous cultures attempt to use a "Mother Earth" metaphor, something vital is lost in the translation. A metaphor that emerges within the language of a tribal people cannot be accurately translated into the language of an oppressive people.

Audre Lorde discusses the problem of the slave using the "master's tools" to dismantle the master's house.[7] This has been an ongoing problem especially for feminists using patriarchal language and philosophical constructs to critique and reconstruct patriarchal ideologies. Often the origin of words and their historical relationship to oppressive ideologies actually contradict the very spirit of liberation that feminists attempt to convey. Within the current patriarchal society, female metaphors and images of nature cannot be abstracted from the patriarchal values, desires, and definitions of women that saturate our media, religion, and education from the day we are born. The metaphor of "Mother Nature" is crafted within a patriarchal ideology that "justifies" women's compulsory heterosexuality, motherhood, and submissiveness. It contains within it the history of what it has meant to be a woman and mother within this society, as well as what it has meant for women within this society to continually be compared to our dualistic idea of nature.

It is absurd to encourage people to "love Mother Nature" when motherhood in this culture is oppressive, devalued, and even despised. Only when all radical ecologists become active participants and allies in women's struggle for liberation from the patriarchal institution of motherhood should we begin to talk about the possibility of an authentic love for "mothers."

Clearly, we have little choice but to use language as a means of expressing our thoughts and desires. However, we must be extremely critical in how we import symbols, metaphors, and theoretical constructs from non-hierarchical, tribal cultures. Therefore, I call for a moratorium on female metaphors of nature such as "Mother Earth" until all *women* are free in this society.

As social creatures, we can never see nature as a "purely" natural thing, stripped of social meaning. We will never uncover nature as a "thing in itself." In fact, nature is not some "thing" that we can separate ourselves from and finally "know," no matter how liberatory our culture or language may be. Nature is the water in our bodies and the wind in our hair. Within our bodies, each of us contains DNA from the first cells of evolution. Instead of trying desperately to know nature solely through language or contemplation, we must also begin to know ourselves. It is vital that we enter into a lifelong process of critical self-reflection, until we become a society conscious of itself as a crucial, potentially liberatory moment in natural history.

## Knowing, Caring, and Labors of Love

Authentic love is a celebration of the distinctiveness of the other, which we begin to see when we begin to know ourselves. However, this knowledge of other people and of nature must be gleaned from actual labor or "caring for" the beloved. Love cannot be "acquired" by meditating in isolation. In her essay "Women and Caring: What Can Feminists Learn About Morality from Caring?" Joan Tronto states that within the sexual division of labor, women are assigned the direct service of "caring for" children, the old, the sick, while men are credited for "caring about" such romantic ideals as "the prosperity of the family."[8] Although women's labor emerges out of patriarchal structures, and is often taxing and undervalued, Tronto points out a liberatory dimension to women's domestic labor. According to Tronto, many women develop a relational way of loving and knowing informed by their direct experience in caring for peoples of different ages, needs, and abilities. Women's love for those in their care does not emerge from an abstract romantic sentiment. Instead, it emerges from an appreciation and knowledge of the particular needs, experiences and level of development of their loved ones.

By discussing this "domestic tradition," I do not intend to romanticize the institutions of compulsory marriage, motherhood, and domestic labor. I also do not imply that women should extend these services to ecology by becoming the movement's janitorial martyrs. Rather, my aim is to highlight a liberatory aspect of women's history that is crucial to the ecology movement as a whole. What is impressive is that this "tradition of relatedness" emerged in spite of women's social alienation and oppression.

In women's work lies the historical intersection between love and ecology. In fact, ecology itself emerged out of the insights of a woman concerned with women's "labors of love" in the home. In the late 1800s Ellen Swallow coined the term "ecology" and founded the science of "home ecology."[9] Concerned with the interrelationship among air, water, food, and human health, Swallow founded America's first "pure food movement," and in 1882 the state of Massachusetts passed the country's first pure food laws. She was among the first to fight for pure water, creating the world's first Water Purity Tables. She also empowered women, isolated in their homes, to become scientists, sending them microscopes, specimens, and lessons on how to maintain health in the domestic workplace. Swallow's "home ecology," later reduced to "home economics" by public schools, highlighted the relationship between a love of nature and a love of humans as a part of nature. She neither romanticized nature nor reduced nature to an expendable resource that one can spoil and waste. She created a science that cared for both social and ecological ecosystems.

It is no coincidence that the U.S. anti-toxics movement has been founded and led primarily by women, many of whom are housewives. Out of their intimate knowledge of and commitment to home ecology emerged their fight against chemical waste dumps that leached into their backyards, poisoning their children. Often a love of nature emerged in these women as they cared for their children, fighting for clean water and food. These women rarely express a sentimental or romantic love of nature. Rather, they rage audaciously, leading the fight for the survival of their eco-communities.

The ecology movement today should also be a "home ecology" that expresses this love of nature through active care for social and ecological eco-communities. Swallow's term "ecology" comes from the Greek words "oikos" and "logos," or "the way of the house." A true "oiko-logy" dissolves the hierarchical separations between the privatized domestic realm of the home and the alienated public realm. As true "oiko-logists," we do not just care about our own private backyards and bodies. We also care for "the world home," in all of its social and ecological diversity.

If we live in an urban setting, and our eco-community is socially permeated on a large scale, then our love of nature will be expressed and learned through enhancing community cooperation—for example, by creating working and living cooperatives, community centers, gardens, and projects. On the Lower East Side of Manhattan, a largely Puerto Rican community created a center called "Charas" that cares for a variety of the community's needs. Through its "sweat equity" project, for example, individuals renovate abandoned buildings in exchange for housing. The center also sponsors political murals and theater projects as well as community gardens, which provide not only food but also an opportunity for mutual aid. Love of nature is learned not only by caring for the soil in the community garden, and crafting windmills and solar panels on top of community buildings, but also by caring for the creative and social needs of human nature within that ecosystem.

Love of nature emerges from knowledge of oppression and potential liberation within our eco-communities. We learn this love by actively caring for our social and natural eco-communities, by fighting all forms of social oppression, and by expressing our potential for cooperation and creative enhancement of nature.

## From Romantic Protection to Allied Resistance

As we begin to know and care for society and nature, the idea of romantically "protecting nature" will become obsolete. Instead, we will strive to know and care for the resistance of all living things that dwell in poisoned eco-communities, offering ourselves as allies in resistance to social and ecological degradation. The question will no longer be how to "protect" nature, but, rather, how to liberate humans within society so that we may create a harmonious, ecological world.

It is time for an ecology movement committed to ending all forms of domination. This movement must force those in power to completely relinquish economic and psychological privileges that weigh down the backs of the oppressed globally, no matter how "big" or "small" that privilege may be. Even if it is the poor man's "privilege" of beating or degrading "his" woman, or making a few more dollars on the hour, it all must go, along with the patriarchal ideologies and institutions that justify this privilege. An ecological society, free of all forms of domination, will express the human ability to participate fully in developing the richness and creativity of both the natural and the social world.

Entering into a social movement is not as romantic as "saving" nature. When we cease to focus exclusively on "protecting nature," we are forced to encounter people. We encounter the rage, desires, and often the rightful mistrust of the oppressed as well as the unrelinquished privilege of those in the ruling class. The decision to become active in a social movement implies meeting oppression within social movements as well as in the world at large. Within every movement, just as within every individual, is a degree of racism, sexism, and anti-Semitism, to name but a few forms of domination. Engaging in work for social change includes confronting and unlearning oppression within our groups and communities.

Becoming an ally in resistance also means relinquishing the desire for romantic heroism. When supporting the struggle of our own or another people, we must let go of our desires to "save" or control others. As discussed earlier, we are still living out the scripts of the romantic era, secretly desiring to control others in the name of helpful "protection." However, true liberation requires collective participation and cooperation in a struggle in which no one is "saved."

Instead of romanticizing the idea of "protecting" the lands and wildlife that are being destroyed by the flooding for the Hydro-Quebec dam, we offer our time, money, and labor to the Inuit and Cree people who have known and cared for their eco-community for thousands of years. Similarly, the forests in India do not need our "protection." Rather, the women in the Chipko "tree-hugging" movement need allies in their fight to maintain the forests on which their survival depends.

We cannot think of nature as a maternal abstraction that we must "preserve." Abstracting natural ecosystems from social ecosystems reflects no love of nature. Instead, it reflects a carelessly racist or sexist dismissal of humanity. Campaigns to "save the whales" or "save the rain forests" that make no connection to the indigenous peoples who struggle within those eco-communities fail to help the public make the connection between social domination and ecocide.

Ecologists often discuss the necessity of "seeing the forest through the trees," or seeing beyond individual environmental problems or solutions to address the ecological crisis in its entirety. I implore us all to "see the *women* through the trees"; to see the women who work in factories packaging the trees once they are reduced to useless objects; to see the women whose cultures and soil are eroded through deforestation; and to see the women whose husbands hit them with trees, honed down to the shape of a baseball bat. In addition, if we do not see all human oppression and suffering through the trees, and the struggle for self-determination through the trees, then the ecology movement will achieve only one big forest "nature preserve," with the oppressed still struggling along the perimeter.

Last, there is a temptation to romanticize one's alliance with struggles of self-determination. Many in radical ecological and social movements are lured by the struggles of people living in what they see as "exotic" cultures. We must be critical of such romantic motivations for becoming allies. We must be conscious of our preconceptions about different cultures, and our misuse of privilege. Often, people are eager to fly to warm, far-off countries to wage a campaign, yet are less enthusiastic about fighting poverty, violence against women, or toxic waste in their own communities.

## Romantic Constraint: Conservatism, Conservation, and Reactionary Nostalgia

"We" are warned to behave chivalrously toward nature, to restrain "our" inclination to despoil, ravage, and plunder nature's splendor. Television campaigns appeal to many Americans' Christian guilt, reinforcing the belief that humans are a flawed and fallen species. We are admonished to solve the ecological crisis personally, by driving less, recycling more, and turning lights out when leaving a room. We are told that "our" careless extravagance has caused the hole in the ozone, the erasure of the rainforests, and the poisoning of the oceans. Each of us is the dragon, we are told, devouring nature with insatiable appetites. We must redeem ourselves by behaving in a knightly manner, promising Lady Nature that we will restrain ourselves.

Implicit within romantic propaganda is a reactionary nostalgia for the "simple life" of the past. The old guy in the Quaker oatmeal commercial suggests that living simply is the "right thing to do." An Emersonian nature romanticism wafts through the air, telling us that all we need is a simple house, a good book, and a chestnut or two to roast on the fire. It is time to end our years of debauchery, time to buckle down. The family is re-romanticized as in the fifties; babies are "in," and "family values" must be restored.

This romantic "conservationism" smacks of political conservatism. Many conservationists and conservatives emphasize the "goodness" of the past. A recent advertisement put out by the manufacturers of Geo says, "In the 90's More People Will Lead Simpler Lives, Protect the Environment, Rediscover Romance And . . . Get to Know Geo." Their full-page ad presents a black-and-white photograph of a hometown-looking teenage boy and girl relaxing wholesomely in a convertible. The girl has long, blond, naturally flowing hair, wears no makeup, and sits in a simple skirt with her knees together. Their clothes are clearly from the late fifties, when the country was still "innocent."

The ad suggests that the nineties will be a time of "restoring" the simplicity of the days before the Vietnam War and the civil rights and women's movements. Romance, which the women's movement "destroyed" by challenging gender roles, will be restored as well. The nineties environmental campaign will attempt to conflate the debauchery of right-wing capitalism with the political struggles of the left as the cause of ecocide. The cause of environmental destruction will quite possibly be portrayed as a breakdown of "simple" Christian family life, and the breakdown of romance and chivalry between the sexes.

The Nazis in Germany also romanticized a connection between nature and the good, "simple" past. They fabricated an entire romantic drama in which German Nationalism sought to preserve the purity of the "blood and soil" of the "Aryan" people. Germans were encouraged to recover their close tie to nature, to the German wilderness, in order to purge themselves of the poison of foreign, decadent influences such as Leftists and Jews. As in our current romantic environmental campaign, Germany romanticized and sought to reclaim a past that never existed. Like ours, the German media also presented images of blond, wholesome youth romantically frolicking in nature, free from the "dark" forces and races that plagued the cities.

There is nothing romantic about living simply. Women and the poor have lived the real "simple life" for centuries, impoverished by the economic and social institutions of compulsory heterosexuality, motherhood, and alienated labor. A life without choices, alternatives, and in many cases material survival is indeed very simple. Women and all oppressed peoples cannot afford to live any more "simply." Because so many of us have lived simply, restrained by authority for centuries, the romantic appeal to conserve nature sounds seductively familiar. So many of us accept these warnings without even thinking. However, when we look closer, we see that the ultimate imperative is not to "conserve" nature, but to release human potential for radical change within society.

These warnings to conserve natural resources and to exercise environmental constraint imply that "we" have been "partying it up" and now must get sober. Nothing could be farther from the truth. The "party" ended when domination emerged within society thousands of years ago, adding capitalism to its list of atrocities only during the last several centuries. Under patriarchy, women and all oppressed peoples have been forced to restrain their desire for freedom, expression, and self-determination. We have constrained, held back, our passions, creativity, and desires for a truly liberatory society.

When George Bush, "the environmental president," instructs us to conserve nature, perhaps he is really warning us to conserve the structure of this authoritarian society. The media campaigns have an authoritarian flavor that appeals to our expectations of social control and direction. Surely these campaigns do not encourage the public to question the economic and social structures that are the true causes of ecocide.

We are asked to conserve more, waste less. However, capitalism itself is never challenged as a system that promotes and depends on wasteful consumption. Ironically, capitalism shapes the false needs that we are chastised for attempting to satisfy. Our lives are vacuous. We are alienated in our work, in our communities, and in our ideas of nature. We live within an economic system that depends on a poor underclass, a system that requires ever-new human and natural "resources" to survive. Yet, again, no one questions whether this system is inherently flawed. Instead, the flaw is assumed to be inherent within "human nature."

Indeed, wasteful consumption must end. But this end must be achieved by abolishing capitalism and social domination, not merely by recycling and encouraging the rich to buy expensive "ecologically sound" products. The slew of new "environmentally friendly" products that crowd even mainstream market shelves are unaffordable to many working- and middle-class consumers. These products alleviate the ecological anxiety of the rich while perpetuating an oppressive economic system that ultimately exploits humans and nature.

The romantic drama of ecology is over. It is time for a new era. The knights can stop protecting nature and restraining their unchivalrous desires. The dragon no longer hovers over the romantic countryside flashing the generic name tag of "technology" or "humanity." The dragon has finally taken off its mask. It wears the face of the capitalist draining the blood from the land and people of the "Third World." The dragon wears the fist of the batterer beating the last breath from the woman who dared survive. The dragon wears the face of domination, the face of all institutions, ideologies, and individuals who strip people of their land, culture, passion, and self-determination.

## Beyond the Cult of the Romantic: Anarchism and an Erotic Love of Nature

Learning to love, know, and care for nature is a process of personal and social transformation. Audre Lorde describes this transformation as a recovery of the erotic, as a resurgence of an "internal sense of satisfaction," or "the power which comes from sharing deeply any pursuit with another person."[10] If this is true, then we are truly in an erotic crisis. We are forced to pawn off our passion, funneling it exclusively into sexual relationships, if we are so lucky. We must revive the full spectrum of the erotic, demanding that all aspects of work and community be infused with a spirit of aliveness and passion.

As we become more alive, we will demand a quality of life that is impossible under the current hierarchy. To make this demand, the ecology movement must also become an anarchist movement, eradicating all forms of hierarchy to release the human, erotic potential for cooperation within society. Social ecology, a body of ecoanarchist theory founded by Murray Bookchin, explains that ecology must embody an anarchist critique and reconstructive vision of society if the movement is to truly achieve its liberatory goals. Bookchin has been active for decades as an activist, educator, and theorist, challenging the ecology movement to become a radical, social movement committed to ending all forms of social and ecological degradation.

Emma Goldman shows how domination deprives people not only of material needs but of sensual and social ones. Authority kills our capacity for self-expression and joy within the context of a cooperative community. People are curious, social creatures with the need to taste, see, and dance in the world. We have a desire to know and to be known, and to explore the perimeters of our imaginations and abilities. However, in exchange for true, erotic love, we have been fed nutritionless food, with romance thrown in as a sweetener. In exchange for feeling connected to others, to our work, and to nature, we are encouraged to connect to lifeless symbols of joy and power in the form of money and possessions. Instead of knowing each other authentically, we are taught to construct romantic ideas and expectations of one another, which can only keep the oppressed down while keeping the oppressors living a destructive illusion. The erotic has been drained from our work and sexuality, reducing them both to alienated relationships of domination and submission.

Within an alienated society, we are recognized only by the number of our possessions. We are afraid of being truly known, for fear of another seeing our emptiness. However, in an erotic, anarchistic society, we desire to know and to be known authentically by the talents expressed through our art, work, and care for others. Cooperative labor and activities of care make our relationships more complex, more interdependent, woven together like a basket that holds our potential for compassion and creativity.

We must create an "erotic democracy" that decentralizes power and allows for direct, passionate participation in the decisions that determine our lives. We must establish a municipal economy that addresses the needs and abilities of all citizens by creating systems including barter and worker cooperatives. We must rethink technology as a creative art form that can add to the splendor of both the social and natural worlds. We can actually choose our technologies, just as an artist chooses her brushes, to paint a vibrant, vital, social and ecological vision. We can choose to make the soils richer, to make the waters flourish with life. Goldman says of anarchism:

> Anarchism, then, really stands for the liberation of the human mind from the dominion of religion; the liberation of the human body from the dominion of property; liberation from the shackles and restraint of government. Anarchism stands for a social order based on the free grouping

of individuals for the purpose of creating real social wealth; an order that will guarantee to every human being free access to the earth and full enjoyment of the necessities of life, according to individual desires, tastes, and inclinations.[11]

Anarchism, then, really stands for the liberation of the human spirit and nature from the dominion of romantic love; the liberation of the woman's body from the dominion of romanticized sexuality, marriage, and motherhood; liberation of all from the shackles of alienated labor and social powerlessness romanticized by ideologies of oppression. Ultimately, an anarchist love of nature emerges from an erotic love of ourselves as human nature; an erotic love, knowledge, and care for our ability to be fully human in the most social and cooperative sense. Only when we have discarded romantic love will we be able to know our true erotic "desires, tastes, and inclinations." Only when we begin to uncover the potential for freedom, diversity, and self-determination among all human beings will we begin to understand and truly appreciate the power and beauty of the natural world.

The cult of romantic love of nature leads us away from the real work of ecology. We must begin to be conscious of that which obscures our knowledge of women and nature, actively knowing and caring for ourselves, each other, and nature. We must relinquish our romantic desire to be protectors, becoming allies in resistance to all who fight for a socially just and ecologically sustainable world. Entering the erotic era means releasing our potential for passionate, creative expression, our desire to know and to be known within a compassionate, ecological society.

The ecology movement will not be truly radical until we radicalize our idea of what it means to love, know, and care for nature. We must transcend the romantic relationships between "man" and nature, "knight" and "helpless lady," and ultimately "master and slave" if we are to abolish all forms of social and ecological degradation. Our role is not to idealize, protect, or restrain, but to care for each other and for nature in a way that truly expresses an authentic love for the natural and social worlds.

NOTES

1. Denis de Rougemont, *Love in the Western World* (Princeton: Princeton University Press, 1983), 106–7.
2. Ibid., 64.

3. Kirkpatrick Sale, "Gaia," in *Dwellers in the Land: The Bioregional Vision* (San Francisco: Sierra Club Books, 1985), 3.

4. Betsy Hartman, *Reproductive Rights and Wrongs: The Global Politics of Population Control and Reproductive Choice* (New York: Harper & Row, 1987).

5. Bill Devall, and George Sessions, "Why Wilderness in the Nuclear Age?" in *Deep Ecology: Living As If Nature Mattered* (Salt Lake City: Peregrine Smith Books, 1985), 127.

6. From a conversation with Murray Bookchin, July 18, 1984.

7. Audre Lorde, "The Master's Tools Will Never Dismantle the Master's House," in *Sister Outsider* (New York: Crossing Press, 1984), 110–13.

8. Joan Tronto, "Women and Caring: What Can Feminists Learn About Morality from Caring?" in *Gender Body Knowledge*, ed. Susan Bordo and Alison Jaggar (New Brunswick, N.J.: Rutgers University Press, 1989), 172–88.

9. Patricia Hynes, "Catalysts of the Environmental Movement," *Woman of Power* 9 (1988): 37–39.

10. Audre Lorde, "Uses of the Erotic: The Erotic as Power," in *Sister Outsider*, 53–59.

11. Emma Goldman, "Anarchism: What It Really Stands For," in *Anarchism and Other Essays* (New York: Dover Publications, 1969), 62.

# CHAPTER 10

# From Heroic to Holistic Ethics: The Ecofeminist Challenge

## Marti Kheel

As the destruction of the natural world proceeds at breakneck speed, nature ethicists have found themselves in search of a theory that can serve to bring this destruction to a halt.[1] Just as the prototypical hero in patriarchal stories must rescue the proverbial "damsel in distress," so, too, the sought-after theory must demonstrate heroic qualities. It must, singlehandedly, rescue the ailing body of "Mother Nature" from the villains who have bound and subdued her. The theoretical underpinnings of environmental and animal liberation philosophies are seen by many ethical theorists as having the necessary "intellectual muscle" to perform this heroic feat.[2] But is a heroic ethic a helpful response to the domination of nature, or is it another conqueror in a new disguise?

It is significant that ecofeminists have, by and large, declined to join the "hunt" for an environmental ethic or "savior theory." The writings within ecofeminism have largely ignored the heated debates engaged in by (predominantly) male philosophers over what should constitute the basis of an appropriate ethic for the natural world. A glance at the vast majority of ecofeminist writings reveals, instead, a tendency to concentrate on exposing the underlying mentality of exploitation that is directed against women and nature within the patriarchal world.[3] Whereas nature ethicists have tended to concentrate on "rescuing" the "damsel in distress," ecofeminists have been more likely to ask how and why the "damsel" arrived at her present plight.

Clearly ecofeminists have taken a different approach to the current crisis in nature. No single theory is sought or expected to emerge, through reasoned competition with the others, as the most powerful or compelling one. In fact, no single ethical theory seems to be sought at all. What have been emerging, rather, are a number of theories or stories that, when woven together into a fabric or tapestry, help to provide a picture or "portrait" of the world in which we currently live.[4] Whereas mainstream nature ethicists have based much of their analysis on abstract principles and universal rules, ecofeminists have tended to highlight the role of metaphors and images of nature. The emphasis has been not on developing razor-sharp theories that can be used to dictate future conduct, but rather on painting a "landscape" (or "mindscape") of the world.

This is not to say that ecofeminists have merely described our current problems, showing no interest in changing the world. On the contrary, ecofeminists have been deeply committed to social transformation. The method of transformation that ecofeminists have subscribed to, however, is premised on the insight that one cannot change what one does not understand. Understanding the inner workings of patriarchal society is emphasized precisely so that society might be transformed. The transformation that ecofeminists wish to bring about is, thus, often implicit in their critiques. If the images of women and nature under patriarchal society have facilitated the exploitation and abuse of both, then, clearly, new ways of perceiving the world must be sought. The natural world will be "saved" not by the sword of ethical theory, but rather through a transformed consciousness toward all of life.

The emphasis on developing new ways of perceiving the world is in keeping with much of the recent work in feminist moral theory. Feminist moral theorists have begun to show that ethics is not so much the imposition of obligations and rights, but rather a natural outgrowth of how one views the self, including one's relation to the rest of the world. Before one can change the current destructive relation to nature, we must, therefore, understand the world view upon which this relation rests. Just as a health-care practitioner would not attempt to treat an illness without understanding the nature and history of the disease, many feminists would argue that it is not possible to transform the current world view of patriarchy without understanding the disease that has infected the patriarchal mind. What, then, is the world view that patriarchy has bequeathed us?

## *The Conquest of Nature: The Damsel Is Distressed*

The predominant image of nature throughout the Western, patriarchal world has been that of an alien force. Nature, which has been imaged as female, has been depicted as the "other," the raw material out of which culture and masculine self-identity are formed. Two major images have been

244

used to achieve separation from nature.[5] One of the most common images has been that of the Beast.[6] The Beast is conceived as a symbol for all that is not human, for that which is evil, irrational, and wild. Civilization is thus achieved by driving out or killing the Beast. On an inward level, this involves driving out all vestiges of our own animality—the attempt to obliterate the knowledge that we are animals ourselves.[7] Outwardly, the triumph over the Beast has been enacted through the conquest of wilderness, with its concomitant claim to the lives of millions of animals driven from their lands.

The triumph over the demonic Beast has been a recurring theme throughout the mythologies of the patriarchal world. Typically, the slain Beast is a former divinity from the earlier matriarchal world. The serpents, dragons, and horned gods, who were at one time worshiped as divine, are transformed in patriarchal mythology into devils and monsters that must be slain. Thus, Apollo slays Gaia's python; Perseus kills the three-headed Medusa (the triple goddess), who is described as having snakes writhing from her head; Hercules defeats the terrible multiheaded Hydra; and the pharaohs of later Egypt slay the dragon Apophys.[8] In the Middle Ages, there were countless renditions of St. George's prowess in killing the dragon—again, to rescue the "damsel in distress."

Frequently the death of the Beast is said to herald the birth of light and order, either at the beginning or the end of time. Thus, in the Sumero-Babylonian *Epic of Gilgamesh*, Marduk kills his mother, the goddess Tiamat, the great whale-dragon or cosmic serpent, and from her body the universe is made. Both Judaism and Christianity continue the dragon-slaying tradition. According to St. John the Divine, at the world's end an angel with a key will subdue the dragon that is Satan. And in the Hebrew legend, the death of the serpentlike Leviathan is prophesied for the Day of Judgment. In Christianity, the task of killing the dragonlike monster was transferred from gods and heroes to saints and archangels. The archangel Michael was a notable dragon-slayer. Faith, prayer, and divine intervention came to be seen as the new dragon-slayers whose task it is to restore the world of order.

These myths of violence and conquest contrast sharply with the mythologies of prepatriarchal cultures. The cosmological stories of these societies typically depicted the beginning of life as emerging from a female-imaged goddess who embodied the earth. Thus, Gaia, in the earliest Greek myths, was thought to give birth to the universe by herself. And the snake, so much feared in our current culture, was worshiped in such societies as divine. By the time of the biblical story of the Garden of Eden, a totally new world view had emerged. Both a woman and an animal were by this time depicted as the source of all evil in the world. And "Man," above all other forms of life, was claimed to have a special relation to the divine.

Today, the heroic battle against unruly nature is reenacted as ritual drama in such masculine ventures as sport-hunting, bullfights, and rodeos. A similar mentality can be seen in the ritual degradation of women in pornography and rape. As Susan Griffin points out, pornography is ritual drama.[9] It is the heroic struggle of the masculine ego to deny the knowledge of bodily feelings and one's dependence upon women and all of the natural world.

The second image of nature appears less heroic but is equally violent in its own way. It is the image of nature as mindless matter, which exists to serve the needs of superior, rational "Man." In this image, animals are depicted as having different, unequal natures rather than as wild or evil creatures that must be conquered and subdued. They are not so much irrational as nonrational beings. Along with women, they are viewed as mere "matter" (a word that, significantly, derives from the same root word as "mother").

Both Aristotelian and Platonic philosophy contributed to the conception of nature as inert or mindless matter. It was the Aristotelian notion of purpose and function, however, that especially helped to shape the Western world's instrumental treatment of women and nature.[10] According to Aristotle, there was a natural hierarchical ordering to the world, within which each being moved toward fulfillment of its own particular end. Since the highest end of "Man" was the state of happiness achieved through rational contemplation, the rest of nature was conveniently ordered to free "Man" to attain this contemplative goal. Thus, plants existed to give subsistence to animals, and animals to give it to "Man"; and the specific function of women, animals, and slaves was to serve as instruments for the attainment of the highest happiness of free, adult men. There is no need to conquer nature in this conception, since nature has already been safely relegated to an inferior realm.

The Jewish-Christian tradition has also contributed to an instrumental and hierarchical conception of nature.[11] The Genesis account of Creation must bear a large share of the guilt for this state of affairs. In the priestly account of the Genesis story of Creation, we are told that God gave "Man" "dominion over every living thing that moveth upon the earth" (Genesis 1:26). And in the Yahwist version, chronologically an earlier account, we are told that nonhuman animals were created by God to be helpers or companions for Adam, and when they were seen as unfit, Eve was created to fulfill this role (Genesis 2:22). Both stories, in their distinct ways, reinforce the notion that women and nature exist only for the purpose of serving "Man."[12]

The conception of nature as an object for "Man's" use was carried to an ultimate extreme by Cartesian philosophy. According to Descartes, since animals were lacking in "consciousness" or "reason," they were mere machines that could feel no pain. Smashing the legs of a monkey, Descartes "reasoned," would hurt no more than removing the hands of a clock. With Cartesian philosophy, the wild, demonic aspect of nature was, thus, finally laid to rest, and the image of nature as a machine was born.

The image of nature (and women) as mindless objects is typically employed for more practical goals—profit, convenience, and knowledge. Division and control, not conquest, are the guiding motives; the rationality of the detached observer replaces the pleasure of conquest as the psychological mode. The use of animals in laboratories, factory farms, and fur ranches exemplifies this frame of mind, as does the image and use of women as "housewives" and "breeding machines." In the earlier (Beastly) image, nature is seen as a harlot; in this conception, nature is more like a slave or wife.

Although the two images of nature may seem unrelated, they merely represent different points along a single scale. In one image, nature is seen as a demonic being who must be conquered and subdued. In the other image, nature has been subdued to the point of death. Behind both images, however, lies a single theme—namely, the notion of nature as the "other," a mental construct in opposition to which a masculine, autonomous self is attained. In one, the violence appears to be perpetrated by an aggressive masculine will; in the other, through the use of reason. But the underlying theme remains the same—namely, the notion of the aggressive establishment of the masculine self through its opposition to all of the natural world.[13]

Feminist psychoanalytic theory has helped to shed light on the psychological motives that lie behind the need men feel to separate violently from the female world. According to object-relations theory, both the boy and the girl child's earliest experience is that of an undifferentiated oneness with the mother figure. Although both must come to see themselves as separate from the mother figure, the boy child, unlike the girl, must come to see himself as opposed to all that is female as well. Thus, the mother figure, and by extension all women, become not just *an* other, but *the* other—the object against which the boy child's identity is formed and defined.[14]

Object-relations theorists, such as Dorothy Dinnerstein, have also argued that it is not just women who become an object against which men establish their sense of self, but that nature becomes objectified as well.[15] Women and nature both come to represent the world of contingency and vulnerability that men must transcend. The twin need to separate from women and from nature can be discerned in typical male rituals of initiation into adulthood. A boy's entrance into manhood is typically marked by separation from women and often by violence toward the nonhuman world. In many tribal cultures a boy is initiated into manhood by being sent off to hunt and kill an animal. In other cultures, "baptisms of blood" occur when a young man goes to war or sexually penetrates a woman for the first time.[16]

## *The Protection of Nature: The Damsel Is Redressed*

If the cult of masculinity has been modeled on the image of predation, the field of nature ethics has been modeled on that of protection. Both animal liberation and environmental ethics spring from a common defensive reaction to the willful aggression perpetrated upon the natural world. Animal liberationists concentrate much of their energies on protecting those animals reduced to the status of inert matter or machines—that is, animals in laboratories and factory farms. Environmental ethicists, by contrast, devote themselves primarily to protecting those parts of nature that are still "wild." But the underlying motive remains the same—namely, the urge to defend and protect.[17]

Various modalities have been proposed for how the defense of nature might best be waged. Typically, nature ethicists have felt compelled to arm themselves with the force of philosophical theory in coming to nature's defense. Whereas patriarchal society has sought to destroy the natural world, nature ethicists have sought to place it under the protective wing of ethical theory. However, as Sarah Hoagland points out, predation and protection are twin aspects of the same world view: "Protection objectifies just as much as predation."[18]

In their attempt to forge iron-clad theories to defend the natural world, nature ethicists have come to rely on the power and strength of a reasoned defense. Reason is enlisted as the new hero to fight on nature's behalf. In the past, humans (primarily men) have conceived of themselves as proprietors of the object-laden natural world.[19] Today, many nature ethicists conceive of themselves not as the owners of nature, but as the owners of value, which it is their prerogative to mete out with a theoretical sweep of their pens. Ethical deliberation on the value of nature is conceived more or less like a competitive sport. Thus, nature ethicists commonly view themselves as "judges" in a game that features competing values out of which a hierarchy must be formed. The outcome is that some must win and others must lose. If a part of nature is accorded high value (typically by being assigned a quality that human beings are said to possess, such as sentience, consciousness, rationality, autonomy), then it is allowed entrance into the world of "moral considerability." If, on the other hand, it scores low (typically by being judged devoid of human qualities), it is relegated to the realm of "objects" or "things," and seen as unworthy of "interests" or "rights." The conferral of value in ethical deliberation is conceived as the conferral of power.[20] "Inherent value" or "inherent worth" (the highest values) accrue to nature to the extent that nature can be rescued from the object world.[21] Much of the heated debate among nature ethicists occurs over what class of entities may rightfully be granted admittance to the subject realm. The presumption behind this conceptual scheme is that if an entity is not graced with the status of "subject," it will become the "object" of abuse.

Both animal liberationists and environmental ethicists seek to curb the willful destruction of the natural world through another act of human will. Reason is, once again, elevated above the natural instincts and asked to control our aggressive wills. The same reason that was used to take value out of nature (through objectification and the imposition of hierarchy) is now asked to give it value once again. A sound ethic, according to this view, must transcend the realm of contingency and particularity, grounding itself not in our untrustworthy instincts, but rather in rationally derived principles and abstract rules. It must stand on its own as an autonomous construct, distinct from our personal inclinations and desires, which it is designed to control. Ethics is intended to operate much like a machine. Feelings are considered, at best, as irrelevant, and at worst, as hazardous intrusions that clog the "ethical machinery." Basing an argument on love or compassion is tantamount to having no argument at all. As Peter Singer boasts in his well-known *Animal Liberation*, nowhere in his book will readers find an appeal to emotion where it cannot be substantiated by rational argument.[22]

In their attempt to forge iron-clad theories to defend the natural world, nature ethicists have, in many ways, come to replicate the aggressive or predatory conception of nature that they seek to oppose. They leave intact a Hobbesian world view in which nature is conceived as "red in tooth and claw," with self-interest as the only rule of human conduct.[23] The presumption is that only reason compels people to submit to sovereign rule—in this case, not that of a king, but that of ethical theory. Ethics, according to this world view, comes to replicate the same instrumental mentality that has characterized our interaction with the natural world. It is reduced to the status of a tool, designed to restrain what is perceived as an inherently aggressive will.

Not all philosophers of nature have relied on axiological or value theory to rescue nature from her current plight. A number of writers, working in what some refer to as the field of ecophilosophy,[24] have sought to ground their philosophy not in the rational calculation of value, but rather in a transformed consciousness toward all of life.[25] Although they share with nature ethicists the urge to rescue nature from the object realm, they reject a "values in nature" philosophy in favor of grounding their philosophy in a particular phenomenological world view.

Often the search for this transformed consciousness is described in terminology that borrows freely from the field of resource development. For example, we read of the search for the "conceptual resources" or the "foundations" of an environmental consciousness.[26] Although various religious and philosophical traditions have been proposed as suitable "resources" for the development of this consciousness, it is the images and metaphors of nature within these traditions that are the primary focus of concern. Some of the images and metaphors for nature that have been proffered as "fertile" grounds for the development of an environmental consciousness include that of an "interconnected web," "a community of living beings," an "organism," and an "expanded Self." The science of ecology has provided additional support for a world view that perceives all of life as an interconnected web or a single living being. The tendency of many ecophilosophers is to "mine" these conceptual systems for an ecological consciousness, rather than to examine their own feelings and emotions toward the natural world.[27]

The underlying motive for the reconceptualization of the natural world is the urge to rescue nature from the aggression that is thought to ensue without these conceptual restraints. History has, in fact, shown that particular conceptions of nature have acted as a restraint against human aggression. As Carolyn Merchant points out:

> The image of the earth as a living organism and nurturing mother has historically served as a cultural constraint restricting the actions of human beings. One does not readily slay a mother, dig into her entrails for gold, or mutilate her body. . . . As long as the earth was considered to be alive and sensitive, it could be considered a breach of human ethical behavior to carry out destructive acts against it.[28]

Many ecofeminists, inspired by the premodern conceptions of Gaia or "Mother Earth," have consciously sought to reclaim these images.[29] For most ecofeminists, however, this attempt to revive the image of Gaia is grounded not in systematic phenomenology but, rather, in a feeling of spiritual connection with the natural world. A female image of the earth simply seems to have resonance for many ecofeminists as a contrast to the patriarchal notion of a male sky god.[30]

Yet the image of the earth as a living being is insufficient in and of itself to bring a halt to the current destruction of the natural world. The attempt by many ecophilosophers to graft a new image onto our current conception of nature fails to challenge the underlying structures and attitudes that have produced the image they seek to supplant. The underlying tendencies toward aggression that exist under patriarchy are thus left intact.

The Gaia hypothesis, proposed by the scientist James Lovelock, illustrates this point. The hypothesis originally was hailed by ecophilosophers for reviving the notion of the earth as a living being. This initial enthusiasm, however, was subsequently tempered when Lovelock concluded that the earth, as a result of its self-regulating mechanisms, was perfectly capable of enduring humanity's insults. Lovelock boldly claimed, "It seems very unlikely that anything we do will threaten Gaia. . . . The damsel in distress [the environmentalist] expected to rescue appears as a buxom and robust man-eating mother."[31] With Lovelock's theory, the earth was "revived," but the underlying structures and attitudes that promote aggression were left unchallenged. Thus, although ecophilosophers have avoided some of the pitfalls of nature ethics, with its attendant notion of obligations and rights, they have often left unchallenged the deeper problem entailed in the notion of ethics as a form of restraint.

The notion of ethical conduct as restraint of aggression is clearly illustrated in the writings of Aldo Leopold, considered by many to be the founder of ecophilosophy and the environmental movement. Deep ecologists have pointed to Leopold's "land ethic" as the embodiment of their ideal of the expanded Self. According to deep ecologists, when one expands one's identity to the "land" or to all of nature, nature will be protected, since to cause nature harm would be to harm oneself as well.[32] Thus, the expanded Self, not axiological theory, is designed to defend the natural world from human abuse. However, if we examine Leopold's land ethic carefully,[33] we find that what it most clearly conveys is the notion of ethics as a means of restraint. Far from eliminating the aggressive drives that are inherent in patriarchy, the expansion of identity merely contains the aggressive impulses so as not to exceed a specified limit, which might thus endanger the "land."

Leopold's land ethic maintains that a thing is right when it tends to preserve the "integrity, stability, and beauty of the biotic community. It is wrong when it tends otherwise."[34] This maxim, however, which has been widely quoted, gives an incomplete picture of Leopold's ideas. Not only are the "beauty, integrity and stability of the biotic community" in no way marred by the killing of individual animals for sport; they are actually *enhanced* by it, in Leopold's view: "The instinct that finds delight in the sight and pursuit of game is bred into the very fiber of the human race."[35] He goes on to state that the desire to hunt lies deeper than the urge to participate in other outdoor sports: "Its source is a matter of instinct as well as competition. . . . A son of Robinson Crusoe, having never seen a racket, might get along nicely without one, but he would be pretty sure to hunt or fish whether or not he were taught to do so."[36] In other words, for Leopold, a boy instinctively learns to shoot a gun, and, moreover, instinctively wants to hunt and kill. As he states: "A man may not care for gold and still be human but the man who does not like to see, hunt, photograph or otherwise outwit birds and animals is hardly normal. He is supercivilized, and I for one do not know how to deal with him."[37]

According to Leopold, all boys and men have this aggressive instinct (interestingly, he had nothing to say about women and girls). Ethics, then, enters into the picture as the need to curb, *not eliminate,* this aggressive drive. The ability to exercise (and curb) this aggressive instinct, through such activities as hunting, is viewed by Leopold as an inalienable right:

> Some can live without the opportunity for the *exercise and control* of the hunting instinct, just as I suppose some can live without work, play, love, business or other vital adventure. But in these days we regard such

deprivation as unsocial. Opportunity for the exercise of all the normal instincts has come to be regarded more and more as an inalienable right.[38]
[Emphasis mine.]

Leopold goes on to complain that "the men who are destroying our wildlife are alienating one of these rights and doing a good job of it."[39] In other
words, wildlife should be preserved not because of the animal's inherent
right to life, but because of the hunter's inherent right to kill! As he explains, "[The individual's] instincts prompt him to compete for his place
in the community but his ethics prompt him also to cooperate (perhaps
in order that there may be a *place to compete for*").[40] (Again the emphasis is mine.) As Leopold summarizes his ideas, "An ethic ecologically is
a limitation on freedom of action in the struggle for existence. An ethic
philosophically is a differentiation of social from antisocial conduct. These
are two definitions of one thing. Good social conduct involves limitation
of freedom."[41]

Leopold's land ethic is, thus, inextricably tied to his ideas about proper
hunting conduct. It involves what he calls "good sportsmanship." Much
of Western ethics is based upon a similar idea of good sportsmanship,
according to which you compete in the game but play by the rules.

The notion that ethical conduct involves restraining the errant or immoral passions can be found not only in Western philosophy but in Western
religion as well.[42] The Christian church changed the focus of morality from
prudence to obedience. The sentiments of the Church fathers are aptly captured by Sarah Hoagland—namely, that "evil results when passion runs
out of (their) [i.e., the Church fathers'] control."[43] The Church was (and
is) fond of buttressing this notion with appeals to biblical authority. We are
told that in the biblical story of Genesis, Adam's sin is precisely a failure of
will. Adam's failure to obey God's command is attributed to Eve, and Eve's
lapse of obedience is in turn ascribed to the snake. Eve has gone down in
history as the embodiment of evil for having trusted the word of an animal
over God's command.

Obedience to a transcendent God or abstract concept has been one of
the most common conceptions of ethics in the Western world. Behind
this notion lies the even more fundamental notion of ethics as restraint.
Indeed, the model of ethics as a form of restraint can be seen in the Jewish-
Christian God Himself. Thus, feeling remorse for having destroyed most
of the world, God forges a covenant with Noah after the flood to restrain
Himself from further outbursts of this kind.[44]

Frequently, aggressive conduct is not prohibited under patriarchy, merely restrained and controlled. Often aggression is explicitly condoned if it is properly channeled into ritualized form. In many cultures, killing a totem animal is customarily condemned, but honored on rare occasions when performed as a sacrifice to a god. Similarly, the laws of Kashrut sanction the killing of animals as long as it is done in a restrained and ritualized fashion, according to "God's command."

The institutionalization of violence in modern society serves a legitimating function similar to that of ritual violence. For example, it is illegal for someone to beat a dog wantonly on the street, but if an experimenter beats the same dog in the protective confines of a laboratory, while counting the number of times the dog "vocalizes," it is considered an honorable activity and called "science." The rules of the experiment operate, like the rules of ritual, to lend legitimacy to the violent act.[45] Animal experimentation is accorded additional legitimation by borrowing the language of ritual. Animals are said to be "sacrificed" in laboratories, not killed. Behind this obfuscation of language lies the tragic belief that somehow, if animals are killed at the altars of science, human beings will be allowed to live.[46]

Aggression is often condoned under patriarchy in the name of an abstract ideal, typically "the greater good." We are told that killing (whether in laboratories, in warfare, or in razing land) is necessary for the greater good of "Mankind." Again, the Christian God himself provides a perfect example of this conduct. Through the killing of his son, "God" is said to have sought the redemption of "Man," and hence the greater good.

Since the Enlightenment, ethical theory has tended to be based less on the Word of God and more on the god of Reason.[47] The theme of controlling the unwieldy passions, however, has remained intact, receiving its most refined expression in the thought of Kant. While science and technology were mining nature for her riches, Kant, in analogous fashion, was attempting to strip human ethical conduct of its immersion in the natural world. As he writes, "To behold virtue in her proper shape is nothing other than to show morality stripped of all admixture with the sensuous and of all the spurious adornments of reward or self love."[48] Moral individuals, according to Kant, rise above their personal inclinations or nature, and act out of duty. Duty is determined first by pure reason or logic, stripped of all feeling, and then by the exercise of the will.

The conception of morality as the rational control of irrational and aggressive desires contrasts sharply with the way in which many women have described their ethical behavior and thought. Research by Carol Gilligan suggests that women's ethical conduct and thought tend to derive more from a sense of connection with others and from the feelings of care and responsibility that such connection entails. Men's sense of morality, on the other hand, tends to derive more from an abstract sense of obligations and rights. According to one of Gilligan's respondents, Amy, "Responsibility signifies response, an extension rather than a limitation of action. Thus, it connotes an act of care, rather than restraint of aggression." For Jake, by contrast, responsibility "pertains to a limitation of action, a restraint of aggression."[49]

For many women, what needs to be explained is not how and why people should be compelled to behave in moral ways, but how and why compassion and moral behavior fail to be sustained. As Alison Jaggar states, "Because we expect humans to be aggressive, we find the idea of co-operation puzzling. If, instead of focusing on antagonistic interactions, we focused on cooperative interaction, we would find the idea of competition puzzling."[50]

## *Truncated Narratives*

The founding of ethics on the twin pillars of human reason and human will is an act of violence in its own right. By denigrating instinctive and intuitive knowledge, it severs our ties to the natural world. But the violence of abstraction operates in other ways as well. Wrenching an ethical problem out of its embedded context severs the problem from its roots.[51] Most nature ethicists debate the value of nature on an abstract or theoretical plane. Typically, they weigh the value of nature against the value of a human goal or plan. For example, we are asked to weight the value of an animal used for research in a laboratory against the value of a human being who is ill. The problem is conventionally posed in a static, linear fashion, detached from the context in which it was formed. In a sense, we are given truncated stories and then asked what we think the ending should be. However, if we do not understand the world view that produced the dilemma that we are asked to consider, we have no way of evaluating the situation except on its own terms.

What, for example, is a mother to say when she is told that the only way that her child can be saved is through the "sacrifice" of animal life? The urgency of the situation leads the mother to believe what she is told and to feel that it is "right" that the animal should die to save her child's life. It is understandable that the mother would choose her daughter's life over that of an anonymous animal. It would also be understandable, however, if the mother chose the life of her daughter over that of an anonymous *child*. This, however, is not the ethical dilemma that she is asked to consider. No one has asked her to juxtapose the life of one human against that of another. Although it would clearly be more helpful to experiment on a human child to help save the life of another child, no one is proposing this. Animals, however, have been relegated to the status of objects or property. As such, their bodies can easily be conscripted into this tragic human story.[52]

The mother of the ailing daughter consumes this story; she does not create it or even enact it. *She* is not the one who will be injecting poisons into animals and watching their bodies writhe in pain. *She* is not the one who will slice into their brains to see what bits of knowledge might lie therein. She is the consumer of a narrative or story from which these details have been conveniently excised.

Currently, ethics is conceived as a tool for making dramatic decisions at the point at which a crisis has occurred.[53] Little if any thought is given to why the crisis or conflict arose to begin with. Just as Western allopathic medicine is designed to treat illness, rather than maintain health, Western ethical theory is designed to remedy crisis, not maintain peace. But the word "ethics" implies something far less dramatic and heroic—namely, an "ethos" or way of life.

According to Iris Murdoch, moral behavior is not a matter of weighing competing values and making the proper, rational choice. Rather, as she argues, what is crucial in the moral life is the act of attention *before* a moral choice is made. In her words, the moral life is "not something that is switched off in between the occurrence of explicit moral choices. What happens between such choices is indeed what is crucial."[54] Murdoch contends: "If we consider what the work of attention is like, how continuously it goes on and how imperceptibly it builds up structures of values round about us, we shall not be surprised that at crucial moments of choice most of the business of choosing is already over."[55] Morality, for Murdoch, is far from the notion of the rational control of an inherently aggressive will. When one directs a "patient, loving regard" upon "a person, a thing, a situation," according to Murdoch, the will is presented not as "unimpeded movement," but rather as "something very much more like obedience."[56]

It is precisely this loving regard that patriarchal culture has failed to attain. Rather, in the patriarchal "look," nature has been reduced to a set of objects or symbols that are used to attain a sense of self that is detached from the rest of the natural world. Nature is imaged as wild and demonic, passive and inert, but never as a community of living beings with instincts, desires, and interests of their own.

The patriarchal mind has managed to look, but not see, act but not feel, think but not know. Claude Bernard, considered by many to be the founder of modern medicine and the widespread use of animals in research, embodies this failure of perception. According to Bernard: "The physiologist is not an ordinary man: he is a scientist, possessed and absorbed by the scientific idea that he pursues. He does not hear the cries of animals, he does not see their flowing blood, he sees nothing but his idea, and is aware of nothing but an organism that conceals from him the problem he is seeking to resolve." [57]

It is this fixation on abstraction (God, Reason, ideas, or the "Word") that has hampered the patriarchal mind from perceiving other forms of life in caring ways. In order to disengage from this fixation on abstraction, it is necessary to engage in practice. If ecofeminists are serious about transforming the patriarchal world view, we must begin to take our own experiences and practices seriously. We might, for example, decide, on an abstract plane, that we are justified in eating meat. But if we are dedicated to an ecofeminist praxis, we must put our abstract beliefs to the practical test. We must ask ourselves how we would feel if we were to visit a slaughterhouse or factory farm. And how would we feel if we were to kill the animal ourselves? Ethics, according to this approach, begins with our own instinctive responses. It occurs in a holistic context in which we know the whole story within which our actions take place. It means rethinking the stories that we have come to believe under patriarchy, such as the belief that we must experiment on animals to save human life, or the belief that we must eat meat to lead healthy lives. [58] As Carol Adams points out, we are brought up to accept that being eaten is the logical ending to the story of a farm animal's life. [59] But stories such as these can only be conceived by a patriarchal mind that is unable to conceive of nature as important apart from human use.

Patriarchal society is adept at truncating stories and then adapting them to its own needs. It is true, for example, that *some* animals are predators; however, the vast majority are not. [60] Most of the animals that humans eat are, in fact, vegetarian (cows, pigs, chickens). We are asked, under patriarchy, to model our behavior not after the vegetarian animals but after the predators. The narrative of predation thus becomes a convenient "pretext" to justify a wide range of violent acts. No other species of animal confines, enslaves, and breeds other animals to satisfy its taste for flesh. Yet, under patriarchy, *this* story remains untold. Nor are we told that predatory animals generally kill other animals only for survival reasons; that, unlike humans, these animals would not survive without eating meat. The story of predation is wrenched out of the larger context and served to us to consume.

Since we live in a fragmented world, we will need to stretch our imaginations to put it back together again. It is often difficult for us to conceive of the impact that our personal conduct has beyond our individual lives. Reason is easily divided from emotion when our emotions are divided from experience. Much of the violence that is perpetrated against the natural world occurs behind closed doors or out of our view. Most of us will never see a slaughterhouse, fur ranch, or animal research laboratory. If we are to engage in an ecofeminist praxis, the least we can do is inform ourselves of what transpires in these places. If we are to make holistic choices, the whole story must be known.

The story of meat eating must include not only the brutal treatment of animals on factory farms and in slaughterhouses, not only the devastating impact of meat eating on the ecology of the earth, on world hunger, and on human health—it must include *all* these and other details, which it must then weave together into a whole. Only when we have all the details of this and other stories will we be able to act holistically with our bodies, minds, and souls. It is the details that we need to live moral lives, not obedience to abstract principles and rules.[61]

Holistic medicine provides a fitting paradigm for holistic ethics. Just as holistic medicine seeks to discover the whole story behind dis-ease, so, too, holistic ethics seeks to discover the whole story behind ethical dilemmas. Western allopathic ethics, on the other hand, is designed to treat the symptoms of patriarchy (its dilemmas and conflicts), rather than the disease embodied in its total world view. Allopathic ethics, like allopathic medicine, operates on the notion of heroism.[62] Just as Western heroic medicine spends most of its time, money, and resources on battling advanced stages of disease and emergency situations, so, too, Western heroic ethics is designed to treat problems at an advanced stage of their history—namely, at the point at which conflict has occurred. It is not difficult to discern why allopathic medicine spends little to no research money on prevention.[63] Prevention is simply not a very heroic undertaking.[64] How can you fight a battle if the enemy does not yet exist? It is far more dramatic to allow disease and conflict to develop and then to call in the troops and declare war.

The drama of illness is seen to lead ineluctably to the climax of a heroic, technological fix.

Heroic medicine, like heroic ethics, runs counter to one of the most basic principles in ecology—namely, that everything is interconnected. Ecology teaches us that no part of nature can be understood in isolation, apart from its context or ecological niche. So, too, I would argue, our moral conduct cannot be understood apart from the context (or moral soil) in which it grows. By uprooting ethical dilemmas from the environment that produced them, heroic ethics sees only random, isolated problems, rather than an entire diseased world view. But until the entire diseased world view is uprooted, we will always face moral crises of the same kind. There is an ecology to ethics, just as to every aspect of the natural world. If we do not care for our moral landscape, we cannot expect it to bear fruit.

## Weaving New Stories

The "environmental crisis" is, above all, a crisis of perception. It is a crisis not only by virtue of what our culture sees, but by virtue of what it does not see. Adrienne Rich has shown how "lies, secrecy, and silence" have been used to perpetuate the exploitation of women.[65] The same may be said to apply to the exploitation of all of the natural world as well. If we are to transform the destructive consciousness that pervades our current culture, we must break through the lies, secrecy, and silence. This is not an individual endeavor. Holistic ethics is a collective undertaking, not a solitary task. It is a process of helping one another to piece together the wider stories of which our lives form a part. It means filling in the missing links. It may mean approaching a woman on the street who is wearing a fur coat and asking her if she is aware of how many animals died to make her coat, and if she is aware of how much suffering the animals had to endure. At the same time, it means understanding the cultural context that leads this woman to see glamour where others see death. She is the product of a society that robs women of their own self-image and then sells it back to them in distorted form. She thinks that she is "dressed to kill"; we must let her know that others have been killed for her to dress.[66]

In order to engage in holistic ethics, we must also disengage from patriarchal discourse. Patriarchal discourse creates dilemmas that it then invites us to resolve. Thus, animal experimenters typically invite us to answer the question, "Who would we save if we had to choose between our drowning daughter and a drowning dog?" The crisis scenario is designed to lead us to believe that only one life can be saved, and only at the other's expense. Disengaging from patriarchal discourse means that we must refuse to dignify these dualistic questions with a response. Even to consider such questions is to give support and validity to the patriarchal world view.[67] The best response to such questions is, perhaps, to pose a question of our own. We might ask why the child is ill to begin with. Was it due to the hormones found in the meat she was fed, or was it perhaps due to the consumption of drugs that had proved "safe" after testing on animals? And why was the proverbial dog touted by research scientists "drowning" to begin with? Had someone thrown the dog in the water (or, rather, the laboratory) in the pathetic belief that somehow, through the dog's death, a young child's life would be saved? And how and why did we develop a culture in which death is seen as a medical failure, rather than as a natural part of life?

As we disengage from patriarchal discourse, we begin to hear larger and fuller stories. Hearing these bigger stories means learning to listen to nature. The voice of women and the voice of nature have been muted under patriarchy. Women and nature are considered objects under patriarchy, and objects do not speak, objects do not feel, and objects have no needs. Objects exist only to serve the needs of others. But despite our society's refusal to listen, nature has been increasingly communicating her needs to us. Nature is telling us in myriad ways that we cannot continue to poison her rivers, forests, and streams, that she is not invulnerable, and that the violence and abuse must be stopped. Nature *is* speaking to us. The question is whether we are willing or able to hear.[68]

The notion of obligations, responsibilities, and rights is one of the tools used by heroic ethics. But genuine responsibility for nature begins with the root meaning of the word—"our capacity for response." Learning to respond to nature in caring ways is not an abstract exercise in reasoning. It is, above all, a form of psychic and emotional health.[69] Heroic ethics cannot manufacture health out of the void of abstraction. Psychic and emotional health cannot be manufactured at all. It can only be nurtured through the development of a favorable environment or context within which it can grow. The moral "climate" must be right.

Ecofeminists and other nature writers have often proclaimed the importance of a "holistic world view." By "holism" they refer to the notion of the "interdependence of all of life." But interdependence is hardly an ideal in and of itself. A master and slave may be said to be interconnected, but clearly that is not the kind of relation that ecofeminists wish to promote.

The *quality* of relation is more important than the fact that a relation of some kind exists. If our society is to regain a sense of psychic health, we must learn to attend to the *quality* of relations and interactions, not just the *existence* of relations in themselves. Thus, when hunters claim to promote the well-being of the "whole" by killing individual animals, or to "love" the animals that they kill, we must challenge their story. Our own notion of holistic ethics must contain a respect for the "whole" *as well as* individual beings.

Re-specting nature literally involves "looking again." We cannot attend to the quality of relations that we engage in unless we know the details that surround our actions and relations. If ecofeminists are sincere in their desire to live in a world of peace and nonviolence for all living beings, we must help each other through the pains-taking process of piecing together the fragmented world view that we have inherited. But the pieces cannot simply be patched together. What is needed is a reweaving of all the old stories and narratives into a multifaceted tapestry.

As this tapestry begins to take shape, I stretch my imagination into the future and spin the following narrative. Many, many years from now, I am sitting by the fireside with my sister's grandchild. She turns to me and asks me to tell her a story of how things used to be, in the distant past. I turn to her and speak the following words:

"Once upon a time," I tell her, "there existed a period we now call the Age of Treason. During this time, men came to fear nature and revolted against the earlier matriarchal societies which had lived in harmony with the natural world as we do now. Many terrible things occurred during this time that will be difficult for you to understand. Women were raped and the earth was poisoned and warfare became routine.

"Animals were tortured throughout the land. They were trapped and clubbed so people could dress in their furs. They were enslaved in cages— in zoos, in laboratories, and on factory farms. People ate the flesh of animals and were frequently ill. Researchers told people that if they 'sacrificed' animals in laboratories they would be cured of disease. People no longer trusted in their own power to heal themselves and so they believed what they were told.

"The men had forgotten that they had formerly worshiped the animals they now reviled. Instead they worshipped a God that told them they had a special place in Creation, above all the other animals on earth. They found great comfort in this thought. And so they continued their cruel-hearted ways."

Marti Kheel

As I conclude my fantasy, I imagine my grandniece turning to me with a look of disbelief.

"Did they *really* used to eat animals?" she queries.

"Yes," I answer gently, "and much, much worse. But now that is all a matter of history. Like a very bad dream. Now, at long last, we can live in peace and harmony with all the creatures of the earth. The Age of Treason has passed."

NOTES

1. I have used the term "nature ethicists" to refer broadly to those writers working in the fields commonly referred to as "environmental ethics" and "animal liberation." I prefer the term "nature ethics" to that of "environmental ethics" since it more clearly implies the inclusion of humans within its parameters. The term "environmental ethics" tends to reinforce a dichotomous view of "humans" and "the rest of nature." For clarity, however, I sometimes use the term "environmental ethics" in order to distinguish this philosophical perspective from that of animal liberation. I also distinguish "nature ethics" from the field of "ecophilosophy" (see n. 24). In contrast to nature ethicists, who seek to develop an *environmental ethic,* ecophilosophers, as referred to in this chapter, seek to develop *ecological consciousness* (see below).

2. In a nationwide march on Washington for animal rights held on June 10, 1990, the Anglican theologian and animal liberation author and activist Andrew Linzey boasted that "we are no longer a movement of little old ladies in tennis shoes; ours is a movement with *intellectual muscle*" (my emphasis). Heroism has been an undercurrent not only in nature ethics and ecophilosophy, but in the environmental movement as well. Phrases such as "the race against extinction," the "fight to save the planet," and the "war against pollution" all betray an underlying heroic stance. Radical environmental groups such as Earth First! also freely employ the terminology of warfare. The back cover of a popular book on the radical environmental movement boldly asserts that "war has been declared—perhaps history's most important war—and it's being waged to save the world from ourselves"; see Rik Scarce, *Eco-Warriors: Understanding the Radical Environmental Movement,* with a foreword by David Brower (Chicago: Noble Press, 1990). The description of a television show reflects the same heroic mentality. The show, geared toward children and billed under the heading "Bashing the Ravagers," is described as featuring five young "planeteers" who are embodied by Gaia, the spirit of the earth, to "battle" a group of "eco-villains." The planeteers, who combine forces during crisis situations, mysteriously generate a (male) superhero, Captain Planet, sporting a form-fitting costume and bearing a distinct resemblance to that popular hero

Superman. John Carman, *TV Week, San Francisco Chronicle*, September 30, 1990, p. 3.

3. Some of the major works on ecofeminism include Leonie Caldecott and Stephanie Leland, eds., *Reclaim the Earth: Women Speak Out for Life on Earth* (London: Women's Press, 1983); Andrée Collard with Joyce Contrucci, *Rape of the Wild: Man's Violence Against Animals and the Earth* (Bloomington: Indiana University Press, 1989); Mary Daly, *Gyn/Ecology: The Meta-Ethics of Radical Feminism* (Boston: Beacon Press, 1978); Irene Diamond and Gloria Feman Orenstein, eds., *Reweaving the World: The Emergence of Ecofeminism* (San Francisco: Sierra Club, 1990); Elizabeth Dodson Gray, *Green Paradise Lost* (Wellesley, Mass.: Roundtable Press, 1981); Susan Griffin, *Woman and Nature: The Roaring Inside Her* (New York: Harper & Row, 1978); *Heresies* 13 (1981): "Feminism and Ecology"; Carolyn Merchant, *The Death of Nature: Women, Ecology and the Scientific Revolution* (New York: Harper & Row, 1983); Judith Plant, ed., *Healing the Wounds: The Promise of Ecofeminism* (Philadelphia: New Society, 1989).

4. The theme of weaving together women's voices recurs throughout both ecofeminist and feminist thought. According to Karen Warren, a feminist ethic is, of necessity, a contextualist ethic, which is properly viewed as a *collage* or *mosaic,* a *tapestry* of voices that emerges out of felt experiences. The point is not to have one *picture* based on a unity of voices, but a *pattern* which emerges out of the very different voices of people located in different circumstances": "The Power and the Promise of Ecological Feminism," *Environmental Ethics* 12 (1990): 139. Support for a pluralist conception of ethics can also be found in the work of Christopher D. Stone, *Earth and Other Ethics: The Case for Moral Pluralism* (New York: Harper & Row, 1987), 115–52; also see Jim Cheney, "Postmodern Environmental Ethics," *Environmental Ethics* 11 (1989): 117–34. For a contrast to the "multivocal" conception of environmental ethics, see Baird Callicott, who argues in "The Case Against Moral Pluralism," *Environmental Ethics* 12 (1990): 99–124, for a "univocal ethical theory" that involves "one metaphysics of morals: one concept of the nature of morality . . . one concept of human nature . . . one moral psychology."

5. The analysis of the images of nature in Western society that follows is drawn from my unpublished manuscript, "Befriending the Beast and the Body: The Ecofeminist Challenge."

6. I am indebted to Mary Midgley, *Beast and Man: The Roots of Human Nature* (New York: Meridien Books, 1978), for my understanding and use of the term "Beast."

7. For an in-depth analysis of how both masculine self-identity and Western civilization are founded upon the attempt to transcend animal and female natures, see Wendy Brown, *Manhood and Politics: A Feminist Reading in Political Theory* (Totawa, N.J.: Rowman & Littlefield, 1988); Marilyn French, *Beyond Power: On Women, Men, and Morals* (New York: Summit Books, 1985); Susan Griffin, *Por-*

*nography and Silence: Culture's Revenge Against Nature* (New York: Harper & Row, 1981).

8. Monica Sjöö and Barbara Mor, *The Great Cosmic Mother: Rediscovering the Religion of the Earth* (San Francisco: Harper & Row, 1987), 250–51.

9. Griffin, *Pornography and Silence*, p. 55.

10. For a detailed analysis of the functionalist conception of women within Western political thought, see Susan Moller Okin, *Women in Western Political Thought* (Princeton: Princeton University Press, 1979).

11. The best-known formulation of this argument was made by Lynn White, Jr., in "The Historical Roots of Our Ecological Crisis," in *The Environmental Handbook*, ed. John Barr, 3–16, reprinted from *Science* 10 (1967): 1203–7. White's thesis instigated an outpouring of literature defending the Christian religion against his critique. Typically, the defense has hinged on the contention that the scriptural notion of "stewardship" implies not only privilege but responsibility. See, for example, Robin Attfield, *The Ethics of Environmental Concern* (New York: Columbia University Press, 1983). Despite valiant attempts to place stewardship in a more benign light, there is no escaping the fact that it still implies a hierarchy with humans at the top.

12. Elizabeth Dodson Gray, *Green Paradise Lost*, 4, argues that the pattern of the first Genesis account reflects a "hierarchical" conception, whereas the second is more accurately described as "anthropocentric," in that "everything is created around the male, including the female [who is] created from his rib to be his helpmate." However, as she argues, "the interpretation through the ages has blended the accounts in Gen. 1 and Gen. 2 into a single Creation Tradition, which has been both hierarchical and anthropocentric."

13. I am indebted to Catherine Keller for my understanding of the multiple manifestations of the masculine "separative self"; see *From a Broken Web: Separation, Sexism, and Self* (Boston: Beacon Press, 1986). For a related theme, see Evelyn Fox Keller, *Reflections on Gender and Science* (New Haven: Yale University Press, 1985).

14. See Nancy Chodorow, *The Reproduction of Mothering: Psychoanalysis and the Sociology of Gender* (Berkeley and Los Angeles: University of California Press, 1978).

15. Dorothy Dinnerstein, *The Mermaid and the Minotaur: Sexual Arrangements and the Human Malaise* (New York: Harper & Row, 1976).

16. For a critique of Anglo-European culture's emphasis on warrior virtues, see Barbara Ehrenreich, "The Warrior Culture," *Time*, October 15, 1990, 100. See also the letter of response by Ward Churchill, co-director of the Colorado American Indian Movement, which critiques Ehrenreich for failing to see the nonviolent ways in which manhood is recognized in many tribal cultures: "Ehrenreich and Indians," *Z Magazine*, November 1990, 5. It is interesting, I feel, that Churchill cites "hunting" as an example of a "nonviolent" rite of passage into adult masculine self-identity.

17. For a more detailed critique of the divisions between the philosophies of

animal liberation and environmental ethics, see my "Liberation of Nature: A Circular Affair," *Environmental Ethics* 7 (1985): 135–49; also see my "Animal Liberation and Environmental Ethics: Can Ecofeminism Bridge the Gap?" paper presented at the Annual Meeting of the National Women's Studies Association, Akron, Ohio, June 20–24, 1990.

18. Sarah Hoagland, *Lesbian Ethics: Toward New Values* (Palo Alto, Calif.: Institute of Lesbian Studies, 1989), 31.

19. Both stewardship ethicists and reform environmentalists merely admonish humans to care for the object-laden world with due respect. Ecotheologians typically remind humans that nature is not the property of "Man," but rather the property of God. The object or property status of nature is, thus, left intact, with God, not humans, seen as the landlord of the world. For example, ecotheologian Richard A. Baer, Jr., argues in "Higher Education, the Church, and Environmental Values," *Natural Resources Journal* 17 (July 1977): 48, that the earth is "property that does not belong to us." As Roderick Nash comments, "From Baer's perspective *Homo sapiens* rents an apartment called nature. God is, quite literally, the landlord. He expects compliance with basic 'principles of etiquette' in the use of his creation . . . humankind does not have unconditional freedom to conquer and exploit what it could never, in the last analysis, own." From *The Rights of Nature: A History of Environmental Ethics* (Madison: University of Wisconsin Press, 1989), 101.

20. Significantly, the word "value" derives from the Latin *valere*, meaning "to be strong, hence well." It derives from the same root word as "valiant" and "valor." Values in ethics confer power and strength.

21. Inherent value is typically defined as the value that an entity possesses independent of its utility or interest to other beings. Thus, those beings that have "inherent value" are said to be valued *for themselves*. According to Tom Regan, *The Case for Animal Rights* (Berkeley and Los Angeles: University of California Press, 1983), 243, only those individuals who are "subjects of a life" may be said to possess "inherent value." Although "inherent value" is supposed to exist independently of a valuing consciousness, there is no escaping the fact that it is humans who determine which entities have it and which do not. Paul Taylor uses the term "inherent worth" in an essentially identical manner to Tom Regan's use of "inherent value." See *Respect for Nature: A Theory of Environmental Ethics* (Princeton: Princeton University Press, 1986).

22. Peter Singer, *Animal Liberation: A New Ethics for Our Treatment of Animals* (New York: Avon Books, 1975), xi.

23. Kenneth Goodpaster has argued that mainstream, modern ethical theory rests on the premise of egoism, and the corollary notion that ethical consideration for others is reached by a process of generalization. "From Egoism to Environmentalism," in *Ethics and Problems of the 21st Century*, ed. K. E. Goodpaster and K. M. Sayre (Notre Dame, Ind.: University of Notre Dame Press, 1979), 21–35.

24. There is considerable fluidity in the terminology of nature writers, and I am

aware that not all writers employ the distinction I make between ecophilosophy and nature ethics. For alternate definitions of ecophilosophy, see Henrik Skolimowski, *Ecophilosophy: Designing New Tactics for Living* (Salem, N.H.: Marion Boyers, 1981); Arne Naess, "The Shallow and the Deep, Long-Range Ecology Movement: A Summary," *Inquiry* 16 (1973): 95–100.

The term "ecosophy" has also been proposed to refer to "ecological wisdom," as opposed to the more abstract, philosophical approach implied by the term "ecophilosophy." This approach seems to bear the closest affinity to an ecofeminist consciousness or ethic; see, for example, Alan Drengson, *Beyond The Environmental Crisis: From Technocrat to Planetary Person* (New York: Peter Lang, 1989); Arne Naess, *Ecology, Community and Lifestyle*, trans. and ed. David Rothenberg (Cambridge and New York: Cambridge University Press, 1990).

25. As George Sessions states, "The search then, as I understand it, is not for environmental ethics but for ecological consciousness." See *Ecophilosophy* 3 (1981): 5a.

26. Examples of this language can readily be found in the pages of the journal *Environmental Ethics*. See, for example, Richard Cartwright Austin, "Beauty: A *Foundation* for Environmental Ethics," *Environmental Ethics* 7 (1985): 197–208; Eliot Deutsch, "A Metaphysical *Grounding* for Nature Reverence: East West," *Environmental Ethics* 8 (1986): 293–316; Ernest Partridge, "Nature as a *Moral Resource*," *Environmental Ethics* 4 (1984): 101–30; "Asian Traditions as a *Conceptual Resource* for Environmental Ethics: Papers from Sessions on Environmental Ethics and Asian Comparative Philosophy," *Environmental Ethics* 8 (1986). (Emphasis added.)

27. Some ecophilosophers do explicitly emphasize the role of feeling, intuition, and experience in ethical consciousness. Baird Callicott, in particular, has argued for the notion of an environmental ethic founded upon "love and respect." See "Elements of an Environmental Ethic: Moral Considerability and the Biotic Community," in *In Defense of the Land Ethic: Essays in Environmental Philosophy* (Albany: State University of New York), 70. However, Callicott also insists in "Intrinsic Value, Quantum Theory," ibid., 160, that this "expanded moral sentiment" is grounded in a *single* phenomenological world view. The single, "seminal paradigm" that Callicott proposes for contemporary environmental ethics rests on Humean axiological foundations, as embellished by the thought of Darwin and Leopold.

Deep ecologists also emphasize the experiential nature of ecological consciousness. According to Bill Devall and George Sessions, "The ultimate norms of deep ecology . . . cannot be grasped intellectually but are experiential": *Deep Ecology: Living As If Nature Mattered* (Salt Lake City: Peregrine Smith, 1985), 69. Jim Cheney, however, has argued that the consciousness that deep ecologists refer to derives from an abstract metaphysic rather than a "narrative embedment in a specific set of relationships." See "The Neo-Stoicism of Radical Environmentalism," *Environmental Ethics* 11 (1989): 324.

For a feminist analysis of the role of feeling in nature ethics and ecological consciousness, see Jim Cheney, "Eco-Feminism and Deep Ecology," *Environmental*

*Ethics* 9 (1987): 115–45; Josephine Donovan, "Animal Rights and Feminist Theory," Chapter 7 in this volume; Kheel, "The Liberation of Nature," 135–49; Warren, "The Power and the Promise of Ecological Feminism," 125–46.

28. Carolyn Merchant, "Mining the Earth's Womb," in *Machina Ex Dea: Feminist Perspectives on Technology*, ed. Joan Rothschild (New York: Pergamon Press, 1983), 100.

29. Some feminists have expressed misgivings about restricting the image of the earth to that of a mother figure. As Linda Vance argues in Chapter 5 in this volume, the image of nature-as-mother acts as "a reminder that our primary role is as caretakers and providers, and that our only source of power is the threat to become angry and withhold our bounty. . . . it sounds like a not very subtle warning to us that only mothers, only women who nurture and provide, deserve to be safe from rape."

30. Linda Vance has provided a refreshingly honest explanation for her decision to characterize the earth as female: "If I didn't think of nature as female, I wouldn't be able to feel such enormous pleasure in her presence." In other words, one might argue genderizing the earth as female is a matter of sexual preference! See Chapter 5 in this volume.

31. James Lovelock, "Gaia: A Model for Planetary and Cellular Dynamics," in *Gaia: A Way of Knowing*, ed. William Irwin Thompson (Great Barrington, Mass.: Lindisfarne, 1987), 96.

32. In the words of deep ecologist Arne Naess, "Care flows naturally if the 'self' is widened and deepened so that protection of free Nature is felt and conceived as protection of ourselves." In "Self-Realization: An Ecological Approach to Being in the World," the Fourth Keith Roby Memorial Lecture in Community Science, Murdoch University, Western Australia, March 12, 1986, 39–40.

33. The following analysis of Leopold's ideas is drawn from my "Ecofeminism and Deep Ecology: Reflections on Identity and Difference," in *Covenant for a New Creation: Ethics, Religion and Public Policy*, ed. Carol Robb and Carl Casebolt (Maryknoll, N.Y.: Orbis Press, 1990). An earlier, abridged form of the article also appeared under the same title in *Reweaving the World: The Emergence of Ecofeminism*, ed. Irene Diamond and Gloria Orenstein (San Francisco: Sierra Club, 1990), 128–37.

34. Aldo Leopold, "Land Ethic," in *A Sand County Almanac: With Essays on Conservation from Round River* (New York and Oxford: Oxford University Press, 1966), 262.

35. Leopold, "Goose Music," ibid., 227.

36. Ibid., 232.

37. Ibid., 227.

38. Ibid., 227.

39. Ibid.

40. Leopold, "Land Ethic," 239.

41. Ibid., 238.

42. For a discussion of the elevation of reason and devaluation of emotion in Western ethical thought, see Hoagland, *Lesbian Ethics*, 157–97; also see Mary Daly, *Beyond God the Father: Toward a Philosophy of Women's Liberation* (Boston: Beacon Press, 1973), 102–6.

43. Hoagland, *Lesbian Ethics*, 158.

44. Genesis 8:20–21: "The Lord said in His heart, 'I will never again curse the ground because of man, for the imagination of man's heart is evil from his youth; neither will I ever again destroy every creature as I have done.'"

45. Other parallels between science and ritual are not hard to detect. Thus, science is an activity that must be conducted in secret, where only the initiated (i.e., other scientists) have the power to cast spells (i.e., perform experiments). The accepted methods of verification in scientific investigation (hypothesis, tests, and results) also operate much like a magical spell. If the procedure is not faithfully followed, the spell (i.e., the experiment) is said to have no effect (i.e., to be inaccurate). The spells and incantations found in ritual also find their parallel in the lingo that scientists have developed, which only the initiated (i.e., other scientists) are able to understand.

46. The sacrificial motive behind animal experimentation was appreciated by many of the early anti-vivisectionists in the 1800s. Anna Kingsford argued, "An almost exact parallel to the modern vivisector in motive, method, and in character is presented by the portrait thus preserved to us of the medieval devil-conjurer. In it we recognise the delusion, whose enunciation in medical language is so unhappily familiar to us, that by means of vicarious sacrifices, divinations in living bodies, and rites consisting of torture scientifically inflicted and prolonged, the secrets of life and of power over nature are obtainable." See her "'Violationism,' or Sorcery and Science," lecture presented to the British National Association of Spiritualists, January 23, 1883, and reprinted in *Light*, February 4, 1882, 55–58.

47. The similarity in the roles played by Reason and Revelation is aptly described by Beverly Harrisson in "Keeping Faith in a Sexist Church," in *Making the Connections: Essays in Feminist Social Ethics*, ed. Carol Robb (Boston: Beacon Press, 1985), 214: "'Reason' replaced 'Revelation,' but both were hypostasized and portrayed as nonrelational qualities, possessions of subjects, the one of God alone, the other of 'man' alone."

48. Immanuel Kant, *Groundwork of the Metaphysic of Morals*, trans. H. J. Paton (New York: Harper Torchbooks, 1964), 94.

49. Carol Gilligan, *In a Different Voice: Psychological Theory and Women's Development* (Cambridge: Harvard University Press, 1982), 37–38.

50. Alison Jaggar, *Feminist Politics and Human Nature* (Totowa, N.J.: Rowman & Allanheld, 1983), 41.

51. The importance of context for ethics is also emphasized by Jim Cheney, who argues in "Eco-Feminism and Deep Ecology," 144, that "to contextualize ethical

deliberation is, in some sense, to provide a narrative or story, from which the solution to the ethical dilemma emerges as the fitting conclusion." See also Warren, "The Power and the Promise of Ecological Feminism," 125–46. The research by Carol Gilligan suggests that the contextual approach to ethical deliberation is, in fact, more characteristic of women. When faced with an ethical problem, women attempt to obtain more information and to reconstruct the dilemma in its contextual particularity, whereas men tend to resolve it through adherence to abstract principles and rules. See *In a Different Voice*.

52. According to Joseph Meeker, Western culture is premised upon a tragic world view in which conflict is presupposed, along with the necessity for its resolution through heroic death. As he argues in *The Comedy of Survival: Studies in Literary Ecology* (New York: Charles Scribner's Sons, 1972), 37, "From the tragic perspective, the world is a battle ground where good and evil, man and nature, truth and falsehood make war, each with the goal of destroying its polar opposite." Meeker holds that the tragic world view lies at the heart of our current environmental crisis. He contrasts the tragic world view with the more environmentally compatible mode of comedy, which is premised on the desirability of adaptation and survival: "Comedy illustrates that survival depends upon people's ability to change themselves rather than their environment, and upon their ability to accept limitations rather than to curse fate for limiting them. . . . When faced with polar opposites, the problem of comedy is always how to resolve conflict without destroying the participants. Comedy is the art of accommodation and reconciliation" (39). Although Meeker draws no connection between the tragic world view and that of patriarchy, I would argue that they are one and the same.

53. For an excellent critique of mainstream philosophy's emphasis on crisis situations, see Joe Mellon, "Nature Ethics Without Theory," Ph.D. diss., University of Oregon, 1989, 56. Mellon argues that "moral crisis cases are not matters of *decision* at all; we act because . . . we must." He explains that "moral crises do not present us with some *right* thing to do. They are extreme situations in which one is forced to act as best one can." The bad faith of animal experimenters, according to Mellon, is that they make no effort to avoid the "crisis situations" that they routinely invoke to justify the use of animals in the "war against disease." As he states, "if no efforts are made to learn, and no steps are taken to avoid, then it seems poor form indeed to claim that what one is facing is a crisis, and that one is entitled to the extreme measures which might be justified in a genuine crisis situation. Vivisectionists do precisely this. They are wedded to their methods, and have no intention of giving them up."

54. Iris Murdoch, *The Sovereignty of Good* (London: Cox and Wyman, 1970), 37.

55. Ibid.

56. Ibid., 40. Linda Peckham expressed to me her dismay over Murdoch's choice of the word "obedience" to refer to the will's role in moral decision-making (conversation, December 5, 1990). She suggested that the word "cooperation" might

convey a less dictatorial sense of the will. The word "obedience" is, in fact, so overlaid with Jewish-Christian connotations that it is difficult to conceive of it as anything other than a commanding voice. Interestingly, the word "obedience" derives from the Latin *ob* (meaning "toward," "facing," or "upon") and *audire* (meaning "to hear"). If "obedience" in its root meaning refers to the notion of listening to one's "inner voice," then perhaps there is some call for retaining this word in reference to ethical thought.

57. Cited in John Vyvyan, *In Pity and in Anger: A Study of the Use of Animals in Science* (Marblehead, Mass.: Micah Publications, 1988), 11.

58. Meat eating has been shown to be a major cause of disease due to the high levels of protein, bacteria, cholesterol, chemicals, hormones, and fat found in meat. For more on the health hazards of meat eating (as well as its other adverse effects), see Barbara Parham, *What's Wrong with Eating Meat?* (Denver: Ananda Marga Publication, 1979); John Robbins, *Diet for a New America* (Walpole, N.H.: Stillpoint, 1987); on health aspects only, see John McDougall, *McDougall's Medicine: A Challenging Second Opinion* (Piscataway, N.J.: New Century, 1985).

59. Carol Adams, *The Sexual Politics of Meat: A Feminist-Vegetarian Critical Theory* (New York: Continuum, 1990), 91–94.

60. Stephan Lackner estimates that, disregarding the creatures slaughtered by humans, "only 5 percent of all animals are killed by other animals. Ninety-five percent of all animal lives are terminated without bloodshed: by old age, sickness and exhaustion, hunger and thirst, changing climates, and the like." *Peaceable Nature: An Optimistic View of Life on Earth* (San Francisco: Harper & Row, 1984), 12.

61. I am indebted to Mellon, "Nature's Ethics Without Theory," for an appreciation of the central role played by "details" in ethical conduct and thought.

62. For more on the heroic, warfare mentality that underlies Western allopathic medicine, see my "From Healing Herbs to Deadly Drugs: Western Medicine's War Against the Natural World," in Plant, *Healing the Wounds*, 96–111.

63. Western medicine's lack of concern for prevention can be seen in the fact that despite estimates showing that 80 percent or more of all cancers are attributable to environmental factors, medical research continues to pour billions of dollars into finding magic (chemical) cures for this and other diseases. See John H. Knowles, "The Responsibility of the Individual," in *Doing Better and Feeling Worse: Health in the United States*, ed. John H. Knowles, M.D. (New York: Norton, 1977), 63.

64. I do not mean to imply that the ethos of heroism is the only reason for Western medicine's dismal neglect of preventive medicine. Certainly the profit motive has been an important contributing factor as well. Preventing disease, as most researchers know, is not profitable. It has been estimated, for example, that as many people make a living from cancer today as die from it: see Hans Reusch, *Slaughter of the Innocent* (New York: Civitas Publications, 1983), 71. Animal experimentation also provides a convenient legal cover to drug manufacturers: thus, when the drug thalidomide was extensively tested on animals and yet went on to produce birth

defects in 10,000 children born to pregnant mothers who took it, the drug's manufacturers were acquitted on the grounds that research on animals could not reliably predict how a drug would affect humans. Ibid., 8–10.

65. Adrienne Rich, *On Lies, Secrecy and Silence: Selected Prose 1966–1978* (New York: Norton, 1979).

66. Some of the anti-fur movement's campaign literature has tended to blame women for the existence of furs. One well-known ad features a woman dragging a coat behind her, trailing a pool of blood. The words of the ad state, "It takes 40 dumb animals to make a fur coat, but only one to wear it." A milder reproach can be found in a Humane Society ad that depicts a woman hiding her face behind her purse. The caption declares, "You should be ashamed to wear fur." Although the latter ad does not stoop to name calling as in the former case, it nonetheless reinforces the traditional function of advertising, which has been to tell women what they should feel or do (in this case, be ashamed). The best approach, in my opinion, is not to blame women, but rather to provide them with the missing narrative pieces that are needed for them to think and feel on their own.

67. In a similar vein, Sarah Hoagland contends that to engage in debate over whether or not women should have rights is to acknowledge implicitly that women's rights are debatable. As she points out in *Lesbian Ethics*, 26, "Men's rights are not debatable. Thus, in agreeing to defend women's rights [one] is solidifying status quo values which make women's but not men's rights debatable in a democracy."

68. Josephine Donovan echoes a similar theme in her suggestion that it is both possible and necessary to ground an ethic for the treatment of animals in "an emotional and spiritual conversation with nonhuman life forms. Out of a women's relational culture of caring and attentive love, therefore, emerges the basis for a feminist ethic for the treatment of animals. We should not kill, eat, torture, and exploit animals because they do not want to be so treated, and we know that. If we listen, we can hear them." See Chapter 7 in this volume.

69. Along similar lines, Mary Daly argues that "unlike 'justice,' which is depicted as a woman blindfolded and holding a sword and scales, Nemesis has her eyes open and uncovered—especially her Third Eye. Moreover, she is concerned less with 'retribution,' in the sense of meting out of rewards and punishments, than with an internal judgment that sets in motion a new kind of psychic alignment of energy patterns": *Pure Lust: Elemental Feminist Philosophy* (Boston: Beacon Press, 1978), 240. Similarly, Sarah Hoagland says in *Lesbian Ethics*, 265, that her desire in writing that book was to participate in a new kind of psychic alignment of energy patterns, a moral revolution.

# CHAPTER 11

# A Cross-Cultural Critique
# of Ecofeminism

## Huey-li Li

Regardless of their different theoretical positions, ecofeminists appear to agree that there are important conceptual connections between the oppression of women and the oppression of nature.[1] They believe that the traditional sex/gender system has had a significant impact on today's environmental problems. Moreover, many ecofeminists in English-speaking countries accept the age-old perception of an affinity between woman and nature as a self-evident explanation for the connections between these two forms of oppression.[2] On the one hand, ecofeminists believe that there are perceived similarities between woman and nature—such as passivity and life-giving nurturing qualities—that make them equally vulnerable to male domination.[3] On the other hand, ecofeminists proclaim that women's association with nature gives women a special stake in healing the alienation between humanity and nature and, eventually, in solving today's environmental problems.[4]

The association of women and nature, however, is not a transhistorical and transcultural phenomenon.[5] At the global level, making the woman-nature affinity the theoretical grounding of ecofeminism appears to be problematic. Moreover, critics of ecofeminism argue that ecofeminists oversimplify the etiology of environmental problems by making men responsible for what actually is beyond male hegemony.

Do ecofeminists overestimate the influence of the sex/gender system on environmental problems? Would there still be significant connections between the oppression of women and the oppression of nature if we left out the age-old perception of a woman-nature affinity? Is it reactionary for ecofeminists to relate today's ecological destruction to the social structure of male domination?

In response to these questions, I examine in this chapter the explanatory accounts of the conceptual connections between the oppression of women and the oppression of nature proposed by Rosemary Radford Ruether, Carolyn Merchant, and Elizabeth Dodson Gray. All overlook the non-Western cultural perception of male-female and culture-nature relations, while correctly identifying gender as the crucial metaphor for constructing culture-nature relations in Western culture, which may be more implicated in today's worldwide environmental degradation than other cultures. Subsequently, I argue that the perception of the woman-nature affinity reveals male hegemony over culture formation and that there are parallels between the operation of sexual oppression and the human exploitation of nature. Nevertheless, I disagree with a reductionist approach in ecofeminist theorizing that tends to attribute the interrelated factors involved in the human exploitation of nature to the polarization of sex/gender differences. Such a view is based on a linear, cause-and-effect paradigm that cannot elucidate the complexity of worldwide environmental problems.

## *The Conceptual Roots of Human Domination and Women's Oppression*

Among ecofeminist works, Ruether's *New Woman/New Earth* (1975), Gray's *Green Paradise Lost* (1979), and Merchant's *The Death of Nature* (1980) systematically explore the common conceptual roots of the oppression of women and the oppression of nature. Their varied perspectives enable us to probe into these oppressive systems from different angles.

### Transcendent Dualism as the Conceptual Root of Oppression

In *New Woman/New Earth*, Rosemary Radford Ruether advocates the view that the feminist "vision of a new society of social justice must reckon with the ecological crises."[6] She argues that both the human destruction of nature and women's oppression are legitimized and perpetuated by a hierarchical social structure that allows one group to dominate another. According to Ruether, this hierarchical social structure is rooted in a dualistic ideology, "transcendent dualism," which stresses separation, polarization, and detachment between sexes, classes, and human and nonhuman beings. In these binary oppositions, man/upper-class/white/human beings are considered superior to woman/lower-class/people of color/nature. The subjugation of the inferior groups is thus accepted as a legitimate social arrangement.

Ruether further claims that women's oppression was historically prior to racism and classism. Thus, sexist ideology can be considered the pivot of the constitution of various forms of oppression: "The psychic organization of consciousness, the dualistic view of the self and the world, the hierarchical concept of society, the relation of humanity and nature, and of God and creation—all these relationships have been modeled on sexual dualism."[7]

Since "sexual oppression" is in this view the primordial model for the operation of any other oppressive system, the lower classes and subjugated racial groups all are said in patriarchal society to share the repressive characteristics ascribed to feminity, such as passivity, sensuality, irrationality, and dependence. In contrast, the dominant race and class are assumed to represent true humanity and to possess rationality and the capacity for autonomy and higher virtues. Ruether concludes that "the structures of patriarchal consciousness that destroy the harmony of nature are expressed symbolically and socially in the repression of women," and that the dismantling of the structure of male domination is the common goal of both the women's movement and the environmental movement.[8]

"Woman as Mother" is a central issue in Ruether's demystification of transcendent dualism. Although she considers the concept of matriarchy unhistorical, she still presumes that there was a woman-identified culture prior to the present patriarchal one. Ruether implies that in this woman-identified culture, the female capacity for human reproduction led women to an implicit acceptance of and identification with the cyclical ecology of death and rebirth. A world view of "coming-to-be-and-passing-away" reveals a total acceptance of human mortality. In contrast, men's inability to bear children induces them to contrive a male deity who creates human beings and transcends finite bodily existence. Rooted in transcendent dualism, patriarchal religion seeks to pursue the infinitude of human existence. Following patriarchal religion, the development of science and technology in the West also seeks to "realize infinite demand through infinite material 'progress,' impelling nature forward to infinite expansion of productive power. Infinite demand incarnate in finite nature, in the form of infinite exploitation of the earth's resources for production, results in ecological disaster."[9] In short, Ruether suggests that patriarchal culture, bound to the pursuit of "transcendence," eventually leads to the annihilation of nature.

Ruether seems to consider transcendent dualism the ultimate cause of various forms of oppression, but she is not clear about its own origin. Thus, Val Plumwood poses the following questions:

> Transcendent dualism itself presumably did not appear in a social vacuum; did it produce inferiorisation of the spheres of women and nature? Or were the foundations already present in the inferior treatment of women, nature and inferior social groups such as slaves? Are women inferiorised because of identification with the female sphere? Or are we faced with a set of interlocking structures of domination which mutually evolve and reinforce one another, in turn both aiding and drawing strength from the conceptual structure of transcendent dualism? [10]

It would appear that Ruether views transcendent dualism as constructed by men in order to compensate for their inability to create life. Thus, the conceptual inferiorization of the female sphere and whatever is associated with it can be regarded as necessary to legitimize the social structure of male domination. In other words, transcendent dualism does not *produce* the inferiorization of the sphere of woman and nature; the inferiorization of the feminine *is part of* transcendent dualism. After all, there might be a "collusion" between the conceptual system (i.e., transcendent dualism) and cultural practices (i.e., the inferior treatment of women). Thus, conceptualization is neither the cause nor the effect of cultural practices. A particular conceptual system can be acquired by individuals through the acculturation process. Yet "acculturation" does not refer only to the indoctrination of abstract conceptual systems. Conceptual systems are already embedded in cultural practices. Hence, it is futile to attempt to determine the causal relationship between transcendent dualism and the inferior social treatment of woman and nature.

Without sufficient historical evidence, it is virtually impossible to determine whether women's oppression is due to the identification with nature or nature is exploited because of its identification with woman. As the woman-nature affinity is taken for granted in Ruether's arguments, I think that she would be likely to agree that these two forms of oppression mutually evolved and reinforced each other.

Since dualism has been a predominant ideology in Western society, Ruether's argument appears to be plausible. However, Plumwood points out that "the reproductively related features of masculinity and feminity . . . were (until recently at least) universal, but the alleged consequent, the transcendent apriority of the rational, is not a universal feature." [11] In other words, men's inability to gestate does not universally lead to the pursuit of transcendence. This casts doubt on Ruether's claim that transcendent dualism is the ultimate cause of both women's oppression and the human domination of nature.

Consider, for example, the puzzling fact that the absence of transcendent dualism in Chinese society does not preclude women's being oppressed. There are no parallels between Chinese people's respectful attitude toward nature and the inferior social position of women. The association of women and nature is not a cross-cultural phenomenon, since nature as a whole is not identified with woman in Chinese society. Following F. W. Mote's characterization of the Chinese vision of nature as the "all-enfolding harmony of impersonal cosmic function,"[12] Tu Wei Mi notes that wholeness, dynamism, and continuity are the three motifs of Chinese cosmology:

> The idea of all-enfolding harmony involves two interrelated meanings. It means that nature is all-inclusive, the spontaneously self-generating life process which excludes nothing. The Taoist idea of tzu-jan ("self-so"), which is used in modern Chinese to translate the English word nature, aptly captures this spirit. To say that self-so is all-inclusive is to posit a nondiscriminatory and nonjudgemental position, to allow all modalities of being to display themselves as they are. This is possible, however, only if competitiveness, domination, and aggression are thoroughly transformed.[13]

In short, Chinese people consider that the enduring pattern of nature is "union rather than disunion, integration rather than disintegration, and synthesis rather than separation."[14] Thus, Tu concludes that "to see nature as an external object out there is to create an artificial barrier which obstructs our true vision and undermines our human capacity to experience nature from within."[15]

Based on "being together with nature," "nature reverence" has been Chinese people's common attitude toward nature. However, this holistic world view did not prevent the establishment of male domination and female subordination and the ensuing oppression of women. At present, the pursuit of economic development, not transcendence, has entailed constant and accelerating exploitation of nature in Chinese society, despite the continuing presence of reverence for nature. Thus, it is doubtful that transcendent dualism is the ultimate cause of various forms of oppression, and that the exploitation of nature is modeled universally after sexual oppression.

## Merchant's Critiques of the Mechanistic World View

Woman's maternal role is a central issue in Carolyn Merchant's analysis. In *The Death of Nature*, Merchant makes a sweeping claim that "the ancient identity of nature as a nurturing mother links women's history with the history of the environment and ecological change."[16] According to Merchant, the identification of nature with a nurturing mother prevented human destruction of nature in early human history: "The image of the earth as a living organism and nurturing mother has served as a cultural constraint restricting the actions of human beings; one does not readily slay a mother, dig into her entrails for gold, or mutilate her body. . . . Not only did the image of nature as a nurturing mother contain ethical implications but the organic framework itself, as a conceptual system, also carried with it an associated value system."[17] Although Merchant does not claim that the organic world view is woman-identified, her connecting it with the nurturing mother is allied to Ruether's valuing of a "coming-to-be-and-passing-away" world view. In other words, Merchant and Ruether alike suggest that the female principle plays an important role in an organically oriented mentality.

Nature can also be identified with a disorderly woman who brings plagues, famines, and tempests. Merchant further argues that such an image called forth human control over nature in the scientific revolution, and she notes that Francis Bacon, the celebrated father of science, was renowned for utilizing female imagery to develop scientific knowledge and methods. Indeed, she suggests that Bacon's new scientific objectives and methods were derived from the European witch trials. More specifically, she likens the use of mechanical devices to interrogate and torture the suspected witches to science's torture of nature through mechanical inventions: "This method, so readily applicable when nature is denoted by the female gender, degraded and made possible the exploitation of the natural environment."[18] Symbolically, Bacon even speculates that relentlessly interrogating nature could regain the human dominion over it—dominion that was lost when Adam and Eve were expelled from paradise.

As a whole, the Baconian doctrine of domination over nature is correlated with the perception of disorder in feminized nature. Thus, Merchant concludes that "for Bacon, . . . sexual politics helped to structure the nature of the empirical method that would produce a new form of knowledge and a new ideology of objectivity seemingly devoid of cultural and political assumptions."[19] This belief paved the way for "the rise of mechanism as a rational antidote to the disintegration of the organic cosmos."[20]

Merchant relates "the change in controlling imagery"—from nurturing mother to disorderly woman—"to changes in human attitudes and behavior toward the earth."[21] As the identification of nature with a nurturing mother apparently impeded the progress of commercialism and industrialization, the image of a disorderly woman emerged in the seventeenth century as a cultural sanction for the domination of nature. In other words, images of nature are socially constructed in order to launch a new scientific epoch. Mechanism, with its emphasis on power and order, became a conceptual instrument to promote the domination of nature. Merchant suggests that a mechanistic world view not only entails the devaluation of traditional femininity, but also results in the human exploitation of nature.

As noted above, Merchant's critique of mechanism complements Ruether's demystification of transcendent dualism. After all, it is dualism that lays the foundation for a mechanistic world view. Conversely, it is mechanism that eventually severs the organic relationship between human beings and nature.

However, Merchant's argument regarding the conceptual links between women's oppression and the human domination of nature is neither well grounded nor fully developed. Above all, her connection of women's history with the history of the environment is based on the ancient conceptualization of nature as a nurturing mother, which she seems to assume precludes the human domination of nature. However, women's oppression occurred long before the machine became the predominant metaphor for reality. Chinese misogyny, in particular, coexisted with an organic world view. Without the sanctions of mechanism, the Baconian doctrine of domination already accepted witch trials as the model for developing natural science. The organic world view may have restrained the human destruction of nature, but it certainly was not the panacea for women's oppression.

On the other hand, a mechanistic world view is not absolutely detrimental to women, even though it aggravates the exploitation of a feminized nature. For instance, Merchant points out that following the rise of mechanism, "a new concept of the self as a rational master of passions housed in a machinelike body began to replace the concept of the self as an integral part of a close-knit harmony of organic parts united to the cosmos and society."[22] The development of individualism within the mechanistic world model produced social changes that may have contributed to the contemporary feminist movement. Hence, Merchant's argument that mechanism sanctions women's oppression appears to be untenable. Regardless of the influence of mechanism on today's ecological crises, an adequate account of the conceptual links between women's oppression and human domination of nature must go beyond critiquing a mechanistic world view.

### Gray's Critiques of Sex/Gender Role Differentiation

Drawing from Nancy Chodorow's and Dorothy Dinnerstein's theories, Elizabeth Gray identifies the psychosexual root of male domination over both women and nature.[23] In *The Mermaid and the Minotaur*, Dinnerstein argues that the feminization of nature can be traced to the human infant's failure to distinguish clearly between its mother and nature. Like Merchant, Gray suggests that the awareness of human dependence upon nature led men in early human history to view the destruction of natural resources as antagonistic toward nature and thus dangerous. As technology advanced, however, a euphoric sense of conquering nature replaced men's fear.

In accordance with Nancy Chodorow, Gray further claims that men's need to conquer women and feminized nature is the result of sexual differentiation in gender role development. Chodorow argues that most human beings experience a sense of oneness with their mother in the state of infantile dependence. The female infant's sense of oneness is sustained by modeling her own gender identity upon her mother, whereas the male infant's gender development leads to rejection and denial of his dependence on and attachment to her. Gray argues that man's ambivalence toward dependence upon the mother has enormous psychosexual repercussions on his relationship with women and whatever is perceived as feminine. Consequently, it is impossible for men, as the dominant sex, to think clearly and feel positively about their dependence upon nature. In order to ensure men's continuous independence and detachment from the mother and the female in general, it is essential for patriarchal culture to prescribe the wife's role as submissive, economically impotent, and generally inferior. To Gray, the advancement of technology mainly aspires to "transform [men's] psychologically intolerable dependence upon a seemingly powerful and capricious 'Mother Nature' into a soothing and acceptable dependence upon a subordinated and non-threatening 'wife'."[24]

There are some major gaps in Gray's argument. First of all, it is difficult to substantiate Dinnerstein's claim because the woman-nature affinity is not a cross-cultural phenomenon. The rooting of oppression in the infant's inability to distinguish mother and nature is challenged by the fact that this infantile experience does not universally develop into the conceptual affiliation between women and nature.

Chodorow's analysis appears to be circular. If there were no well-established sex/gender role system, the development of masculinity would not require a rejection of man's early dependence upon his mother. Undoubtedly, the presence of a woman as the child's primary caretaker reduces the influence of male adults, especially fathers, on the development of male infants, but it is still likely that men in their early years develop some identification with their fathers. In other words, Chodorow may overstate the abruptness of the rejection of the mother. Hence, her argument fails to verify her claim that sexual differentiation in the development of gender identity is the conceptual root of male domination of women and feminized nature.

In addition, Gray assumes that man's rejection of his dependence on his mother eventually results in a desire to dominate both woman and nature. Gray may intend to imply that men's striving for total independence underlies their cult of toughness and their aggression against woman and nature. Still, she does not give us a satisfactory account of why a need for independence must turn into a desire for domination.

To ecofeminists, a recognition of the conceptual connections between the oppression of women and the oppression of nature is essential for any adequate understanding of both forms of oppression.[25] Yet the analyses outlined above are based mainly on Western culture. A lack of global cultural awareness in the theorizing of ecofeminism inevitably weakens ecofeminists' claims. The origins of the woman-nature affinity require further elaboration from a cross-cultural perspective. My suggestion is that this affinity is probably a social construction. Women's closeness to nature, as perceived by Western people, is not biologically determined, and the perception of an affinity between woman and nature is not an essential feature of the human unconscious. We need more cross-cultural studies of the relations between various conceptualizations of nature and the corresponding social treatment of women, and these studies must take sociohistorical conditions into consideration. After all, the women's movement and the environmental movement alike deal with global issues. If the goal of developing theory is to "represent our experience of the world in as comprehensive and inclusive a way as possible,"[26] then it is important for ecofeminists to expand the scope and depth of their theoretical investigation.

## The Woman-Nature Affinity in
## Western Language and Ideology

Warwick Fox suggests that Western culture might be far more implicated in today's ecological breakdown than non-Western cultures.[27] Because Western culture has to a large extent homogenized world culture, ecofeminists' analyses (though not universally valid) may still shed significant light on a Western construction—the woman-nature affinity—a construction which may play a central role in generating today's global environmental problems.

The social construction of the woman-nature affinity in the West indicates that the image of woman has been used as an available and powerful metaphor to describe as well as prescribe the human perception of nature. An ever-increasing number of philosophers and cognitive scientists have argued that metaphors are not merely the ornaments of language. By providing a critical link between experience and abstract thinking, metaphors play a significant role in human conceptualization.[28] Hence, woman as metaphor, exemplified by the identification of nature with woman, deserves our further attention.

In the process of metaphorization, the subject who utters the metaphor and the metaphoric vehicle represent two distinct groups—for example, men and women. Eva Feder Kittay argues that women are persistently used as metaphors for men's activities and projects, while there are no equivalent metaphors using men as vehicles for women and women's activities.[29] Women's disinclination to employ men as metaphoric vehicles and women's lower participation, compared with men's, in the conceptualization process (which presumably involves the employment of metaphors) reveal a fundamental inequality between men and women.

From Simone de Beauvoir's standpoint, it is woman's secondary status in the sexual hierarchy that provides motivation for the metaphoric use of woman.[30] Beauvoir's claim is based on Hegelian metaphysics. In the Hegelian schema, the category of the Other, as distinctively opposite to the Self, provides epistemological and ontological conditions for the development of self-consciousness. In a male-dominated society, woman, as the subordinated sex, is perceived as the Other in man's conception. As an Other to man, woman is always available as the metaphoric vehicle for his self-conception. Women, too, internalize man's perception of man as "Self" and woman as "Other," and are therefore unlikely to employ man as a metaphoric vehicle.

Invoking Chodorow's "object-relations" psychoanalytic theory, Kittay further explains that women have never reciprocally constituted men as Other because of the asymmetrical gender-differentiated relations between men and women.[31] The sex/gender role system dictates that men's gender identity must be in opposition to the mother. In other words, mother as Other is essential to men's self-formation. In contrast, women's self-formation is based on a continuing identity with the mother. As a result, the mother does not necessarily appear to be an Other to woman. By continuously identifying with the mother, a woman is less likely than a man to need to employ the category of Other for self-formation.

Focusing on individual psychosexual development, the explanations provided by Beauvoir, Chodorow, and Kittay may account for the prominence of women as metaphoric images in an already sex/gender–differentiated society. With regard to women's lower participation in the conceptualization process on a larger scale, it is essential to inquire into the implications of women's exclusion from the creation of symbol systems.

According to Gerda Lerner: "When humankind made a qualitative leap forward in its ability to conceptualize large symbol systems which explain the world and the universe, women were already so greatly disadvantaged that they were excluded from participation in this important cultural advance."[32] The development of monotheism (i.e., the Judeo-Christian tradition) in particular institutionalized the exclusion of women from the creation of symbol systems.[33] Thus, Mary Daly considers Adam's "naming" of the animals and the woman as the prototype of male dominance over symbol systems, cultural institutions, and methods.[34] Naming is a powerful instrument for ordering and structuring our perception of the world. Conversely, our understanding of the world is restricted by prefigured patterns in language and thought, which are the very product of a systematic process of naming. This is why Ernest Schachtel states, "Nature is to man whatever name he wants to give her. He will perceive nature according to the names he gives her, according to the relations and perspective he chooses."[35] In male-identified monotheism, the symbolic constructs of this world are "based on the counterfactual metaphor of male procreativity and redefine female existence in a narrow and sexually dependent way."[36] Within this patriarchal framework, the very metaphors for gender have expressed the male as norm and the female as deviant, while "man" is used to subsume "woman."[37] Consequently, the exclusion of women from naming leads to the marginalization and even omission of women's experiences in human culture formation. Men, by holding a monopoly on naming, are able to indoctrinate and to reinforce male-identified values in women who do not necessarily share men's world view.

Following patriarchal religion, science not only utilizes metaphoric images of woman to develop a methodology for manipulating nature but also deliberately devalues and further excludes femininity. Merchant's critiques of the mechanistic world view indicate the significance of sexual metaphor in the early development of science. Evelyn Fox Keller relates sexual metaphors in science to sociopolitical developments at the end of the seventeenth century: "Definition of male and female were becoming polarized in ways that were eminently well suited to the growing division between work and home required by early industrial capitalism."[38] The male-female polarity also corresponded with "an ever greater polarization of mind and nature, reason and feeling, objective and subjective" in the development of modern science.[39] From the polarization of man and woman, a new ideal of womanhood—"a chaste, desexualized, and harmless dependent"—gradually emerged to facilitate "a deanimated, desanctified, and increasingly mechanized conception of nature."[40] At the same time, science in conjunction with masculinity became the active agent initiating and effecting the transformation of both nature and culture. Thus, Keller concludes:

> Given the success of modern science, defined in opposition to every female, fears of both Nature and woman could subside. With the one reduced to its mechanical substrate, and the other to her asexual virtue, the essence of Mater could be both tamed and conqured; male potency was confirmed.[41]

In short, the woman-nature affinity reveals women's role in male-identified conceptual apparatuses as well as the male monopoly of symbol systems. Ecofeminists do not specifically address and discuss the above implications of the woman-nature affinity, but their critiques of male domination, with emphases on patriarchal religion (Ruether and Gray) and the masculinization of the development of science (Merchant), show how androcentric fallacies have been built into Western culture. This is why ecofeminists argue that human destruction of nature should be attributed to androcentrism rather than anthropocentrism.[42]

Huey-li Li

## Sexual Oppression and the Human Exploitation of Nature: Action and Immobilization

Although human actions that are destructive of nature are occasionally described as rapes of nature, the connections between the oppression of woman and the exploitative treatment of nature have not been fully brought to light. This may be due to the perceptible differences between the oppression of woman and the oppression of nature. To many people, it is simply absurd to associate strip mining, toxic ocean dumping, and nuclear weaponry with sexual harassment of women, wife battering, and female sexual slavery. Notwithstanding the age-old woman-nature affinity, a further exploration of how the oppressive systems operate may be beneficial for a better understanding of the parallels between them.

The term "oppression" has been widely used to refer to the forceful subordination of women in patriarchal society. Gerda Lerner argues that "oppression" involves the malicious intention of the oppressor and a power struggle that results in the dominance of one group over the other. Since "the oppression of women" inevitably misleads us to "conceptualize women-as-a-group primarily as victims" and to overlook the fact that women "have collaborated in their own subordination through their acceptance of the sex/gender system," Lerner claims that "oppression" is inadequate to describe women's situation in society.[43]

I agree with Lerner that the sex/gender role system is a historical institution constructed by both women and men. In other words, the female-subordinate and male-dominant social structure is sustained mainly by an elaborate sex/gender role system rather than by a constant power struggle between men and women. However, through centuries of acculturation, individuals have been indoctrinated into accepting the sex/gender role system as a natural and immutable arrangement. Without developing gender awareness, women individually or collectively may not be aware of their complicity in the maintenance and perpetuation of the sex/gender role system. As the establishment of the sex/gender role system sets up a male-dominated and female-subordinated sexual hierarchy, the powerlessness of women especially restrains their ability to confront sexual inequality and gender injustice. Consequently, women as a group share their vulnerability to male violence, discrimination by male dominant cultural institutions, and the mystification of male superiority, regardless of their different ages, classes, and ethnic backgrounds. Thus, the forceful subordination of women is not merely a collusion between men and women at a conscious

284

level. The oppressiveness of women's situations in patriarchal society cannot be erased by emphasizing women's acceptance of the sex/gender role system.

In short, oppression is not necessarily constituted by the deliberate intention of the oppressor (the dominant) and the unconscious acceptance of the oppressed (the subordinant) at an individual level. An examination of oppression should emphasize how the oppressive system operates in society.

Marilyn Frye's illuminating analysis provides us with a better understanding of this operative process. According to Frye, oppression is "a system of interrelative *barriers* and *forces* which *reduce, immobilize,* and *mold* people who belong to a certain group, and effect their subordination to another group (individually to individuals of the other group, and as a group, to that group" (emphasis mine).[44] Evidently, the structure of an oppressive system presupposes two distinct and well-defined groups. In the case of sexual oppression, women, through socialization and acculturation, must be *molded* into the subordinate group, and men into the dominant group. Women's internalization of female inferiority, the cultivation of female self-abnegation, and nurturant training are all indispensable to the fabric of the male-dominated and female-subordinated social structure. In order to make the hierarchical relationship between men and women appear to be natural and immutable, interrelated barriers and forces (i.e., patriarchal religion, sexist legislation, the educational deprivation of women) are erected and maintained. The sexual division of labor and the separation between the public and the domestic spheres in particular are essential to confine and *immobilize* women in "the service sector."[45] The *immobilization* of women eventually reduces their own needs, values, and capacities.

*Reduction, immobilization,* and *molding* can also be considered the key elements of the oppression of nature. Ecofeminists argue that both the nature/culture and the male/female polarity are rooted in dualistic ideology. In Western society, the conceptualization of nature especially stresses the separation of nature and human culture. Nature is defined as the "inherent power or force by which the physical and mental activities of man [*sic*] are sustained" and "the material world, or its collective objects and phenomena . . . the features and products of earth itself, as contrasted with those of human civilization"—a definition that categorizes nature and human civilization as two opposite systems.[46] A sense of an organic continuum between natural and cultural is missing.[47] In this dualistic system, nature has been *reduced* to a resource reservoir for providing the material needs of human beings. In other words, the instrumental values of natural resources to human beings have eclipsed the intrinsic values of nature. In contrast to the dynamic process of human civilization, nature has to be regarded as static, fixed, and immutable. The *immobilization* (to speak metaphorically) of nature then highlights human innovation and creativity. Following the Scientific Revolution, the advancement of technology in particular enhanced the human capacity to control, manipulate, and further *mold* the natural environment. Pollution of air, water, and soil, large-scale deforestation, and the destruction of wildlife and wilderness demonstrate the power of human technology in molding the natural environment.

Ecofeminist analyses shed valuable light on these undeniable parallels between the oppression of women and the exploitative treatment of nature, enhancing our understanding of the interlocking structure of oppression.

## Problems of Reductionism in Ecofeminism

Ecofeminists contend that an adequate understanding of the human exploitation of nature cannot overlook the pervasive role of the ideology of male domination in the formation of human culture. By applying a sex/gender analysis, ecofeminists also alert us to the profound impacts of gender on environmental problems. Yet some ecofeminists tend to trace all of today's interrelated ecological problems to sexual polarization, relating ecological destruction to traits associated with men (aggression, competitiveness, and militarism), and ecological sensibility to traits associated with women (nurturing, caring, and compassion). However, there are problems with such a reductionistic analysis.

Technology appears to be the most powerful instrument in gaining mastery over nature, and destructive technology (e.g., escalating pesticide use, nuclear weaponry) exacerbates ecological problems. Merchant's critique of Baconianism clearly shows the masculinization of the early development of science, which paved the way for the advances of modern technology, and there is no denying that the current population of scientists and engineers is overwhelmingly male. However, the development of science and technology cannot be exclusively identified with male gender characteristics. John Burke points out that human inquisitiveness plays an important role in technological invention and innovation,[48] and inquisitiveness is a characteristic shared by both men and women. In *The Myth of the Machine*, Lewis

Mumford argues that women as domesticators made significant contributions to the development of technology in early cultures:

> Protection, storage, enclosure, accumulation, continuity—these contributions of neolithic culture largely stem from woman and woman's vocation. In our current preoccupations with speed and motion and spatial extension, we tend to devaluate all these stabilizing processes. . . . But without this original emphasis on the organs of continuity . . . the higher functions of culture could never have developed.[49]

Autumn Stanley's reexamination of the history of technology also shows women's significant achievements in taming animals, making fire, and introducing rotary motion.[50] Men and women share an equal capacity for technological inventions, based on the human need to improve material life. Thus, women's relatively low involvement in the invention of destructive modern technology can be attributed to the sex/gender segregation of work, rather than inherent differences between men and women.

The tendency toward growth, expansion, and accumulation is inherent in capitalism. The enticement of profit not only maximizes production but also actuates consumption. Exponential economic growth is continuously pursued, at the cost of considerable damage to the natural environment and the diminishing of nonrenewable resources. The sexual division of labor, established before the rapid development of science/technology and the rise of capitalism, has excluded most women from executive and decision-making positions in economic institutions. As a result, women's participation in the labor force following industrialization has not changed their secondary status in society. In a male-dominated society, women, as the subordinated sex, have little control over the socioeconomic structure.

Ecofeminists tend to claim that the asymmetrical power relationship between men and women is the fundamental cause of socioeconomic injustice, which is then extended to the exploitative treatment of nature. In other words, ecofeminists presume that the development of capitalism is in accordance with male gender characteristics, especially aggression and competitiveness. But there is no evidence that women have an inherent ecological sensibility while men have an inherent impulse toward the destruction of nature. In fact, it is more likely that both men and women share a common desire for an affluent and comfortable material life, which may significantly contribute to the development of capitalism. Thus, it is untenable to assume that an egalitarian relationship between men and women or an elimination of sexual differentiation can preclude the establishment of exploitative economic institutions or limit commercial expansion. Indeed, such a reductionistic approach can easily lead back into a conceptual trap— the dichotomy between males and females that presumably is the basis of oppression.

The splitting of humanity into femininity and masculinity deprives human beings of personality traits, behavioral patterns, and value systems that could be common to both men and women. The polarization of maleness and femaleness is in line with the establishment of the male-dominated and female-subordinated sexual hierarchy. Male aggression is justified by the ideology of the dominant class, males. Overgenderization in human culture not only produces women's oppression but also constructs an aggression-oriented society. While genetic factors may contribute to male aggressiveness, other factors are also important. In accordance with the primary ecological principle that everything is interconnected with everything else, an inquiry into the impact of genderization must also include a consideration of interrelated sociohistorical conditions, events, and processes.

## *Ethics and Reintegration*

Acid rain, toxic wastes, the greenhouse effect, and nuclear meltdown are no respectors of persons. The deterioration of our living environments reveals the lethal effects of our oppressive and exploitative treatment of nature. Speaking of women's concerns for today's environmental problems, ecofeminism has emerged as a relatively new version of feminism.

I have pointed out that the woman-nature affinity, while true of Western cultures, is not a cross-cultural phenomenon. As the theoretical ground of ecofeminism, this alleged affinity fails to account for the conceptual connections between the human exploitation of nature and women's oppression at the global level. Yet the ideology of human domination over nature does indeed reflect a male-identified world view that is not necessarily shared by women. Applying Marilyn Frye's analysis of oppression to the natural world highlights the true parallels between the oppression of women and the oppression of nature, even without invoking the woman-nature affinity, or engaging in a reductionistic and reactionary attribution of ecological destruction to the "male" character.

Ecofeminists correctly observe that gender ideology had profound influences on our world view and the construction of cultural institutions. The ecofeminists' sex/gender analyses have undertaken a fundamental reexamination of the Western historical and cultural roots of today's ecological breakdown. Although their contextual analyses are limited (based as they are on Western culture), ecofeminist critiques of dualism and mechanism still shed valuable light on the conceptual roots of the global ecological destruction that may ensue from Western economic, military, and scientific imperialism.

Moreover, the ecofeminist analysis of oppression does not merely focus on the binding relations between the oppression of women and the oppression of nature. What is highly stressed is how the operation of one oppressive system is intimately interrelated with other forms of oppression. Sheila Collins succinctly states that "racism, sexism, class exploitation, and ecological destruction are four interlocking pillars upon which the structure of patriarchy rests."[51] In the preface to *New Woman/New Earth*, Rosemary Radford Ruether indicates that an examination of ideologies that support sexism must not overlook "the interrelationship of sexism with other structures of oppression, such as race, class, and technological power."[52] In other words, the praxis of ecofeminism aims at ending many interrelated oppressive systems. For non-Western women, this approach appears to be more plausible to ensure the solidarity of the global ecofeminist movement than an argument based solely on the woman-nature affinity.

Speaking of women's acute awareness of ecological crises in India, Vandana Shiva's analysis of "development" lucidly explains how the interrelated oppressive systems entail ecological degradation in the Third World. According to Shiva, the "ideology of development is in large part based on a vision of bringing all natural resources into the market economy for commodity production."[53] From the standpoint of a market economy, natural forests are unproductive, even though Indian women's self-sufficient subsistence economy is based on forests, and forests are central to Indian civilization. Thus, forests must be "developed into monoculture plantations of commercial species."[54] Through *military power,* the British introduced the "scientific management" of forests, which aimed at transforming them into timber mines for commercial purposes. The reduction of forests to timber mines sunders forestry from water management, from agriculture, and from animal husbandry. By focusing on economic growth, the postcolonial pursuit of "development" continues the process of colonization. As local people's needs are managed through market mechanisms, nature's productivity and renewability are deeply impaired. Thus, Shiva argues that "development is equivalent to maldevelopment, a development bereft of the feminine, the conservation, the ecological principle."[55] Since the causes of wide-scale deforestation are interrelated, Shiva concludes that a comprehensive understanding of ecological disasters can not overlook "the scientific-military-industrial complex of capitalist patriarchy."[56]

Shiva's criticisms of "development" are based on Indian women's experience of multiple oppression—sexism, imperialism, colonialism, and capitalism—which has made them keenly aware of how ecological breakdown and socioeconomic inequalities are interrelated. Understanding the inseparability of social and ecological issues, stressed and illuminated by Shiva's analysis of "development," is essential for constructing a framework of environmental ethics.

Aldo Leopold, an early advocate of environmental ethics, claims, "We have a well articulated human-to-human ethic; what we need is a comparable human-to-land ethic."[57] Here, "land" refers to an ecosystem that includes soil, water, plants, and animals. To delineate an ethics that can "supplement and guide the economic relation to land," we must, Leopold says, "presuppose the existence of some mental image of land as a biotic mechanism."[58] Some environmental ethicists are inclined to see human affairs as irrelevant to environmental issues. For instance, Holmes Rolston III contends that "in an environmental ethic, what humans want to value is not compassion, charity, rights, personality, justice, fairness or even pleasure and the pursuit of happiness. Those values belong in interhuman ethics— in culture, not nature—and to look for them here is to make a category mistake."[59]

It is true that environmental ethics is beyond the conventional scope of ethics, which focuses on interpersonal relationships. Environmental ethics must specifically define the normative presuppositions regarding our behavior toward nature, such as the value of protecting the diversity in an ecosystem. Yet environmental ethics should not be established on a human-nature binary system. From the vantage point of ecofeminism, human beings are part of nature, and nature and culture are interrelated. From this perspective, Rolston's attempt to separate environmental ethics from inter-human ethics is based on a false dichotomy. To ecofeminists, nature is not an abstract, static, and fixed entity, but rather a complex and interconnected web of life. Ecofeminists' ethical concerns regarding environmental issues are extended to any indication of brokenness and disharmony in the web of life. War, class exploitation, poverty, and animal experimentation are not regarded as peripheral to other urgent ecological issues, such as air and water pollution, oil spills, and the extinction of wilderness and wildlife. Consequently, the ecofeminist movement encompasses anti-militarism, the anti-nuclear movement, protests against the misuse of reproductive technology, and opposition to the economic exploitation of the Third World.

The framework of environmental ethics envisioned by ecofeminists is integrative as well as inclusive. Ecofeminists' critiques of the social structure of male domination, transcendent dualism, mechanism, and sex/gender role differentiation make us aware that a fundamental reconstruction of patriarchal culture is needed to solve the ecological dilemma. Moreover, ecofeminists' elucidation of the interrelatedness of oppressive systems indicates that interhuman and environmental ethics are also inseparable. Ecofeminists' transformative vision of environmental ethics underscores the ecological principle: everything is connected with everything else. Hence, ecofeminism can be the key to harmony, sustainability, and diversity in the age of science and technology.

### NOTES

*Acknowledgments:* I wish to express my gratitude to Nan M. DiBello, Greta Gaard, Clyde Nabe, Ralph Page, and Thomas Paxson for their helpful comments on this paper. Special thanks go to Sheila Ruth for her encouragement, inspiration, and warmth.

1. See, for example, Karen J. Warren, "Feminism and Ecology: Making Connections," *Environmental Ethics* 9 (1987): 3–20.

2. Karen J. Warren, "The Power and the Promise of Ecological Feminism," *Environmental Ethics* 12 (1990): 125–46.

3. Susan Griffin, *Woman and Nature: The Roaring Inside Her* (San Francisco: Harper & Row, 1978).

4. Ynestra King, "Toward an Ecological Feminism and a Feminist Ecology," in *Machina Ex Dea: Feminist Perspectives on Technology*, ed. Joan Rothschild (New York: Pergamon Press, 1983).

5. Carol P. MacCormack and Marilyn Strathern, eds., *Nature, Culture, and Gender* (Cambridge: Cambridge University Press, 1980), offer a fuller cross-cultural analysis of woman-nature connections.

6. Rosemary Radford Ruether, *New Woman/New Earth: Sexist Ideologies and Human Liberation* (New York: Seabury, 1975), 31.

7. Ibid.

8. Ibid., 106.

9. Ibid., 194.

10. Val Plumwood, "Ecofeminism: An Overview and Discussion of Positions and Arguments," *Australasian Journal of Philosophy*, supp. to vol. 64 (1986): 120–37.

11. Ibid.

12. F. W. Mote, *Intellectual Foundations of China* (New York: Knopf, 1971).

13. Tu Wei Mi, "The Continuity of Being: Chinese Visions of Nature," in *On Nature*, ed. L. S. Rouner (Notre Dame, Ind.: University of Notre Dame Press, 1984), 118.

14. Ibid., 119.

15. Ibid., 125. Tu does not address the complexity of Chinese religion, nor does he discuss a variety of folk definitions of nature. However, his interpretation of Chinese visions of nature, in general, is consistent with Confucianism, Taoism, and Neo-Confucianism. While Ruether's articulation of "transcendent dualism" represents the predominant world view in the West, Tu's interpretation of Chinese visions of nature also captures the prevalent world view in Chinese society. The following articles offer further discussion on the relations between Chinese traditions and environmental ethics: R. T. Ames, "Taoism and the Nature of Nature," *Environmental Ethics* 8 (1986): 317–49; J. Baird Callicott, "Environmental Ethics in Asian Traditions of Thought: A Propaedeutic," *Philosophy East and West* 37 (1987): 115–30; C. Cheng, "On the Environmental Ethics of the Tao and Ch'i," *Environmental Ethics* 8 (1986): 351–70; D. L. Hall, "On Seeking a Change of Environment: A Quasi-Taoist Proposal," *Philosophy East and West* 37 (1987): 160–71.

16. Carolyn Merchant, *The Death of Nature: Women, Ecology, and the Scientific Revolution* (New York: Harper & Row, 1980), xvi.

17. Ibid., 3, 5.

18. Ibid., 5.

19. Ibid., 172.

20. Ibid., 192.

21. Ibid., 172.

22. Ibid., 214.

23. Nancy Chodorow, "Family Structure and Feminine Personality," in *Women, Culture, and Society: A Theoretic Overview*, ed. Michelle Z. Rosaldo and Louise Lamphere (Stanford, Calif.: Stanford University Press, 1974); Dorothy Dinnerstein, *The Mermaid and the Minotaur: Sexual Arrangements and the Human Malaise* (New York: Harper & Row, 1976); Elizabeth D. Gray, *Green Paradise Lost* (formerly *Why the Green Nigger?*) (Wellesley, Mass.: Roundtable Press, 1981).

24. Gray, *Green Paradise Lost*, 42.

25. Warren, "Feminism and Ecology."

26. Evelyn Fox Keller, *Reflections on Gender and Science* (New Haven: Yale University Press, 1985).

27. Warwick Fox, "The Deep Ecology–Ecofeminism Debate and Its Parallels," *Environmental Ethics* 11 (1989): 5–26.

28. George Lakoff and Mark Johnson, *Metaphors We Live By* (Chicago: University of Chicago Press, 1980); S. C. Pepper, *World Hypotheses* (Berkeley: University of California Press, 1942).

29. Eva Feder Kittay, "Woman as Metaphor," *Hypatia* 3.2 (1988): 63–86.

30. Simone de Beauvoir, *The Second Sex*, trans. H. M. Parshley (New York: Knopf, 1952).

31. Kittay, "Woman as Metaphor."

32. Gerda Lerner, *The Creation of Patriarchy* (New York: Oxford University Press, 1986), chaps. 9 and 10.

33. Ibid., 180–98.

34. Mary Daly, *Beyond God the Father: Toward a Philosophy of Women's Liberation* (Boston: Beacon Press, 1973).

35. Ernest Schachtel, *Metamorphosis* (New York: Basic Books, 1959).

36. Lerner, *The Creation of Patriarchy*, 220.

37. Ibid.

38. Keller, *Reflections on Gender and Science*, 62.

39. Ibid., 63.

40. Ibid., 63–64.

41. Ibid., 64.

42. Ariel K. Salleh, "Deeper Than Deep Ecology: The Eco-Feminist Connection," *Environmental Ethics* 6 (1984): 339–45.

43. Lerner, *The Creation of Patriarchy*, 234.

44. Marilyn Frye, *The Politics of Reality: Essays in Feminist Theory* (Freedom, Calif.: Crossing Press, 1983), 33.

45. Ibid., 10.

46. *The Oxford English Dictionary* (Oxford: Clarendon Press, 1983).

47. R. A. F. Thurman, "Buddhist Views of Nature: Variations on the Theme of Mother-Father Harmony," in Rouner, *On Nature*.

48. John G. Burke, "Comment: The Complex Nature of Explanation in the Historiography of Technology," *Technology and Culture* 11 (1970): 22–26.

49. Lewis Mumford, *The Myth of the Machine* (New York: Harcourt Brace Jovanovich, 1966), 144.

50. Autumn Stanley, "Women Hold Up Two-Thirds of the Sky: Notes for a Revised History of Technology," in Rothschild, *Machina Ex Dea*.

51. Sheila D. Collins, *A Different Heaven and Earth* (Valley Forge, Pa.: Judson Press, 1973).

52. Ruether, *New Woman/New Earth*, xi.

53. Vandana Shiva, *Staying Alive: Women, Ecology and Development* (London: Zed Books, 1988), 9.

54. Ibid., 4.

55. Ibid.

56. Ibid., 31.

57. Aldo Leopold, *A Sand County Almanac: And Sketches Here and There* (New York and Oxford: Oxford University Press, 1949), 204.

58. Ibid.

59. Holmes Rolston III, *Environmental Ethics: Duties and Values in the Natural World* (Philadelphia: Temple University Press, 1988), 225.

# CHAPTER 12

# Ecofeminism and Native American Cultures: Pushing the Limits of Cultural Imperialism?

## Greta Gaard

Questions of racism and cultural imperialism have been brought to the foreground of the women's movement in the United States, most notably at the 1990 convention of the National Women's Studies Association (NWSA).[1] White academic feminists have been charged with theorizing about "women" in a way that universalizes and therefore does not account for differences among women based on culture, race, and class. Ecofeminists striving to create a theory that is inclusive of both humans and nature cannot afford, in our respect for the natural world, to ignore or dismiss these questions as "already answered" or "solved." In particular, three areas of debate within ecofeminism have the potential to create theory that borders on cultural imperialism with regard to Native American cultures:[2] the place of animals within ecofeminist theory, the feminization of nature as "Mother Earth," and the movement to reclaim the goddess in an ecofeminist theory of spirituality. If it is to be a truly viable and inclusive theory, ecofeminism can and must address these three issues—and others—in a way that is respectful to other cultures. In this chapter, and writing as a white woman, I will address each of these issues in turn to illustrate the ways in which ecofeminism has the potential to coopt Native American cultures, and to suggest methods for creating theory that avoid cultural imperialism.

As a preface, it is worth noting that in the United States ecofeminist theory has been articulated largely from a white feminist viewpoint. Perhaps Native American women have not needed to build ecofeminist theory because their own cultures provide them with an ample understanding of the interconnectedness and interdependence of humans and nature. But for those feminists who have no such heritage to rely upon, ecofeminism has much to offer.

## Toward an Understanding of
## Animals in Ecofeminism

In "The Power and the Promise of Ecological Feminism," Karen Warren proves that environmental theories and feminist ethics which do not account for the interconnected dominations of women and nature are inadequate.[3] However, Warren's theory provides no adequate grounding for an ethic that can describe relationships among animal species, specifically those between humans and nonhumans. In this section, I will first provide a critique of the ecofeminism put forth by Warren, then offer what I believe is a more inclusive, nonimperialist theory of ecofeminism which can address human and nonhuman ethical relations.

While Warren spends a good deal of time addressing nature and women, she leaves no space for addressing animals and how humans should interact with them. In fact, while a central portion of the essay discusses ethical ways of rock climbing, the conclusion romanticizes the slaughter of an animal. It would be easy (though incorrect) to infer, from the juxtaposition of these two narratives, that Warren believes a rock is more worthy of moral concern than is an animal.

Warren's essay communicates this value judgment through a sleight of hand: while the climber is unmarked and anonymous, and therefore white and privileged according to Warren,[4] the "four-legged"-slayer is a "Sioux" (Lakota).[5] For this reason, I question the implication on which Warren's article concludes: that is, that killing another animal, if done "respectfully" in one culture, can be determined an ethical practice in another culture. In fact, deep ecologists are most notably involved in this kind of overgeneralization, borrowing here and there from Native American and Eastern cultures the pieces that fit into their theory, while ignoring other aspects of those cultures.[6] This type of conceptualization is cultural cannibalism. Warren claims that an ecofeminist ethic is contextualist,[7] yet by excerpting the animal-slaying narrative from the context of the Lakota culture, and providing no analysis of our differing conceptual frameworks, she strays beyond the very boundaries of ecofeminism that she describes. "What counts as appropriate conduct toward both human and non-human environments is largely a matter of context,"[8] according to Warren, but where is the contextual analysis of the differences between precolonized Lakota culture and modern-day white Western culture?

In the Lakota narrative, one creature's need to survive is subordinated to another creature's need to "have food to eat and clothing to wear." Here, the cultural and historical context comes into play. In America in the 1990s, most humans no longer need to rely on animals for either food or clothing. Nutritious sources of food and warm supplies of clothing are available without taking the lives of other animals. To continue this killing, this domination, now entails subordinating the *needs* of one creature to the *desires* of another. In fact, the current practice of factory farming in America leaves no room for the Lakota narrative Warren describes. When animals are routinely boxed, caged, injected with hormones, forcibly inseminated, denied access to their young, and made to suffer immeasurably in transit to their deaths, it would be ludicrous indeed to graft the Lakota narrative onto the end of the American factory farming story.[9] Yet this is the only place for animals in the ecofeminism set forth in Warren's essay.

Warren defines ecofeminism as "quintessentially anti-naturist. Its anti-naturism consists in the rejection of any way of thinking about or acting toward nonhuman nature that reflects a logic, values, or attitude of domination."[10] This statement sets up a bifurcated definition by which beings can be described as either human nature or nonhuman nature. I have no trouble with the description of both as parts of nature; I simply question whether the most salient way of classifying nature is in terms of a human/nonhuman dichotomy, as this division seems rather anthropocentric. But accepting this pair of definitions for just a moment, one can see that since animals are not human (one might more properly say that humans are in fact animals), they must be classified as nonhuman nature. Thus, if ecofeminism as defined by Warren truly opposes the domination of nonhuman nature, we must ask if killing is an act of domination.

Warren defines the logic of domination as "a structure of argumentation which leads to a justification of subordination."[11] Now we must wonder if subordination is involved when one human being kills another being. I think this riddle can be solved. One being often kills another in the belief that its own needs are more important than the needs of the being it kills. In essence, the first being subordinates the needs and desires of the second being to its own, and through this subordination authorizes killing the other being. One may reasonably conclude, then, that killing is an act of domination. If ecofeminism opposes the domination of nonhuman nature, then ecofeminism must also oppose the killing of animals.

As a qualification, it is worth noting that this argument must be applied contextually: that there are contexts in which subordinating the needs of others, even the lives of others, is necessary to one's own survival or that of one's family or loved ones.[12] In Chapter 10 Marti Kheel addresses the situation in which a mother is asked to choose between her daughter's life and a dog's life. Kheel points out that "it would also be understandable . . . if the mother chose the life of her daughter over that of an anonymous *child*." Instead of pursuing the ethics of such a choice, Kheel suggests we challenge the crisis mentality that brings about such ethical dilemmas in the first place. Internationally, the problems of poverty and hunger are indeed at crisis level, brought about by a global scheme of economic underdevelopment,[13] and those people struggling to survive under such circumstances operate under a different set of ethical standards entirely. One has only to consider the lifestyles of many poor, indigenous, or Third World people to envision cases in which killing and eating other beings, human or nonhuman, could be necessary to the survival of the group and thus could be ethically justified in those contexts. I am not certain, however, that such killing would not involve a justification of subordination—and thereby invoke the logic of domination.

Here, some may object that we depend for our very existence on some form of domination, subordinating the needs of certain others to our own. For example, some may argue that in eating salad or rice pilaf, we have subordinated the needs of those plants to our own, just as meat-eaters subordinate the needs of nonhuman animals. To this type of objection, there are two replies: (1) the needs that plants may be said to have cannot be compared to the needs animals may be said to have, because the two kinds of being are not alike; and (2) if it is true that our diet and hence our survival depend upon some form of subordination, the most ethical course is clearly the path of least subordination. For human nature, where such choices exist, a vegetarian diet is ethically preferable to a carnivorous diet because a vegetarian diet involves the least amount of subordination, domination, and oppression.

Finally, I would like to respond to the words used in the Lakota narrative to describe the killing of the "four-legged." I would also like to contextualize this analysis by noting that in the Lakota language, the words may be entirely different and hold entirely different meanings—another argument against importing favored aspects of other cultures into our own.[14] This said, I want to consider the description of the "four-legged" as "brother," and the words describing the "four-legged's" acts toward its killer.

In Judeo-Christian culture, the crime of one brother slaying another, as in the Cain and Abel story, is the source of strife in civilization. Biblically, to "set brother against brother" was seen as a horrid curse. Certainly these mythic meanings are not part of the Lakota culture, in which "brother" human kills his "brother," the "four-legged." For those of us inheriting a Judeo-Christian ethic, however, brother killing brother is highly unethical; brother eating brother afterward is simply cannibalism.

In the Lakota narrative the "four-legged" is described as "offering his body to you just now," yet the word "offer" implies a kind of choosing, a willingness. But in the context of Judeo-Christianity, the fact that the four-legged is shot in the hind quarters so that its throat may be slit leads me to believe that this is no free-will offering. If the "four-legged" were a human, this killing would be described as unethical. Thus, this Lakota narrative, when translated from its original language, extracted from its cultural context, and imported into ecofeminist theory, now seems to imply some sort of neo-Renaissance Great Chain of Being, with nonhuman animals positioned beneath humans in a value hierarchy, and placed there for our use. In fact, in Native American cultures humans are seen as the last and lowest form of life, since all other life forms were created before us.[15]

The problem here is cultural difference: Warren's essay uproots only a desired portion of Native American culture as needed to justify her own version of ecofeminism. This strategy is conceived of by Marti Kheel as a "truncated narrative"—a case in which a portion of one culture's "story" is grafted onto another cultural context. Warren has argued that a feminist ethic must be a contextualist ethic as well, yet by decontextualizing the act of deer-slaying from the entire Lakota culture, and using it to justify meat eating in another culture, Warren's logic breaks down. In fact, in the United States there can be little justification for killing or eating animals outside the context of traditional Native American culture.[16]

To illustrate the centrality of vegetarianism to ecofeminism, I would like to use a recent feminist-vegetarian text. Carol Adams' *The Sexual Politics of Meat: A Feminist-Vegetarian Critical Theory* illustrates the connections between feminism and vegetarianism in an attempt to expand our understanding of patriarchal ideology.[17] Adams' central thesis is that meat eating is a manifestation of patriarchal values; that in white Western culture, meat is associated with masculinity and virility, whereas vegetarianism is considered effeminate and is associated with women. Using the fairly standard feminist technique of deconstructing the language, she explains that "meat" no longer means all foods, but rather "the essential or principal part of something." "Vegetable" represents the least desirable characteristics of a thing; "to vegetate is to lead a passive existence, just as to be feminine is to lead a passive existence."[18] Thus, "men who become vegetarians challenge an essential part of the masculine role. They are opting for women's food. How dare they? Refusing meat means a man is effeminate, a 'sissy,' a 'fruit.'"[19] We need look no further than the humorous *Real Men Don't Eat Quiche* to understand that gender is played out at the dinner table as it is in the rest of our culture.

Adams finds the intersection of sexual violence and meat eating in the "bondage equipment of pornography—chains, cattle prods, nooses, dog collars, and ropes," all of which suggest the control of animals. "When women are victims of violence," she writes, "the treatment of animals is recalled."[20] It is no surprise that rape survivors often describe their experience as "being treated like a piece of meat." But if the experience is unpleasant and degrading for women, what holds us back from acknowledging the brutal quality of that experience for other animal species, who are indeed "treated like pieces of meat" rather than whole, sentient beings?

Adams perceives "a cycle of objectification, fragmentation, and consumption."[21] Once women's bodies are objectified and fragmented in popular slang—tits, cunt, pussy, hole, *ad nauseam*—women are seen as less than human, and more appropriately as objects to be raped, dismembered, murdered. In other systems of oppression, we can observe the same process of renaming: in Nazi Germany, the Jews were referred to as "units"; in the Vietnam War, the Vietnamese were not people but "gooks"; in hunting, the animals to be killed are called "game." After she or he is killed, the animal is dismembered, and the animal's body parts are renamed in such a way as to obscure the fact that they were once part of a living, breathing being. In response to euphemisms that authorize oppression and annihilation, Adams quotes Emarel Freshel, an early twentieth-century vegetarian: "'If the words which tell the truth about meat as food are unfit for our ears, the meat itself is not fit for our mouths.'"[22]

In fact, the parallels between the exploitation of women and that of animals are numerous. It is a commonplace of feminist theory that tokenism is a symptom of oppression. When a woman is applauded at work because she "thinks like a man," we understand the meaning of token acceptance. When animals other than humans are categorically described as either pets or food, and the minority are accepted as pets while the majority are consumed as food, we are suddenly blind to this kind of tokenism. We understand how women are exploited by compulsory motherhood, yet our awareness skips over the realities faced by females of other species in the enslavement and prostitution of factory farms. We understand the fragmentation and objectification that take place in pornography as symptomatic of domination, yet when real body parts show up on our dinner plates, in our caps or shoes, we are suddenly blind. What can account for this systematic denial?

Comfort. It is almost embarrassing. If we acknowledge the connection between these systems of exploitation, we will have to make a change in the way we live—in what we eat, in what we wear. And it is simply not convenient to make such a change. The pleasure of our palates is more important than the agony of thousands of animals who live painful lives ending in brutal and violent deaths. Yet if we can see the intertwining oppressions of women of different colors and different nations, if we can understand how racism and classism function like sexism, if we can understand, in essence, that it is the claim of difference that authorizes these oppressions—what prevents us from understanding the oppression of other animal species?

More than comfort, it may be the fact, horrifying to some, that we too are animals. And the inability to accept this simple fact recalls the liberal split between mind and body. It is a split that denies the body, denies our feelings. By eating the dead bodies of other animals, we deny our connection to our own bodies, to our feelings, to the rest of nature. In doing so, we reinforce the assumptions of patriarchy. For white Western ecofeminists positioned outside Native American cultures, then, vegetarianism is an integral part of ecofeminist praxis.

## The Problem of "Mother Earth"

Of the many examples that could be cited to illustrate the woman-nature connection in Western culture, perhaps the most commonplace is the metaphor of "Mother Earth." Ecofeminists and environmentalists alike invoke this metaphor in calling for a halt to environmental degradation and destruction (for example, a popular bumper sticker features a shot of the earth from space, and the caption "Love Your Mother"). Some theorists point to the Native American conception of Mother Earth, urging Westerners to adopt this relationship to nature in the belief that such a notion will curb the ruthless violation of the natural world. But like the deer-slaying example cited earlier, the image of Mother Earth cannot be stolen from Native American cultures and used in Western culture while retaining the same meaning. This notion grows out of a constellation of values, and deprived of that cultural context, assumes meanings from our own culture instead.[23]

In white Western culture, mothers are expected to be selfless, generous, and nurturing. Their very existence derives its sole meaning from tending to the needs of their children. Mothers are expected to give endlessly, even after their children are grown. This maternal giving merits no economic value, as Marilyn Waring's *If Women Counted* has amply demonstrated. In fact, the institution of mothering has been a primary locus of women's subordination, according to Nancy Chodorow and Adrienne Rich.[24]

In thinking of the white Western cultural devaluation of mothers, I am reminded of a book that was widely read when I was young. In Shel Silverstein's *The Giving Tree* (1964), the story is told of a child—a boy, of course—who slowly took all the gifts of the tree: first the fruit for food, then the branches for play, and later the entire trunk and branches for building a house. Then he left for many years, not returning to visit the tree. But when the boy was old and disillusioned with life, he returned to the tree again. Since the tree had given him everything but still retained the desire to give, it offered itself to the boy as a stump to sit on and rest. This simple story makes clear the connection between all-giving human mothers and the idea of nature as an all-giving mother. Until Western culture changes its conception of motherhood to one in which the mother's needs are also respected, the metaphor of Mother Earth will only serve to perpetuate the very notion ecofeminism seeks to eradicate.[25]

Recently, while thinking about these problems, I had the opportunity to visit Niagara Falls, where again the fundamental difference between Western and traditional Native American cultures was demonstrated to me. There, for a small fee, visitors are given yellow rain ponchos and allowed to tour the caves behind the Falls. At one of these openings, the icy floor of the cave was covered with copper and silver coins. But of what value or use is money to nature? At first I thought it was a pleasant if misguided gesture of appreciation from an inherently capitalist viewpoint. But then the real difference struck me: whereas a Native American would offer tobacco as a gesture of gratitude toward nature, white culture traditionally interprets throwing money into water as an opportunity to ask for something more. In the two cultures, the human-nature relationship is interpreted respectively as a site of reciprocal give-and-take or a locus of unmoderated taking. The coins in the waterfall (and their frequently disproportionate or token quality in comparison with the coin-thrower's request) are consistent with the image of "Mother Nature" as the all-giving caretaker of humans.

The notion of the mother's generosity is based on the related concept of the mother's fecundity and bounty. Mother never tires of giving precisely because her supplies are limitless. And yet we have only to turn once again to Western culture to find a deep hatred of women's fertility. Women who have more than two children are somewhat disdained by the middle class; their fertility is regarded even more harshly if they are nonwhite mothers. Moreover, if a woman's body becomes more matronly as a result of multiple births, this bounty of flesh is also despised.[26]

The notion of the mother's fecundity becomes especially dangerous, then, when it is associated with "Mother Earth." The idea that old-growth forests are inexhaustible, for example, has authorized unrestrained logging for industry. Because there is always "more" in mother's generous apron, human children have not worried about dumping raw sewage or garbage into the waters. But the earth's resources are not only limited; they are rapidly being depleted, even devastated. It is time for humans to stop behaving like children.

A final aspect of the "Mother Earth" symbolism is, of course, the feminization of the earth. In the English language, nature and natural forces (hurricanes, tornadoes), many animals (cats, deer, rabbits), and, in general, whatever cannot be controlled take the feminine pronoun. But "she" is not merely a value-free pronoun; when applied to nature, "she" still carries the connotations of femininity. "We should check carefully whether we really want to view our relationship with the Earth through genderized lenses," warns Yaakov Garb. "What baggage will carry over from one domain to another (especially in a culture whose relation to both women and mothers is as misogynous as ours is)?"[27] While there are numerous examples of this carryover, I will select only a few.

One problem with feminizing the earth is that nature has now become a "damsel in distress," as Chaia Heller and Marti Kheel point out in Chapters 9 and 10. Recently I received a two-decal postcard from an organization called "Campaign for the Earth" that utilized this heroic mentality. On the back of the postcard, in a cursive typefont, was the following note: "Dear Children, Thank you for opening your hearts and taking part in this wonderful Campaign for me. I have been hurting, but feel better just knowing that you care. With Love, Mother Earth." On the front, the postcard's decals depicted spaceship earth, with just one change: the earth was not round, but heart-shaped. Such appeals rely upon the same mentality that is responsible for so much environmental destruction: the notion that humans have the power to save the earth, that we are in control, and that the earth is depending on us. This is a gross inversion of fact. The earth will be here long after humans have destroyed its capacity to support our form of life. The entity needing heroic efforts is us.

Another example of how feminizing the earth backfires can be found in a cartoon that appeared in the *Duluth News Tribune* on October 24, 1989, shortly after the San Francisco earthquake and the hurricane in Charleston.[28] The cartoon depicts a buxom, almost Valkyrie-like woman towering above the cities of San Francisco and Charleston, whose buildings are quaking, swaying, or crushed. On her dress is the word "Nature," and her voice-bubble says, ". . . just in case you've forgotten how insignificant you really are." This is feminine nature "out of control"—human control, that is, or technological control. The fear is that if "we" (and somehow humans become masculinized here) do not control "her," nature will destroy us.

A final example of the connection between gender and dominance in our cultural attitudes toward nature can be found in the pesticide ads of industrial agriculture. In an issue of *Statewatch*, Brian Ahlberg describes how "agribusiness agri*culture* sees nature as a force to be conquered."[29] There has been "a virtual explosion of products with military-associated names," such as "Surefire, Colonel, TopGun, Marksman, Salute, Bladex, Scepter, Squadron, and Bayonnet," Ahlberg observes. For example, the ad for Command depicts a hand grenade with the pin pulled out, set beneath a weed; it is captioned, "Everything you've ever wanted to do to a weed." Going one step farther, a magazine ad for the SIGCO seed company encourages farmers to "ruin Mother Nature's reputation," depicting a young, tough-looking Mother Nature who's "made it her business to challenge farmers." The message is that a nature that is feminine—even maternal—must still be controlled. And as feminist theorists have observed, rape is an extreme form of dominance and control.[30]

In Western culture, to feminize nature is to sexualize nature. Phrases like "virgin forest" and "rape of the land" suggest various "uses" and "potentials" for nature. In these constructions, rape is something that simply "happens" to nature and to women. But where is the agent for that verb in this passive construction? Who performs the "rape of the land"? When nature is feminized and therefore sexualized in such constructions, culture is masculinized, and the human-nature relationship becomes one of compulsory heterosexuality.[31]

In the final analysis, however, the feminization of nature remains problematic because it involves a fundamentally flawed, anthropomorphic projection of self that obscures our ability to know a different other. And this is Elizabeth Dodson Gray's argument against feminizing nature. "The truth is that nature is itself," Gray writes. "It is neither male human nor female human."[32] In the context of dominant Western culture, feminizing the earth entails not only anthropomorphizing nature; it also dooms the earth to endless subjugation.

Anthropomorphizing the earth—projecting our human characteristics onto a nonhuman environment—is disrespectful in the same way that racism is disrespectful, for it seeks to understand another not on her or his own terms but as a projection of ourselves. In "Have We Got a Theory for You!" María Lugones and Elizabeth Spelman suggest two ways of "learning" about others that are inherently racist, and one is "the case in which I observe myself and others like me culturally and in other ways and use that account to give an account of you. In doing this, I remake you in my own image."[33] Gray reaches a similar conclusion: "Projection, then, is very convenient for the one who does the projecting. It gives that person the illusion of knowledge. And the projection itself functions to hide and obscure the true identity of that which is projected upon."[34] Thus, the metaphor of "Mother Earth" dooms nature to a female way of being, which in Western culture means a subordinate way of being. If women were not the targets of sexism in Western culture, feminizing nature might take on a whole other meaning.

If the earth is not feminine, then how can we think of it? To answer this question, I like to think about the questions posed by Garb: "Isn't the fantasy that we can somehow contain the Earth within our imagination, bind it with a single metaphor, the most mistaken presumption of all? What would it be to live with multiple images of the Earth—fragmented, partial, and local representations that must always be less than the Earth we try to capture through them?"[35] In fact, the best vehicle for envisioning our relationship with the earth may be ecofeminist spirituality.

## Ecofeminist Spirituality

A final illustration of the potential for cultural imperialism and the need to respect cultural contexts comes from the emerging women's spirituality movement. Beginning with such pivotal works as Mary Daly's *Beyond God the Father* (1973) and *The Church and the Second Sex* (1968), the feminist spirituality movement blossomed in the seventies and eighties with works by Starhawk (*Dreaming the Dark* and *The Spiral Dance*), Carol Christ (*Womanspirit Rising*), Merlin Stone (*When God Was a Woman*), Charlene

Spretnak (*The Politics of Women's Spirituality* and *The Spiritual Dimension of Green Politics*), and Monica Sjöö and Barbara Mor (*The Great Cosmic Mother*), to name a few. More recently, the trend has been toward a reclaiming of the goddess, as witnessed by the production and immediate popularity of two educational videos distributed by the National Film Board of Canada, "The Burning Times" and "Goddess Remembered" (both 1990), along with the publication of Gloria Feman Orenstein's *The Reflowering of the Goddess*. Certain thinkers believe ecofeminism is the bridge between political theory and the goddess spirituality movements.

Uncovering the history of goddess worship is extremely important, as Carol Christ suggests in "Why Women Need the Goddess": the Goddess affirms "female power, the female body, the female will, and women's bonds and heritage." Christ argues that "religions centered on the worship of a male god . . . keep women in a state of psychological dependence on men and male authority, while at the same time legitimating the *political* and *social* authority of fathers and sons in the institutions of society."[36] According to Orenstein, Goddess spirituality "does not separate heaven and earth, spirit and matter, human and animal; [it is] a spirituality that images the Earth as sacred, and the Goddess as the Great Mother of all life."[37] For this reason, Orenstein believes Goddess spirituality is an important dimension of ecofeminism, and considers "the return of the Goddess as a sign of the return to an attitude of reverence for the Earth, our Mother, and of an ecological as well as a nonsexist consciousness."[38] The role of the Goddess in reclaiming feminist history is also important: "The Goddess symbol also reminds women that our legitimate history has been buried, and that through its excavation we are learning how short the patriarchal period in human history has been in comparison with the 30,000 or more years of matristic history in which goddess-centered cultures flourished in central Europe, Anatolia and the Near and Middle East."[39]

Certainly uncovering history is important for women and other nondominant groups. In "Resisting Amnesia: History and Personal Life," Adrienne Rich remarks, "It is nothing new to say that history is the version of events told by the conqueror, the dominator. Even the dominators acknowledge this. What has more feelingly and pragmatically been said by people of color, by white women, by lesbians and gay men, by people with roots in the industrial or rural working class is that without our own history we are unable to imagine a future because we are deprived of the precious resource of knowing where we come from: the valor and the waverings, the visions and defeats of those who went before us."[40] In the program brochure for the 1991 Heart of the Earth PowWow, an article titled "500 years after Columbus: The Legacy of Genocide" echoes Rich's sentiments: "The gala events surrounding the Columbus Quincentennial (1492–1992) will serve to reinforce the epidemic historical amnesia in this country. Any party honoring the Columbus expedition only will obscure the true history of the genocidal era which began in 1492." Remembering and reclaiming the past is an important affirmation for many nondominant cultures. But does ecofeminism really need Goddess spirituality? Is this movement yet another manifestation of cultural imperialism?

The Goddess revival has been challenged most notably by Janet Biehl, who argues that there is no necessary correlation between Goddess worship and an equal or elevated status for women.[41] Moreover, there is no proof that the Goddess worshiped by people in various Neolithic cultures was a nature Goddess, since there was no separate concept of nature in prehistory: "The realms of nature and humanity were not distinguished until Hellenic times," Biehl objects. How much of the Goddess myth is historical reality? According to Biehl, the Goddess is more myth than fact, and "the politics of myth facilitates manipulation" of believers. Perhaps no deity is entirely factual, hence the problems of proving their existence. The better question might be a rephrasing of Biehl's second point: whose interests do these myths serve?[42] Whose history is this really?

As Orenstein acknowledges, the Goddess cults now being discovered were located in central Europe and the Near and Middle East. For women living in those areas today, these may be important discoveries, but how relevant are they to the history of women in the United States? The importance of place—and not merely culture, gender, or class alone—is neatly stated by Paula Gunn Allen when she speaks of Native American ceremonies and literatures: "The greater and lesser symbols incorporated into the ceremonies take their meaning from the context of the ceremony—its purpose and its meaning. Attempts to understand ceremonial literature without knowledge of this purpose often have ludicrous results. The symbols cannot be understood in terms of another culture, whether it be that of Maya or of England, because those other cultures have different imperatives and have grown on different soil, under a different sky within the nexus of different spirits, and within a different traditional context."[43] Thus, there are two questions women living in the United States must answer in terms of an ecofeminist or a Goddess spirituality: is it appropriate to adopt the traditions of a white European culture that developed in relation to an entirely different natural context? And is it appropriate to adopt the traditions of a culture different from our own, but rooted on this same continent?

To focus the first question, one may ask in turn how much do women living in the United States have in common with the women of agricultural societies in Crete, for example, over 30,000 years ago? Can women in the United States really call this our "heritage"? While we can acknowledge the importance of this mythical or historical precedent as empowering us to believe in the possibility of another similar occurrence today, it would seem highly awkward to most women to begin offering thanks and devotion to a Corn Goddess or a Queen Bee. While I am in no way censuring those women who find such worship or rituals useful, I do believe that the majority of women will find it foreign.

The second question is less easily dismissed. In fact, many white and nonwhite women in the United States have turned to Native American cultures to find their spirituality, a move that on the surface would seem more logical, since those cultures preceded us on this part of the earth. But, once again, to do this is to participate in cultural imperialism. As Andrea Smith writes in a position paper distributed at the 1990 conference of the National Women's Studies Association, white feminists who attempt to extract spiritual rituals from Native American communities are "continuing the same exploitative and genocidal practices of their forefathers/mothers" and perpetuating a form of "Indian spiritual abuse."[44] Native American spirituality is inseparable from Native American cultures, a unity little understood by white Euro-Americans. "A message a white woman would be more likely to hear from a medicine woman," writes Smith, "is to look into your *own* culture and find what is liberating in it." Thus, the answer to both questions is "no." Implicit in ecofeminist theory is the importance of being "grounded" in a particular context, while respecting cultural differences. An ecofeminist spirituality must evolve naturally from a specific geographic and cultural location. Fortunately for those who seek a spiritual perspective, the theory and practice of ecofeminism is in itself equal to the task Smith sets forth.

The fundamental principle of ecofeminism is the interconnectedness of all life. While this principle can be found in Native American thought, it is also characteristic of Hinduism, Zen, and other philosophies as well. In fact, the essence of god consciousness, buddha consciousness, and the Hindu yogi's state of samadhi is the consciousness of interconnection, an awareness of oneness that transcends mere ego identity. Quite simply in its understanding of interconnection, ecofeminism bridges politics and spirituality.

But this was an artificial duality to begin with. "Spirituality is indeed political," writes Judith Antonelli, "[in] that it deals with the distribution of power."[45] Because "spirit and matter are not dichotomized but are the inside and outside of the same thing," when ecofeminists speak of the interconnectedness of all natural life, they can be understood to be making a political and a spiritual statement simultaneously.[46] The only thing left is for us to realize that.

And many people are finding a real need for spirituality. The recent popularity of "meditation, New Age spiritualities and the revival of fundamentalist religions is a reflection of our great hunger for contact with our inner selves," writes Hallie Iglehart. "This need will not go away."[47] So many women and men have been drawn to ecofeminism out of a basic respect for nature, a sense of wonder. Ecofeminism, for these people, is a way of describing a political theory and practice for what we know intuitively to be true. Knowledge and awareness of our interconnectedness provide the impetus for ecofeminist political acts as well as ecofeminist spirituality.

Some political activists have hesitated to incorporate spirituality out of fear that all spirituality is apolitical, that a focus on the "inner" life will detract from activity in the "outer" life. For ecofeminism, this assumption is patently untrue. "When we understand that everything is interconnected," writes Starhawk, "we are called to a politics and set of actions that come from compassion, from the ability to literally feel *with* all living beings on the Earth."[48] This spirituality motivates and requires political work, according to Jonathon Porritt of the Green party: "The spiritual dimension is the most compelling reason why we should be involved in politics. One cannot sustain that which one does not revere."[49] It is this reverence for the natural world, along with the simple logic of the theory, that draws people into action on behalf of the Earth.

Ecofeminist spirituality is ecofeminist politics is ecofeminism.

Without stealing pieces from other cultures and other traditions, ecofeminists can arrive at this answer on our own.

## Ecofeminism and Cultural Context

Ecofeminism and Native American cultures have many values in common. To avoid cultural imperialism, however, ecofeminists must resist the urge to import "convenient" pieces of Native American cultures, Middle Eastern cultures, or any other cultures to construct a mosaic of theories from varying cultural sources. Such a theory would lack the regard for context that is the common goal of all authentically feminist theories. However, there are mutually respectful ways for ecofeminists to build coalitions or to build theory with women of color.

In "Have We Got a Theory for You!" Lugones and Spelman offer a guide for white women interested in building theory with women of color. Addressing white women, Lugones writes, "I do not think that you have any obligation to understand us. You do have an obligation to abandon your imperialism, your universal claims, your reduction of us to your selves simply because they seriously harm us."[50] Moreover, building theory with women of color does not mean presenting them with an argument to critique: "There is a very important difference between (a) developing ideas together in a 'pre-theoretical' stage, engaged as equals in joint inquiry, and (b) one group developing, on the basis of their own experience, a set of criteria for good change for women—and then reluctantly making revisions in the criteria at the insistence of women to whom such criteria seem ethnocentric and arrogant. The deck is stacked when one group takes it upon itself to develop the theory and then have others criticize it."[51] Lugones concludes, "If white/Anglo women are to understand our voices, they must understand our communities and us in them."[52] The best way to achieve such understanding is through friendship and what Marilyn Frye has called "loving perception," which is a genuine desire to know a different other.[53] Such knowing may require some repositioning on the part of the knower, for it entails seeing each potential friend at home, in her own cultural context. Yet it is this kind of "world-travelling"[54] white feminists and ecofeminists must undertake if we are to understand and to build friendship, resistance, and theory with women across the boundaries of class, color, and culture.

In contrast to other areas of the world, ecofeminism in the United States has been articulated largely from a white perspective. The fact that white Westerners can arrive at the same insights as other cultures seems so amazing to some that we have been quick to import portions of those other cultures to validate our insights. Not only is this cultural imperialism, it is entirely unnecessary. To those feminists who respect the earth and understand the interconnectedness of all life, ecofeminism is its own validation.

## NOTES

*Acknowledgments:* I am deeply grateful to Jesse Ehlert, Lori Gruen, Marti Kheel, and Stephanie Lahar for their careful readings and suggestions on earlier drafts of this chapter.

1. Regarding the 1990 NWSA convention and the problem of racism, for the viewpoint of the NWSA steering committee, see Patsy Schweickart, "Reflections on NWSA '90," *NWSAction* 3 (Fall 1990): 3–4, 9–10; for the viewpoint of the Women of Color Caucus, see "Speaking for Ourselves," *Women's Review of Books* 8 (February 1991): 27–29.

2. Within Native American communities, there is debate over whether the term "Native American" or "American Indian" should be used. Some argue for the use of specific tribal names only, as a way to retain the uniqueness of each group. In the interim, I have chosen to use the term "Native American," and to acknowledge the continuing debate.

3. See Karen Warren, "The Power and the Promise of Ecological Feminism," *Environmental Ethics* 12 (1990): 125–46. I want to acknowledge here the tremendous contributions Warren has made in developing ecofeminist theory (see Bibliography), and my own intellectual indebtedness to her on many points. My critique is offered in the spirit of advancing ecofeminist debate, which is vital to the growth and development of the theory.

4. Warren writes in "The Power and the Promise of Ecological Feminism," 144: "In contemporary sex-gendered, raced, classed, and naturist culture, an unlabeled position functions as a privileged and 'unmarked' position." Because Warren's climber is unnamed and unlabeled, by virtue of her own theory, the climber functions from a privileged position.

5. "Sioux" is a French word meaning "enemy." The native people called themselves "Lakota," which means "the original people" (personal communication with Jesse Ehlert, Bois Forte Reservation mental health outreach worker, February 22, 1991). In this chapter, therefore, I have chosen to replace Warren's "Sioux" with "Lakota."

6. For an analysis of the inherent racism and classism of such positions, see Ramachandra Guha, "Radical American Environmentalism and Wilderness Preservation: A Third World Critique," *Environmental Ethics* 11 (1989): 71–83.

7. Warren, "Power and Promise," 141.

8. Ibid., 143.

9. For the concept of truncated narratives, I am indebted to Marti Kheel's "From Heroic to Holistic Ethics: The Ecofeminist Challenge" (Chapter 10 in this volume).

10. Warren, "Power and Promise," 141.

11. Ibid., 128.

12. For ecofeminist analyses of the importance of context in relation to vegetarianism, see Deane Curtin, "Toward an Ecological Ethic of Care," *Hypatia* 6

(Spring 1991): 60–74, and Deborah Slicer, "Your Daughter or Your Dog?" *Hypatia* 6 (Spring 1991): 108–24.

13. For a feminist analysis of global economics, development policies, and their impact on women's lives, see Vandana Shiva, *Staying Alive: Women, Ecology and Development* (London: Zed Books, 1988), and Marilyn Waring, *If Women Counted: A New Feminist Economics* (San Francisco: HarperCollins, 1988).

14. Cf. María Lugones writes in regard to the racism of white/Anglo feminists: "We and you do not talk the same language. . . . Since your language and your theories are inadequate in expressing our experiences, we only succeed in communicating our experience of exclusion. We cannot talk to you in our language because you do not understand it." See María C. Lugones and Elizabeth V. Spelman, "Have We Got a Theory for You! Feminist Theory, Cultural Imperialism and the Demand for 'The Woman's Voice,'" *Women's Studies International Forum* 6 (1983): 573–81.

15. Personal communication from Jesse Ehlert, February 27, 1991.

16. For a vegetarian-feminist argument that advocates that all feminists, regardless of their cultural traditions, should be vegetarian, see Jane Meyerding, "Feminist Criticism and Cultural Imperialism (Where Does One End and the Other Begin)," *Animals' Agenda* (November–December 1982): 14–15, 22–23.

17. Carol Adams, *The Sexual Politics of Meat: A Feminist Vegetarian Critical Theory* (New York: Continuum, 1990).

18. Ibid., 36.

19. Ibid., 38.

20. Ibid., 43.

21. Ibid., 47.

22. Ibid., 67.

23. Carolyn Merchant, in both *The Death of Nature: Women, Ecology, and the Scientific Revolution* (New York: Harper & Row, 1980), and *Ecological Revolutions: Nature, Gender, and Science in New England* (Chapel Hill and London: University of North Carolina Press, 1989), shows that whatever the term "mother" means to a particular culture will metaphorically infect the meanings that culture attaches to the term "Mother Earth." For an analysis of this metaphorical transfer in contemporary culture, see Ellen Cronan Rose, "The Good Mother: From Gaia to Gilead," *Frontiers* 11 (1991): 77–97.

24. See Nancy Chodorow, *The Reproduction of Mothering: Psychoanalysis and the Sociology of Gender* (Berkeley: University of California Press, 1978), and Adrienne Rich, *Of Woman Born: Motherhood as Experience and Institution* (New York: Bantam Books, 1976).

25. Marti Kheel suggests a different tactic: "We need to challenge the spurious images of both women and nature. One could equally argue that we should not use the word 'lesbian' to describe ourselves, since lesbians are held in low regard in our culture and it would be much better to use a word or image that didn't threaten people so much. But of course it is the negative regard in which lesbians

are held that needs to be addressed. I would argue that the same is true for women and nature" (personal communication, March 10, 1991). I agree with Kheel's analysis as a long-term solution, and something we should strive for; but until we can eradicate the sexism and misogyny that has dominated Western culture since the inception of patriarchy, I believe the Mother Earth metaphor will continue to be a harmful one and one that must be rejected. Cf. Catherine Roach, "Loving Your Mother: On the Woman-Nature Relation," *Hypatia* 6 (Spring, 1991): 46–59: "As long as we perceive women as closer to nature within a model which perceives nature to be on the one hand mechanical, on the other hand semihuman, and in both cases legitimately exploitable, then we will see women as a resource, and both women and the environment will suffer."

26. The politics of population growth, mothering, and birth control are explored in Betsy Hartmann, *Reproductive Rights and Wrongs: The Global Politics of Population Control and Contraceptive Choice* (New York: Harper & Row, 1987). For a feminist analysis of the relationship between mothering, woman's flesh, and nurturance, see Kim Chernin's *The Hungry Self: Women, Eating and Identity* (New York: Harper & Row, 1986), and *Reinventing Eve: Modern Woman in Search of Herself* (New York: Harper & Row, 1987).

27. Yaakov Jerome Garb, "Musings on Contemporary Earth Imagery," in *Reweaving the World: The Emergence of Ecofeminism*, ed. Irene Diamond and Gloria Feman Orenstein (San Francisco: Sierra Club, 1990), 264–78, at 277.

28. I am indebted to Kate Basham for drawing this cartoon to my attention.

29. Brian Ahlberg, "Pesticide Ads Conquer Nature with Images," Minnesota Public Interest Research Group (MPIRG) *Statewatch*, Spring–Summer 1988, 7.

30. See, for example, Susan Griffin, *Rape: The Politics of Consciousness* (San Francisco: Harper & Row, 1986).

31. Cf. Adrienne Rich, "Compulsory Heterosexuality and Lesbian Existence," in *Blood, Bread, and Poetry: Selected Prose 1979–1985* (New York: Norton, 1986), 23–75. From a lesbian perspective, an interesting exception is posed in Linda Vance's chapter in this volume (Chapter 5). There she envisions a relationship of sisterhood with nature, a separate-yet-connected relationship of respect and struggle.

32. See Elizabeth Dodson Gray, "Nature: Our Cultural Assumptions," *Creation* 5 (May–June 1989): 31–33.

33. Lugones and Spelman, "Have We Got a Theory," 577.

34. Gray, "Nature," 32.

35. Garb, "Musings," 278.

36. Carol Christ, "Why Women Need the Goddess," in *Womanspirit Rising: A Feminist Reader in Religion*, ed. Carol P. Christ and Judith Plaskow (New York: Harper & Row, 1979), 276, 275.

37. Gloria Feman Orenstein, *The Reflowering of the Goddess* (New York: Pergamon Press, 1990), 6.

38. Ibid., 14.

39. Ibid., 6.

40. Rich, "Resisting Amnesia," in *Blood, Bread, and Poetry*, 136–55.

41. See Janet Biehl, "The Politics of Myth," *Green Perspectives* 7 (June 1988): 1–6.

42. I am indebted to Lori Gruen for this observation.

43. Paula Gunn Allen, *The Sacred Hoop: Recovering the Feminine in American Indian Traditions* (Boston: Beacon Press, 1986), 73–74.

44. See also Andy Smith, "For All Those Who Were Indian in a Former Life," *Ms.*, November–December 1991, 44–45.

45. Judith Antonelli, "Feminist Spirituality: The Politics of the Psyche," in *The Politics of Women's Spirituality: Essays on the Rise of Spiritual Power Within the Feminist Movement*, ed. Charlene Spretnak (New York: Anchor Books/Doubleday, 1982), 399–403.

46. Rosemary Radford Ruether, "Toward an Ecological-Feminist Theory of Nature," in *Healing the Wounds: The Promise of Ecofeminism*, ed. Judith Plant (Santa Cruz, Calif., and Philadelphia: New Society Publishers, 1989), 145–50, at 145.

47. Hallie Iglehart, "The Unnatural Divorce of Spirituality and Politics," in Spretnak, *Politics of Women's Spirituality*, 404–14, at 409–10.

48. Starhawk, "Power, Authority, and Mystery: Ecofeminism and Earth-Based Spirituality," in Diamond and Orenstein, *Reweaving the World*, 73–86, at 74.

49. Jonathon Porritt, "Seeing Green: How We Can Create a More Satisfying Society," *Utne Reader* 36 (November–December 1989): 70–77.

50. Lugones and Spelman, "Have We Got a Theory," 576.

51. Ibid., 579.

52. Ibid., 581.

53. For Marilyn Frye's distinction between arrogant and loving perception, see "In and Out of Harm's Way: Arrogance and Love," in *The Politics of Reality: Essays in Feminist Theory*, ed. Marilyn Frye (Trumansburg, N.Y.: Crossing Press, 1983), 52–83.

54. María Lugones articulated this concept in "Playfulness, 'World'-Travelling, and Loving Perception," in *Lesbian Philosophies and Cultures*, ed. Jeffner Allen (Albany: State University of New York Press, 1990), 159–80.

# Selected Bibliography

Abzug, Bella. "Women and the Fate of the Earth: The World Women's Congress for a Healthy Planet." *Woman of Power* 20 (Spring 1991): 26–30.

Adams, Carol J. "Anima, Animus, Animal." *Ms.*, May/June 1991, 62–63.

——. "Developing Courses That Integrate Animal Rights and Feminism." *APA Newsletter on Feminism and Philosophy* 90 (Fall 1991): 135–43.

——. "Ecofeminism and the Eating of Animals." *Hypatia* 6 (Spring 1991): 125–45.

——. *The Sexual Politics of Meat: A Feminist-Vegetarian Critical Theory*. New York: Continuum, 1990.

——., ed. *Ecofeminism and the Sacred*. Mary Knoll, N.Y.: Orbis Books, 1992.

Allen, Paula Gunn. *The Sacred Hoop: Recovering the Feminine in American Indian Traditions*. Boston: Beacon Press, 1986.

Benhabib, Seyla. "The Generalized and the Concrete Other: The Kohlberg-Gilligan Controversy and Feminist Theory." In *Feminism as Critique: On the Politics of Gender*, ed. Seyla Benhabib and Drucilla Cornell, 77–95. Minneapolis: University of Minnesota Press, 1987.

Bertell, Rosalie. "Charting a New Environmental Course." *Women and Environments* 13 (Winter/Spring 1991): 6–9.

——. "Radioactivity: No Immediate Danger?" *Ms.*, September/October 1991, 27–30.

Biehl, Janet. "Ecofeminism and Deep Ecology: Unresolvable Conflict?" *Our Generation* 19 (1988): 19–31.

——. "The Politics of Myth." *Green Perspectives* 7 (June 1988): 1–6.

——. *Rethinking Ecofeminist Politics*. Boston: South End Press, 1991.

——. "What Is Social Ecofeminism?" *Green Perspectives* 11 (October 1988): 1–8.

Brown, Margaret. "Ecofeminism: An Idea Whose Time Has Come." *Utne Reader* (April 1988).

Brown, Wilmette. *Roots: Black Ghetto Ecology*. London: Housewives in Dialogue, 1986.

Caldecott, Leonie, and Stephanie Leland, eds. *Reclaim the Earth: Women Speak Out for Life on Earth*. London: Women's Press, 1983.

Cantor, Aviva. "The Club, the Yoke, and the Leash: What We Can Learn From the Way a Culture Treats Animals." *Ms.*, August 1983, 27–29.

Cheney, Jim. "Eco-Feminism and Deep Ecology." *Environmental Ethics* 9 (1987): 115–45.

Chodorow, Nancy. *The Reproduction of Mothering: Psychoanalysis and the Sociology of Gender*. Berkeley: University of California Press, 1978.

Collard, Andrée, with Joyce Contrucci. *Rape of the Wild: Man's Violence Against Animals and the Earth*. Bloomington: Indiana University Press, 1989.

Collins, Sheila. *A Different Heaven and Earth*. Valley Forge, Pa.: Judson Press, 1973.

Conn, Sarah A. "The Self-World Connection: Implications for Mental Health and Psychotherapy." *Woman of Power* 20 (Spring 1991): 71–77.

Corea, Gena. "Dominance and Control: How Our Culture Sees Women, Nature and Animals." *Animals' Agenda* (May/June 1984): 37.

Corrigan, Theresa, and Stephanie T. Hoppe. "Lives on Earth: Developing Animal Rights Consciousness." *Woman of Power* 20 (Spring 1991): 59–63.

Curtin, Deane. "Toward an Ecological Ethic of Care." *Hypatia* 6 (Spring 1991): 60–74.

Davies, Katherine. "Historical Associations: Women and the Natural World." *Women and Environments* 9 (Spring 1987): 4–6.

———. "What is Ecofeminism?" *Women and Environments* 10 (Spring 1988): 4–6.

Diamond, Irene, and Gloria Feman Orenstein, eds. *Reweaving the World: The Emergence of Ecofeminism*. San Francisco: Sierra Club, 1990.

DiPenna, Donna. "Truth vs. 'Facts.'" *Ms.*, September/October 1991, 21–26.

Doubiago, Sharon. "Deeper Than Deep Ecology: Men Must Become Feminists." *New Catalyst Quarterly* 10 (Winter 1987/88): 10–11.

Easlea, Brian. *Science and Sexual Oppression: Patriarchy's Confrontation with Women and Nature*. London: Weidenfeld & Nicholson, 1981.

Echols, Alice. "The New Feminism of Yin and Yang." In *Powers of Desire: The Politics of Sexuality*, ed. Ann Snitow, Christine Stansell, and Sharon Thompson, 439–59, New York: Monthly Review, 1983.

Eisler, Riane. *The Chalice and the Blade*. San Francisco: Harper & Row, 1988.

Feldsien, Pat. "Creation Spirituality: Present to the Earth." *Creation* 5 (May/June 1989): 31–33.

Fox, Warwick. "The Deep Ecology–Ecofeminism Debate and Its Parallels." *Environmental Ethics* 11 (1989): 5–26.

George, Susan. *A Fate Worse Than Debt*. New York: Grove, 1988.

Gilligan, Carol. *In a Different Voice: Psychological Theory and Women's Development*. Cambridge: Harvard University Press, 1982.

Gilligan, Carol, Janie Ward, Jill McLean Taylor, and Betty Bardige, eds. *Mapping the Moral Domain*. Cambridge: Harvard University Press, 1988.

Glasheen, Laurie Corliss. "Building Coalitions for Our Earth: An Interview with Ellie Goodwin about 'Race, Poverty, and the Environment' Newsletter." *Woman of Power* 20 (Spring 1991): 32–35.

Graham, Pat. "A Matter of Respect: The Dissection Hotline for Students and Educators." *Woman of Power* 20 (Spring 1991): 56–58.

Gray, Elizabeth Dodson. *Green Paradise Lost*. Wellesley, Mass.: Roundtable Press, 1981.

———. "Nature: Our Cultural Assumptions." *Creation* 5 (May/June 1989): 31–33.

———. "Seeing and Hearing the Living Earth." *Woman of Power* 20 (Spring 1991): 18–21.

Griffin, Susan. *Pornography and Silence: Culture's Revenge Against Nature*. New York: Harper & Row, 1981.

———. "Split Culture." *ReVISION* 9 (Winter/Spring 1987): 17–23.

———. *Woman and Nature: The Roaring Inside Her*. New York and San Francisco: Harper & Row, 1978.

Griscom, Joan L. "On Healing the Nature/History Split in Feminist Thought." *Heresies* 13: "Feminism and Ecology" (1981): 4–9.

Gruen, Lori, and Peter Singer. *Animal Liberation: A Graphic Guide*. London: Camden Press, 1987.

Guha, Ramachandra. "Radical American Environmentalism and Wilderness Preservation: A Third World Critique." *Environmental Ethics* 11 (1989): 71–83.

Hamilton, Cynthia. "Women, Home, and Community: The Struggle in an Urban Environment." *Woman of Power* 20 (Spring 1991): 42–45.

Haraway, Donna. *Primate Visions: Gender, Race, and Nature in the World of Modern Science*. New York: Routledge, 1989.

Hartmann, Betsy. "The Ecology Movement: Targeting Women for Population Control." *Ms.*, May/June 1991, 83.

———. *Reproductive Rights and Wrongs: The Global Politics of Population Control and Contraceptive Choice*. New York: Harper & Row, 1987.

Hynes, H. Patricia. *The Recurring Silent Spring*. New York: Pergamon Press, 1989.

Kelly, Petra. "Women and Global Green Politics: A Call for the Formation of a New Political Party in the United States." *Woman of Power* 20 (Spring 1991): 24–25.

Kheel, Marti. "Animal Liberation Is a Feminist Issue." *New Catalyst Quarterly* 10 (Winter 1987/88): 8–9.

———. "Ecofeminism and Deep Ecology: Reflections on Identity and Difference." *The Trumpeter* 8 (1991): 62–72.

———. "The Liberation of Nature: A Circular Affair." *Environmental Ethics* 7 (1985): 135–49.

———. "Speaking the Unspeakable: Sexism in the Animal Rights Movement." *Feminists for Animal Rights Newsletter*, Summer/Fall 1985.

King, Roger J. H. "Caring About Nature: Feminist Ethics and the Environment." *Hypatia* 6 (Spring 1991): 75–89.

———. "Noddings, Care, and Environmental Ethics." *APA Newsletter on Feminism and Philosophy* 90 (Fall 1991): 127–30.

King, Ynestra. "The Eco-Feminist Imperative." In *Reclaim the Earth: Women Speak Out for Life on Earth*, ed. Leonie Caldecott and Stephanie Leland, 9–14. London: Women's Press, 1983.

———. "The Ecology of Feminism and the Feminism of Ecology." In *Healing the Wounds: The Promise of Ecofeminism*, ed. Judith Plant, 18–28. Philadelphia: New Society; Ontario: Between the Lines, 1989.

———. "Feminism and the Revolt of Nature." *Heresies* 13: "Feminism and Ecology" (1981): 12–16.

———. "Healing the Wounds: Feminism, Ecology, and the Nature/Culture Dualism." In *Reweaving the World: The Emergence of Ecofeminism*, ed. Irene Diamond and Gloria Feman Orenstein, 106–21. San Francisco: Sierra Club, 1990.

———. "Making the World Live: Feminism and the Domination of Nature." In *Women's Spirit Bonding*, ed. Janet Kalven and Mary I. Buckley, 56–64. New York: Pilgrim Press, 1984.

———. "May the Circle be Unbroken: The Eco-Feminist Imperative." *Tidings* (May 1981): 1–5.

———. "Toward an Ecological Feminism and a Feminist Ecology." In *Machina Ex Dea: Feminist Perspectives on Technology*, ed. Joan Rothschild, 118–29. New York: Pergamon Press, 1983.

———. "What Is Ecofeminism?" *The Nation*, December 12, 1987, 702, 730–31.

Lahar, Stephanie. "Ecofeminist Theory and Grassroots Politics." *Hypatia* 6 (Spring 1991): 28–45.

———. "Towards an Expanded View of Nature in Women's Psychology." *NWSA Journal* 1 (Winter 1988/89): 183–98.

Lugones, María. "Playfulness, 'World'-Travelling, and Loving Perception." In *Lesbian Philosophies and Cultures*, ed. Jeffner Allen, 159–80. Albany: State University of New York Press, 1990.

Lugones, María, and Elizabeth V. Spelman. "Have We Got a Theory for You! Feminist Theory, Cultural Imperialism and the Demand for 'The Woman's Voice.'" *Women's Studies International Forum* 6 (1983): 573–81.

Macauley, David. "On Women, Animals and Nature: An Interview with Susan Griffin." *APA Newsletter on Feminism and Philosophy* 90 (Fall 1991): 116–27.

McGuire, Cathleen, and Colleen McGuire. *What Is Ecofeminism Anyway?* New York: Ecofeminist Visions Emerging, 1991.

Manushi Collective. "Drought: God-Sent or Man-Made Disaster?" *Heresies* 13: "Feminism and Ecology" (1981): 56–58.

Mason, Jim, and Peter Singer. *Animal Factories*. New York: Crown Publishers, 1990.

Meeker-Lowry, Susan. "An Economy for the Living Earth." *Woman of Power* 20 (Spring 1991): 78–79.

Merchant, Carolyn. *The Death of Nature: Women, Ecology, and the Scientific Revolution*. New York: Harper & Row, 1980.

———. "Earthcare: Women and the Environmental Movement." *Environment* 23 (1981): 2–13, 38–40.

———. *Ecological Revolutions: Nature, Gender, and Science in New England*. Chapel Hill and London: University of North Carolina Press, 1989.

Meyerding, Jane. "Feminist Criticism and Cultural Imperialism (Where Does One End and the Other Begin)." *Animals' Agenda* (November/December 1982): 14–15, 22–23.

Midgley, Mary. *Animals and Why They Matter*. Athens: University of Georgia Press, 1983.

Mies, Maria. *Patriarchy and Accumulation on a World Scale*. Atlantic Highlands, N.J., and London: Zed Books, 1986.

Mills, Mary Ann. "From the First Beginning: The Sovereign Indigenous Women of the Arctic Assist Their People." *Woman of Power* 20 (Spring 1991): 36–39.

Mills, Patricia Jagentowicz. "Feminism and Ecology: On the Domination of Nature." *Hypatia* 6 (Spring 1991): 162–78.

———. *Woman, Nature, and Psyche*. New Haven, Conn.: Yale University Press, 1987.

Monagle, Katie. "Ghana: An Enterprising Woman." *Ms.*, May/June 1991, 16.

Murphy, Patrick. "Ground, Pivot, Motion: Ecofeminist Theory, Dialogics, and Literary Practice." *Hypatia* 6 (Spring 1991): 146–61.

———. "Sex-Typing the Planet." *Environmental Ethics* 10 (Summer 1988): 155–68.

———, ed. "Feminism, Ecology, and the Future of the Humanities." Special issue of *Studies in the Humanities* 15 (December 1988).

Nyoni, Sithembiso. "Africa's Food Crisis: Price of Ignoring Village Women?" *Women and Environments* 8 (Fall 1986): 20.

Orenstein, Gloria Feman. *The Reflowering of the Goddess*. New York: Pergamon Press, 1990.

Ortner, Sherry B. "Is Female to Male As Nature Is to Culture?" In *Woman, Culture, and Society*, ed. Michelle Z. Rosaldo and Louise Lamphere, 67–87. Stanford, Calif.: Stanford University Press, 1974.

Pele Defense Fund. "The Violation of the Goddess Pele: Geothermal Development on Mauna Loa Volcano." *Woman of Power* 20 (Spring 1991): 40–41.

Peterson, Abby, and Carolyn Merchant. "'Peace with the Earth': Women and the Environmental Movement in Sweden." *Women's Studies International Forum* 9 (1986): 465–79.

Pietila, Hilkka. "The Daughters of Earth: Women's Culture As a Basis for Sustainable Development." In *Ethics of Environment and Development*, ed. J. Ronald Engel and Joan Gibb Engel, 234–44. Tucson: University of Arizona Press, 1990.

Plant, Judith. "Revaluing Home: Feminism and Bioregionalism." In *Home! A Bioregional Reader*, ed. Van Andrass, Christopher, Judith Plant, and Eleanor Wright,

21–23. Philadelphia and Lillooet, British Columbia: New Society Press, 1990.

———. "Searching for Common Ground: Ecofeminism and Bioregionalism." *New Catalyst Quarterly* 10 (Winter 1987/88): 6–7.

———, ed. *Healing the Wounds: The Promise of Ecofeminism*. Philadelphia: New Society, 1989; Ontario: Between the Lines, 1989.

Plumwood, Val. "Ecofeminism: An Overview and Discussion of Positions and Arguments." *Australasian Journal of Philosophy*, supp. to vol. 64 (1986): 120–38.

———. "Nature, Self, and Gender: Feminism, Environmental Philosophy, and the Critique of Rationalism." *Hypatia* 6 (Spring 1991): 3–27.

Prentice, Susan. "Taking Sides: What's Wrong with Eco-Feminism?" *Women and Environments* 10 (Spring 1988): 9–10.

Regan, Tom. *The Case For Animal Rights*. Berkeley and Los Angeles: University of California Press, 1983.

Roach, Catherine. "Loving Your Mother: On the Woman-Nature Relationship." *Hypatia* 6 (Spring 1991): 46–59.

Robbins, John. *Diet for a New America*. Walpole, N.H.: Stillpoint, 1987.

Rose, Ellen Cronan. "The Good Mother: From Gaia to Gilead." *Frontiers* 11:1 (1991): 77–97.

Ruether, Rosemary Radford. *New Woman/New Earth: Sexist Ideologies and Human Liberation*. New York: Seabury, 1975.

Sale, Kirkpatrick. "Ecofeminism—A New Perspective." *The Nation*, September 26, 1987, 302–5.

Salleh, Ariel. "Deeper Than Deep Ecology: The Eco-Feminist Connection." *Environmental Ethics* 6 (1984): 339–45.

———. "Eco-Socialism/Eco-Feminism." *Capitalism, Nature, Socialism* 2 (1991): 129–34.

———. "Epistemology and the Metaphors of Production: An Eco-Feminist Reading of Critical Theory." *Studies in the Humanities* 15 (1988): 130–39.

———. "Living with Nature: Reciprocity or Control?" In *Ethics of Environment and Development*, ed. J. Ronald Engle and Joan Gibb Engel, 245–53. Tucson: University of Arizona Press, 1990.

Sells, Jennifer. "An Eco-feminist Critique of Deep Ecology: A Question of Social Ethics." *Feminist Ethics* (Winter 1989/90): 12–27.

Sen, Gita, and Caren Grown. *Development, Crises, and Alternative Visions: Third World Women's Perspectives*. New York: Monthly Review, 1987.

Sessions, Robert. "Deep Ecology Versus Ecofeminism: Healthy Differences or Incompatible Philosophies?" *Hypatia* 6 (Spring 1991): 90–107.

Shiva, Vandana. *Staying Alive: Women, Ecology and Development*. London: Zed Books, 1988.

———. "Where Has All the Water Gone? Women and the Water Crisis." *Ecoforum* 10 (April 1985): 16.

Singer, Peter. *Animal Liberation*. New York: New York Review of Books, 1990.

————, ed. *In Defense of Animals*. New York: Blackwell, 1985.

Sjöö, Monica, and Barbara Mor. *The Great Cosmic Mother: Rediscovering the Religion of the Earth*. San Francisco: Harper & Row, 1987.

Slicer, Deborah. "Your Daughter or Your Dog?" *Hypatia* 6 (Spring 1991): 108–24.

Smith, Andy. "For All Those Who Were Indian in a Former Life." *Ms.*, November/December 1991, 44–45.

Spiegel, Marjorie. *The Dreaded Comparison: Human and Animal Slavery*. New York: Mirror Books, 1989.

Spretnak, Charlene. "Ecofeminism: Our Roots and Flowering." *Elmwood Newsletter* 4 (Winter Solstice 1988): 1.

————. "Gaian Spirituality." *Woman of Power* 20 (Spring 1991): 10–17.

————. *The Spiritual Dimension of Green Politics*. Santa Fe, N. Mex.: Bear & Co., 1986.

————, ed. *The Politics of Women's Spirituality: Essays on the Rise of Spiritual Power Within the Feminist Movement*. New York: Anchor Books/Doubleday, 1982.

Stone, Merlin. *When God Was a Woman*. New York: Dial Press, 1976.

Timberlake, Lloyd, and Laura Thomas. *When the Bough Breaks . . . Our Children, Our Environment*. London: Earthscan Publications, 1990.

Tronto, Joan. "Beyond Gender Difference to a Theory of Care." *Signs* 12 (1987): 644–63.

Tuana, Nancy, and Karen Warren, eds. "Feminism and the Environment." Special issue of *APA Newsletter on Feminism and Philosophy* 90 (Fall 1991).

Van Gelder, Lindsy. "It's Not Nice to Mess with Mother Nature." *Ms.*, January/February 1989, 60–63.

Waring, Marilyn. *If Women Counted: A New Feminist Economics*. San Francisco: HarperCollins, 1988.

Warren, Karen J. "Feminism and Ecology: Making Connections." *Environmental Ethics* 9 (1987): 3–21.

————. "Feminism and the Environment: An Overview of the Issues." *APA Newsletter on Feminism and Philosophy* 90 (Fall 1991): 108–16.

————. "The Power and the Promise of Ecological Feminism." *Environmental Ethics* 12 (1990): 125–46.

————. "Toward an Ecofeminist Ethic." *Studies in the Humanities* 15 (1988): 140–56.

————. "Water and Streams: A Feminist Perspective." *Imprint* 6 (Summer 1989): 5–7.

————, ed. "Ecological Feminism." Special issue of *Hypatia* 6 (Spring 1991).

Warren, Karen, and Jim Cheney. "Ecological Feminism and Ecosystem Ecology." *Hypatia* 6 (Spring 1991): 179–97.

Warren, Karen, and Nancy Tuana, eds. *APA Newsletter on Feminism and Philosophy* 90 (Fall 1991): 103–63.

Westra, Laura. "Towards Integrity in the Great Lakes Region: Some Feminist Considerations." *APA Newsletter on Feminism and Philosophy* 90 (Fall 1991): 130–35.

*Woman of Power* 20 (Spring 1991). Special issue: "The Living Earth."

Wyman, Miriam. "Explorations of Ecofeminism." *Women and Environments* 9 (Spring 1987): 6–7.

Young, Iris. "'Feminism and Ecology' and 'Women and Life on Earth': Eco-Feminism in the 80's." *Environmental Ethics* 5 (1983): 173–80.

Zimmerman, Michael E. "Feminism, Deep Ecology, and Environmental Ethics." *Environmental Ethics* 9 (1987): 21–44.

# *About the Contributors*

CAROL J. ADAMS is a feminist writer and activist who has been involved over the past fifteen years with the issues of domestic and sexual violence, vegetarianism and animal rights, low-income housing, and challenges to white racism. She has a Master of Divinity from Yale University and is author of *The Sexual Politics of Meat: A Feminist Vegetarian Critical Theory*, which won the first Crossroad-Continuum Women's Studies Award. Adams has edited *Ecofeminism and the Sacred* (Orbis Press, 1992), and written about ecofeminism and its relationship to the other animals for *Hypatia, Ms.*, and other publications. She is completing books on *Abortion and Animal Rights* and *Pastoral Care and the Problem of Abusive Men*.

JANIS BIRKELAND teaches architecture at the University of Tasmania, Australia, in the Departments of Urban Planning and Architecture. She worked as a city planner, attorney, and architect in San Francisco until her move to Tasmania, where she is completing her doctoral degree in Environmental Law and Planning. She has delivered numerous lectures on ecofeminism and environmental planning, and has been active in peace, environmental, and social justice movements for many years. Most recently, she has originated and promoted the concept of organic playgrounds in collaboration with her two children.

JOSEPHINE DONOVAN is professor of English at the University of Maine. She is the author of *Feminist Theory: The Intellectual Traditions of American Feminism, New England Local Color Literature: A Women's Tradition*, and *After the Fall: The Demeter-Persephone Myth in Wharton, Cather, and Glasgow*. Her essay on "Animal Rights and Feminist Theory" originally appeared in *Signs*.

JANE EVERSHED is an ecofeminist artist living in Minneapolis. She is devoted to bringing the awareness of human geocide, among other issues, to the mainstream through the distribution of her notecards.

GRETA GAARD is assistant professor of composition and women's studies at the University of Minnesota, Duluth. The course planner for her class, "Ecofeminist Theories and Practices," appeared in the Fall 1991 *APA Newsletter on Feminism and Philosophy*. Her essays have appeared in *Feminist Teacher, Hurricane Alice*, the *Hungry Mind Review*, the *Collective Voice, Equal Time*, and the *Women's Review of Books*. She has spoken widely on the topic of ecofeminism and is a member of the Minnesota Greens.

LORI GRUEN teaches classes on social and political philosophy, feminist philosophy, and environmental ethics at the University of Colorado, Boulder, where she is associated with the Center for Values and Social Policy. She is the co-author of *Animal Liberation: A Graphic Guide*, and has written a number of articles pertaining to women, animals, and nature, including "Gendered Knowledge? Examining Influences on Scientific and Ethological Inquiries" in *Interpretation and Explanation in the Study of Animal Behavior: Comparative Perspectives*; "Animals" in *A Companion to Ethics*; and a review of *Rape of the Wild* and *Healing the Wounds* in *Hypatia* 6 (1991). Before returning to academe, she was an activist in Washington, D.C., and an organic farmer in West Virginia.

CHAIA HELLER is a political philosopher, writer, and activist. She has spent the last ten years living in Iowa and Vermont, where she has taught ecofeminism at Burlington College and the Institute for Social Ecology in Plainfield, Vermont. She is an active member of the Left Greens and of the "Speak Out" speakers bureau sponsored by South End Press. Currently she writes and tours nationally, speaking on issues of ecofeminism, anarchism, and social ecology.

MARTI KHEEL is a writer and activist in the areas of ecofeminism and animal liberation. Her articles have been translated into several languages and appeared in a variety of journals and anthologies, including *Environmental Ethics, The Green Reader, Woman of Power, Creation*, and *New Catalyst*. Kheel's essays have figured prominently in two ecofeminist anthologies, *Healing the Wounds* (1989) and *Reweaving the World* (1990). She is co-founder of Feminists for Animal Rights, and a regular contributor to its newsletter.

STEPHANIE LAHAR directs the Counseling/Human Relations Program at Woodbury College in Montpelier, Vermont. She previously taught in the Environmental Program at the University of Vermont, where she has also served on the Commission on the Status of Women. She is a writer and activist, and a founding member of the Burlington, Vermont, Conservation Board. Her recent contributions to ecofeminism include "Towards an Expanded View of Nature in Women's Psychology," which appeared in *NWSA Journal* 1 and "Ecofeminist Theory and Grassroots Politics," in *Hypatia* 6.

HUEY-LI LI acquired her undergraduate degree in Chinese literature from National Taiwan University. Now a doctoral student in the field of educational policy studies at the University of Illinois, Li has lived most of her life in Taiwan. Her research and critical inquiry focus on the conceptual linkages among sexism, racism, classism, and the human exploitation of nature. Her chapter in this volume was originally presented at the 1990 convention of the National Women's Studies Association in Akron, Ohio.

ELLEN O'LOUGHLIN holds a bachelor's degree from Smith College and a master's in American Studies/Women's Studies from the State University of New York at Buffalo. She designed and taught a course on ecofeminism for her master's thesis project and has recently completed an apprenticeship in farm and garden ecological horticulture at the University of California, Santa Cruz. She currently lives in Los Angeles.

LINDA VANCE is an attorney and associate professor of women's studies and social policy in the Adult Degree Program of Vermont College, where she supervises independent studies on women, law, environmental history and policy, and social history. Her activism ranges from backcountry trail maintenance and environmental reconstruction projects in wilderness areas of the United States to legal representation of citizens' groups opposing large-scale gold-mining ventures in New Mexico. Vance has chaired the Ecofeminist Task Force of the National Women's Studies Association (NWSA) since 1989. Her chapter in this volume, "Ecofeminism and the Politics of Reality," was first presented at the 1990 NWSA conference in Akron, Ohio.

# Index

Contrucci, Joyce, 4
Corea, Gena, 67–68
Cosmetics, 70–71; cruelty-free, 87n.34
Critical Theory, 27, 174
Cronon, William, 104–6
Crosby, Alfred, 101, 104, 107
Culture and nature, separation of, 62–64, 96–100, 124–25, 180, 199–200

Daly, Mary, 282
Deep ecology, 15, 29, 109; idealizing nature, 223–24; and identification, 49–51; and Leopold's land ethic, 252; as liberalist strategy, 43; and population, 224; and projection as a way of knowing, 230
Descartes, Rene, 247
Devall, Bill, 225–26
Diamond, Irene, 4
Dinnerstein, Dorothy, 76, 248, 279
Domination, 235
Donovan, Josephine, 8, 323
Doubiago, Sharon, 42
Dualism, 20, 79–80, 96, 180, 184, 204, 273–76; Platonic, 220; of reason and emotion, 175

Earth First! 262n.2; male orientation of, 132, 142n.16; on population, 224
Earth images, 219, 223, 224, 227. *See also* Nature
Ecofeminism: and construction of gender, 79–81; defined, 1, 17–20, 133–36, 146; differences within, 135; feminist reaction to, 132–33; misconceptions about, 21–23; origins of, 1; praxis of, 135–40, 184–85, 257; problems of reductionism (essentialism) in, 286–88; and spirituality, 305–9
Ecological framework, 108
Eco-Marxism, 27
Ecophilosophy, 250–51
Ecosocialism, 15, 28
Eisler, Riane, 97
Either/or thinking, 184, 255–56, 259–60
Environmental "crisis," as a crisis of per-

ception, 259; psychosexual roots of, 247–48
Environmental Defense Fund, 227
Environmental philosophy: male orientation of, 131; as romantic constraint, 226–28
Erotic, the, 239–41
Essentialism, 22–23, 26; potential within ecofeminism for, 147, 286–88
Ethics: axiological theory, 250; holistic, 258–59; as restraint, 252–54; rights vs. responsibilities, 2
European migration, 101, 104–5; from an ecofeminist perspective, 107–12; production and reproduction in, 105–6
Evershed, Jane, 323

Factory farming, 72–74, 203, 258, 297
Farm workers, conditions of, 151–52, 155–56, 161–62
Fawcett, Jane, 102
Feminism, as anthropocentric, 74–78; liberal, 75–76; Marxist, 76; radical, 77–78; socialist, 77; as species-specific, 204
Fisher, Elizabeth, 63
Fox, Warwick, 281
Freire, Paulo, 205, 212–13
French, Marilyn, 180–81
Fraser, Nancy, 198–99, 210, 214, 216n.13
Frye, Marilyn, 123, 285, 310

Gaard, Greta, vii, 10, 324
Gaia hypothesis, 223–24, 245, 251
Gender: and militarism, 35–37; and population, 34; and technology, 32–33; and Third World development, 33
Gilligan, Carol, 2, 111, 184, 254–55
Gilman, Charlotte Perkins, 168–69
Global "housekeeping," 233–34
Goddess, the, 306–8
Goldman, Emma, 197, 240
Goodman, Ellen, 198, 201, 205, 207, 212
Gray, Elizabeth Dodson, 279–80, 305
Greens: androcentrism of, 26–32; Australian, 14; and cooptation, 52–53; philosophy of, 13; and sexism, 51–52
Griscom, Joan, 22